The Complete Idiot's Reference Card

Thirty American Events Worth Knowing

1. Columbus lands, October 12, 1492. Old World meets new.

2. Slaves come to America, 1619. They are sold to Virginia tobacco farmers, and the hurt has yet to heal.

3. The Pilgrims land at Plymouth, Massachusetts, November 19, 1620. Many believe our nation started then and there.

4. General Braddock suffers defeat in frontier Pennsylvania, July 9, 1755. This and other French and Indian War disasters make some colonials start thinking about independence.

5. Continental Congress convenes, September 1774. A revolution is made, a nation planned.

6. The Constitution is ratified, June 21, 1788. The states approve a blueprint for union and an enduring democracy.

7. Washington is elected, April 6, 1789. He creates the office of president and wins credibility for the new nation.

8. The Bill of Rights is ratified, December 15, 1791. The first ten amendments to the Constitution spell out the rights we identify as our American heritage.

9. The Louisiana Purchase is made, May 2, 1803. The West becomes a part of the United States, a place for expansion, dreams, and conflict.

10. The Indian Removal Act is passed, May 28, 1830. The eastern tribes are forced to move west to make way for white settlement.

11. War with Mexico breaks out, May 13, 1846. This controversial war expands the United States into the Southwest.

12. Fort Sumter falls, April 12, 1861. The Civil War begins.

13. The Homestead Act is passed, May 20, 1862. The agricultural settlement of the western plains commences.

14. Emancipation is proclaimed, September 23, 1862. This first step toward ending slavery gives the Civil War its moral motive.

15. Lincoln is murdered, April 14, 1865. With him dies all hope for rapidly healing the wounds of civil war, and Reconstruction is doomed to destructive vindictiveness.

alpha
books

16. The Golden Spike is driven, May 10, 1869. The Central Pacific and Union Pacific are joined, completing the nation's first transcontinental railroad.

17. Indians die at Wounded Knee, December 28, 1890. The massacre ends 400 years of white-Indian warfare and is the culmination of a long Native American tragedy.

18. The Model T is launched, 1908. Henry Ford perfects mass production of the automobile, which will shape the physical and social landscape of 20th-century America.

19. The United States enters World War I, April 6, 1917. American troops fight in the Great War.

20. The 18th Amendment is ratified, 1919. Prohibition bans liquor and makes "organized crime" a big business.

21. The stock market crashes, October 29, 1929. The Roaring Twenties give way to the Great Depression, an emergency that redefines government.

22. Pearl Harbor is attacked, December 7, 1941. The United States is thrust into the century's second world war.

23. Hiroshima is vaporized, August 6, 1945. The greatest military weapons project in history culminates in the atomic bomb, which ends World War II and transforms global politics.

24. Senator Joseph McCarthy sees red, February 9, 1950. The Wisconsin senator tells a gathering of the Women's Republican Club in Wheeling, West Virginia, that he has the names of 205 communists in the State Department, and the "McCarthy Era" begins, undermining American democracy.

25. The Supreme Court outlaws segregation, May 17, 1954. The decision in *Brown v. Board of Education of Topeka* gives the civil rights movement the force of law.

26. John F. Kennedy is murdered, November 22, 1963. The assassination ends an era of youthful national hope and spawns endless conspiracy fears, but it also gains support for the martyred president's social programs.

27. Congress passes the Tonkin Gulf Resolution, August 7, 1964—a blank check for presidential war powers in Vietnam.

28. Men walk on the moon, July 20, 1969. Apollo 11 astronauts Neil A. Armstrong and "Buzz" Aldrin are the first human beings to walk on the moon.

29. Nixon's "Plumbers" are nabbed, June 17, 1972. The Watergate scandal rocks the nation and ultimately forces Richard Nixon to become the first president ever to resign office.

30. The Berlin Wall falls, 1988–89. The ugly central icon of the Cold War is torn down piece by piece, ushering in what President Bush calls a "new world order."

The COMPLETE IDIOT'S GUIDE TO American History

by Alan Axelrod

alpha books

A Division of Macmillan General Reference
A Simon & Schuster Macmillan Company
1633 Broadway, New York, NY 10019

48535
Non Fic
970

©1996 Alan Axelrod

International Standard Book Number: 0-02-861275-2
Library of Congress Catalog Card Number: 96-08462-0

98   8   7   6   5   4

Interpretation of the printing code: the rightmost number of the first series of numbers is the year of the book's printing; the rightmost number of the second series of numbers is the number of the book's printing. For example, a printing code of 96-1 shows that the first printing occurred in 1996.

Printed in the United States of America

Publisher
Theresa Murtha

Editor
Nancy Mikhail

Production Editor
Lynn Northrup

Copy Editors
Christy Prakel
Jama Carter
Mike Thomas

Cover Designer
Michael Freeland

Illustrator
Judd Winick

Designer
Barbara Kordesh

Indexer
Brad Herriman

Production Team
Angela Calvert, Dan Caparo, Kim Cofer, Tricia Flodder,
Beth Rago, Erich J. Richter

Contents at a Glance

Contents

Foreword

History is fun. It should never be approached like a dose of medicine, but like a big bowl of ice cream. Since our first conscious beginnings, the human race has had an instinctive, quizzical hunger to know where we all came from, what went before us, and how we got here. That yearning is a big part of what sets us above the beasts. Primitive artists carving crude likenesses on the interior walls of caves and tribal story tellers reciting incantations memorized from their fathers fed this longing centuries before the first printed words began linking us up formally with earlier generations in what we celebrate as history.

Alan Axelrod has produced here a marvelous telling of the fascinating story of America—of all those wondrous folk who preceded us on this piece of earth, to our contemporaries. He spins the tale, with grace and ease and knowledge, in an informal and often humorous style that is easily readable, clearly understandable, and immensely enjoyable.

The Complete Idiot's Guide to American History can be read with profit and pleasure by any literate person regardless of his or her previous level of exposure to the subject. The author doesn't overestimate our sophistication nor underestimate our intelligence. He takes us right where we are and starts telling us interesting things, beginning with those ancient Asians who ventured across the Bering Strait more than 10,000 years ago. Then he brings the story up to the present time with people like Bill Clinton and Ross Perot, Rodney King, and O.J. Simpson.

A random thought about one word in the title is probably unnecessary for those who have read other titles of this series. But the word may have peculiar application to this volume. That term, *idiot*, for all its pejorative connotation, isn't really intended here as a reproach. Interestingly enough, the word is Greek in origin. *Idiotes*, in the early Athenian democracy of Pericles, was a specific reference to those who did not take part in public life. Non-voters. So maybe for some of those people—the alienated or uninvolved—this specific work is written, with the hope that they may discover in its pages an unexpected identity with what we are, have been, and can be as a nation.

Axelrod, a consummate scholar and accomplished American folklorist, employs an intriguing combination of writing techniques that catch our fancy with little-known facts at each stage in the telling of his tale. In a sidebar he gives us, for example, an occasional *Word for the Day*. We learn the sometimes surprising origin of words like *wampum*, *telegraph*, *cowboy*, or *brinkmanship*. In another innovative enrichment of the text, the author sprinkles his narrative at appropriate places with *Real Life*, little thumbnail biographies of scores of fascinating folks like Stephen F. Austin, Christopher (Kit) Carson, and Dwight David Eisenhower.

Each chapter of the rapidly unfolding drama begins with a box of brief phrases—subheads—that give an intriguing foretaste of the chapter's contents. Every chapter ends with a terse summary condensation, maybe three spare sentences, titled *The Least You Need to Know*. I suppose that somebody just skimming through and reading these end-of-chapter summations might come up with a coherent bare-bones digest of American history. But don't do that! You'll miss all the fun!

Part of the fun is savoring the actual *Voice from the Past*, a feature interspersing at appropriate points a box containing the actual words of some critical declaration on which history turned. You'll be stunned at the undisguised and, at the time, not unshocking arrogance of the Supreme Court's 1857 decision in the Dred Scott case. And you'll thrill at the verbatim transcript of Winston Churchill's May 13, 1940, acceptance of the Prime Minister's role: "I have nothing to offer but blood, toil, tears and sweat."

And it isn't all politics. Far from it. You'll learn here of the cotton gin, the Overland Trail, the days of Jesse James and Billy the Kid, the discovery of the wireless, the origins of the movie industry—and much, much more. But I'm delaying you with this drivel. Crack open the text and get going. Just try to be careful. History is addictive. You may get hooked on it!

Jim Wright
Former Speaker of the House and author of *Balance of Power: Presidents and Congress from the Era of McCarthy to the Age of Gingrich*

Introduction

Most of the world's nations are *places*—places with a past, certainly, and with traditions and a heritage, but places nevertheless. The United States is different. It's a place, but it's also an *idea*. Sure, democracy was not exactly a new idea in 1776—the word "democracy," meaning government by the people, was coined in ancient Greece—but no one had really tried it before. Few people thought it would actually work.

The story of gambling on an untried notion is bound to be fascinating. When you have a stake in that gamble, the story can be downright riveting. And make no mistake, living in a world where most people are hungry, terrified, tortured, and not free, you do have a big stake in the story.

My purpose is to give you a quick and comprehensive overview of American history. While I've tried not to grind any axes, I'd be less than a living, breathing human being if I told you what I've written is totally impartial and neutral. Obviously, a book of this length is also grossly incomplete. Walk through a bookstore or library and thousands of books on American history will leap at you from the shelves. The great thing is that many of them are well worth reading. However, you now hold in your hands a good place to start, a road map of the American story.

Part 1 takes us back some 45,000 years to the epoch of the first immigrants, the people who crossed the long-vanished Bering "land bridge" from Asia to North America. The discussion then shifts to the collision of Old World and New as Europe invaded the realm of the Native American beginning in the 15th century, transforming the continent into a battlefield on which the basis of a nation was forged.

Part 2 covers the period of the American Revolution, from origins to outcome, including issues of economic, political, and spiritual independence.

Part 3 discusses the creation of the Constitution, the War of 1812, the rise of Andrew Jackson, and the era of the common man, as well as the forced removal of the Indians from the East to the West.

Part 4 analyzes the causes of the Civil War, the early steps toward western expansion—including the Mexican War, by which much of the Southwest was acquired—the Civil War itself, and the Reconstruction era following the Civil War.

Part 5 covers the major period of western expansion, including the homestead movement, the building of the transcontinental railroad, the Indian Wars, the growth of the western cattle empire, and the economic and technological boom of the later 19th century. This section also discusses the immigrant experience, the labor movement, and the rise of urban political machines.

Part 6 charts the nation's evolution as a world power (beginning with the Spanish-American War and World War I), the isolationist reaction against that evolution, the culture of the "Roaring Twenties" (including the heyday of Prohibition Era gangsterism), the stock market crash, and the Great Depression. This section also outlines the origins of World War II and the nation's fight to victory in that war, from which it emerged as a nuclear superpower.

Part 7 covers the Cold War years, the Korean War, the Civil Rights movement, and the social revolution wrought during the administrations of John F. Kennedy and Lyndon Johnson. The section concludes with the Vietnam War.

Part 8 surveys the turbulent home front during the Vietnam era, including such high points as the Apollo 11 moon landing, and such low points as the Watergate scandal. The women's movement is also discussed in this section, as are the energy crisis and the economic crises of American cities and industry, which created fertile ground for the growth of "Reaganomics."

Part 9 begins with the Reagan years and covers the end of the Cold War, including the experience of the Persian Gulf War. The final chapter in this section looks at recent events, which indicate the challenges and the possibilities American democracy faces in the coming millennium.

Finally, at the back of this book, you'll find two helpful appendixes that contain a list of our nation's presidents and vice presidents, and recommendations for further reading.

Extras

In addition to the main narrative of *The Complete Idiot's Guide to American History*, you'll also find other types of useful information, including capsule histories of major events and brief biographies of key people in American history, digests of important statistics, and quick definitions of historical buzzwords. Look for these features:

Main Event

Here you'll read about the most significant or representative single event of an era, ranging from historical milestones to pop culture landmarks.

Word for the Day
This feature defines the buzz-words that defined a time and place.

Stats
Here you'll find key numbers relating to an era or event, including such items as population statistics, war casualties, costs, and so on.

Real Life
This feature provides biographical sketches of an era's most significant and representative figures.

Voice from the Past
These are memorable statements from historically signifi-cant figures and documents.

Special Thanks from the Publisher to the Technical Reviewer

The Complete Idiot's Guide to American History was reviewed by an expert who not only checked the technical accuracy of what you'll learn in this book, but also provided invaluable insight and suggestions. Our special thanks are extended to Harry Oster.

Emeritus Professor of American Literature and Folklore at the University of Iowa, Mr. Oster has degrees from Harvard (A.B.), Columbia (M.B.A.), and Cornell (M.A., Ph.D.). He has taught courses in literature, folklore, drama, and ethnic studies. He wrote *Living Country Blues* on a Guggenheim Fellowship, and has received numerous other grants and awards, including most recently a BBC Radio Third Program series of five programs called "Oster's Blues." He is currently serving as co-editor on an encyclopedia of American Folklore.

Part 1
Exploration? Invasion? Whatever...

*The "New World" was new only to Old World eyes. North America has been popu-
lated for probably as many as 50,000 years, and the people Christopher Columbus
misnamed Indians may well be members of the oldest identifiable human race on the
planet. Except for a brief visit from Vikings about A.D. 1000, the "New" World and
the Old remained unknown to one another until October 12, 1492, when Columbus,
the prodigal son of a Genoese weaver, claimed a Caribbean island for Spain. For the
next 150 years, the people of Europe carved up the land of the Indians, and for the
next 400 years the colonists, settlers, and citizens of Euro-America fought the Indians,
fought one another, and managed eventually to forge a nation. This part of the book
tells the story of that long, exciting, and often tragic process.*

Chapter 1

Who's On First? (50,000 B.C.- A.D. 1500s)

In This Chapter

➤ Where the "first Americans" came from

➤ The Mayas, Incas, and Aztecs

➤ The Anasazi, Mound Builders, and Pueblos

➤ Leif Eriksson, first European in America

Look at a map that shows the north Pacific Ocean. You'll find the Bering Sea, an arm of the Pacific bounded on the east by Alaska, on the south by the Aleutian Islands, and on the west by Siberia and the Kamchatka Peninsula. Near the north end of the Bering Sea is the Bering Strait, which, lying between Alaska and Siberia, connects the Bering Sea with the Chukchi Sea of the Arctic Ocean. At its narrowest, the strait is only 55 miles across, the shortest distance between the continents of North America and Asia. Fifty-five miles in icy cold water is a long swim, but not much of an ocean voyage. Historians believe that once upon a time, there wasn't even that 55 miles of water between the continents.

A Stroll Across the Bering Sea

Several times during what paleontologists call the Quaternary Period—that's their name for the last two million years—a "land bridge" emerged in the Bering and Chukchi Seas as the sea level dropped due to the expansion of the ice cap surrounding the North Pole. The theory is that anywhere from 10,000 to 45,000 years ago, human beings used the Bering land bridge to enter the New World, migrating from what is now northeast Asia to northwestern North America. Beringia, as the land bridge is sometimes called, disappeared when the major continental ice sheets and other glaciers melted, causing the sea level to rise again.

45,000 Years of American History (Abridged Version)

The trek across Beringia was not really an evening's stroll. It must have consumed thousands of years. By 9000 B.C., it's likely that the former Asians reached Patagonia, at the southern tip of South America. In between, in the area that is the present-day United States, the population of what we now call Native Americans may have reached 11 million.

Stats

Eleven million is the current consensus. However, estimates of the prehistoric population of the area encompassed by the United States range wildly—from 8.4 million to 112 million. For comparison, in 1990, 1,959,234 Indians, including Eskimos and Aleuts, lived in the United States.

These Native Americans, thinly distributed over a vast area in bands of a hundred or even fewer individuals, lived for thousands of years on the ragged edge of subsistence. They didn't develop great cities, but, as nomads, wandered, hunted, and foraged together. Then, perhaps 9,000 years ago, some bands began to domesticate plants in order to supplement foraged and hunted food. By the beginning of the 16th century, when Europeans first made contact with Native Americans, they were cultivating maize, beans, and squash, as well as manioc, potatoes, and grains.

Word for the Day

Native American is the term used by most historians and anthropologists to describe the aboriginal peoples of the Western Hemisphere. In this book, I also use the more familiar term "Indian." That designation was coined by Christopher Columbus, who, on October 12, 1492, thought that he had landed in Asia—"the Indies"—and therefore called the people he encountered *Indians*. The name stuck.

Agriculture fostered a more stable lifestyle than hunting and gathering, and the horticultural groups lived in tribes. Along with relatively stable sources of sustenance and substantial populations came more or less permanent houses organized into villages, usually led by a recognized chief.

The Anasazi

Living at a subsistence level, it's not surprising that, within the area of the United States, the Native Americans left little material evidence of their ancient cultures. In the Southwest, archaeologists have identified a people they call the Anasazi (from a Navajo word meaning "the ancient ones"). The Anasazi appeared as early as 5500 B.C. and are also called the Basket Makers, because of the many skillfully woven baskets that have been discovered in sites associated with their culture. The Anasazi built communal dwellings consisting of wood and thatch, and even occupied shallow caves closed off with rocks. By A.D. 400–700, Anasazi communities evolved into collections of somewhat more sophisticated pit houses, built over shallow excavations. During the period of A.D. 700–1100, the Anasazi began building what Spanish invaders would later call *pueblos* (Spanish for "town" or "village" and also "people"). These were fantastic groupings of stone and adobe "apartment buildings," cliff dwellings seemingly hewn out of lofty ledges, the most spectacular of which survive at Mesa Verde in southwest Colorado.

The Mound Builders

In the meantime, to the east, in a vast area stretching from the Appalachian Mountains to the eastern edge of the prairies, and from the Great Lakes to the Gulf of Mexico, other Native Americans were building cultural monuments of a different kind. From about 1000 B.C. to after A.D. 1500, many different Indian societies constructed earthworks that modern archaeologists classify as burial mounds, platform or temple mounds (which served as the foundations for important public and private buildings), and circular and geometric ceremonial earthworks. Archaeologists further recognize two traditions among the mound-building cultures: the Woodland and the Mississippian.

The Woodland mounds were built in eastern North America from about 1000 B.C. to the beginning of the 18th century. The earliest were simple, enclosing only a few burials, but later mounds often reached 80 feet in height, took many years to construct, contained numerous burials, and even included log tombs. The largest and most elaborate of the mounds was built in southern Ohio by people of the Hopewell culture (named after mounds found near the Ohio hamlet of Hopewell).

The mounds of the Mississippian tradition reflect the development of larger-scale farming among the Native Americans. Beginning around A.D. 700, in the flood plains of the central and lower Mississippi River, various tribes built villages consisting of palisades and flat-topped, rectangular mounds that served as bases for temples and other important structures. The Cahokia Mounds, which are found in Illinois, just across the Mississippi from Saint Louis, must have once contained as many as 50 platform mounds and probably supported a population numbering in the thousands.

South of the Border

Pueblos, mounds, some baskets, a few pots—these are the chief material remains of Native American culture before Europeans set foot in what is today the United States. But, to the south, in present-day Mexico and Central and South America, Native American civilization took a very different turn.

The Maya

The Maya lived in southern Mexico and in Belize, Guatemala, and adjacent Honduras. In contrast to the Native Americans, the Maya kept written historical records, extending back to 50 B.C. and ending with the Spanish conquest in the 16th century.

By 5000 B.C., the Maya were installed along the Caribbean and Pacific coasts. Within the next 3,000 years, they began to move inland, turning from fishing to agriculture. By about 1200 B.C., another Native people, the Olmec of the Gulf Coast, dominated trade in Central America and began greatly influencing Mayan culture. By 1000 B.C., the Maya adopted Olmec styles of pottery and jades and also took on Olmec religious symbols. Maya culture and power reached its height by A.D. 900, when it seems to have collapsed, probably due to famine, disease, and chronic warfare among Maya city-states. A landscape adorned with spectacular stepped-pyramid temples and other structures endured, and various Mayan groups continued to prosper in varying degrees until the 16th century, when the Spanish conquistadors invaded.

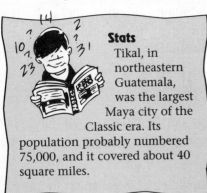

Stats

Tikal, in northeastern Guatemala, was the largest Maya city of the Classic era. Its population probably numbered 75,000, and it covered about 40 square miles.

Most of what is today called Mexico fell under the domination of another great Native American civilization, the Aztecs. Their own myths place their origin at Aztlan, somewhere in north or northwest Mexico, where they lived as a small, nomadic collection of tribes.

During the 12th century A.D., the Aztec tribes migrated southward, settling in the central basin of Mexico by the 13th century. Their existence was a precarious one, as they were repeatedly attacked and routed by other groups. Finally, the Aztecs took refuge on small islands in Lake Texcoco where, in 1325, they founded Tenochtitlan on the site of present-day Mexico City.

From their new base, the Aztecs evolved into ruthless and well-organized warriors. By the 15th century, they subdued and subjugated the peoples of Mexico, thereby creating an empire second in size only to the Incas in Peru. Extending from the Gulf of Mexico to the Pacific and from the Valley of Mexico south into Guatemala, the Aztec empire was peopled mostly by slaves, whose work was supremely manifest in the capital.

As the conquistadors later noted, Tenochtitlan was a city as large as Cordoba or Seville; however, most remarkably, it was situated entirely within Lake Texcoco, two miles from the mainland. Four great causeways led to the city, which was watered by a system of magnificently engineered aqueducts. The streets, lined with splendid temples, issued onto great public squares, which served as marketplaces. And there were priests. Legions of black-robed holy men continually marched through Tenochtitlan's boulevards, for the Aztec capital was the home of God himself as incarnated in the emperor, Montezuma II.

Splendid though it was, the empire was founded in blood for the purpose of shedding blood. In Tenochtitlan, the temple of human sacrifice was more spectacular than the other temples, sprouting forty towers. There were three main halls, from which various windowless chapels branched. The idols that lined its halls were molded of a paste of seeds and plants kneaded together with the blood of prisoners and slaves taken in battle. Blood was the fuel that drove the Aztec government, economy, and culture. It was said that the very ground of Tenochtitlan was black with it.

The Incas

Maya civilization was magnificent, and the Aztecs ruled with terrible splendor, but the Incas of Peru controlled the largest native empire in the Americas. Toward the end of the 14th century, the Incas fanned out from their base in the Cuzco region of the southern Andes. For the next century and a half, their holdings increased until the Inca world was invaded by Conquistadors under the command of Francisco Pizarro in 1532. At the time of that clash, the Incas held sway over some 12 million people in what is now Peru and Ecuador, as well as parts of Chile, Bolivia, and Argentina.

The origin of the Incas is shrouded in mystery, but what is known is that they expanded into a New World empire under the ruler Pachacuti. Pachacuti's sons continued the conquests. One of them, Topa Inca (who reigned from 1471 to 1493), took much of present-day Ecuador, the south coast of Peru, northern Chile, and most of northwestern Argentina, as well as a portion of the Bolivian plateau.

War was a constant Inca activity, but when the Incas weren't fighting, they were building. The greatest surviving monument of Inca architecture is the citadel of Machu Picchu. Situated on a lofty precipice between steep mountain peaks 7,875 feet above sea level on the eastern slopes of the Andes, the fortified town boasts fine stone buildings with extensive agricultural terraces that make the settlement look as if it had been physically carved out of the mountainsides.

Beyond the Aztec Frontier

Look at the Americas in the days before the European invasion. What you see are great empires in South and Central America, but, for the most part, a collection of thinly distributed and, in a political and material sense, less highly developed civilizations in North America. In what is now the southwestern region of the United States, the Anasazi ("Basket Makers") evolved into the people of the Pueblo culture. For many years, these were the people who lived just beyond the Aztec frontier.

Pueblo Culture: The First American Frontier

Archaeologists say that Pueblo culture developed out of the Basket Makers, beginning around A.D. 700. From then until about 1100, these frontier people began using cotton cloth and started building their houses above ground, using stone and adobe masonry. Next, during 1100 to 1300, the modest above-ground dwellings evolved (in some places) into the spectacular multiroom "apartment" complexes, terraced into the sides of cliffs, which continue to awe visitors to such places as Mesa Verde National Park.

Impressive though the Pueblo culture was, it never became as varied or as advanced as the Native cultures to the south. Even before the Spanish entered the American Southwest in the sixteenth century, Pueblo culture began to decline. Between 1276 and 1299, the Pueblos were devastated by drought and famine. Many migrated to more adequately watered regions in New Mexico and northeastern Arizona. Descendants of the Pueblos—the Zunis, the Hopis, and the Rio Grande Pueblos—still live in these areas.

Atlantic Presence

Far to the northeast of the Pueblos, agriculture was well established in the Mississippi valley by the 1st century A.D. We have already glanced at the burial and ceremonial mounds some of these people left. These cultures eventually reached from the Gulf of Mexico to Wisconsin, and from New York to Kansas. It is believed that the thatched houses built by "Temple Mound" people resembled dwellings found in Mexico, and that their pyramidal mounds harked back to the pyramids of Mesoamerica. For these and other reasons (including similarities in religious ritual and in pottery design), many historians believe that the first Indians of the Mississippi valley and Atlantic coastal regions may have descended from Mayan and other Central and South American immigrants to the northern hinterlands.

However they came to populate North America, the Indians of this vast region developed in diverse ways, creating more than 2,000 distinct cultures. Some of these cultures barely subsisted as hunter-gatherers; others became stable and relatively prosperous agricultural societies.

Unlike the Maya, Aztec, and Inca, these North American groups had no written language and left no historical records, so it is impossible to present a "history" of the North American Indians before their contact with Europeans. In fact, some scholars have gone so far as to suggest that most North American Indians lived apart from linear time, harmonizing their lives with the cycles of the seasons and the biological processes of propagation, birth, and death. Europeans, forever *doing* and *getting*, were obsessed with recording *events* and measuring time. The Native Americans were focused instead on *being*. Time itself was therefore different for them.

Leif the Lucky

Momentously—and tragically—the *time* of the Old World would collide with the *time* of the New. For 400 years, from a clash between "Indians" and Christopher Columbus's men in 1493 to the massacre of Native Americans by the U.S. 7th Cavalry at Wounded Knee on December 29, 1890, the history of America would be in large part the history of racial warfare between white and red.

The first European contact, some 500 years before Columbus sailed, ignited no great tragedy, however. It seems likely that Vikings reached the Faeroe Islands by A.D. 800, and that they landed in Greenland in 870. The very first Old World dweller to set eyes on the continent of North America was most likely a Norseman named Bjarni Herjulfsson in A.D. 986. But that sighting came as a result of a mistake in navigation. Herjulfsson had been blown off course, and he had no interest in actually exploring the land he sighted.

It was not until the next decade, about the year 1000, that the Norse captain Leif Eriksson led an expedition that touched a place called Helluland (probably Baffin Island) and Markland (most likely Labrador). Most historians believe that Leif—celebrated as Leif the Lucky in the great Icelandic *sagas* of the 13th century—and his men spent a winter in rude Viking huts hastily erected in a spot abundant with berries and grapes and, for that reason, called Vinland.

Real Life

The adventures of Leif Eriksson (ca. 970–1020) are known exclusively through semilegendary, sometimes contradictory sagas. Leif the Lucky (as he was called) was the son of Eric Thorvaldsson, better known as Eric the Red, who established in Greenland the first enduring European settlement in the New World about 985. Through his fearsome father (Eric was banished from Iceland after having murdered a man), Leif Eriksson was descended from a line of Viking chieftains. Leif explored the lands that had been first sighted by Bjarne Herjulfsson.

Nobody knows for certain just where Vinland was. Some have suggested a location as far south as the Virginia Capes, although most historians believe that it was in Newfoundland, perhaps at a place called L'Anse aux Meadows on the northernmost tip of the Canadian province.

After Leif the Lucky left Vinland, his brother Thorvald paid a visit to the tenuous settlement about 1004. Next, in 1010, Thorfinn Karlsefni, another Icelandic explorer, attempted to establish a more permanent settlement at Vinland. According to two Icelandic sagas, Thorfinn, a trader as bold as he was wealthy, brought women as well as men with him. They carried on a lively trade, but they also fought fiercely with the Native Americans, whom the sagas call Skraelings—an Old Norse word signifying "dwarfs" or "wretches" or, perhaps, "savages." The Skraelings attacked tenaciously and repeatedly.

After three lethal winters, Thorfinn and his would-be settlers abandoned Vinland forever. The Viking expeditions to North America led, then, to nothing—at least not right away. Christopher Columbus, half a millennium removed from the Vikings, heard of the Vinland tradition and was excited by stories about a New World across the "Ocean Sea."

The Least You Need to Know

➤ Native Americans almost certainly immigrated to the Americas from Asia across an Ice Age "land bridge" where the Bering Strait now is.

➤ Pre-Columbian Native American cultures varied widely, with the most elaborately developed living in South and Central America.

➤ The European discoverer of America was (most likely) Leif Eriksson about 1000.

Chapter 2

Columbus Days (1451–1507)

In This Chapter

- ➤ The round earth hypothesis
- ➤ Columbus's early life and struggle for a sponsor
- ➤ The voyages of Columbus
- ➤ Contact—and clash—with Native Americans
- ➤ The voyages of Amerigo Vespucci and the naming of America

Wow. Columbus. This is an *old* story. You've heard it more often than the story of Adam and Eve, more often than the tale of how your Aunt Agnes once met Spiro T. Agnew, and more often than you've watched Ed Norton and Ralph Kramden try to teach each other how to play golf on the umpteenth *Honeymooners* festival of reruns.

It's so old, so tightly tied up with all the other half-learned rote lessons of childhood, that we forget to imagine the combination of creativity, the capacity for wonder, the courage, and the sheer madness that sent a Genoese seafarer and crew in three small ships across an unknown expanse of ocean to (it turns out) they knew not where.

It's a Round World After All

But first there's that business about the roundness of the world. Generations of school-children have been taught that, when Columbus sailed, he was about the only person in the world advanced enough to believe that the earth is round. His task (we were told) was to convince King Ferdinand and Queen Isabella of Spain to finance an expedition to sail *west* in order to reach the *East*. And that, of course, was predicated on the assumption that the world is a globe.

In fact, the idea of a round earth was hardly new by the end of the 15th century. Ancient Greeks such as Pythagoras and Aristotle said the earth was a sphere, and, in the 3rd century B.C., Eratosthenes of Cyrene (ca. 276–195 B.C.) performed a remarkable measurement that determined the earth's circumference with great accuracy.

Son of a Weaver

But Columbus was hardly alone in differing from the conservative view, which, by the late 1400s, was downright unfashionable among the enlightened and educated. Not that Cristoforo Colombo—to use the native Italian form of his name—was well educated. He had been born in Genoa in 1451 to a weaver and would not learn to read and write until he reached adulthood. As a youth, he took to the sea. In 1476, shipwrecked off Portugal, he went to Lisbon, then sailed as far as Ireland and England and even claimed to have sailed from England to Iceland (where, perhaps, he heard stories of an ancient place called Vinland, across the "Ocean Sea"). Columbus returned to Genoa in 1479, then went back to Portugal, where he married. His wife died while giving birth to their child Diego the following year. But, by this time, the seafarer's thoughts were far from his family.

Having learned to read, he devoured shadowy accounts of westward voyages. He decided that the world was indeed round. And he was right about that. What he was wrong about was believing Marco Polo's calculations concerning the location of Japan—1,500 miles east of China—and the work of the Greek astronomer Ptolemy (A.D. ca. 100–70), who grossly underestimated the circumference of the earth and overestimated the size of the Eurasian land mass. Further encouraged by the miscalculations of the Florentine cosmographer Paolo dal Pozzo Toscanelli, Columbus concluded that Japan (which Columbus called Cipangu) was a 3,000-mile voyage *west* of Portugal, over an ocean covering a round earth. Now, that was a long trip, but it was one that (Columbus believed) could be made by the vessels of the day.

Stats
For your information, the actual circumference of the earth at the equator is 24,902 miles. The distance from the Spanish coast to the Bahamas, via the route Columbus took, is about 3,900 miles.

In 1484, Columbus secured an audience with King John II of Portugal and tried to persuade him to back a voyage to Japan. Now, there were excellent reasons for going to the East—all of which involved lucrative trading opportunities, chief among which was the commerce in spices. In the time of Columbus, aromatic spices were not just pleasant condiments. They were rare and precious substances *essential* to the preservation of food in an age long before refrigeration was invented. Spice was as highly valued as gold. But King John II turned Columbus down just the same, believing that even a trip of three thousand miles was beyond the capabilities of existing ships.

Undaunted, the seafarer approached Don Enrique de Guzmán, Duke of Medina Sidonia, only to be rebuffed. He next asked Don Luis de la Cerda, Count of Medina Celi, who was sufficiently intrigued to arrange an audience, on or about May 1, 1486, with Queen Isabella I of Castile. For the next half-dozen years, Columbus, his son Diego in tow, cooled his heels in the Spanish court of Isabella and her husband, Ferdinand II of Aragon. During this time, he made many influential friends and enemies. Among the most powerful of the former was a courtier named Luis de Santangel, who, after the monarchs apparently turned down Columbus once and for all early in 1492, actually persuaded the pair to sponsor the voyage, which was financed by a combination of royal money and private funds. Commissioned "Admiral of the Ocean Sea," as well as viceroy and governor of whatever lands he might discover, Columbus set sail from Palos on August 3, 1492. He was in command of three small ships, the *Niña* (skippered by Vincente Yáñez Pinzón), the *Pinta* (under Vincente's brother, Martin Alonso Pinzón), and his own flagship, the *Santa Maria*.

Trouble on the Horizon

During its first month and a half, the voyage went well, as the three vessels were propelled by highly favorable winds. Then, between the 20th and 30th of September, the winds turned bad and trailed off into doldrums. The fearful crews of all three ships began to grumble their doubts concerning their commanders. Columbus himself must have started to consider how it was one thing to believe in such enlightened ideas as a round earth, yet quite another to stake one's life on the notion. Certainly, he came to realize that he had seriously miscalculated transoceanic distances. He began to keep two logbooks—one, for the benefit of the crew, containing fictitious computations of distances, and another, for his own records, consisting of accurate figures. Despite this deception, the crews of all three ships verged on mutiny by the second week in October.

10/12/92—That's Fourteen 92

Then it happened. On October 12, 1492, the *Santa Maria*'s lookout sighted land. It was a place the natives called Guanahani and Columbus named San Salvador. Most modern historians believe this first landfall was present-day Watling Island, although, in 1986, a group of scholars suggested that the true landfall was another Bahamian island, Samana Cay, 65 miles south of Watling.

The seafarers were greeted by friendly Arawak tribespeople. Believing that he had reached Asia—the "Indies"—Columbus logically enough called these people *Indians*. He then sailed on to Cuba in search of the court of the Mongol emperor of China, with whom he hoped to negotiate a trade in spices and gold. Disappointed in this, Columbus pushed on to Hispaniola (modern Santo Domingo), where, in a Christmas Day storm, the *Santa Maria* was wrecked near Cap–Haitien. Columbus ushered his crew safely onto the shore. Seeing that the Indians were friendly, he left a garrison of 39 at the place he christened La Navidad and, on January 16, 1493, returned to Spain on the *Niña*. Pausing at the Canary Islands on February 15 to replenish supplies, he dispatched a letter to his patron Luis de Santangel, who immediately had it printed and, in effect, published worldwide.

Voice from the Past

The letter of Christopher Columbus to Luis de Santangel, February 15, 1493:

Sir—

As I know you will be rejoiced at the glorious success that our Lord has given me in my voyage, I write this to tell you how in thirty-three days I sailed to the Indies with the fleet that the illustrious King and Queen, our Sovereigns, gave me, where I discovered a great many islands, inhabited by numberless people; and of all I have taken possession for their Highnesses by proclamation and display of the Royal Standard without opposition.

The land there is elevated, with many mountains and peaks. They are most beautiful, of a thousand varied forms, accessible, and full of trees of endless varieties, so high that they seem to touch the sky, and I have been told that they never lose their foliage. I saw them as green and lovely as trees are in Spain in the month of May. Some of them were covered with blossoms, some with fruit, and some in other conditions, according to their kind. The nightingale and other small birds of a thousand kinds were singing in the month of November when I was there. There were palm trees of six or eight varieties, the graceful peculiarities of each one of them being worthy of admiration as are the other trees, fruits and grasses. There are wonderful pine woods, and very extensive ranges of meadow land. There is honey, and there are many kinds of birds, and a great variety of fruits. Inland there are numerous mines of metals and innumerable people.

Hispaniola is a marvel. Its hills and mountains, fine plains and open country, are rich and fertile for planting and for pasturage, and for building towns and villages. There are many spices and vast mines of gold and other metals in this island. They have no iron, nor steel, nor weapons, nor are they fit for them, because although they are well-made men of commanding stature, they appear extraordinarily timid. The only arms they have are sticks of cane, cut when in seed, with a sharpened stick at the end, and they are afraid to use these.

First Blood

In addition to the observations Columbus made in his letter regarding the Indians' timidity, he recorded in an October 14, 1492, journal entry his opinion that no fortress was required at La Navidad, "for these people are very simple as regards the use of arms." The garrison Columbus left behind at unfortified La Navidad when he went back to Spain set about pillaging goods and raping women as soon as he departed. The "timid" Indians retaliated. When Columbus returned in November 1493, on his second voyage, no Spaniards were left alive.

Carving Up a New World

Columbus made four voyages to America. His first triggered a dispute between Spain and Portugal, whose king had rebuffed the Great Navigator back in 1484. The failure to back him notwithstanding, the Portuguese crown pressed claims to Columbus's discoveries, which soon led Pope Alexander VI to issue a pair of papal bulls (*Inter Caetera* and *Inter Caetera II*) in 1493 that divided the newly discovered and yet-to-be-discovered world between Spain and Portugal. The two nations formalized this decree with the Treaty of Tordesillas (June 7, 1494), which established a line of demarcation at 370 leagues west of the Cape Verde Islands.

Three More Voyages

In the meantime, Ferdinand and Isabella sent Columbus on his second voyage (from Cadiz, on September 25, 1493), this time grandly outfitted with a fleet of 17 ships and nearly 1,500 men. After discovering the grim fate of La Navidad, Columbus set up a new colony, named Isabella, about 70 miles east of that bloody site. Columbus explored the Caribbean for some five months, then tried to govern the fledgling colony he had planted, but instantly proved to be a disastrously inept administrator. He returned to

Spain in 1496, leaving his brother Bartolome in charge with instructions to move the settlement to the south coast of Hispaniola. Renamed Santo Domingo, this became the first permanent European settlement in the New World.

In June 1496, when Columbus landed at Cadiz, it was not to a hero's welcome. Although he continued to protest that he had found a shortcut to gold- and spice-rich Asia, he had clearly failed to find the mainland (where, presumably, the treasure was stashed), and discouraged colonists trickled back to Spain with complaints about the Great Navigator's abusiveness and ineptitude. Nevertheless, growing competition from Portugal, which sent Vasco da Gama to India in 1497, prompted Isabella and Ferdinand to fund a third voyage. With difficulty—on account of his tarnished reputation—Columbus gathered a crew to man six ships, which departed Spain in May 1498, reaching Trinidad on July 31, 1498. On August 1, they landed on the mainland, and Columbus thereby became the discoverer of South America.

He also discovered pearls at islands near the coast. This must have been a great relief, for his royal sponsors were continually fuming about Columbus's failure to harvest the treasure trove they had anticipated. But then came the bad news. Sailing across the Caribbean to Santo Domingo, Columbus found the colonists in revolt. In the meantime, the disgruntled Spanish sovereigns had dispatched a royal commissioner, Francisco de Bobadilla, who arrived from Spain in 1500 to straighten matters out. He summarily stripped the Columbus brothers of governing authority and sent them back to Spain in chains.

The captain of the returning vessel thought Columbus had gotten a raw deal and removed the shackles, but Columbus dramatically insisted that he appear before Isabella and Ferdinand in chains. The conscience-stricken pair immediately ordered him freed. In May 1502, they even sent him on a fourth and final voyage. Landing briefly at Martinique, Columbus sailed on to Santo Domingo, only to be refused permission to land. He explored the Central American coast and was marooned for a year in Jamaica because his wooden vessels had been thoroughly rotted by shipworm. Subsequently rescued, he reached Spain in November 1504 and died two years later (on May 20, 1506) at Valladolid, still claiming that he had reached Asia and arguing fruitlessly for his family's right to a share of whatever wealth and power his discoveries might yet yield.

Why We're Not Called Columbia

In the end, Columbus was cheated even of the honor of having his major discovery named for him. The Florentine explorer Amerigo Vespucci (1454–1512) claimed to have made four Atlantic voyages between 1497 and 1504, although only two have been absolutely confirmed: one in 1499, commissioned by Spain and resulting in the discovery of Brazil and Venezuela, and another in 1501, to Brazil on behalf of Portugal. Following the 1501 voyage, Vespucci coined the phrase *Mundus Novus*—New World—to describe the region. The name stuck. Then, in 1507, the German cartographer Martin Waldseemuller published an account of Vespucci's voyages, along with a map and *Cosmographiae introductio* (*Introduction to Cosmography*), a treatise on mapmaking. It was Waldseemuller who used a Latinized form of Vespucci's first name to label the region Amerigo Vespucci had explored.

The Least You Need to Know

➤ Columbus was hardly unique in believing the earth to be round. However, he did set sail and persuade a crew that they would not fall off the edge of a flat world.

➤ Despite the Native Americans' friendly overtures, the Spanish attacked and suffered retaliation. This inaugurated four hundred years of white–Indian warfare in the Americas.

➤ Columbus derived little benefit from his four voyages; even the land mass he discovered, America, was named for a later explorer, *Amerigo* Vespucci.

Chapter 3

New Spain, Same Old Spaniards (1400–1600s)

In This Chapter

➤ Spanish voyages after Columbus

➤ Conquest of the Aztecs and Incas

➤ Coronado's search for the Seven Cities of Cibola

➤ The "Black Legend" and native revolts

In the wake of Columbus, the Portuguese scrambled to launch a series of expeditions, including that of Amerigo Vespucci and, in 1500, an expedition to India led by Pedro Alvares Cabral. To put it mildly, Cabral went wide in the South Atlantic and ended up in Brazil.

Yet another Portuguese, Ferdinand Magellan, sailed not under the flag of his native country, but on commission from Spain, charged with proving that the aptly named Spice Islands lay on the Spanish side of the line of demarcation established by the Treaty of Tordesillas.

Magellan sailed west in 1519, found the Strait of Magellan separating the southern tip of South America from Tierra del Fuego, and crossed the Strait into the Pacific. That ocean had been discovered on September 25 or 27, 1513, by Vasco Nuñez de Balboa, but it was Magellan who named it. Magellan explored the Philippine Islands and even persuaded the ruler of Cebu, one of the islands, to accept Christianity. That soon embroiled Magellan in a local war, however; and on April 27, 1521, he was killed by natives on Mactan Island. One of Magellan's captains, Juan Sebastian del Cano, brought his ship, the *Victoria*, back to Spain, thereby completing (in 1522) the first circumnavigation of the globe.

The voyages of Spain, as well as those of Portugal, were undertaken not for the sake of exploration, but for the purpose of conquest and colonization—and also to convert the "heathen" New World to the cause of Christ. Accordingly, two classes of professionals were represented among the early Spanish explorers: *conquistadors* ("conquerors") and priests.

The Way of the Conquistador

The New World was opened up to Spain just in the nick of time. Like much of Europe, that nation was dominated by primogeniture, meaning that the first son in a family would inherit all titles and property upon the death of the father. This cramped the style of younger sons, who were left to fend for themselves. The problem was that Spain, in effect, had been all used up—all titles were taken, all property was claimed. For the lower classes, prospects were (as they always are) even more limited. The New World represented a new chance, offering a world of opportunity.

Word for the Day

The word *primogeniture* is Latin, meaning first (*primo*) birth (*geniture*). It signifies the right of the firstborn child—almost exclusively the *male* child—to inherit the whole of his family's wealth, titles, and privileges.

Plumed Serpent

The conquistadors followed in the footsteps of Columbus. Puerto Rico was subjugated during 1508–1509 by Juan Ponce de Leon (ca. 1460–1521), who, according to partially credible legend, had come to the New World in search of the fabled Fountain of Youth. (He didn't find youth, but death: Ponce de Leon was mortally wounded by an Indian arrow in Florida.) Next, Jamaica and Cuba fell easily to the Spaniards in 1510 and 1511.

Far more spectacular was the battle for Mexico. It was led by Hernan Cortés, a minor nobleman who had rejected a university education to become an adventurer in the New World. In 1519, Cortés led an expedition into the present-day region of Tabasco, defeating the Tabascan Indians on March 25. By September 5, he moved against the Tlascalas as well. After triumphing over the Tlascalas, he made them allies in his campaign against their traditional enemies, the powerful Aztecs, who dominated Mexico.

Surprisingly, when Cortés landed at what is today Veracruz, he was met not with hostility, but cordially and humbly greeted by ambassadors of Montezuma II, the Aztec emperor. This fact has mystified generations of historians. Some have concluded that, unlike the ruthlessly brilliant warrior kings who had preceded him, Montezuma II was indecisive and possessed of a weak character. Others have speculated that the Aztecs, having never before seen men mounted on horseback—strange and strangely attired men at that—thought the Spaniards were incarnations of their gods. Some have suggested that Cortés deliberately posed as Quetzalcoatl, the Aztec "plumed serpent" deity. Still other scholars believe that Montezuma II hoped to appease the intruders with gifts of great beauty and value—gems and gold—in the hope that, satisfied, they would simply depart.

If that was Montezuma's hope, it was a tragic misjudgment. Receiving the gifts, Cortés remarked: "Send me some more of it, because I and my companions suffer from a disease of the heart which can be cured only with gold." After an embittered battle, the Aztecs surrendered on August 13, 1521, and the Aztec Mexican empire fell to Hernan Cortés.

Borderlands

Cortés had achieved what all the conquistadors sought: access to unimaginable wealth. However, the only other Spaniard whose success began to approach that of Cortés was Francisco Pizarro, who twice attempted to invade the Incas of Peru during the 1520s and finally achieved his objective on a third try in 1531.

Pizarro, like Cortés, was regarded as a great conqueror, and his exploits stimulated Spanish expeditions into the borderlands—that is, the area of the present United States. The hope was that, somehow, somewhere, another Aztec or Inca realm would be discovered. Indians had told Columbus tales of villages containing vast treasuries of gold. Alvar Nuñez Cabeza de Vaca, a member of a calamitous 1520 expedition led by Cortés's rival, Panfilo Narvaez, journeyed throughout the American Southwest for eight years and brought back to Spain tales of rich pueblos—the Seven Cities of Cibola—though he never claimed to have visited them personally. Another survivor of the Narvaez expedition, a black slave named Estevan, joined an expedition led by Marcos de Niza in 1539 to locate the Seven Cities. Zuni Indians killed the unfortunate Estevan in a battle outside the Hawikuh pueblo, but de Niza returned to Mexico City and there rendered a vivid account of the pueblo and its treasures. Never mind that he had failed to gain entry into Hawikuh.

But, then, Francisco Vazquez de Coronado did not insist on proof. As with so many others who would journey to the American West in the centuries to come, all that was necessary to propel Coronado was a *dream* of riches. During 1540–42, he traveled throughout the Southwest, as far as present-day Kansas. Early in the expedition, during July 1540, he and his troops rode into the Zuni pueblo of Hawikuh in central New Mexico. Imperiously, he demanded the surrender of the pueblo. In response, the usually peaceful Zuni showered stones upon the conquistadors, knocking Coronado himself unconscious. Within an hour, however, Hawikuh fell, Coronado and his men entered it, and they found—very little. Certainly, there was no gold.

Coronado pressed on, in fruitless search of the elusive Seven Cities. Traveling through the pueblo region along the Rio Grande, he took one Zuni or Hopi town after another, forcing the inhabitants into slavery and taking from them whatever food and shelter they required. In the wake of Coronado's visit, during the summer of 1541, the pueblos, led by an Indian named Texamatli, rebelled, but were quickly defeated by the forces of Niño de Guzmán, governor of New Spain.

Oñate the Terrible

With Coronado's disappointment, the legend of the Seven Cities of Cibola diminished, and Spain's interest in the American Southwest likewise dimmed. Then, in 1579, the English sea dog Sir Francis Drake landed on the central California coast and laid claim to what he christened "New Albion," using the old poetic name for England. This spurred the Spanish viceroy at Mexico City to alert the royal court in Madrid that Spain's New World monopoly was imperiled. Embroiled in costly European wars, the Spanish crown did nothing to reinforce the apparently worthless northern frontier of its colonies for another twenty years. Finally, in 1598, an expedition was launched northward from Mexico under the ambitious Don Juan de Oñate. When he reached the site of present-day El Paso, Texas, Oñate claimed for Spain—and his own governance—all of "New Mexico," by which he meant a region extending from Texas to California.

Word for the Day
Whereas Spanish seafarers favored such grandiose titles as "Admiral of the Ocean Sea" and marquis of this or that, the great British navigators who sailed for Queen Elizabeth I gloried in the title of *sea dog*, coined during the 16th century and used to describe only the most daring and seasoned salts.

With 400 men, women, and children in tow—plus 7,000 heads of cattle—Oñate colonized deep into pueblo country, depositing settlers at various sites. In no place, except at the Acoma pueblo, in western New Mexico, did he meet resistance. At Acoma, as usual, he sent an advance squad of conquistadors to tell the Indians that they were hereafter to consider themselves subjects of the Spanish crown. In response, the Indians killed 13 of the Spanish soldiers. Perched atop a high-walled mesa, the defenders of the pueblo believed their position was impregnable. But in January 1599, Oñate's troops fought their way to the top of the mesa, killed most of the pueblo warriors, then took captive 500 women, children, and noncombatant men. Of the latter, 80 over the age of 25 were condemned to the amputation of one foot and a period of 20 years' enslavement. (Whether or not Oñate considered the usefulness of 80 one-footed slaves is not recorded.) The women—as well as children over age 12—were permitted to retain their extremities, but were likewise enslaved. Children under 12 were considered ripe for conversion to Christianity and were committed to the care of priests. A pair of Hopis who had the ill fortune to be visiting Acoma at this time were seized. The governor caused their right hands to be severed, and he sent the maimed Hopis back to their own pueblo as a bloody warning of the consequences of rebellion.

Birth of the "Black Legend"

In 1514, the Spaniard Bartolome de Las Casas (1474–1566), known as the "Apostle of the Indies," catalogued with outrage a litany of his countrymen's atrocities in his *Historia de las Indias* (*History of the Indies*).

Through the writings of Las Casas and other witnesses to Spanish colonial history, a "Black Legend" grew up around Spain in the New World. The conquistadors came to the Americas thoroughly grounded in a bloody tradition of racial warfare, having fought the Moors for eight centuries to gain control of the Iberian peninsula. Moreover, colonizers such as Oñate financed operations with their personal funds. When Oñate failed to turn up the gold he had hoped for, he relentlessly worked the Indians in an effort to make a profit from agricultural enterprise. As it turned out, the people he had subjugated failed to produce enough food even to sustain the colonists, let alone to sell for profit, and, after Oñate's cruelty became obnoxious even to royal officials, he was fined and stripped of all honors.

The Black Legend was also fostered and sustained by the *encomienda* system, which dominated Spanish colonial government from the 16th through the 18th centuries. By 1503, the crown began granting loyal colonists a type of deed (called an *encomendar*) to specific tracts of land with the additional proviso that the Indians living on the land could be used as laborers for a specific number of days per year. The majority of *encomenderos* abused their Indian charges, brutally forcing them to work for nothing more than mere token wages and showing not the least concern for their health.

The cruelty of the *encomienda* system was, to some degree, balanced by the beneficent intentions of the Spanish missionaries. It is true that the Indians were given no choice in deciding whether or not they *wanted* to be "saved" by conversion to Christianity, but the best of the missionaries, beginning with Las Casas, did have an abiding concern for the spiritual as well as physical welfare of their charges. Ironically, such concern may have served to perpetuate the horrors that Oñate and others visited upon the Indians. On economic grounds alone, it is not likely that Spain would have continued to support its colonial outposts north of the Rio Grande. Gold was not forthcoming, and agricultural enterprises produced marginal profits at best and, in most cases, ruinous losses. But all during the Spanish experiment in the Southwest, the friars had been creating a population of new Christians, whose now-sanctified souls, they argued, could not simply be abandoned.

The First American Revolutions

By the middle of the 17th century, after half a century of tyranny, certain of the Pueblo Indian groups were moved to a desperate action. They forged an alliance with their hereditary foes, the Apaches, who were envied and feared for their skill as warriors (the very word *apache* comes from a Zuni term meaning "enemy"). After several abortive attempts at rebellion, the Apaches seized the initiative and, during the 1670s, terrorized the Spanish Southwest. In this they were soon joined by people of the pueblos, who waged a long and disruptive guerrilla war against their Spanish masters. At last, Governor Antonio de Oterrmín moved against 47 so-called medicine men whom he identified as ringleaders of the rebellion. He hanged three and imprisoned the remainder in Santa Fe, the territorial capital. Among the prisoners was an Indian leader from the Tewa pueblo named Popé. Released after several years of cruel imprisonment, Popé went into hiding in Taos and began covertly organizing what he planned as a final, decisive rebellion.

Despite almost universal outrage among the pueblos, achieving unified action was no easy task. Popé managed to persuade all but the most remote pueblos (which were least oppressed by the Spanish) to join him. Next, in order to coordinate action, he sent runners to the various towns, each bearing a knotted cord designed so that the last knot would be untied in each pueblo on the day set for the revolt: August 13, 1680. So determined was Popé to maintain secrecy that he had his brother-in-law murdered when he suspected him of treachery. Despite such precautions, word of the rebellion leaked to the colonial authorities, and Popé was forced to launch his revolution early, on the 10th. Despite the sudden change in schedule, the rebellion was devastating to the Spanish. The major missions at Taos, Pecos, and Acoma were burned and the priests murdered, their bodies heaped upon the altars of their despised religion. The lesser missions were crushed as well, and ranches were destroyed. Those who did not flee were killed. At last, on August 15, Popé led a 500-man army into Santa Fe. Four hundred settlers and 21 of 33 missionaries perished. Although the armed garrison at Santa Fe consisted of only 50 men, they were equipped with a brass cannon, which they used to resist the invasion for four days before evacuating—Governor Oterrmín included—on August 21. Some 2,500 survivors of the onslaught fled as far as present-day El Paso, Texas, abandoning all their possessions to looters.

Sadly for the Native people of the pueblos, Popé capped his triumph by installing himself as absolute dictator and one who was as oppressive as any Spanish overlord had been. For the next eight years, he extorted a ruinous tax from his people, executing anyone who resisted. By the time of Popé's death (from natural causes) in 1688, the pueblo region was in a state of chronic civil war. The Indians were vulnerable, and, a year after Popé's death, the Zia Pueblo was retaken by the Spanish. In 1692, Governor Don Diego de Vargas laid siege to Santa Fe, entirely cutting off its water and food until it collapsed in surrender. During the course of the next four years, all of the pueblos submitted once again to Spanish rule, except for the Hopis, who were somehow simply overlooked by colonial authorities.

All was not entirely quiet. In 1695, the Pima Indians of lower Pimeria Alta—the region of present-day Sonora, Mexico, and southern Arizona—looted and burned Spanish settlements. The uprising was quickly suppressed, and more than 50 years would pass before the Pimas—these of upper Pimeria Alta, many descended from earlier rebels who had fled north—staged another uprising, which degenerated into a century and a half of smoldering guerrilla wars—first against the Spanish, then the Mexicans, and finally the Americans.

From Black Legend to Black Robes

Enslavement and warfare were not the sole legacies of the Spanish in the American Southwest. The priests—the Indians called them "black robes"—who accompanied the conquistadors not only brought their religion to the Americas, but also created a Euro-Indian culture centered around the many missions they established. The first of these, in New Mexico, were founded during the administration of Oñate in 1598. In the course of the next century, Franciscan friars founded more than 40 more, mainly along the Rio Grande. By 1680, missions had been built among most of the Indians in New Mexico as well. As the presence in California of the Englishman Sir Francis Drake had stirred Spanish concerns in 1579, a French landing led by Robert Cavelier, sieur de La Salle, on the Texas coast in 1684 prompted the Spanish to build missions in that area.

Between 1687 and 1711, Father Eusebio Kino established many missions in northern Mexico and Baja California as well as some in southern Arizona, the most famous of which was Mission San Xavier del Bac. But it is for the chain of 21 Franciscan missions, linked together by El Camino Real ("The Royal Road"), extending along the California coast from San Diego in the south to Sonoma in the north, that the Spanish missionaries are best known. The first, Mission San Diego de Alcala (at San Diego) was founded by Father Junipero Serra in 1769. Serra would go on personally to found nine more.

The missions were communities, and, like any other communities, they varied widely in their success. Some faltered and collapsed, while others spawned fertile fields, vineyards, and vast herds of cattle. By bringing large numbers of Indians into a small space, the missions also tended to spread epidemic disease, and they disrupted native culture and traditions.

The way of the conquistador and the way of the Black Robe represent two distinctive aspects of the Hispanic Southwest. But whereas the conquistadors treated the Indians as bestial enemies, to be subdued and enslaved, the Catholic padres regarded them as miscreant children to be supervised and regulated. Neither extreme admitted a full appreciation of their humanity, but both traditions shaped the character of the Southwest in an enduring fashion. Both, too, created enmities between white and red, leaving scars on the history of the region so deep that they would not begin to fade until the end of the 19th century. As to the missions themselves, the last one, San Francisco Solano, in the Sonoma Valley of Northern California, was built in 1823, and the mission system endured until 1833–34, when the revolutionary Mexican Republic—which then encompassed the American Southwest—secularized Church properties.

The Least You Need to Know

> ➤ The sensational exploits of Cortés in Mexico and Pizarro in Peru inspired exploration of the "borderlands" (the area of the present American Southwest).

> ➤ Don Juan de Oñate was typical of the oppressive colonial authorities who ruled the borderlands.

> ➤ In addition to a hunger for wealth and power, the Spanish colonizers were also driven by a desire to convert the Indians of the New World to Christianity.

Chapter 4

England's Errands (1497–1608)

In This Chapter

➤ Search for a Northwest Passage

➤ The "Lost Colony" of Roanoke

➤ Jamestown: first permanent English settlement in America

➤ Captain John Smith and Pocahontas

Some time in the 21st century, people of Hispanic heritage will become the single largest ethnic group in the United States. History is always getting rewritten, and, doubtless, it will get rewritten then as well. However, up to the present, most American history has been told from a distinctly Anglo point of view. There is no doubt that Spain often acted cruelly in the New World, but it is also true that the history of Spain in the New World has been written, mostly, by Anglo historians who, over the years, have narrated that record of cruelty with great relish and even an attitude of superiority. In particular, they have tended to contrast the Spanish colonial experience—driven by greed for gold and absolute power—with the English experience, motivated by a quest for religious freedom.

Well, things weren't quite so simple.

O, Brave New World

Henry VII (1457–1509) ascended the throne of England after he killed Richard III in the Battle of Bosworth Field on August 22, 1485, thereby ending the Wars of the Roses, a series of clashes between the houses of Lancaster and York, rivals for the English throne. Not that it was much of a throne. The costly, bloody wars had drained off resources and manpower at a time when the rest of Europe was building great empires. Separated from the Continent by the English Channel, England had always been European, yet also apart from Europe—a comparatively tiny backwater, in fact, habitually torn by internal conflict among tribes, clans, and families.

King Henry decided to put his hard-won reign on the path to greatness. Having defeated Richard, the Lancastrian monarch sought to end the conflict between the branches of the royal family once and for all by marrying Elizabeth of York, daughter of King Edward VI. (The union produced one of England's greatest —and most terrifying—kings, Henry VIII.) Henry VII built a strong central government, replenished the treasury, and, in 1497, sponsored the first English voyage of exploration in the New World.

Stats

Just *how* small is England? Exclusive of Wales and Scotland, which were not part of the nation in the 1500s, England is only 50,363 square miles in area.

For the sleepy island nation, this was a momentous step. Years later, about 1610 or 1611, during the reign of the first Stuart king, James I, William Shakespeare wrote what was probably his last play. Called *The Tempest,* it is about the beautiful young Miranda and her father-magician, who are exiled to an enchanted island across the ocean. Shakespeare drew much of his inspiration for this magical realm from reading contemporary accounts of the English voyages. There is one particular line in the play that seems to summarize the excitement of the "Age of Discovery" Henry VII had launched a little more than a century earlier. "O, brave new world..." it begins.

Henry VII Backs an Italian Sailor

Giovanni Caboto, born in Genoa about 1451 but a citizen of the seafaring city-state of Venice, finally settled in England with his family. A cartel of merchants in the seaport town of Bristol hired Caboto—whom they called John Cabot—to pioneer a direct route to the spice-rich Indies. The plan was logical and potentially highly lucrative. England, on the westernmost end of the traditional overland caravan routes from the East, paid premium prices for spice. If the East could be reached more directly by sailing *west*, English merchants would get a jump on the worldwide spice market and enjoy unheard of levels of prosperity. King Henry VII made it official by granting Cabot letters of patent, empowering him to claim hitherto unspoken for territories. He sailed from Dursey Head,

Ireland, in May 1497 with no more than 20 men on the ship *Matthew* and landed in Newfoundland on June 24. It is likely that he probed as far south as Maine. After looking around for no more than three weeks—long enough for him to come to the confident conclusion that he had reached the northeast corner of Asia—Cabot returned to England with the exciting news. Eager to believe that Cabot had indeed opened a door to the wide world, a grateful Henry VII granted him an annual pension of £20.

Cabot rushed to outfit a second voyage, bound for what he thought was Japan. Setting out in May 1498, this time with 200 men in five ships, he and his crews were lost at sea. (Some authorities claim that one ship did return to Ireland, but there is no official record of the expedition's fate.)

Passage to India? No Way

The loss of John Cabot was hardly the end of English exploration. His son Sebastian (ca. 1482–1557) was commissioned by Henry VII to make a voyage in 1508 and probably reached what would later be called Hudson Bay. Appointed Henry's official cartographer, Sebastian Cabot nevertheless later transferred his allegiance to England's great rival, Spain, for which he became pilot-major and official examiner of pilots in 1518. After failing, in 1526, to complete a mission intended to follow the route of Ferdinand Magellan, he was prosecuted by his Spanish paymasters in 1530 and found his way back to England in 1548. There King Edward VI granted him a pension, and he became governor for life of the English Muscovy Company. In that capacity, he worked with Sir Hugh Willoughby and Richard Chancellor in search of a "Northeast Passage" connecting the Atlantic and Pacific oceans along the northern shores of Eurasia. Under Cabot's direction, Willoughby and Chancellor looked for the passage. Willoughby and his crew were lost, but Chancellor, though he failed to find the passage, did reach Moscow and trade was opened up between English merchants and those of Russia. Later voyages in search of the Northeast Passage undertaken by Henry Hudson during 1607–1609 were blocked by polar ice.

Main Event

It was Russian sailors who finally found the Northeast Passage in 1648. Semen Ivanov Dezhnev sailed from the Kolyma River through the Bering Strait to the mouth of the Anadyr River on the Pacific Ocean. Vitus Bering, the Danish seafarer for whom the strait is named, sailed from the Pacific to the Arctic Ocean between 1725 and 1730, and Baron Nils A. E. Nordenskjold, a Swede, made the first through passage from west to east in 1878–79, wintering off the Chukchi peninsula.

In the meantime, an even greater interest developed in the prospect of a North*west* Passage. Despite the claims of Columbus and John Cabot that they had reached Asia, it began to dawn on explorers and cartographers alike that the New World really was a *new* world—a continental land mass separating the Atlantic and Pacific oceans and, therefore, separating Europe from Asia, at least as far as any western shortcut was concerned. However, the early explorations had also revealed the presence of many bays and rivers along the northern coast of the new continent, and this suggested the possibility of a water passage clear through the land mass, maybe all the way to the Pacific Ocean and spice-rich Asia. As it became increasingly clear that the Americas would yield no great treasures of gold—no Seven Cities of Cibola—the New World was perceived by some as less of an objective than an obstacle.

The search for the Northwest Passage may be traced to the 1534 voyage of the French navigator Jacques Cartier, who explored the St. Lawrence River with the express purpose of finding a passage to China. The English weighed in when 29-year-old Sir Humphrey Gilbert (c. 1539–83) published *A Discourse to Prove a Passage by the Northwest to Cathia* ("Cathia" = Cathay = China) in 1566 which, 11 years later, indirectly led Sir Francis Drake to sail his famed vessel, the *Golden Hind*, down the Atlantic coast of South America, round Tierra del Fuego, and northward, just beyond San Francisco, California. But Martin Frobisher (ca. 1539–94)—a typically colorful Elizabethan sea dog, who had sailed twice to Africa, had been captured by the Portuguese, and had even gotten his living through high seas piracy—was the first Englishman who deliberately searched for a Northwest Passage. He took three swings. The first, in 1576, yielded the discovery of an inlet in Baffin Island, now known as Frobisher Bay, which Frobisher believed was the opening of the Northwest Passage. He also became excited by the presence of an ore that looked a lot like gold. (Hey, maybe America was not such a bad place after all!) And Frobisher was not the only one who thought he had struck gold. The ore attracted a substantial cartel of investors who created the Company of Cathay, which backed a second voyage in 1577, and a third in 1578.

Neither subsequent expedition found gold, but in July 1578, Frobisher sailed up what was later named Hudson Strait, which was an interesting discovery in itself, but hardly the Northwest Passage. Frobisher named it "Mistaken Strait," gave up the search for the passage, and became vice-admiral in Sir Francis Drake's 1585–1586 expedition to the West Indies and later (1588) served ably in the defense against the Spanish Armada. In the meantime, another Englishman, John Davis (ca. 1550–1605), made three voyages between 1585 and 1587, exploring the western shores of Greenland, Davis Strait, and Cumberland Sound. Failing to find the Northwest Passage, he became one of the first explorers of the Arctic, then, in the opposite hemisphere, discovered the Falkland Islands, 480 miles northeast of Cape Horn, which would become the object of a brief and violent 1982 war of possession between Argentina and Great Britain.

Davis met his end in 1605 at the hands of Japanese in Sumatra. Henry Hudson, the next seeker after the "passage to India," became the victim of his own crew. In 1610–11, after fruitlessly exploring Hudson Bay—an inland body of water so vast that it seemed certain to be the fabled passage—his crew mutinied, casting adrift and to their deaths Hudson and a few loyal men.

Still, the search continued. Between 1612 and 1615, Thomas Button, Robert Bylot, and William Baffin, Englishmen all, made additional voyages to Hudson Bay—looking not only for the Northwest Passage, but for any sign of the missing Henry Hudson. While these expeditions failed to achieve either of their objectives, they did create interest in the region and led, in 1670, to the creation of the Hudson's Bay Company, which became one of the most powerful forces for trade and settlement in North America.

A Colony Vanishes, a Colony Appears

A passage to the East was not the only reason for English interest in the New World. Sir Humphrey Gilbert, author of the provocative tract on the Northwest Passage, earned renown as a soldier in the service of Queen Elizabeth I. She knighted him in 1570 and, eight years later, granted him a charter to settle any lands not already claimed by Christians. The ambitious Elizabeth wanted her island nation to become the center of a new world, the locus of a great trading empire—and she wanted to do this before Spain and Portugal succeeded in grabbing all of that new world for themselves. With her blessing, then, Gilbert sailed in 1579, but was compelled to return when his fleet broke up. He set sail again in June 1583 and reached St. John's Bay, Newfoundland, in August, claiming that territory for the queen. On his way back to England, however, Gilbert's ship, badly overloaded, foundered and sank with the loss of all hands. The charter was inherited by Gilbert's half brother, Sir Walter Raleigh, the 31-year-old favorite of Queen Elizabeth.

Roanoke Lost

In 1584, Raleigh sent a small reconnaissance fleet to what would become Croatan Sound in the Outer Banks of North Carolina. They returned with glowing reports of a land inhabited by "most gentle, loving and faithful" Indians who lived "after the manner of the Golden Age." Knighted by his "Virgin Queen," Raleigh named the new land after her: Virginia. In 1585–86, he dispatched Sir Richard Grenville with a small group of would-be settlers. Sir Francis Drake encountered them a year later, starving and wanting nothing so much as passage back to England. Nothing daunted, Raleigh launched three ships and 117 people (men, women, and children) to what is now called Roanoke Island, off the coast of North Carolina, in 1587. After establishing them on the swampy island, their leader, John White, decided to sail back to England to fetch the supplies that Raleigh had promised to send. (Unknown to White, the supply ships were stalled because of the attack of the Spanish Armada against England.)

When White returned to the colony in 1590, he found no settlers and only the barest trace of a settlement—a few rusted items and what was apparently the name of a neighboring island carved into a tree: CROATOAN.

Had the colonists fallen prey to disease? Starvation? Hostile Indians (who took them captive to "Croatoan")?

Who knows?

Real Life

Sir Walter Raleigh was a favorite courtier of Queen Elizabeth I, who knighted him in 1584, the year he obtained Gilbert's patent. By the 1590s, Raleigh fell out of favor with a jealous Elizabeth after he married one of her maids of honor, and the queen imprisoned him briefly in 1592. He was later "rehabilitated," however, and went on to serve with distinction in naval expeditions to the Guiana coast of South America (1595), Spain (1596), and the Azores (1597). In 1600, he was appointed governor of the Isle of Jersey, serving until 1603, when advisers to Elizabeth's successor, James I, persuaded the new king that Raleigh had conspired against his ascension to the throne. Raleigh was sentenced to death, but execution was stayed for 13 years, during which he languished in the Tower of London. In 1616, he appealed to James to send him on an expedition in search of South American gold. When he returned empty-handed, he was sent back to the Tower—at least in part because the Spanish crown demanded that he be punished for having sacked a Spanish settlement in Guiana. James then ordered his execution, for the original conspiracy conviction, on October 29, 1618.

Jamestown Hangs by a Thread

Raleigh's disaster did not shatter English dreams of colonial expansion. At the start of the 17th century, England was still militarily and commercially weak in comparison with Spain and Portugal. Domestically, as the ancient feudal system decayed, the nation was burdened on the one hand by a displaced peasant class it could no longer feed, and, on the other, it was seeing the rise of a merchant and artisan class whose markets were exceedingly limited. Like Spain, then, England *needed* a new world. In 1605, two groups of merchants, one calling itself the Virginia Company of London (often abbreviated to the London Company) and the other the Plymouth Company, recruited a cartel of investors and joined in a petition to James I for a charter to establish a colony in the territory of Raleigh's patent (which, as far as anyone knew, encompassed whatever portion of North America had not been claimed by Spain). The Virginia Company was granted a charter to colonize southern Virginia, while the Plymouth Company was given rights to northern Virginia.

The Virginia Company moved swiftly to recruit a contingent of 144 settlers, including the families of moneyed gentlemen as well as poor people. The latter purchased their passage to America and the right of residence in the colony by binding themselves to serve the Virginia Company for a period of seven years, working the land and creating a settlement. In December 1606, the hopeful band of men, women, and children boarded the *Susan Constant,* the *Discovery*, and the *Goodspeed.* Thirty-nine perished in the course of the voyage. The remaining 105 arrived at the mouth of a river—they called it the James—on May 24, 1607, and they scratched out Jamestown.

Word for the Day

Most of the colonists obtained passage to the New World by signing a contract called an *indenture*, thereby becoming *indentured servants*—in effect, slaves for the seven-year term of the agreement. This would prove a very popular method of bringing settlers to the fledgling English colonies.

Historians blithely refer to Jamestown as "the first permanent English colony" in the New World. "Permanent," in this case, is a highly relative term. Jamestown was established in a malarial swamp well past the time of season appropriate for planting crops. In any case, the "gentlemen" of the venture—those who were not indentured servants—were unaccustomed to manual labor, and hacking a colony out of the wilderness required the hard work of *all* hands. Within months, half the colony was dead or had fled to the mercies of the local Indians.

Then matters grew worse.

John Smith and Pocahontas

In 1609 came what the colonists called "the starving time." Desperate, the survivors resorted to acts of cannibalism and even looted the fresh graves of their own number as well as those of local Indians.

Jamestown would certainly have joined the Roanoke colony in a common oblivion had it not been for the presence of the soldier of fortune the Virginia Company had hired to look after the military defense of the colony. The intrepid Captain John Smith (ca. 1579–1631) managed to get himself adopted by the local Indians, who were led by the powerful old chief Powhatan, and, from them, obtained enough corn and yams to keep the surviving colonists from starving. He also instituted martial law in the colony, sternly declaring that only those who worked would eat. Enforcing this iron discipline, Smith saved the fledgling colony.

Relations between the colonists and the "Powhatans" (the English named the numerous Algonquin Indian villages after the single chief who controlled them) were always strained. Simply by refusing to share their food, the Powhatans could have wiped out the struggling colony at will. Yet they did not do so, albeit they repeatedly threatened war. Doubtless in an effort to intimidate Chief Powhatan and his people into maintaining peaceful relations, in 1613, Captain Samuel Argall kidnapped his daughter Pocahontas and took her to Jamestown (and, later, to Henrico) as a hostage. Fascinated by the English, the "Indian princess" quickly learned their language and customs—and rapidly evolved from hostage to ambassador. In 1614, with the blessing of her father, she married John Rolfe, a tobacco planter. The union brought eight years of peace between the Indians and the settlers, a period crucial to the survival and development of the colony. (Rolfe took his bride on a voyage back to England, where she was a favorite with London society as well as the royal court. Sadly, this remarkable young woman succumbed to an illness and died, in England, on March 21, 1617, at the age of 22.)

Voice from the Past

Here is the original Pocahontas–John Smith story, as related in *A History of the Settlement of Virginia*, by the early Virginia merchant Thomas Studley and Smith himself—

At last they brought Captain Smith to Powhatan, their emperor. At Captain Smith's entrance before the king, all the people gave a great shout. The queen was appointed to bring him water to wash his hands, and another brought him a bunch of feathers, instead of a towel, on which to dry them. Having feasted him after the best barbarous manner they could, a long consultation was held. At last two great stones were brought before Powhatan. Then as many as could lay hands on Captain Smith dragged him to the stones, and laid his head on them, and were ready with their clubs to beat out his brains. At this instant, Pocahontas, the king's dearest daughter, when no entreaty could prevail, got his head in her arms, and laid her own head upon his to save him from death. Thereupon the emperor was contented to have him live.

To what must have been the great surprise of anyone who had witnessed the first terrible year at Jamestown, the colony survived and even prospered. The indentured colonists, having fulfilled their obligations, took control of their own land, on which they planted tobacco, as the Indians had taught them. A great fondness for the weed developed in Europe, and America found its first cash crop and significant export product. The prospect of growing rich from the cultivation of tobacco attracted more settlers. The Virginia enterprise was, at long last, successfully launched, and the world—New and Old—would never be the same.

The Least You Need to Know

➤ The earliest English interest in the New World was motivated by a desire to strengthen the tiny nation through dominance in trade.

➤ In 1607, Jamestown became the first permanent—albeit precarious—English settlement in America.

Chapter 5

A Rock and a Hard Place (1608–1733)

In This Chapter

➤ Puritans, Separatists, Pilgrims

➤ Settlement of Plymouth and Massachusetts Bay colonies

➤ Religious tolerance in Rhode Island, Maryland, and Pennsylvania

➤ Oglethorpe's utopian experiment

➤ Introduction of slavery

The settlement of Virginia was motivated by a combination of commercial enthusiasm and the intense social and economic pressures of an England that had outgrown its ancient feudal system. Farther north in America, in the area still known as New England, settlement was motivated more immediately by religious zeal.

As early as the reign of Elizabeth I, certain members of the Church of England (which the queen's father, Henry VIII, severed from the Roman Catholic Church during 1536–40) had become extremely critical about what they considered compromises made with Catholic practice. A group of Anglican priests, most of them graduates of Cambridge University, advocated such articles of religion as direct personal spiritual experience, rigorously sincere moral conduct, and radically simple worship services. They felt that the mainstream Anglican church had not gone far enough in reforming worship and purging it of Catholic influence. When James I ascended the throne in 1603, Puritan leaders clamored for reform, including the abolition of bishops. James refused, but Puritanism (as the new reform movement came to be called) gained a substantial popular following by the early 17th century. The government and the mainstream Anglican Church, especially under Archbishop William Laud, reacted with repressive and discriminatory measures amounting to a campaign of persecution. Some Puritans left the country, settling in religiously tolerant Holland, while others remained in England and formed a powerful bloc within the parliamentarian party that, under the leadership of Oliver Cromwell, ultimately defeated (and beheaded!) Charles I in the English Civil War (1642–46).

The New Israel

The Puritans who left England were, logically enough, called Separatists. Most of them were farmers, poorly educated, and of lowly social status. One of the Separatist congregations was led by William Brewster and the Reverend Richard Clifton in the village of Scrooby, Nottinghamshire. This group left Scrooby for Amsterdam in 1608, then, the following year, moved to another Dutch town, Leyden, where they lived for 12 years. Although the Scrooby group had found religious freedom, they were plagued by economic hardship and were concerned that their children were growing up Dutch rather than English. In 1617, they decided on a radical course of action. They voted to immigrate to America.

Brewster knew Sir Edwin Sandys, treasurer of the Virginia Company of London, and, through him, the Scrooby congregation obtained a pair of patents authorizing them to settle in the northern part of the company's American territory. With supplementary financial backing from a London iron merchant named Thomas Weston, somewhat less than half of the congregation finally chose to leave Leyden. They boarded the *Speedwell*, bound for the port of Southampton, England, where they were to unite with another group of Separatists and pick up a second ship. However, both groups were dogged by delays and disputes. Ultimately, 102 souls (fewer than half of whom were Separatists) piled into a single vessel, the *Mayflower*, and embarked from Plymouth on September 16, 1620.

After a grueling 65-day voyage, the Pilgrims (as their first historian, William Bradford, would later label them) sighted land on November 19. Apparently, rough seas off Nantucket forced the *Mayflower*'s skipper, Captain Christopher Jones, to steer away from the mouth of the Hudson River, where the Pilgrims were supposed to establish their "plantation," to a landing at Cape Cod. This lay beyond the Virginia Company's jurisdiction, and some historians believe that the Pilgrims actually bribed Captain Jones to alter course precisely in order to insure the group's independence from external authority. Be that as it may, the *Mayflower* dropped anchor off present-day Provincetown, Massachusetts, on November 21.

There remained two problems. First, the settlers consisted of two distinct groups: the Separatists, united by their religious beliefs, and the others (whom the Separatists called "Strangers") united by nothing more or less than a desire for commercial success. Second, neither group had a legal right to settle in the region, which was beyond the boundary of their charter. While riding at anchor, the two groups drew up the "Mayflower Compact"—in effect, the first constitution written in North America—in which they all agreed to create a "Civil Body Politic" and abide by laws created for the good of the colony.

Plymouth Rock

The settlers probed for a good place to land and soon discovered Plymouth Harbor, on the western side of Cape Cod Bay. They set foot on shore—supposedly on a rock now carved with the year 1620—on December 21, with the main body of settlers disembarking on December 26.

They could hardly have picked a less favorable time and place for their landing. A bitter New England winter was already under way, and the site boasted neither good harbors nor, given its flinty soil, extensive tracts of fertile land. As at Jamestown, people began to die: during the first winter, more than half of them. But these settlers were also very different from their earlier Jamestown counterparts. They were neither moneyed gentlemen, on the one hand, nor indentured servants on the other. Most were yeoman farmers, hard workers who were by right and inclination free.

From their number emerged a succession of able leaders, including John Carver (ca. 1576–1621), the first governor of Plymouth Colony; William Bradford (1590–1657), governor for more than 30 years and the colony's most able early historian, the author of *History of Plymouth Plantation, 1620–1647*; William Brewster (1567–1644); Edward Winslow (1595–1655), the colony's indispensable diplomat, who negotiated a treaty with local Indian chief Massasoit, established vital fur-trading enterprises, and managed relations with England; and Myles Standish (ca. 1584–1656), a professional soldier who served as the colony's military adviser, established its defenses, negotiated with Indians, represented the interests of Plymouth in England (1625–26), and was a founder of Duxbury, Massachusetts, in 1632. But even able leadership would have failed to bring the colony through the first dreadful winter without the aid and succor of the neighboring Wampanoag Indians. Two in particular, Squanto (a Pawtuxet living among the Wampanoags) and Samoset (an Abnaki), gave the Pilgrims hands-on help in planting crops and building shelters. Samoset introduced the settlers to Massasoit, principal leader of the Wampanoags, and Squanto served as interpreter between the chief and the Pilgrim leaders. Throughout his lifetime, Massasoit (that was what the English called him; his Indian name was Wawmegin, "Yellow Feather") treated the settlers as friends.

Main Event

In the fall of 1621, the Pilgrims invited their Native American bene-factors to a feast in celebration of the first harvest, in which Indian aid had been so instrumental. The event was the first Thanksgiving (unless you count the collective prayer of thanksgiving offered on December 4, 1619, by members of the Berkeley plantation near present-day Charles City, Virginia). Our first president, George Washington, proclaimed the first national Thanksgiving Day, on November 26, 1789, but it wasn't until 1863 that President Abraham Lincoln made Thanksgiving an annual holiday to be commemorated on the last Thursday in November. During 1939–41, by proclamation of President Franklin D. Roosevelt, the day was celebrated on the third Thursday in November, but then was returned by act of Congress to the date set by Lincoln.

Massachusetts Bay

Inspired by the success of the settlement of Plymouth (and overlooking the hardships involved in it), another group of Puritans—these only somewhat less radical than the Pilgrims—landed at Massachusetts Bay in five ships in 1630. Eleven more ships arrived the next year. Under the auspices of the Massachusetts Bay Company, a joint stock trading organization chartered by the English crown in 1629, 20,000 immigrants, mostly Puritans, would arrive by 1642, authorized to colonize a vast area extending from three miles north of the Merrimack River to three miles south of the Charles River. Led by John Winthrop, the new Massachusetts Bay Colony was centered in a city called Boston, and it soon prospered.

City on a Hill

The Puritans wanted to create in the New World a new center of right religion, to build what their sermons (with reference to the Old Testament) frequently called a "city on the hill"—a place of holiness that would be an example for all humankind. Toward this end, the Puritans laid great emphasis on family life and, in particular, on the education of children as well as the education of a class of clergymen sufficiently learned to interpret the Scriptures as authentically as possible. For the Puritans intended to guide their actions by an intensive interpretation of the Bible, since they saw themselves as living out a kind of Biblical allegory and prophecy in which they were on an "errand into the wilderness," chosen by God to build the "New Jerusalem." The most immediate practical effects of these beliefs were the creation of Boston's High and Latin Schools as early as 1635, and Harvard College the very next year. Moreover, the Puritan character rapidly evolved into an unlikely combination of a limitless appetite for brilliant religious disputation and flinty intolerance of nonconforming beliefs. Needless to say, although they were smart folks, you wouldn't want to spend a cocktail evening with one.

Main Event

In February 1692, two daughters of the Reverend Samuel Parris and some of their friends are diagnosed by a Salem, Massachusetts, physician as victims of witchcraft. Under questioning, the girls accuse certain women of being witches. The town magistrates proceed against the accused on February 29. By the end of the year, accusations multiply: 140 are accused, 107 of them women. The royal governor of Massachusetts, Sir William Phips, establishes a special court to try more than 70 of the cases. Of 26 individuals convicted, 19 are executed.

The Salem witchcraft epidemic, though extreme, was hardly unique. Witches had been tried before 1692 in Massachusetts as well as Connecticut and, even more frequently, throughout Europe. Who stood accused in *all* of these places? "Witches" were usually poor, elderly women (sometimes men) who quarreled with their neighbors and were generally disruptive, disagreeable social misfits.

Rhode Island: Haven for the Heterodox

One of the most brilliant masters of religious disputation was the Reverend Roger Williams (ca. 1603–1683), who immigrated from England to Boston in 1631. He declined an offer to become minister of the first Boston congregation because it had not formally separated from the Anglican Church. Instead, Williams moved first to Salem, then to Plymouth, and back to Salem. In each place, he was criticized for his "strange opinions," which included a conviction that the lands chartered to Massachusetts and Plymouth belonged by right to the Indians, that a civil government could not enforce religious laws, and that religion itself ultimately rested on profoundly individual conscience and percep-tion. Ordered by the Puritan hierarchy to change his views, Williams refused and was finally expelled from the colony by the Massachusetts General Court in October 1635. He and a handful of followers found refuge in January 1636 among the Indians on Narragansett Bay. At the head of that bay, Williams purchased from his protectors a small tract and founded a town he called Providence—the first settlement in Rhode Island.

During the next four decades, Williams welcomed to Rhode Island those of all persua-sions. In 1644, during the English Civil War, he secured a patent for the colony from the Puritan-controlled Parliament, and he established a genuinely representative government founded on the principle of religious freedom. Williams returned to England again, where he successfully defended his colony's grant against the onslaught of Puritan objections, and after the restoration of Charles II to the British throne, he secured a royal charter in 1663, sanctioning the liberal institutions he had created.

Maryland: Catholics Welcome

The founding and survival of heterodox Rhode Island made it clear to the Puritans that their "city on a hill" would not stand alone in America. In yet another colony, the interests of a group even more repugnant to the Puritans were taking root.

In 1632, King Charles I of England, under siege from the Puritan faction that would soon overthrow him, granted the Roman Catholic George Calvert, First Baron Baltimore a charter to settle North American lands between the 40th parallel and the south bank of the Potomac. The First Baron Baltimore died before the papers were executed, and the charter passed to his son Cecil Calvert, Second Baron Baltimore. In November 1633, 200 Catholic colonists set sail from England in the *Ark and the Dove*, which landed on March 24, 1634, on an island at the mouth of the Potomac they named Saint Clement (it is now called Blakistone Island). The colonists purchased the Indian village of Yaocomico and called it St. Mary's (it is present-day St. Mary's City), which served for the next 60 years as the capital of the colony. Under Lord Baltimore's direction, in 1649, the Colonial Assembly passed the Act Concerning Religion, the first law in the American colonies that explicitly provided for freedom of worship—although it applied only to Christians.

Pennsylvania: Quaker Colony

Freedom of worship was the theme for the creation of yet another non-Puritan colony. The Society of Friends—commonly called Quakers—was founded in 17th-century England by a visionary leader named George Fox. His belief was in the *immediacy* of Christ's teaching; that is, divine guidance was not "mediated" by Scripture, ceremony, ritual, or clergy, but came ultimately to each individual from an "inward light." Accordingly, worship meetings were held in silence, unless some members of the meeting were "moved" or "inspired" to speak. No minister officiated.

By its nature, Quakerism is subversive of authority imposed from the outside, and although a prime tenet of Quakerism is nonviolence and supreme tolerance of all points of view, the religion was quickly perceived as a threat to the dominant order. Quakers were officially and unofficially persecuted. Some immigrated to America, settling in the Middle Atlantic region as well as North Carolina. An early enclave was established in Rhode Island.

The Quakers did have some powerful adherents, one of whom was William Penn, the brilliant young son of a prominent British admiral. On March 14, 1681, Penn obtained from King Charles II a charter granting him proprietorship of the area now encompassed by Pennsylvania. In 1682, Delaware was added to the charter. The region was occupied by some 15,000 Delaware, Shawnee, and Susquehanna Indians, as well as tribes associated with the Iroquois League. During the 17th century, it was claimed by Dutch, Swedish, and English interests. Penn landed at the site of present-day New Castle, Delaware, and performed "livery of seisin," legally taking possession of his grant by pulling up a tuft of grassy turf in his hand. In 1682, he founded Philadelphia, a name Penn formed from two Greek words signifying "brotherly love." The name expressed the intent of what Penn planned as a "holy experiment" of living in harmony.

> **Word for the Day**
>
> *Pennsylvania*, which means "Penn's Woods," was named by King Charles II not after the colony's founder and proprietor, but in honor of Penn's father, also named William, a great British admiral.

Under Penn, "The Great Law of Pennsylvania" extended male suffrage to those who professed a belief in God and met modest property requirements; imprisonment for debt—one of the great scourges of life in England—was all but eliminated; and the death penalty, liberally applied in the Mother Country, was restricted to cases of treason and murder. In a combination of the best tradition of English common law and a dramatic foreshadow of the United States Bill of Rights, the Great Law specified that no person could be deprived of life, liberty, or "estate" (property) except by due, fair, and impartial trial before a jury of 12.

Georgia: Utopia and Prison

Founded on firm—though diverse—religious principles, Plymouth, the Massachusetts Bay Colony, Rhode Island, Maryland, and Pennsylvania were all expressions of hope, variations on a theme of desire for a better life. The origin of Georgia was even more frankly utopian.

In 1732, James Edward Oglethorpe, whose character combined military discipline (he was a general) with a passion for philanthropy, organized a group of 19 wealthy and progressive individuals into a corporation that secured a royal charter to colonize Georgia as the southernmost of Britain's North American colonies. Oglethorpe's bold plan was to create a colony as a haven for various Protestant dissenters, but, even more importantly, for the vast and ever-growing class of insolvent debtors who languished in British prisons and also for persons convicted of certain criminal offenses. Oglethorpe reasoned that the colony would give the debtors a fresh start and would reform and rehabilitate the criminals.

Selflessly, Oglethorpe and the other philanthropists agreed to act as trustees of the colony without taking profits for a period of 21 years. To promote a utopian way of life, Oglethorpe prohibited the sale of rum and outlawed slavery in the colony. He also set regulations limiting the size of individual land holdings in an effort to create equality. The first colonists who arrived with Oglethorpe in 1733 were placed on 55-acre farms, which they were forbidden to sell or transfer. But this arrangement, key to the project, was quickly abandoned. To begin with, few of the original 100 colonists were debtors or sufferers of religious persecution or even criminals ripe for rehabilitation. They were speculators looking for opportunity. They soon found ways of circumventing the 55-acre limit to land holding, and once large plantations were established, slavery followed. Georgia was now no different from England's other southern colonies.

The Slaves of Virginia

The introduction of slaves into Georgia was the hardest blow to Oglethorpe's dream, and he returned to England, disgusted with the entire enterprise. Like most other even modestly enlightened individuals, Oglethorpe regarded slavery as evil. Yet it persisted—even in a would-be utopia—and would persist until it tore a nation apart. Just as Georgia was a latecomer into the British colonial fold, so it had adopted slavery late in the scheme of things. In 1619, just 12 years after Jamestown got its shaky start, Dutch traders imported African slaves at the behest of the Virginia tobacco farmers. The first 20 or so were landed at Jamestown and were not racially discriminated against, but were classed with white indentured servants brought from England under work contracts. Indeed, many years passed before African slaves were brought to the colonies in large numbers. At first, they were purchased primarily to replace indentured servants who had either escaped or had served out the term of their indentures.

As the plantations of the southern colonies, Virginia, the Carolinas, and Georgia, expanded, demand for slavery grew, as did commerce in slaves. The so-called "triangle trade" developed: Ships leaving England with trade goods landed on the African west coast, traded the merchandise for African slaves, transported this "cargo" via the "Middle Passage" to the West Indies or the mainland English colonies, where the slaves were exchanged for the very agricultural products—sugar, tobacco, and rice—slave labor produced. The final leg of the triangle was back to England, laden with New World produce. Nor were the northern colonies untouched by the "peculiar institution" of slavery. Although a later generation of New Englanders would pride themselves on being fierce abolitionists, fighters for the freedom of the slaves, their forefathers had profited from the trade. New England ports became a regular stop for vessels about to return to Old England. The sugar and molasses acquired at southern ports was often unloaded here in order to manufacture rum, an important New England export.

The Least You Need to Know

➤ The Pilgrims were Puritans who left England, settling first in Holland and then in New England (at Plymouth) in 1620. Separatists were somewhat less radical Puritans who settled there (at Massachusetts Bay) beginning in 1630.

➤ The other major English colonies were also established as havens for freedom of worship; Georgia was meant to be a utopia.

➤ Intolerance among the Puritans and slavery in the South marred the colonies' ideal of liberty.

They Could've Been Contenders (1608–1680s)

Compared to the Spanish, the English got off to a slow start in the New World, but they soon became one of the two principal forces in the Americas. The other was France, which directed its main efforts at settlement along the St. Lawrence River in present-day Canada and in the West Indies. Although "black robes"—Catholic priests—came in the wake of French exploration and set up missions to the Indians, religion was never as strong a *component* of settlement as it was for the Spanish, nor so compelling a *motive* for settlement as it was for the English. The fact was that the ambitious Cardinal Richelieu (1585–1642), who, in effect, ruled France as prime minister under the weak-willed Louis XIII, needed money to finance his campaign to make France the dominant power in Europe. And the New World offered opportunity for profit.

Enter Champlain

As a boy growing up in France, Samuel de Champlain (ca.1570-1635) showed a real flair for drawing. He especially liked to design maps—inspired in large part by the tales of adventure his naval captain father brought home. Champlain followed in his father's footsteps and was commissioned by the French government no fewer than a dozen times between 1603 and 1633 to probe the waters of North America and also explore inland. As with so many other explorers at this time, Champlain's primary objective was to find a Northwest Passage through to Asia, but he also worked to promote trade in furs and other commodities. When Richelieu became convinced that money was to be made from North America, even if a Northwest Passage were never found, he also authorized Champlain to establish colonies and (for Richelieu was a cardinal of the Roman Catholic Church, after all) to promote Christianity.

Word for the Day
Canada and the northeastern United States are filled with Frenchified Indian place names. *Quebec* is how an Algonquian Indian word meaning "abrupt narrowing of the river" sounded to Champlain's French ears. Quebec City is located at the narrow head of the St. Lawrence River estuary.

Word for the Day
The terms *Algonquin* and *Algonquian* cause confusion. "Algonquin" describes any of various Native American peoples who live or lived in the Ottawa River valley of Quebec and Ontario. "Algonquian" is a family of Indian languages. Tribes linguistically related through dialects of this language are collectively referred to as Algonquian—*not* Algonquin. The other major Indian linguistic family in eastern North America is the Iroquoian.

Champlain established a broad beachhead for France in North America. During the seven voyages made between 1603 and 1616, he thoroughly mapped northern reaches of the continent (accurately charting the Atlantic coast from the Bay of Fundy to Cape Cod), he established settlements, he got the French fur trade off to a most promising start, and he struck alliances with the Algonquin tribes and Hurons against the tribes of the powerful Iroquois League. These alliances would strengthen the French position in the New World at the often bloody expense of their archrivals, the British, who, during the next 150 years, would make few Indian allies but many Indian enemies. Beginning with Champlain, the lines of alliance and enmity among Frenchman, Englishman, and Indian were sharply drawn. These would, by the middle of the next century, deepen into the wounds of the long and tragic French and Indian War.

Champlain erected a crude settlement at Sainte-Croix in 1604, then moved it to Port Royal the following year. This was the nucleus around which the colony of Acadia would be formed. In July 1608, Champlain directed the digging of a ditch and the erection of a stockade. He called this Quebec.

In 1609, operating from his base in Quebec, Champlain sailed up the St. Lawrence and the river he named after his patron, Richelieu, to the lake that was subsequently named after Champlain himself. Here he attacked a group of Iroquois, on behalf of his Algonquin allies, thereby cementing the French–Algonquin alliance all the more strongly. Later, in 1615, he would venture farther west, across the eastern end of Lake Ontario, and help the Huron Indians in an attack on the Oneida and Onondaga (two tribes of the Iroquois League). In these actions, Champlain was determined to secure the St. Lawrence region for France. He saw that this served as a major avenue of trade for the Indians. Whoever commanded the region would also command trade in the upper Northeast. Of course, securing alliance with one Indian group meant incurring the wrath of another. And the Iroquois were enemies to be feared. Highly organized, the Iroquois League—five tribes, whose territory stretched from the east coast west to Lake Ontario—waged war mercilessly, employing tactics of torture and terror to intimidate their enemies.

Champlain was an enthusiastic booster of Canada, promoting it in the French court of Louis XIII and Richelieu, yet he initially discouraged out-and-out colonization. Little wonder. For Champlain was interested in operating Quebec as a kind of private trading post, with himself in a position to collect a healthy portion of the profits. Nevertheless, the settlement was the nucleus of a French North American fur-trading empire that would endure for the next 125 years.

The Sun King Casts His Rays

Louis XIV was born to Louis XIII and his queen, Anne of Austria, on September 5, 1638. Four years later, Louis XIII died, and his son ascended the throne under the regency of Cardinal Mazarin. Only on the death of Mazarin in 1661 did Louis XIV begin to rule in his own right, and thoughts of New France, while not uppermost in his mind, were at least *in* his mind. Unlike his father—and Cardinal Richelieu—Louis XIV did not want New France to be merely a source of quick trade profit. He understood that, in order to hold the colony, it had to be a genuine colony, populated not just by *coureurs de bois*, but by sturdy, stable yeoman farmers.

Word for the Day

Coureurs de bois—runners of the woods—was a name applied to a class of men who got their living by trapping fur-bearing animals. Their profession required them to combine the roles of explorer, woodsman, diplomat, trader, hunter, and trapper. The *coureurs*, though often barely civilized themselves, were the pioneers of civilization in the upper Northeast.

What happened in 1671, then, shouldn't have been a surprise. Pierre-Spirit Radisson and Médart Chouart, two *coureurs,* proposed to the emperor a scheme to create a company that would effectively monopolize the northern fur trade. But that wasn't all. They promised also to find the Northwest Passage, which (they said) would become an exclusively French route for the transportation of fur directly to Asia. In Japan and China, a little fur would buy a lot of spice. But the king was not interested in sending his subjects on such errands. In response to the proposal, he sent women to New France in order to entice trappers like Radisson and Chouart to settle down; he also offered a bounty to be paid for those who sired large families in New France; and, finally, he urged the Church to excommunicate men who left their farms without the government's permission. In turn, Radisson and Chouart made their own response: They went to the English and secured backing to create the Hudson's Bay Company, which would be for many years the single most powerful mercantile force on the North American continent.

Two years later, the French intendant (chief administrator) in Canada, Jean Baptiste Talon, stuck his neck out and went against official policy by hiring a fur trader named Louis Joliet to follow up on something he had heard from the Indians—tales concerning a "father" of all the rivers. Perhaps this would prove to be the passage to the Pacific, Talon thought. The Indians called it the "Mesippi." But Talon despaired of ever actually getting Joliet on the move, because a new governor was due to arrive from France, and surely he would nip the expedition in the bud.

To Talon's surprise and delight, the governor, Le Comte de Frontenac, a crusty old man who nevertheless possessed a combination of shrewd practicality and vision for the future, approved the expedition. Even if Joliet failed to find a passage to the Pacific, Frontenac reasoned, pushing the claims of France westward was of great strategic importance in and of itself.

Joliet, with a Jesuit priest named Jacques Marquette, did not find a shortcut to the western ocean, but did find the Mississippi, thereby establishing France's claim to a vast portion of what one day would be the United States. In honor of their monarch, they called the territory Louisiana, and it encompassed (as the French saw it) a vast expanse of land between the Appalachian and Rocky Mountains.

Not that the French really knew what to do with all they had found. Louis XIV—called the "Sun King" because of the magnificence of his opulent court and his even more opulent dreams of greatness for a French empire—had visions of a vast agricultural kingdom to reflect in the New World the glories of the Old. But, by the end of Louis's long reign and life, New France consisted of nothing more than a scattering of precarious settlements in Nova Scotia, along the St. Lawrence, and one or two isolated outposts in Louisiana.

The Dutch Invest $24 in Manhattan Real Estate

So, let's see. The English set up Jamestown in 1607. Quebec was founded by France the next year. And, in 1609, Henry Hudson, sailing in the Dutch service, reached the site of present-day Albany. Like everybody and his brother, he was looking for the Northwest Passage. And like everyone who looked for it, he failed. However, his search did give the Netherlands a claim to the richest fur-bearing region of North America south of the St. Lawrence.

This did not bring a rush of colonization. A handful of Dutch sea captains traded for furs with the Indians—often bartering hard liquor—but a colonial movement did not get underway until the Dutch West India Company was founded in 1621. Although it strikes us today as culturally and geographically bizarre, Holland was once controlled by Spain. It was one of that nation's seven Northern Provinces until 1581, when it declared independence. Unfortunately, Spain did not recognize this claim, and the Dutch West India Company was founded by the young Dutch Republic as part of a long, ongoing struggle to remain free. The company was authorized to commission privateers to disrupt Spain's trade with its American colonies and, a little later, to undertake colonization efforts in Brazil, Dutch Guiana (now Surinam), the Antilles, and in the North American region staked out by Henry Hudson, which, in 1623, was christened New Netherland. The following year, the company established a trading post at Fort Orange (present-day Albany), and in 1626 dispatched Peter Minuit (ca. 1580-1638) to serve as the colony's first director-general.

The conquistadors of Spain, when they came to the Americas, simply took the Indians' land. But most of the other European colonizers made attempts to *buy* the land. It seemed more legal that way. Minuit's first step, then, was to legitimate Dutch claims to New Netherland by purchasing Manhattan Island from the Manhattan Indians, a band of the Delaware tribe, for trade goods valued in 1624 at 60 guilders. Now, that figure was computed by a 19th-century historian as being the equivalent of $24, but, with a hundred and more years' worth of inflation, that computation hardly stands as an eternal truth. Still, it is interesting to contemplate the fact that, today, all $24 will buy you is a slot in a Manhattan parking garage near Radio City Music Hall for about 12 hours, and generations of self-satisfied readers of history have chuckled over what has been called the greatest real estate bargain in history. Few have stopped to think, however, that the joke was not on the Indians. After all, *they* never claimed to own Manhattan Island. The concept of land ownership was foreign to most Native American cultures. For them, land was part of the natural world, and you could no more own the land you walked on than you could own, say, the air you breathed. If Minuit wanted to part with a load of trade goods just because an island was named after them, the Manhattan Indians were not about explain to him the error of his ways. In any case, Minuit built a fort at the tip of the island and called it New Amsterdam.

A Tale of Two Governors

The Dutch established a profitable trade with the Indians of New Netherland during the 1620s and 1630s—a period (as we shall see in the next chapter) during which New England settlers were locked in bloody war with their Native American neighbors. It wasn't that the Dutch were kinder and gentler than the English, but that, at first, they were interested in trading rather than settling down on farms. Once the local supply of beavers (whose pelts were the principal trade commodity) became depleted due to over-hunting, the Dutch also started to stake out farms, thereby displacing the Indians.

By 1638, when Willem Kieft (1597–1647) arrived in New Netherland as the colony's fifth governor, two intimately related truths were operative: Violence between the Dutch and Indians was frequent, and aggressive territorial expansion had become a prime Dutch objective. Kieft was appalled by the condition of New Amsterdam. Its defenses were practically nonexistent, and its capacious harbor boasted only one seaworthy vessel. Assuming dictatorial powers, he made sweeping reforms in civil and military administration. Among these was a heavy tax imposed on the local Indians in return for defending them against "hostiles"—mainly the Mohawks. In truth, the Mohawks had become important trading partners with the Dutch and were now allies—henchmen, really—whom Kieft deliberately used to terrorize other tribes. The "defense" tax was actually protection money, and Kieft was behaving no better than a gangster.

When the Raritan Indians, living near New Amsterdam, refused to pay the protection money in 1641 and attacked an outlying Dutch colony, Kieft declared brutal war on them. Two years later, he put the squeeze on the Wappinger Indians, who lived along the Hudson River above Manhattan. To convince them of the wisdom of paying tribute, he unleashed the Mohawks on them. The Wappingers fled down to Pavonia (present-day Jersey City, New Jersey), just across the Hudson from Manhattan. Failing to understand the situation, they appealed to Kieft for aid. In response, he dispatched the Mohawks to Pavonia, then sent Dutch troops in to finish off the refugees. During the night of February 25–26, 1643, Dutch soldiers killed men, women, and children in what was later called the "Slaughter of the Innocents." The heads of 80 Indians were brought back to New Amsterdam, where soldiers and citizens used them as footballs. Thirty prisoners were publicly tortured to death.

Following the atrocity, 11 local tribes united in waging war against the settlers of New Netherland. Kieft frantically parleyed with the Indians, fruitlessly seeking peace. His own colony, panic-stricken, threatened rebellion. At last, in 1645, the Dutch West India Company recalled Kieft to Holland and replaced him with a crotchety one-legged son of a Calvinist minister, Peter Stuyvesant.

The autocratic Stuyvesant immediately set about whipping the colony into shape, restricting the sale of alcohol and persecuting Quakers and Lutherans, whom he feared would lead the impending revolt. On the positive side, he tried earnestly to provide an honest and efficient administration, including a limited public works campaign of improving roads, repairing fences, constructing a wharf on the East River, and building a defensive wall on the northern edge of New Amsterdam along a "crosstown" pathway that would be named for it: Wall Street.

As to the Indians, Stuyvesant strove to reestablish trading relationships, but he continued Kieft's policy of ruthlessness, especially against the Esopus, whose children he took and held as hostages in 1659 to insure the tribe's "good behavior." And when the Esopus refused to yield *all* of their children as directed, Stuyvesant sold those he held into the West Indian slave trade. Their parents never saw them again.

It was, however, Stuyvesant's despotism in governing the colony itself that led to the decay of his power, as the burghers of New Amsterdam clamored for increased self-government, which the West India Company finally granted them. Beyond the confines of New Netherland, Stuyvesant had mixed success in dealing with the colonies of other European powers, beginning with New Sweden.

Sweden in the Delaware Valley

In 1655, Stuyvesant expanded his colony into the Delaware Valley. The fact that the region was already held by Sweden did not deter him. He simply invaded, and New Sweden just as simply yielded. The colony had been founded by Manhattan's own Peter Minuit, who, having been recalled from New Netherland to Holland in 1631, subsequently entered into the service of Sweden (Minuit was neither Dutch nor Swedish by nationality, but had been born in the Duchy of Cleves, a Germanic state). In any case, the New Sweden Company, formed in 1633, was a joint Swedish and Dutch enterprise. Minuit led the company's first expedition in 1638 and established a settlement on the site of present-day Wilmington, Delaware, which he named Fort Christina in honor of the Swedish queen. Within a short time, the Dutch dropped out of the colony, and New Sweden, lying along Delaware River in what is now Delaware, New Jersey, and Pennsylvania, became exclusively Swedish. Under the administration of governors Johan Bjornsson Printz (1643–53) and Johan Claesson Rising (1654–55), friction developed with New Netherland, and Stuyvesant invaded, annexing the territory. Thus concluded the cameo appearance of Sweden as an actor on the New World stage.

New Netherland Becomes New York

But for Stuyvesant, it was win a little, lose a little—and then lose it all. Relations between New Netherland and New England became increasingly strained as the colonies competed for Indian loyalty and trade. The Dutch were at a disadvantage not just militarily, but also as victims of the settlement scheme established by the Dutch West India Company. Whereas the English settled New England, Virginia, and the other southern colonies with relative speed, putting in place a combination of wealthy planters and yeoman farmers, Dutch settlement was hampered by the patroon system, a process whereby land grants of approximately 16 miles along one side of the Hudson (and other navigable rivers) or about 8 miles on both banks (and extending for unspecified distances away from the river) were made to absentee landlords who installed tenant farmers. Thus New Netherland was largely a colony of tenants rather than property holders, and this state of affairs retarded settlement and made patriotism among the New Netherlanders pretty much a lost cause. Even in the 17th century, tenancy, as opposed to ownership, went counter to the American Dream.

Word for the Day

The landlords of New Netherland were called *patroons*. They were investors in the Dutch West India Company who were granted estates along the Hudson and other navigable rivers on the condition that they send 50 settlers within four years to occupy the land. The system never worked well, in part because the landlords—many of whom remained in Holland—were unable to manage their lands efficiently, and the tenants felt they had little stake in the colony.

By the 1660s, New Netherland was weak and torn by dissension. Peter Stuyvesant stumped about on his peg leg and rattled his saber, but he could not rally his countrymen. On September 8, 1664, a fleet of British warships sailed up the Hudson. The Dutch colonists simply declined to offer resistance, leaving a supremely frustrated Stuyvesant no choice but to surrender, albeit on the important condition that the West India Company continue to enjoy substantial trading rights. The British promptly renamed both the colony and its chief town after the Duke of York (the future King James II), and Stuyvesant retired peacefully to his farm, which he called the Bouwerie. Through the years, the tranquil country path passing through his farm was transformed. In the 19th century, it became a racy street of inexpensive theaters, and, by the early 20th, a gray and dilapidated avenue of cheap bars known as the Bowery and symbolic of other American dreams that somehow went awry.

The Least You Need to Know

➤ The French claimed vast tracts of land, but failed to adequately colonize them.

➤ Although they set up a lively trade with the Indians, the Dutch likewise failed to create an enduring colony.

Fires in the Wilderness (1636–1748)

America was and remains a synonym for hopes and dreams. America has brought out the best of which humanity is capable—a dream of justice, a hope for liberty—and it has brought out the worst. First it became a battleground on which Native Americans fought against an invasion from Europe. Then it became a battlefield on which the invaders fought one another, often embroiling the Native Americans in their conflicts. Often, the invaders retreated into the distance and let the Native Americans fight their wars for them. All in all, it was a very bloody beginning.

New England Bleeds

The only thing that's certain is that the murder of Captain John Stone in 1634 was *not* the work of Pequots. As to the rest, the accounts of the Indians and the Englishmen differ.

The Pequots were a powerful Algonquian tribe settled along the Connecticut River. Resenting the intrusion of Dutch traders in the Connecticut valley, they waged a small, bitter war against the Dutch. Then, in 1634, Stone, an Englishman, was killed as his ship lay at anchor at the mouth of the Connecticut River. Never mind that Stone was a pirate, who had tried and failed to hijack a vessel in New Amsterdam, had brandished a knife before the governor of Plymouth Colony, and had been deported from the Massachusetts Bay Colony for drunkenness and adultery, and never mind that the Indians claimed Stone had kidnapped some of their people. Tensions were so high between colonists and Indians that the New Englanders demanded action against the Pequots for the murder of John Stone.

The Pequot War

For their part, the Pequots didn't want any trouble. Although no one accused any Pequot of having laid a finger on Stone, the murder was clearly the work of western Niantics, a tribe that was nominally under Pequot control. Seeking to avert a war, the Pequots accepted responsibility and signed a treaty with the Massachusetts Bay Colony in which they promised to surrender those guilty of the murder. They also agreed to pay an exorbitant indemnity, relinquish rights to a vast tract of Connecticut land, and trade exclusively with the English rather than the Dutch. A part of the indemnity was paid, but the Pequots claimed that, of the murderers, all were dead (one at the hands of the Dutch, the others of smallpox), except for two, who had escaped.

For two years, the Massachusetts Bay colonists did nothing. Then, on June 16, 1636, Mohegan Indians warned the English that the Pequots, fearful that the colonists were about to take action, had decided on a preemptive strike. A new conference between the Pequots and the colonists was called at Fort Saybrook, Connecticut, and agreements were reached, but word soon arrived of the death of another captain, John Oldham, off Block Island. This time, the perpetrators were Narragansetts (or a tribe subject to them), and although the Narragansett sachems immediately dispatched 200 warriors to avenge the deaths on behalf of the colony, the English sent Captain John Endecott to

> **Word for the Day**
>
> *Wampum* is the Anglicized version of the Algonquian word *wampompeag*. Although the term came to describe any kind of valuable item used as the equivalent of money, it originally was applied to cylindrical seashells strung on strings or beaded into belts and used as money or as tokens of good faith (wampum belts were exchanged at treaty signings, for example).

Block Island with orders to seize the Indians' stores of wampum, slaughter all the men they could find, and take captive the women and children for sale as slaves in the West Indies.

The Indians, anticipating just such behavior, had fled. A frustrated Endecott paid a visit to the Pequots just beyond Fort Saybrook and set about burning their villages.

Soon, all of the Connecticut valley burned, as the enraged Indians retaliated, putting to the torch one English settlement after another, and the colonists responded against the Pequots in kind.

What motivated Endecott to bring down a bloody war upon Indian and colonist alike? Racial hatred? Blind stupidity? Certainly, both of these things. But, as would be the case with all the white–Indian wars of the colonial period, there was a motive of power politics as well, in which the Indians figured as pawns ruthlessly played by the competing European powers. In the case of the Pequot Wars, both of the competitors were English. The Massachusetts Bay Colony and the settlers of the Connecticut valley disputed over possession of the valley. Whoever asserted dominion over the Pequots, whose country lay precisely within the disputed territory, would have a strong *legal* claim to the region. Endecott, a soldier in service to Massachusetts Bay, was eager for a fight in order to dominate the Pequots and thereby beat out the Connecticut settlers. But the very competitiveness of the New England colonies made effective unified action against the Indians almost impossible, and it wasn't until the spring of 1637 that the disorganized colonial forces were able to enlist the aid of the Narragansetts, Eastern Niantics, and Mohegans—all rivals of the Pequots—in order to mount a counter-offensive. Captain John Mason, in command of the colonial–Indian coalition, attacked a village at Mystic, Connecticut, where he killed 600–700 Pequots—mostly women, children, and old men—in the space of an hour.

Following the Mystic massacre, the Pequots were defeated at every turn. On September 21, 1638, the Treaty of Hartford divided the Pequot prisoners of war as slaves among the allied tribes—Mohegans, Narragansetts, and Niantics—and further stipulated that no Pequot could inhabit his former country again. Indeed, the treaty proclaimed, the very name "Pequot" would be forever expunged.

> **Word for the Day**
> Among the Algonquian tribes, a *sachem* was the equivalent of a chief. Within the Iroquois confederacy of tribes, a sachem was a member of the ruling council. Neither chiefs nor sachems were absolute rulers in the European sense of a monarch, but were influential and powerful tribal leaders.

King Philip's War

An even more destructive war broke out in New England less than 40 years later, again over a murder. On June 11, 1675, a farmer saw an Indian looting his cattle. He killed the Indian. The local Wampanoag chief, called Metacomet by the Indians and (with contempt) King Philip by the English, sought justice from the local garrison. Rebuffed, the Indians took justice into their own hands and killed the hot-tempered farmer, then killed his father and five other settlers.

But the war had actually been brewing for some time. King Philip was the son of Massasoit, the chief who had been so friendly to the New Englanders. Faced with the colonists' insatiable land hunger, their rising population, and their highhanded, contemptuous treatment of himself, King Philip was not inclined toward friendship. Beginning about 1662, he stirred rebellion among the Narragansetts and the Nipmucks as well as his own Wampanoags. At first, the colonists were hobbled by the same problem they had during the Pequot War. Disorganized and apparently incapable of unified action, the New Englanders suffered very heavy losses during the first months of the war. It was only after they managed to join forces as the United Colonies that Massachusetts, Plymouth, Rhode Island, Connecticut, and the more remote "Eastern Colonies"—Maine and New Hampshire—began to take the initiative.

Stats
Among the colonists, 1 in 16 men of military age was killed in King Philip's War. At least 3,000 Indians died; many more were deported and sold into slavery in the West Indies.

King Philip's War was an unmitigated catastrophe for colonists and Indians alike. During 1675–76, half the region's towns were badly damaged and at least 12 utterly wiped out. The colonial economy was left in tatters because of the disruption of the fur trade, coastal fishing, and the West Indian trade. The Wampanoags, Narragansetts, and Nipmucks lost a great many of their number. As for the colonists, proportional to the population at the time, King Philip's War stands to this day as the costliest conflict in American history.

The French and Indian Wars

The Pequot War and King Philip's War were strictly colonial tragedies. The series of wars that followed, however, were reflections of conflicts that had engulfed Europe.

King William's War

King William III ascended the English throne in 1689, after James II had been ousted in a Protestant revolt. William almost immediately (May 12, 1689) committed his nation to the Grand Alliance, joining the League of Augsburg and the Netherlands to oppose

French king Louis XIV's invasion of the Rhenish Palatinate. In Europe, this resulted in an eight-year conflict known as the War of the League of Augsburg. In America, the struggle was called King William's War and pitted the French and Abnaki Indians (of Maine) against the English and their allies among the Iroquois.

The New World theater of this war gave rise to a new kind of fighting. In 1689, Louis XIV dispatched Louis de Buade, comte de Frontenac, to America as governor of New France. He had served in that capacity before—from 1672 to 1782—but was so dictatorial that he was recalled to France at the request of those he governed. Louis understood that what his colonies needed just now was precisely what this tough 70-year-old had to offer: a stomach for relentless aggression. Frontenac pro-posed not merely a defensive strategy against the British, but an invasion of New York. His only problem, he soon realized, was that he did not have the manpower to invade anybody. The solution, Frontenac decided, was to fight a "little war," one that consisted not of grand strategies and the mass movement of great armies fighting European-style battles, but of ambushes, murders, and terror—mostly carried out by Indian allies. Properly coordi-nated, such action would demoralize the English settlers while simultaneously draining their military resources.

Word for the Day
In French, "little war" is *la petite guerre*. This phrase soon evolved into the single word *guerrilla* to describe a limited, covert style of warfare as well as the combatants who fight such wars.

Frontenac's "little war" was a dreary pattern of raid and counter-raid, without much decisive action, but with plenty of misery to go around from July 1689, when La Chine, Quebec, was ravaged by Iroquois, to September 1691, when Benjamin Church, aged hero of King Philip's War, was called out of retirement to defend Saco, Maine. By the end of the month, the English struck a truce with Abnakis, which, however, was soon violated.

In September 1697, the Treaty of Ryswyck ended the War of the League of Augsburg in Europe and, therefore, officially ended King William's War in America, but raids and counter-raids continued through the end of the 17th century.

Queen Anne's War

Now it's time to return to the cheerful precincts of "civilized" Europe. England, Holland, and Austria had the jitters over an alliance struck between France and Spain when King Charles II of Spain, a Hapsburg (that is, originally an Austrian), died in 1700, having named a Bourbon (that is, originally a Frenchman) as his successor. The French, natu-rally, backed Charles's nominee, Philip of Anjou, the grandson of Louis XIV. England, Holland, and Austria threw their support behind the Bavarian Archduke Charles, second son of the Hapsburg emperor Leopold I. These three nations then formed a new Grand Alliance in 1701, and the War of the Spanish Succession was declared between the Grand Alliance and France and Spain on May 4, 1702. In America, the conflict was called Queen Anne's War. The war began on September 10, 1702, when the South Carolina legislature authorized an expedition to seize the Spanish-held fort and town of Saint Augustine, Florida. When a combined force of 500 colonists and Chickasaw Indians failed to breach the fort, they settled for burning the town instead.

Not unexpectedly, this act brought a series of counter-raids from Spanish-allied Appalachee Indians, which prompted South Carolina governor James Moore to lead a force of militiamen and Chickasaws in a destructive sweep of western Florida during July 1704. The result: Seven villages and 13 Spanish missions (out of 14 in the area) were razed, and the Appalachee were effectively annihilated as a tribe. Strategically, Moore's campaign opened a path into the heart of French Louisiana. Anticipating this, French colonial authorities heavily bribed the Choctaws into an alliance which blocked Moore's advance into Louisiana.

In the meantime, up north, the French had managed to gather even more Indian allies, especially among the Abnakis, who ravaged English settlements in Maine (where Queen Anne's War was called the Abnaki War). Farther north, in Nova Scotia, Benjamin Church, now so enfeebled by old age that he had to be carried into battle, terrorized the French Acadian settlements of Minas and Beaubassin during July 1704, while, in Newfoundland, French and Indian forces retaliated during August by destroying the English settlement at Bonavista. The war raged—from Saint Augustine, Florida, to St. Johns, Newfoundland (captured by the French just before Christmas 1708)—not in a series of great battles, but in a string of murders, raids, and counter-raids.

In 1713, Louis XIV, weary of war and crushed under heavy debt, was ready to end the wars in Europe and America. The cause of the War of the Spanish Succession had become a moot point. The 11-year-old Bavarian archduke backed by the Grand Alliance had died, and Louis's grandson Philip of Anjou ascended the Spanish throne by default. The Treaty of Utrecht (July 13, 1713) ended the European and American wars, with Hudson Bay and Acadia becoming English and the St. Lawrence islands becoming French. The Abnakis swore allegiance to the English crown, but continued to raid the English settlements of Maine for years.

Tuscarora and Yemasee Wars

At about the time Queen Anne's War was winding down, the Tuscarora Indians in North Carolina were growing tired of being cheated and abused by colonial traders, to whom they continually lost goods and land and at whose hands they even suffered abduction for sale into the West Indies slave trade. Wishing to avoid war, the Tuscaroras, in 1709, obtained permission from the government of Pennsylvania to migrate there. The government of North Carolina refused to furnish the required certificate to make the migration possible. After all, the North Carolina traders enjoyed making a profit from the Indians. In 1710, a Swiss entrepreneur named Baron Cristoph von Graffenried founded the settlement of New Bern at the confluence of the Neuse and Trent rivers in North Carolina. Graffenried chose not to purchase his land from the Tuscaroras, but instead secured the blessing of North Carolina's surveyor general to "appropriate" the property and drive the Indians off.

That was the final straw for the Tuscaroras. On September 22, 1711, they attacked New Bern, killing 200 settlers, including 80 children. Remarkably, Graffenried, captured and released, managed to negotiate peace, only to have it broken by William Brice, who, thirsting for revenge, captured a local chief of the Coree tribe (allies of the Tuscaroras) and roasted him alive. The war was renewed, and, as if Brice's act had set its tone, was filled with more than the usual quota of atrocities, including the death-by-torture of scores of captive soldiers and settlers.

North Carolina called on South Carolina for help. In 1713, South Carolina's Colonel James Moore combined 33 militiamen and 1,000 allied Indians with the troops of North Carolina to strike all the principal Tuscarora settlements. This force killed hundreds of Tuscaroras and captured some 400 more, whom the governor sold into slavery to defray the costs of the campaign. A peace treaty was signed in 1715, and those Tuscaroras who managed to escape death or enslavement migrated north, eventually reaching New York. In 1722, they were formally admitted into the Iroquois League as its "sixth nation."

No sooner was the 1715 treaty concluded than the Yemasees, a South Carolina tribe, rose up against their white neighbors for much the same reasons that had motivated the Tuscaroras: abuse, fraud, and enslavement. The military response, led by South Carolina governor Charles Craven, was swift and terrible. With the aid of Cherokee allies, the Yemasees were hunted to the point of tribal extinction.

Stats
How much was a human being worth? The wholesale price for the Tuscaroras sold on the West Indies slave market was £10 each at a time when £100 per year was considered a handsome living.

King George's War

Men have seldom needed to look very hard for a reason to start a war. This one began with the loss of an ear. Following Queen Anne's War (or, if you prefer, the War of the Spanish Succession), England concluded the "Assiento" with France's ally, Spain. This was a contract permitting the English to trade with the Spanish colonies in goods and slaves.

English traders soon abused the privileges granted by the Assiento, however, and Spanish officials responded harshly. In one case, Spanish coast guards seized Robert Jenkins, master of the British merchant ship *Rebecca*, and cut off his ear during an interrogation. Word of this outrage triggered the "War of Jenkins's Ear" in 1739 between England and Spain, resulting in an abortive invasion of Spanish Florida by Georgia's James Oglethorpe in 1740.

During this time, the War of Jenkins's Ear dissolved into a larger conflict, known in Europe as the War of the Austrian Succession (1740–48). The death of the Holy Roman Emperor Charles VI in 1740 brought several challenges to the succession of daughter Maria Theresa as monarch of the Hapsburg (Austrian) lands. It looked as if the Hapsburg territories were ripe for the plucking, and King Frederick the Great of Prussia moved first to claim his slice by invading Silesia. France, Spain, Bavaria, and Saxony joined Frederick's fold, while Britain came to the aid of Maria Theresa. Once again, the European conflict also appeared in an export version: King George's War.

It was fought mainly by New Englanders against the French of Nova Scotia and again resulted in a wilderness in flames. Territory changed hands, but only temporarily; for the 1748 Treaty of Aix-la-Chapelle, which ended the War of the Austrian Succession, also ended King George's War, restoring (as treaty language puts it) the *status quo ante bellum:* the way things were before the war. But treaty language can be misleading, and the *status* was no longer quite *quo.* Enmities and alliances among the French, the Indians, and the English were now not only lines drawn on a map, but scars seared into the souls of all involved. Wait a few more years. There would be a new, far bigger, far more terrible war.

The Least You Need to Know

➤ Wars were fought with the Indians to gain their land.

➤ Colonies often used Indians as pawns in violent struggles with one another.

➤ North America frequently was a theater of wars that originated in Europe.

Chapter 8

Global War— American Style (1749–1763)

In This Chapter

➤ Conflict over the Ohio Valley

➤ Braddock's defeat at Fort Duquesne

➤ Forbes's victory at Fort Duquesne

➤ Wolfe's takeover of Quebec

➤ Aftermath: Pontiac's Rebellion

The treaty of Aix-la-Chapelle, which ended King George's War on October 18, 1748, brought no more than fleeting peace to the American frontier. On March 27, 1749, King George II granted huge wilderness tracts to a group of entrepreneurs called the Ohio Company, stipulating that, within seven years, the company must plant a settlement of 100 families and build a fort for their protection. The grant and the stipulation accompanying it rekindled the hostility of the French and their Indian allies, who feared an English invasion.

Their fears were valid. Throughout 1749, an influx of British traders penetrated territories that had been the exclusive trading province of the French. In response, on June 26, 1749, Roland-Michel Galissonière, marquis de La Galissonière, governor of New France, dispatched Captain Pierre-Joseph Céleron de Blainville with 213 men to the Ohio country. By November 20, 1749, Céleron had made a round trip of 3,000 miles, burying at intervals lead plates inscribed with France's claim to sovereignty over the territory. The lines of battle were drawn.

The French and Indian War

La Galissonière was replaced as governor by Jacques-Pierre de Jonquière, marquis de La Jonquière, in August 1749. He decided it would take more than buried lead plates to control North America, and he began to build forts. He also attacked the Shawnees, the most powerful of the Ohio country tribes who traded with the English. In the meantime, an English trader named Christopher Gist negotiated a treaty (1752) at Logstown (Ambridge), Pennsylvania, between Virginia and the Ohio Company, and the Six Iroquois Nations (plus the Delawares, Shawnees, and Wyandots). This treaty secured for Virginia and the Ohio Company deeds to the vast Ohio lands. However, French-allied Indians drove the English out of this wilderness country by 1752, and yet another governor of New France, Ange Duquesne de Menneville, marquis Duquesne, quickly built a string of forts through the Ohio country that ultimately stretched from New Orleans to Montreal. Lord Halifax, in England, pushed the British cabinet toward a declaration of war, arguing that the French, by trading throughout the Ohio Valley, had invaded Virginia.

Word for the Day
Most of the colonial–Indian conflicts of the 17th and early 18th century (King William's War, Queen Anne's War, and King George's War) are collectively called the French and Indian *Wars*. The cataclysmic North American war of 1754-63 is the French and Indian *War*.

First Blood for the Father of Our Country

In the heat of war fever, Governor Robert Dinwiddie of Virginia secured authority from the crown to evict the French from territory under his jurisdiction. He commissioned 21-year-old Virginia militia captain George Washington to carry an ultimatum to the French interlopers: *Get out or suffer attack.* Washington set out from Williamsburg, Virginia's capital, on October 31, 1753, and delivered the ultimatum to the commandant of Fort LeBoeuf (Waterford, Pennsylvania) on December 12, 1753. Captain Legardeur, 30 years older than Washington, politely but firmly declined to leave. In response, Governor Dinwiddie ordered the construction of a fort at the strategically critical "forks of Ohio," the junction of the Monongahela and Allegheny rivers, the site of present-day Pittsburgh.

In the meantime, up in Nova Scotia, British authorities demanded that the Acadians—French-speaking Roman Catholic farmers and fishermen who freely intermarried with the Micmac and Abnaki Indians—swear loyalty to the British crown. These people had the misfortune of living in the midst of the most important fishery in the world, waters coveted by all the nations of Europe. While the British threatened the Acadians with expulsion from Nova Scotia, the French threatened to turn their Indian allies against any Acadians who took the loyalty oath. Tensions mounted.

Back at the forks of the Ohio, the French, having patiently watched the construction of Dinwiddie's fort, attacked. Badly outnumbered, Ensign Edward Ward, in command of the new outpost, surrendered on April 17, 1754, and was allowed to march off with his men the next day. The English stronghold was now christened Fort Duquesne and occupied by the French. Unaware of this takeover—and on the very day that the fort fell—Dinwiddie sent Washington (now promoted to lieutenant colonel) with 150 men to reinforce it. En route, on May 28, Washington surprised a 33-man French reconnaissance party. In the ensuing combat, 10 of the Frenchmen were killed, including Ensign Joseph Coulon de Villiers de Jumonville, a French "ambassador." This battle, then, was the first real battle of the French and Indian War.

"Who Would Have Thought It?"

Realizing that the French would retaliate, Washington desperately sought reinforcement from his Indian allies. A grand total of 40 warriors answered the call. It was too late to retreat, so at Great Meadows, Pennsylvania, Washington built a makeshift stockade and christened it Fort Necessity. On July 3, Major Coulon de Villiers, brother of the man Washington's small detachment had killed, led 900 French soldiers, Delawares, Ottawas, Wyandots, Algonquins, Nipissings, Abnakis, and French-allied Iroquois against Fort Necessity. When the outpost's defenders had been reduced by half, on the 4th of July, Washington surrendered. He and the other survivors were permitted to leave, save for two hostages, who were taken back to Fort Duquesne.

With the loss of the Ohio fort and the defeat of Washington, it was the English rather than the French who had been evicted from the Ohio country. A desperate congress convened at Albany from June 19 to July 10, 1754, and produced a plan for colonial unity. The plan managed to please no one. In the meantime, from Fort Duquesne, the French and their many Indian allies raided freely throughout Pennsylvania, Maryland, and Virginia. Finally, in December 1754, the English crown authorized Massachusetts governor William Shirley to reactivate two colonial regiments.

These 2,000 men were joined by two of the British army's absolutely worst regiments, commanded by one of its dullest officers, Major General Edward Braddock. The French responded by sending more troops as well, and British forces were expanded to 10,000 men. On April 14, 1755, Braddock convened a council of war and laid out a plan of attack. Brigadier General Robert Monckton would campaign against Nova Scotia, while Braddock himself would capture Forts Duquesne and Niagara. Governor Shirley would strengthen and reinforce Fort Oswego and then proceed to Fort Niagara—in the unlikely event that Braddock was detained at Fort Duquesne. Another colonial commander, William Johnson, was slated to take Fort Saint Frédéric at Crown Point.

Main Event

One of the best-loved poems in American literature is *Evangeline*, published in 1849 by Henry Wadsworth Longfellow. The poem takes as its subject the separation of lovers brought about by an incident of the French and Indian War. In July 1755, the Acadians of Nova Scotia refused to submit to the loyalty oath the victorious British demanded. On July 28, 1755, Governor Charles Lawrence ordered the Acadians' deportation, and on October 13, 1,100 Acadians were sent into exile. Many others followed—6,000 to 7,000 in all—resettling throughout the colonies, but especially in Louisiana, where, through a contraction of the word *Acadians*, they became *Cajuns*.

Monckton and John Winslow (a colonial commander) achieved early success in Nova Scotia, but General Braddock struggled to get his expedition under way to Fort Duquesne. Braddock managed to alienate would-be Indian allies, and even insulted the Delawares so profoundly that they went over to the French side. Braddock also alienated the "provincials," of whom he was so thoroughly contemptuous that the colonial governors resisted collecting war levies and generally refused to cooperate with the general.

At long last, Braddock led two regiments of British regulars and a provincial detachment (under George Washington) out of Fort Cumberland, Maryland. It was an unwieldy force of 2,500 men loaded down with heavy equipment. Along the way, French-allied Indians sniped at the slow-moving column. Washington advised Braddock to detach a "flying column" of 1,500 men to make the initial attack on Fort Duquesne, which Braddock believed was defended by 800 French and Indians. By July 7, the flying column set up a camp 10 miles from their objective.

Spies out of Fort Duquesne made Braddock's forces sound very impressive, and the fort's commandant, Claude-Pierre Pécaudy de Contrecoeur, was prepared to surrender. But Captain Liénard de Beaujeu convinced him to take the initiative and attack. All he had available were 72 regulars of the French Marine, 146 Canadian militiamen, and 637 assorted Indians. These he threw against Braddock's encampment on the morning of July 9, 1755. The result was panic among the British. Troops fired wildly—or at each other. It is said that many of the British regulars huddled in the road like flocks of sheep. Braddock, stupid but brave, had five horses shot from under him as he vainly tried to rally his troops. At last, mortally wounded, he continued to observe the disaster. Of 1,459 officers and men who had engaged in the Battle of the Wilderness, only 462 would return. (George Washington, though unhurt, had two horses shot from under him and his coat pierced by four bullets.) As he lay dying, Braddock said simply: "Who would have thought it?"

Panic, Retreat, Retrenchment

The defeat at the Battle of the Wilderness drove many more Indians into the camp of the French and laid English settlements along the length of the frontier open to attack. To make matters worse, the French had captured Braddock's private papers, which contained his main war plan. French governor Vaudreuil had intended to move against Fort Oswego on the south shore of Lake Ontario; learning from Braddock's abandoned papers that Forts Niagara and Saint Frédéric would be the objects of attack, he reinforced these positions, using the very cannon the routed English had left behind.

While the Pennsylvania, Maryland, and Virginia frontiers were convulsed by Indian raids, William Johnson was victorious at the Battle of Lake George and built the strategically important Fort William Henry on the south end of the lake. Washington, returned from the Battle of the Wilderness, persuaded authorities to build more forts, extending from the Potomac and James and Roanoke rivers, down into South Carolina. These forts, Washington said, were the only effective means of combating the widespread Indian raids unleashed by the French.

By June 1756, British settlers in Virginia had withdrawn 150 miles from the prewar frontier. George Washington complained to Governor Dinwiddie: "the Bleu-Ridge is now our Frontier...there will not be a living creature left in Frederick-County: and how soon Fairfax, and Prince William may share its fate, is easily conceived."

Main Event
The British so hated and feared the Indians that, on April 10, 1756, the colonial council of Pennsylvania began to offer a "scalp bounty" on Delawares: $50 for a woman's scalp; $130 for the scalp of each man above ten years of age. How officials were supposed to determine sex and age, let alone tribe, based on the appearance of the scalps was not specified.

Seven Years of Bad Luck

For its first three years, the French and Indian War had been strictly a North American conflict. In 1756, it became a world war as Prussia invaded Saxony. The following year, the Holy Roman Empire (in effect, Austria) declared war on Prussia, which then invaded Bohemia. Through a complex of interests, intrigues, and alliances, the French, the British, the Spanish, and the Russians also joined the war, which eventually encompassed more than 30 major battles in Europe, India, Cuba, the Philippines, and North America. The world conflict was given the generic title of the Seven Years War.

Paths of Glory

As part of its commitment to an expanded war, France sent the dashing and highly capable Louis Joseph, marquis de Montcalm to take charge of Canadian forces on May 11, 1756. For their part, the British forces suffered defeat after defeat. At last, in December 1756, William Pitt became British secretary of state for the southern department, a post that put him in charge of American colonial affairs. He took command away from inept, politically chosen officers and gave it to those with genuine military skill—colonial commanders included. The result was a gradual reversal of Britain's ill fortune.

Pitt chose Brigadier General John Forbes, one of his best commanders, to assault—for the third time in the war—Fort Duquesne. Despite many delays, mainly caused by the incompetence and corruption of the British quartermaster (supply) corps, an army of 5,000 provincials, 1,400 Highlanders, and an ever-diminishing number of Indian allies lumbered toward the stubborn objective at the forks of the Ohio. When the main force became bogged down in the mud not far from the fort, one of Forbes's subordinates, Colonel Henry Bouquet, became impatient and, on September 11, hastily ordered 800 Highlanders to attack. They were cut down by French and Indians, who killed a third of their number.

This triumph, however, proved a Pyrrhic victory for the French. Losses among their Indian allies were so heavy that most of the Indians, after seizing plunder, deserted the cause. In the meantime, a treaty concluded at Easton, Pennsylvania, in October 1758 brought peace between the French-allied Delaware and the English. Colonel Bouquet, still reeling from defeat, proclaimed with relief that the Treaty of Easton had "knocked the French on the head."

On November 24, Forbes was at last ready to make his advance on Fort Duquesne. Suddenly, a distant explosion was heard. Rather than allow the English to capture the fort, the French had blown it up. The heads of Bouquet's Highlanders, captured earlier, had been skewered on upright stakes, the soldiers' kilts tied below them. It was a grisly greeting, yet Forbes knew that the nation in control of the forks of the Ohio—the confluence of the Monongahela, Allegheny, and Ohio rivers—held the gateway to the West. And that gateway was now in British hands.

If the year 1758 marked the turning of the tide in favor of the British, 1759 was the year of French disaster, culminating in the siege, battle, and loss of Quebec on September 18, 1759. This loss effectively brought to an end French power in North America.

Although the war had been decided with the surrender of Quebec, the fighting did not stop. Montreal remained in French hands, and Quebec had to be held. For the next two years, however, the British steadily contracted the circle around French Canada. At last into the fray, during its waning months, came Spain, which sided with France. England declared war on the new combatant on January 2, 1762, and crushed the adversary with sea power alone. As it became clear to everyone involved that the war in America and in Europe was about to end, France rushed to conclude in secret the Treaty of San Ildefonso with Spain (November 3, 1762), in which it ceded to that country all of its territory west of the Mississippi and the Isle of Orleans in Louisiana. This offering was intended as compensation for the loss of Spain's Caribbean holdings to the British. On February 10, 1763, the great Treaty of Paris followed, which officially ended hostilities in America and abroad.

The score? France ceded all of Louisiana to Spain and the rest of its North American holdings to Great Britain. Spain recovered Cuba (in compensation for the loss of territories in Florida and in the Caribbean), and France retained the Caribbean islands of Guadeloupe, Martinique, and St. Lucia.

Pontiac's Rebellion

In far-off Paris, pens had been put to paper. Within a few days of the Treaty of Paris, on April 27, 1763, Pontiac (ca. 1720–69), war chief of the Ottawa Indians, called a grand council of Ottawa and other tribes—most notably the Delaware, Seneca (as well as elements of other Iroquois tribes), and the Shawnee. The chief pushed for an attack on Detroit. This decision ignited a series of bloody assaults on the western outposts that the French had just officially surrendered to the English. Although many Indian war leaders participated, this coda to the French and Indian War would be called Pontiac's Rebellion.

Pontiac had been moved to war by British general Jeffrey Amherst's refusal to continue the French custom of giving presents to the Indians, especially gifts of ammunition, on which the tribes had come to depend for hunting. This outrage, combined with the bellicose pronouncements of an Indian mystic named Neolin—better known to the whites as the Delaware Prophet—fanned the flames. Neolin, Pontiac, and others urged action against the English now, before they became too numerous to drive from the land.

Pontiac's Rebellion tore the white frontier apart, as Indian warriors tortured, mutilated, and killed with exuberance. Amherst, in desperation, decided to wage total war, giving orders to take no prisoners, but to kill all belligerents. He even instituted biological warfare, directing one of his officers deliberately to infect the tribes with smallpox. Although this plan was officially abandoned for fear of spreading the infection among the white settlements, Simon Ecuyer, a Swiss mercenary temporarily acting as commander of the besieged Fort Pitt (the former French Fort Duquesne), called a peace conference with his Delaware attackers. As a token of esteem, he presented them with two blankets and a handkerchief. They had been provided by Captain William Trent from the fort's smallpox hospital. "I hope they will have the desired effect," Trent remarked to Ecuyer.

They did. An epidemic swept through the Delaware, and this misfortune, along with the Indians' realization that the supply of English settlers was apparently inexhaustible, brought Pontiac to the peace table at the end of 1763. By the following year, other disaffected tribal leaders had also surrendered—but not before a band of renegade white settlers had gone on their own rampage.

On December 14, 1763, a mob of 57 Scotch-Irish Presbyterians from Paxton and Donegal, settlements in the heart of the raid-racked Pennsylvania frontier, butchered a party of six Conestoga Indians, notwithstanding the fact that the Conestogas were and had always been peaceful. Despite Governor John Penn's call for the arrest of the "Paxton Boys," frontier Pennsylvania approved of their action and encouraged more. The magistrates of Lancaster County gathered the remaining Conestogas into a public workhouse for their protection. The Paxton Boys raided the building on December 27, killing 14 Indians as they knelt in prayer. The survivors—again, for their "protection"—were once more removed, this time to a barren island in the middle of the windswept Delaware River. Safe from the Paxton Boys, the Indians were ravaged by the elements of a brutal winter. Fifty-six Indians sickened and died.

This sordid end to a brutal period of war would prove but a prelude to yet another, even more momentous, struggle in the wilderness.

The Least You Need to Know

➤ The French and Indian War was the American phase of the Seven Years War, which historians consider the first "world" war.

➤ Although the English had more colonists, the French had more Indian allies and were far better at wilderness combat tactics than the inflexible British regulars.

➤ Pontiac attempted to unite several tribes in a campaign to stem the tide of English immigration into the Ohio Valley.

Part 2
The World Turned Upside Down

A few years ago, so-called "revisionist" historians set themselves up in the business of "debunking" American history, and it was common to hear talk about how the American Revolution was about economics rather than such "ideals" as freedom and equality. Well, to a colonist struggling to make ends meet, economics was freedom and equality. It's true, the roots of the American Revolution were tangled up in money, but they grew into a great tree of liberty that all the world has gazed on with envy and wonder. The chapters in this section discuss the origin and course of our war for independence.

WANNA GO...

INVITE

Chapter 9

Invitation to a Tea Party (1763–1775)

In This Chapter

➤ Proclamation Line of 1763

➤ Taxation without representation

➤ The Boston Massacre and Boston Tea Party

➤ First Continental Congress

➤ Battles of Lexington and Concord

➤ The misnamed "Battle of Bunker Hill"

➤ *Common Sense* and The Declaration of Independence

Britain finally won the French and Indian War, but in the process, started losing its North American colonies. For most of the war, colonial leaders were the brunt of royal contempt, and provincial military men saw how ineffectual the British regulars were in fighting wilderness wars. The "Mother Country" began to seem unresponsive, uncaring, arrogant, and even incompetent. The colonies, traditionally competitive with one another, emerged from the crucible of war feeling stronger bonds among themselves than with an aloof and unfeeling government across the sea.

King George Draws a Line

The Treaty of Easton, concluded in 1758, had helped turn the tide toward the British in the French and Indian War. By formally agreeing to prohibit white settlement west of the Allegheny Mountains, British authorities persuaded the war-weary Indian allies of the French that they no longer needed to fear invasion by the English. But another product of the French and Indian War, the road that General John Forbes had hacked through the Pennsylvania wilderness to deliver his unwieldy army to do battle at Fort Duquesne, ensured that the treaty would be violated almost immediately. The Forbes Road was the first great avenue into the North American interior. It led to the confluence of the Ohio, Allegheny, and Monongahela rivers—the site of present-day Pittsburgh and the gateway to the trans-Allegheny West. Even before the war was over, settlers began to use the road, and the Easton agreement was breached.

With the French neutralized in North America, the British crown saw the next and continuing threat of war to be conflict with the Indians. But as long as a buffer zone existed between the Indians and the colonists, peace could be maintained. Accordingly, on October 7, 1763, King George III issued a new proclamation redrawing the limit of western settlement at the Appalachian Mountains.

At first, the Proclamation of 1763 worked like magic to calm the Indians and to bring to an end the bloody coda to the French and Indian War known as Pontiac's Rebellion. What the British government hadn't reckoned on was that, while pacifying the Indians, the Proclamation line enraged the settlers, who went ahead and pushed settlement across the forbidden mountains. When resentful Indians responded with raids, the illegal settlers appealed to royal authorities for aid. They were rebuffed. The gulf that had been created between the colonies and England during the French and Indian War widened. As the frontier regions became more populous and powerful, the allegiance of many authorities in the Tidewater (the more established coastal settlements) leaned westward rather than back toward Europe.

Taxation Without Representation

Fighting any war is expensive, and no war is more costly than one fought across an ocean. During the French and Indian War, the English treasury had amassed a huge debt. The English government, led by Chancellor of the Exchequer George Grenville, decided that it was fitting and proper for the colonies to pay their fair share. Grenville pushed through Parliament heavy duties on numerous commodities imported into the colonies, most notably molasses and sugar, and the laws became known collectively as the Sugar Act. Passed in 1764, this was the first act the English Parliament passed for the specific purpose of raising tax revenues in the colonies.

At the same time, Parliament passed the Currency Act, which forbade the colonies from issuing paper money and required the use of gold in all business transactions. This act thereby guaranteed that the colonies would be economically dependent on England. Parliament also decided to enforce the Acts of Trade and Navigation, which had been passed during the 1650s but never really put into effect. England used these acts to raise additional duty revenue.

The colonists, reeling from a business recession caused by the French and Indian War, and the frontier regions, resentful of the Proclamation Line, were stunned and outraged at being taxed without the benefit of parliamentary representation. After a Boston town meeting denounced "taxation without representation," the phrase evolved into a battle cry that spread from that city to the other colonies.

The action Boston proposed was nonviolent. The colonies made a Non-Importation Agreement, pledging to boycott a wide variety of English goods. Parliament, taking little heed of this protest, passed the Quartering Act in 1765, requiring colonial governments to furnish barracks and provisions for royal troops. The next year, the act was extended to require the billeting of soldiers in taverns and inns at the expense of the colonists. Not only were these measures a further financial hardship on the colonies, they rankled in a way that reached beyond economics. The Quartering Act was seen as an invasion of privacy and an affront to personal liberty. Even colonists who were not directly affected by the revenue acts were enraged by the Quartering Act.

Stamps of Tyranny

Parliament had an even more offensive measure in store. In 1765, it passed the Stamp Act, which required that every paper document—ranging from newspapers, to deeds, to playing cards—bear a revenue stamp purchased from royally appointed colonial stamp agents. Worse, violations of the act were to be tried summarily by vice-admiralty courts, in which there were no juries. Not only did the colonists see the stamps as evil, but denial of trial by jury attacked a right as old as the Magna Carta.

The Stamp Act united the colonies in opposition to the "tyranny" of the Mother Country. Subversive secret societies such as the Sons of Liberty were formed in many towns, the boycott of English goods was stepped up, and a Stamp Act Congress was called in New York in October 1765 (eight colonies sent delegates). The congress drafted a "Declaration of Rights and Grievances," claiming that the colonists had the rights of British subjects and that taxation without parliamentary representation was a violation of those rights. Parliament repealed the Stamp Act in March 1766, but simultaneously delivered a political slap in the face by passing the Declaratory Act, which affirmed Parliament's authority to create laws for the colonies "in all cases whatever."

Act II

Chancellor of the Exchequer Charles Townshend (1725–67) next pushed through Parliament a bundle of acts intended to raise revenue, tighten customs enforcement, and assert imperial authority in America. Enacted on June 29, 1767, the so-called Townshend Acts levied import duties on glass, lead, paint, paper, and tea. Additional bills in the package authorized "writs of assistance" (blanket search warrants), created additional jury-less vice-admiralty courts, established a board of customs commissioners headquartered in Boston, and suspended the New York assembly for its defiance of the Quartering Act of 1765.

Samuel Adams, of the Massachusetts Sons of Liberty, sent a "circular letter" to the other 12 colonies calling for renewal of the non-importation agreements. Royal customs officials in Boston were attacked after they seized a ship belonging to the merchant John Hancock. The beleaguered officials requested a contingent of English troops to occupy Boston.

During 1768–69, all the colonies except New Hampshire boycotted English goods, and the Virginia House of Burgesses, led by Patrick Henry, created the Virginia Association to enforce the boycott. At this, the royal governor of Virginia dissolved the House of Burgesses, thereby further inflaming anti-British passions. However, in April 1770, Parliament again bowed to the pressure and repealed all the Townshend duties—except for a tax on tea.

Real Life

Samuel Adams (1722–1803) inherited a one-third interest in his father's prosperous brewery but lost most of his fortune through mismanagement. If he was not very adept at handling money, Adams was highly skilled at politics; after attending Harvard, he attracted a wide following among members of Boston's many political clubs. Adams was instrumental in creating the most influential and radical of the clubs, the Sons of Liberty. In 1765, Adams organized the protest against the Stamp Act.

Elected to the lower house of the Massachusetts legislature, Adams served from 1765 to 1774 and composed the great protest documents of the era, including the Circular Letter (1768) against the Townshend Acts. He fanned the flames of resistance and rebellion in the popular press, and after 1770, was chief architect of intercolonial "committees of correspondence," which coordinated the developing revolution. Adams was a prime mover behind the Boston Tea Party of 1773.

A principal member of the First Continental Congress, Samuel Adams participated in drafting the 1781 Articles of Confederation, precursor of the Constitution.

Massacre in Boston

The British troops sent to Boston at the request of the beleaguered customs officials were, to put it mildly, not popular. On March 5, 1770, one of the soldiers got into a brawl with a civilian workman. This triggered an evening of protests by bands of colonists who roamed the streets. Finally, a squad of Redcoats, led by Captain Thomas Preston, fired into a small mob agitating in front of the hated Customs House. Three colonists died instantly, and two others were mortally wounded.

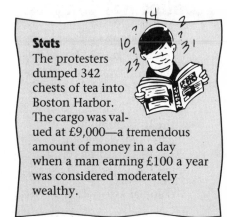

Main Event
First to die in the cause of American liberty was the leader of the Boston mob, Crispus Attucks (born about 1723). He was almost certainly a black man, perhaps of partly Indian descent.

Prudently, British authorities immediately withdrew the troops from town. But the "Boston Massacre" became the focal point of anti-British propaganda and heightened American fears about standing armies established in the colonies. The committees of correspondence became increasingly active, and the colonies drew closer together in opposition to the crown.

From Tea Party to Continental Congress

By 1773, the only duty remaining from the Townshend Acts was the tax on tea. To modern ears, this sounds rather trivial. Don't want to pay a tax on tea? Well, then stop drinking tea!

But going without tea was never a viable option for *English* men and women. Moreover, in the 18th century, tea was an extremely valuable trade commodity—almost a second currency. The East India Company, England's chief tea producer, was vital to British government interests because it had extensive influence in India. Expenses, however, were high, and by the 1770s, the company was close to bankruptcy. To bail out the firm, Parliament suspended the tax paid on tea in England but retained the import tax on tea sold in the colonies. Worse, the government ruled that the East India Company could sell the tea directly to agents at a set price rather than through colonial merchants at public auction. Not only was the tax unfair, but colonial merchants, cut out of the profit loop, resented the crown's intrusion into free enterprise.

Stats
The protesters dumped 342 chests of tea into Boston Harbor. The cargo was valued at £9,000—a tremendous amount of money in a day when a man earning £100 a year was considered moderately wealthy.

The committees of correspondence worked overtime to spread the word of opposition to the tea duty and to impose an absolute boycott of English tea. On one occasion, the royal governor of Massachusetts refused demands to send recently arrived tea ships back to England. So on the night of December 16, 1773, a band of Bostonians—lamely disguised as Indians—boarded three ships in Boston harbor and dumped a cargo of tea chests overboard. The act triggered similar "tea parties" in ports up and down the coast.

Intolerable Acts

King George III of England (1738–1820) has always gotten a bad rap in American schoolbooks, which traditionally have painted him as a tyrant seeking to squeeze out of the colonies not only their cash, but their liberty as well. In truth, George was a popular monarch, as earnest as he was mediocre and incapable of thinking on his own. During the period immediately preceding the American Revolution, he depended entirely on the advice of his prime minister, Lord North, an aggressive autocrat. Following the Tea Party, it was North who sponsored what the colonists called the Intolerable Acts.

The first of these acts, the Boston Port Act (March 31, 1774), closed the harbor to commerce until such time as Boston paid for the destroyed tea. Next, the Massachusetts Government Act (May 20) reserved for the crown the power to appoint members of the upper house of the legislature. The Government Act also increased the royal governor's patronage powers, provided that juries be summoned by sheriffs rather than elected by colonists. Most onerous of all, the Government Act banned town meetings not explicitly authorized by law or by the governor. At the same time, the Impartial Administration of Justice Act authorized a change of venue to another colony or even to England for crown officers charged with capital crimes while performing official duties.

Intended to restore order to Massachusetts, the Intolerable Acts boomeranged, leading the colonies to recognize their common cause and to convene the First Continental Congress.

Continental Congress

The Congress met in Philadelphia during September 1774, and only Georgia failed to send delegates. The 56 delegates who convened represented the full spectrum of colonial thought, from radicals who wanted to sever all ties with England, to conservatives who wanted to find a way to heal the breach. The Massachusetts delegation produced the Suffolk Resolves, which the radicals supported, calling for the people to arm, to disobey the Intolerable Acts, and to collect their own colonial taxes. The conservatives countered with a plan of union between England and the colonies. With modifications, the Suffolk Resolves were adopted by a margin of six to five. The Intolerable Acts were declared unconstitutional, and the non-importation boycott was given teeth by the creation of a colonial association to enforce it.

Following the Continental Congress, Thomas Jefferson (in his pamphlet, *Summary View of the Rights of British America*) and John Adams (in a series of published letters he signed "Novanglus") proposed dominion status for the colonies, whereby the colonies would govern themselves but acknowledge the crown as the head of state. At the time, Parliament rejected this idea as too radical, but liberals in the English government did formulate a plan of conciliation in 1775, which would have granted a considerable degree of self-government to the colonies. The hyper-conservative House of Lords rejected the plan, however, and Parliament as a whole declared Massachusetts to be in rebellion. In a sense, then, it was the British Parliament that declared the American Revolution.

The Shot Heard 'Round the World

Massachusetts responded to the Parliamentary declaration by organizing special militia units that could be ready for battle on a minute's notice. They were called the Minutemen.

General Thomas Gage, commander of British regulars, ordered to use force against the defiant colonials, dispatched Lieutenant Colonel Francis Smith with a column from Boston to seize the gunpowder stored at the Massachusetts Provincial Congress in the town of Concord. On the morning of April 19, 1775, Smith's troops dispersed a company of Minutemen at Lexington, unintentionally killing several in an unauthorized burst of musket fire. Smith reached Concord but found only a small portion of the gunpowder. He had not reckoned with the resourcefulness of a small band of swift riders.

Paul Revere (1735–1818) was a prosperous and highly skilled Charlestown, Massachusetts, silversmith, who was a leader of the Sons of Liberty and had been a participant in the Boston Tea Party. A courier for the Massachusetts Committee of Correspondence, Revere rode, on the night of April 18, from Charlestown to Lexington, alerting the populace to the approach of British troops. In Lexington, he also warned John Hancock and Samuel Adams, the chief leaders of the Massachusetts rebels, to escape. Accompanied by two other riders, Charles Dawes and Samuel Prescott, Revere rode on to Concord but was intercepted by a British patrol. Although Prescott was the one who actually managed to reach Concord, it was Revere whom Henry Wadsworth Longfellow celebrated in his famous, if fanciful, poem of 1863, "Paul Revere's Ride."

While the battles of Lexington and Concord were not colonial victories, they were certainly not British triumphs, either. As Smith's column returned to Boston, it was harassed by continual Patriot gunfire,

> **Voice from the Past**
>
> "By the rude bridge that arched the flood, / Their flag to April's breeze unfurled, / Here once the embattled farmers stood, / And fired the shot heard round the world."—Ralph Waldo Emerson, "Hymn Sung at the Completion of the Concord Monument, April 19, 1836"

resulting in the deaths of 73 British soldiers and the wounding of an additional 200. The pattern would prove typical of the war. British forces, trained to fight European-style open-field battles, would often win such engagements, only to be cut up piecemeal by colonial guerrilla groups firing from concealed ambush.

Washington Backs a Long Shot

Soon after the battles at Lexington and Concord, colonial militia forces from all over New England converged on Boston and laid siege to the city. In May 1775, a Vermont land-owner named Ethan Allen led a militia outfit he had organized—the Green Mountain Boys—against Fort Ticonderoga between Lake Champlain and Lake George in New York and seized it from British regulars. Next, Crown Point, on the western shore of Lake Champlain, fell to rebel forces. Despite these early triumphs, anyone who assessed the situation with a cold eye would have put money on the British and not the Colonial Americans. Britain was an established imperial power, with deep pockets, a tested army, and the most powerful navy in the world. Moreover, while the *colonies* had acted in unity, the *colonists* were hardly unanimous in the desire to rebel. Each colony contained a large "Loyalist" population.

Then there was the matter of leadership. The English had a king and a prime minister, while the colonies had no king or other chief executive. And that wasn't the half of it. The colonies had no government at all, no treasury, and no regular army. True, a Conti-nental Congress had convened, but 13 separate colonial assemblies vied with it for power and authority.

Forty-three-year-old George Washington, now a prosperous Virginia planter, was accus-tomed to long odds. He had played them during his militia service in the French and Indian War. Sometimes he had won. Mostly, he had lost. On June 15, 1775, at the suggestion of John Adams of Massachusetts, the Second Continental Congress asked Washington to lead the as-yet nonexistent Continental Army. Washington accepted.

A Thousand Fall Near Bunker Hill

The colonies' new commander set off for New England to lead the Minutemen. Before Washington arrived, however, British General Thomas Gage (who had been reinforced on May 25 by fresh troops from Britain and additional generals, including John Burgoyne, William Howe, and Henry Clinton) offered to call the Revolution quits—no harm, no foul. General Gage would grant an amnesty to everyone except Sam Adams and John Hancock, the two chief troublemakers. In response, the Massachusetts Committee of Public Safety ordered General Artemus Ward to fortify Bunker Hill on Charlestown Heights, overlooking Boston harbor. Ward instead sent Colonel William Prescott with 1,200 men to occupy nearby Breed's Hill, which was lower and more vulnerable.

Gage opened up on Breed's Hill with a naval bombardment at dawn on June 17, 1775. Then he launched an amphibious attack with 2,500 men under General Howe. Twice, the superior British force attempted to take the hill, and twice they were repelled. A third assault, with fixed bayonets, succeeded only after the colonials had run out of ammunition. Misnamed for Bunker Hill (the superior position that *should* have been defended), the battle was a tactical defeat for the colonists, but it was a tremendous psychological victory for them. They had been defeated only because of a shortage of ammunition.

Stats
Of the 2,500 British troops engaged at Bunker Hill, 1,000 perished, a devastating casualty rate of 42 percent—the heaviest loss the British would suffer during the long war.

An Olive Branch Breaks and a Declaration Is Written

The Second Continental Congress made its own final attempt to stop the revolution by sending to King George III and Parliament the so-called Olive Branch Petition. Meanwhile, Washington formed the first parade of the Continental Army on Cambridge Common in Cambridge, Massachusetts, on July 3, 1775. In September, Britain contemptuously rejected the Olive Branch Petition. Georgia, final holdout from the Second Continental Congress, joined that assembly and the Revolution. Congress next moved to organize a post office department, a commission for negotiating with Indians, and a navy. By December 1775, Virginia and North Carolina militia defeated the forces of the royal governor of Virginia and destroyed his base at Norfolk.

Common Sense and Confederation

With the rebellion in full swing, it was time to create a feeling of historical purpose to catch up with the rush of events. In January 1776, Thomas Paine, a Philadelphia patriot and orator, anonymously published a modest pamphlet called *Common Sense*. In brilliant, even melodramatic prose, Paine outlined the reasons for breaking free from England, portraying the American Revolution as a *world* event, an epoch-making step in the history of humankind.

Voice from the Past

"These are the times that try men's souls. The summer soldier and sunshine patriot will, in this crisis, shrink from the service of his country; but he that stands it now, deserves the love and thanks of man and woman. Tyranny, like hell, is not easily conquered."—*Common Sense*

With the colonies united as never before, the next great document to emerge from the gathering storm was a formal declaration of independence. On July 1, 1776, Richard Henry Lee, one of Virginia's delegates to the Continental Congress, presented a draft proposal for a document asserting that "these United Colonies are, and of a right ought to be, free and independent States." Congress passed the draft document but sent it to a committee for discussion, debate, and amendment. Thomas Jefferson of Virginia, who had a fine reputation as a writer, was selected to revise the committee's draft. He ended up wholly rewriting it.

The Declaration of Independence, like Thomas Paine's *Common Sense*, cast the American struggle for independence in a noble light as a profound gesture "in the course of human events." Inspired by the great English political philosopher John Locke (1632–1704), Jefferson listed the "inalienable rights" of humankind. These included life and liberty, but where Locke had listed *property* as the third right, Jefferson specified "the pursuit of happiness." The purpose of government, Jefferson declared, was "to secure these rights," and the authority of government to do so derived "from the consent of the governed." When a government ceased to serve its just purpose, it was the right and duty of "the governed" to withdraw their allegiance. And that is precisely what the colonies had done. Jefferson's document was adopted by Congress on July 4, 1776.

The Least You Need to Know

➤ Unfair taxation, limits on westward settlement, and the involuntary quartering of British soldiers united the colonies in rebellion.

➤ Thomas Paine (*Common Sense*) and Thomas Jefferson (The Declaration of Independence) helped elevate a *colonial* revolution to the status of a momentous world event.

➤ American troops were citizen soldiers, fighting at home and committed to their cause. The British soldiers were a professional army doing a grim job in a distant land.

Chapter 10

The Fires of Liberty (1776–1783)

In This Chapter

➤ Articles of Confederation

➤ Early Patriot triumphs and losses

➤ Victory at Saratoga

➤ Surrender of Cornwallis

Great though it is, the Declaration of Independence, a human document, is imperfect. It failed to deal with the issue of slavery (Jefferson's fellow southerners struck the references he had included), and it failed to specify just how the separate colonies, each with its own government and identity, could unite in a single government. Throughout the early years of the Revolution, the Continental Congress struggled with this issue and finally produced, in November 1777, the Articles of Confederation.

A timid document, the Articles gave the individual states—not the federal government—most of the power, including the authority to levy taxes; after all, "taxation without representation" had triggered the rupture with England. Eventually, the Articles would be scrapped in favor of a brand-new, much bolder Constitution. But the earlier document, the product of agonizing debate, would hold the nation together through a Revolutionary War that, like most wars, went on much longer than either side had any reason to expect.

The Longest Odds

While the framers of the Articles of Confederation in Philadelphia did battle with words and ideas, soldiers in the field fought with powder and lead. Politician and militiaman alike were well aware that, if King George earnestly willed it, if he sent to America everything he had, the colonies would, in all likelihood, be defeated. But during the early years of the war, Britain was surprisingly slow to take the offensive.

Siege of Boston

Most of the "Lobsterbacks" (as the colonials called the red-coated British troops) were bottled up in Boston, to which Washington's forces laid siege. Try as they might, the British were unable to break out of their entrenchments. Then, when Washington arrayed his artillery on Dorchester Heights, British commanders gave the order to evacuate by sea in March 1776, reestablishing their headquarters at Halifax, Nova Scotia.

Down South

While His Majesty's forces were being humiliated in New England, Sir Henry Clinton sailed with his troops along the southern coast. His purpose was to rally property-rich Loyalists against the upstart, ragtag rabble of the newly established "American" governments in the Carolinas and Georgia. As he prepared to disembark at Cape Fear, North Carolina, Clinton received news that a Loyalist uprising had been squelched by Patriot forces at the Battle of Moore's Creek Bridge near Wilmington, North Carolina, on February 27, 1776. Clinton pressed southward, reaching Charleston Harbor. Seeking to establish a base for Loyalist resistance, Clinton bombarded Charleston's harbor fortifications, but Patriot forces drove off the British by June 28, 1776. It was a valuable triumph, which stalled British activity in the South for more than two years.

A Pale Flush of Victory

The first 12 months of the war had gone far better than any self-respecting oddsmaker would have predicted. The British had been forced out of New England and the South. However, a key American hope had also been dashed. The Patriots had tried to persuade the French citizens of Quebec to make common cause with them against the British. American strategists understood that, as long as the British conducted the war from far-off London, the Patriot cause would enjoy a great advantage. However, if the British should begin to use nearby Canada as the staging area for an invasion of the colonies, that advantage would evaporate. Unfortunately, the French Canadians were unwilling to initiate any action themselves. But, fortified by successes in defending against the British in New England and the South, the Americans decided to take the offensive.

An army under General Richard Montgomery marched from upper New York and captured Montreal on November 10, 1775. Simultaneously, troops commanded by Colonel Benedict Arnold advanced through the wilderness of Maine to unite with Montgomery's units in an attack on the walled city of Quebec. The invaders were beaten back, and Montgomery was killed on December 30. American forces maintained a blockade of the Canadian capital through May 1776, but the offensive in Canada had petered out, and Americans would stay out of the region for the rest of the war.

The British Lion Roars

There was worse, much worse, to come.

Beginning in the summer of 1776, British forces wrested the initiative from the Americans. British general Guy Carleton, the very able governor of Quebec, was ordered to chase the Americans out of Canada and down through the region of Lake Champlain and the Hudson River. This action would sever the far northern tier of colonies from the southern. Simultaneously, a much larger army led by General William Howe (who had replaced Gage as supreme commander of Britain's North American forces) was assigned to capture New York City and its strategically vital harbor.

Carleton succeeded handily in driving the remaining Americans out of Canada, but, plagued by supply problems and the approach of winter, was unable to pursue them back below the border. This setback, however, did not stop Howe, who hurled against New York City the largest single force the British would ever field in the Revolution: 32,000 troops, 400 transports, 73 warships (commanded by his vice-admiral brother, Richard Howe, with whom he shared the American supreme command). It was all too apparent to General Washington that, militarily, the situation in New York was hopeless. In the course of the war, the American commander would prove highly skilled at the art of the strategic withdrawal, pulling back in a manner that cost the attacker and yet left his own forces intact to fight another day. This is precisely what he wanted to do in the case of New York, but Congress, fearing that the loss of a major city would dispirit Patriots throughout the colonies, ordered him to defend the position. Washington met with defeat on Long Island on August 27, 1776.

If Washington and the Continental Congress had weighed the odds more soberly, perhaps they would have raised the white flag. But Washington did not surrender. Instead, he fought a series of brilliant rearguard actions against Howe on Manhattan Island, which cost the British time, money, and energy. It took Howe from August to November to clear Washington's forces from New York City and its environs. Then, instead of moving inland via the Hudson, Howe simply pushed Washington across New

Jersey. If he had hoped to corner and fight the Continental Army to a standstill, Howe was mistaken. The Americans escaped across the Delaware River into Pennsylvania on December 7, 1776.

Recrossing the Delaware

"These are the times that try men's souls," Thomas Paine had written just two years earlier. The present times transformed Washington's men into a determined and disciplined army, even in the depths of the war's first vicious winter. Washington, as General Howe saw the situation, was defeated, crushed. Certainly, he had no business striking back, especially not in this inclement season. Howe was a competent European general. In Europe, the proper times of year for fighting were spring, summer, and fall. In Europe, armies did not fight in winter. But Washington understood: This was not Europe. Collecting his scattered regulars and militiamen, General Washington reorganized his army and led it back across the Delaware River, from Pennsylvania to New Jersey.

On December 26, 1776, Washington surprised and overran a garrison of Hessian mercenaries at Trenton, New Jersey, then went on to an even bigger victory at Princeton on January 3, 1777. The triumphs were a sharp slap in General Howe's face. Fortified by these miraculous victories, Congress rejected the peace terms the Howe brothers, in their capacity as peace commissioners, proposed. The fight for independence would continue.

Word for the Day

Following the practice of the day, King George III paid foreign mercenary troops to do much of his fighting in America. The *Hessians* came from the German principality of Hesse-Kassel. Although not all of the German mercenaries employed in the war came from this principality, most of them did. The name was applied to all the hired soldiers—about 30,000 in all—who fought in most of the major campaigns, usually answering to British commanders. Some Hessians stayed here after the war and became American citizens.

Saratoga Morning

Wearily, the British laid out plans for a new assault on the northern colonies. Major General Burgoyne was in charge of Britain's Canadian-based army, but he and Howe failed to work out a plan for coordinating their two forces. Burgoyne led his army down the customary Lake Champlain–Hudson River route, while Howe was stalled by indecision. Finally, he decided not to support Burgoyne's offensive but to leave a garrison under

Sir Henry Clinton in New York City and to transport the bulk of his army by sea to attack Philadelphia. It was a fatal blunder.

Burgoyne's operation began promisingly, as the American Northern army, suffering from lack of supply and disputes among its own commanders, fell back before the British advance. Burgoyne, popularly known as "Gentleman John," was so confident of victory that he invited officers to bring wives and mistresses on the campaign. He staged sumptuous dinner parties for all engaged in the grand enterprise of teaching the rebels a lesson they would never forget. At his arrogant leisure, Burgoyne advanced on and recaptured Fort Ticonderoga on July 5, 1777, but he moved at such an unhurried pace that American forces had plenty of time to regroup for guerrilla combat in the wilderness of upstate New York. The Americans destroyed roads, cut lines of communication and supply, and generally harassed Burgoyne's columns. At Bemis Heights, on the west bank of the Hudson River, he was met by the revitalized Northern forces of the Continental Army commanded by Horatio Gates and supported by Benedict Arnold and Daniel Morgan. At the opening of the Battle of Saratoga, Burgoyne charged the Americans twice, on September 19 and October 7, 1777, only to be beaten back with heavy losses both times. Blocked to the south and without aid from Clinton, Gentleman John surrendered 6,000 regulars plus various auxiliaries to the Patriot forces on October 17, 1777.

Trouble in the City of Brotherly Love

Despite the triumph at Saratoga, the news was not all good for the Americans. Howe took his army by sea and landed on upper Chesapeake Bay, 57 miles outside of Philadelphia, poised for an assault on that city. On October 4, 1777, Howe won Philadelphia, the American capital.

But what, really, had the British gained? An entire army, Burgoyne's, was lost. Howe had paid dearly for the prize he now held. In contrast, the American forces remained intact, and the rebellion continued. Most important of all, the French were deeply impressed by the American victory at Saratoga, not the British capture of Philadelphia.

Viva La France!

As early as 1776, Louis XVI's foreign minister, the Comte de Vergennes, persuaded his king to aid—albeit secretly—the American cause. Prudently, Vergennes withheld overt military aid until he was confident of the Americans' prospects for victory. He did not want to risk a *losing* war with Britain. The victory at Saratoga, rumors that Britain was going to offer America major territorial concessions to bring peace, and the extraordinary diplomatic skills of Benjamin Franklin (whom Congress had installed in Paris as its representative during this period) finally propelled France openly into the American camp. An alliance was formally concluded on February 6, 1778, whereby France granted diplomatic recognition to the "United States of America." Shortly after the treaty of alliance was signed, Spain, a French ally, also declared war on Britain.

A Hard Forge

Nations may *disagree* and fight one another, and they may *agree* and fight together, but nature takes no notice in either case. The winter of 1778 visited great suffering on the Continental Army, which was encamped at Valley Forge, Pennsylvania. Yet on the cruel, cold anvil of that terrible winter, a stronger army was forged, in large part through the efforts of Baron von Steuben (1730–94), a Prussian officer who trained American troops to European standards. (A number of Europeans played valiant roles as volunteers in the service of the American Revolution. In addition to Baron von Steuben, these included Johann, Baron de Kalb [1721–80], a German in the French army, and two Polish patriots, Tadeusz Kocluszko [1746–1817] and Kasimierz Pulaski [ca. 1747–79]. Most famous of all was the Marquis de Lafayette [1757–1834], a brilliant commander fiercely loyal to Washington.) Spring brought Washington new recruits and the promise of French auxiliary forces, while it brought the British nothing but new pressures. The Howe brothers, having failed to crush the Revolution, resigned their commands and returned to England. Sir Henry Clinton assumed principal command in North America and evacuated his army from Philadelphia (which had proved a prize of no military value), concentrated his forces at New York City, and dispatched troops to the Caribbean in anticipation of French action there.

Washington pursued Clinton through New Jersey, fighting him to a stand at Monmouth Courthouse on June 28, 1778. The result, a draw, was nevertheless a moral victory for the Continentals, who had stood up to the best soldiers England could field. If Monmouth was not decisive, it did mark the third year of a war in which the British could show no results whatsoever.

White War, Red Blood

The American Revolution was really two wars. Along the eastern seaboard, it was a contest of one army against another. Farther inland, the fighting resembled that of the French and Indian War. Both sides employed Indian allies, but the British recruited more of them and used them as agents of terror to raid and burn outlying settlements. From the earliest days of the war, the royal lieutenant governor of Detroit, Henry Hamilton, played a key role in stirring the Indians of the Indiana-Illinois frontier to wage ferocious war on Patriot settlers. Hamilton's Indian nickname tells the tale: they called him "Hair Buyer." In 1778, the young George Rogers Clark (1752–1818), a hard-drinking Kentucky militia leader, overran the British-controlled Illinois and Indiana region and took "Hair Buyer" prisoner. Even more celebrated in the western war campaign—albeit less militarily significant—was the intrepid frontiersman Daniel Boone.

Bloody though the Kentucky frontier was, conditions were even worse on the New York–Pennsylvania frontier, which was terrorized by the Iroquois. Washington dispatched Major General John Sullivan into western New York with instructions to wipe out tribal towns wherever he found them. Nevertheless, the Iroquois persisted in raiding, as did the tribes throughout the Ohio country. They were supported and urged on by Loyalist elements in this region, and their combined activity would not come to an end even with the conclusion of the war. Indeed, this western frontier would smolder and be rekindled periodically, bursting into open flame as the War of 1812.

On Southern Fronts

In the lower South, the British found effective Indian allies in the Cherokee, who, despite suffering early defeats at the hands of the American militia in 1776, continued to raid the frontier. As the war ground on, the British regular army, which had generally neglected the South following early failures there, began to shift attention to the region by late 1778. The British reasoned that the region had a higher percentage of Loyalists than any other part of America and also offered more of the raw materials—indigo, rice, cotton—valued by the British.

In December 1778, British forces subdued Georgia, then, during 1779, fought inconclusively along the Georgia–South Carolina border. A combined French and American attempt to recapture British-held Savannah was defeated. In February 1780, Sir Henry Clinton arrived in South Carolina from New York with 8,700 fresh troops and laid siege to Charleston. In a stunning defeat, Charleston was surrendered on May 12 by American General Benjamin Lincoln, who gave up some 5,000 soldiers as prisoners. Quickly, General Horatio Gates led a force to Camden in upper South Carolina but was badly defeated on August 16, 1780, by troops under Lord Cornwallis, whom Clinton, returning to New York, had put in command of the Southern forces.

With the Tidewater towns in British hands, the Piedmont shouldered the task of carrying on the resistance. Such legendary guerrilla leaders as the "Swamp Fox" Francis Marion and Thomas Sumter cost the British dearly. Then, on October 7,

Word for the Day

The *Tidewater* is the traditional name for the coastal South. In colonial times, the *Piedmont* (literally, "foot of the mountains") was the region just east of the Blue Ridge Mountains. The Tidewater was the more settled and affluent region, whereas the Piedmont was the poorer, more sparsely settled frontier region.

1780, a contingent of Patriot frontiersmen—most from the Watauga settlements in present-day eastern Tennessee—engaged and destroyed a force of 1,000 Loyalist troops at the Battle of King's Mountain on the border of the Carolinas.

Triumph at Yorktown

Fresh from his seaboard conquests, Cornwallis was now pinned down by frontier guerrillas. A third American army under Major General Nathanael Greene launched a series of rapid operations in brilliant coordination with the South Carolina guerrillas. Dividing his small army, Greene dispatched Brigadier General Daniel Morgan into western South Carolina, where he decimated the "Tory Legion" of Lieutenant Colonel Banastre Tarleton at the Battle of the Cowpens on January 17, 1781. Breaking free of the guerrillas, Cornwallis pursued Morgan, who linked up with Greene and the main body of the Southern army. Together, Morgan and Greene led Cornwallis on a punishing wilderness chase into North Carolina, then fought him to a draw at Guilford Courthouse on March 15, 1781.

Cornwallis, effectively neutralized, withdrew to the coast. Greene returned to South Carolina, where he retook every British-held outpost, except for Charleston and Savannah. Although the enemy would hold these cities for the rest of the war, its possession was of negligible military value, because the occupying garrisons were cut off from the rest of the British forces.

Cornwallis had withdrawn to Virginia, where he joined forces with a raiding unit led by the most notorious turncoat in American history, Benedict Arnold. Cornwallis reasoned that Virginia was the key to possession of the South. Therefore, he established his headquarters at the port of Yorktown.

Real Life

Benedict Arnold (1741–1801) was born in Norwich, Connecticut, and served as a teenager in the French and Indian War. During the Revolution, he handled himself brilliantly, but became embittered when he was passed over for promotion. When he served as commander of forces in Philadelphia, Arnold was accused of overstepping his authority, and he made matters worse by marrying Margaret Shippen (1779), the daughter of a prominent Loyalist. His new wife, accustomed to affluence, encouraged Arnold to spend freely, and he was soon buried in debt. Arnold saw the British as a means of gaining promotion and cash. He offered them a plan to betray the fortifications at West Point, New York, but his treachery was revealed when British Major John André was captured in

September 1780 carrying the turncoat's message in his boot. André was executed as a spy, but Arnold escaped to enemy lines and was commissioned a brigadier general in the British army. In that capacity, he led two expeditions, one that burned Richmond, Virginia, and another against New London in his native Connecticut. However, he never received all of the career advancement and fortune the British had promised. He went to England in 1781, was plagued by a "nervous disease," and died in London in 1801.

General Washington combined his Continental troops with the French army of the Comte de Rochambeau and laid siege to Yorktown on October 6, 1781. Simultaneously, a French fleet under Admiral de Grasse prevented escape by sea. Seeing the situation, General Clinton dispatched a British naval squadron from New York to the Chesapeake, only to be driven off by de Grasse. Washington and Rochambeau relentlessly bombarded Yorktown. At last, the British general surrendered his 8,000 troops to the allies' 17,000 men on October 19, 1781. As Cornwallis presented Washington with his sword, the British regimental band played a popular tune of times. It was called "The World Turned Upside Down."

The Least You Need to Know

➤ George Washington's greatest accomplishments were to hold his armies together during a long, hard war, to exploit British strategic and tactical blunders effectively, and to make each British victory extremely costly.

➤ The Revolution did not end in American victory, so much as in the defeat of England's will to continue to fight.

➤ The Revolution was instantly perceived as a worldwide event—a milestone in the history of humankind.

Part 3
Building the House

With independence achieved, the citizens of the new United States were faced with the task of building a nation, of creating laws without renewing tyranny, of representing the will of the majority without trampling the rights of the minority, and of proclaiming liberty without bringing down upon themselves the curse of anarchy. Then, with a strong Constitution in place, the new nation took its place among the other nations of the world—barely surviving the War of 1812 in the process. Following that conflict, as the United States pushed westward, a new kind of leader emerged, not from the patrician ranks of the Tidewater states, but from the western frontier. The "Age of Jackson" saw the expansion of the nation and the growth of democracy, but also the hard doom of Indian men, women, and children, who were set marching along a bitter Trail of Tears. Here is a narrative of the years that proved the United States a viable nation.

Chapter 11

From Many, One (1787–1797)

In This Chapter

➤ Treaty of Paris and the end of the Revolution

➤ Government of territories by the Northwest Ordinance

➤ Creation and ratification of the Constitution

➤ The Bill of Rights

➤ Hamilton vs. Jefferson

For all intents and purposes, the Battle of Yorktown ended the American Revolution. Yet triumph here did not mean total victory for the Americans. Sir Henry Clinton still occupied key cities, and Britain continued to skirmish in this hemisphere with France and Spain. But Yorktown marked the end of Britain's will to fight its colonies, and it put America's treaty negotiators, Benjamin Franklin (1706–90) and John Jay (1745–1829), in a strong bargaining position. They understood that Britain was anxious to pry America free of the French sphere of influence; therefore, they correctly calculated that the British negotiators would be inclined to hammer out generous peace terms. Jay and Franklin obtained not only British recognition of American independence, but also the cession of the vast region from the Appalachians to the Mississippi River as part of the United States.

The treaty also made navigation of the Mississippi free to all signatories (France, Spain, and Holland), restored Florida to Spain and Senegal to France, and granted to the United States valuable fishing rights off Newfoundland. The definitive Treaty of Paris was signed on September 3, 1783, and ratified by the Continental Congress on January 14, 1784.

Rope of Sand

Drafted in 1777 and ratified in 1781, the Articles of Confederation became the first constitution of the United States. As the document was conceived by John Dickinson (1732–1808) in 1776, it provided for a strong national government. But the states clamored for more rights—especially the power of taxation—and Dickinson's document was watered down by revision and amendment. Instead of a nation, the Articles created a "firm league of friendship" among 13 sovereign states. The Articles provided for a permanent national Congress, consisting of two to seven delegates from each state (yet each state was given one vote, regardless of its size or population), but did not establish an executive or judicial branch. Congress was charged with conducting foreign relations, declaring war, making peace, maintaining an army and navy, and so on, yet it was essentially powerless, since it was wholly at the mercy of the states. Congress could issue directives and pass laws, but it could not enforce them. The states either chose to comply or not. Miraculously, the Articles held the states together during the Revolution, but it soon became clear that the Articles had created no union, but what various lawmakers called "a rope of sand."

Word for the Day

The eagle on the Great Seal of the United States of America holds in its beak a ribbon on which the Latin motto *e pluribus unum* is inscribed. The words mean "from many, one" and express the formidable nature of the task that faced the founding fathers: to forge a single nation from several states and many individuals. The motto was chosen by a committee appointed by the Continental Congress on July 4, 1776, and was officially adopted on June 20, 1782. The phrase is a quotation from "Moretum" by the Roman poet Vergil (70–19 B.C.) but was borrowed more immediately from *Gentleman's Magazine*, a popular British periodical on whose cover the phrase had appeared for many years.

Northwest Ordinance

Under the Articles of Confederation, Congress enacted at least one momentous piece of legislation. The Northwest Ordinance (July 13, 1787) spelled out how territories and states were to be formed from the western lands won in the Revolution. What was then called the Northwest—the vast region bounded by the Ohio and Mississippi rivers and by the Great Lakes—was to be divided into three to five territories. Congress was empowered to appoint a governor, a secretary, and three judges to govern each territory. When the adult male population of a territory reached 5,000, elections would be held to form a territorial legislature and to send a nonvoting representative to Congress. When the territorial adult male population reached 60,000, a territory could write a constitution and apply for statehood. Whereas Britain had refused to make its American colonies full members of a national commonwealth, the Articles ensured that the frontier regions would never be mere colonies of the Tidewater, but equal partners in a common enterprise.

Of equal importance, the Ordinance was the first national stand against slavery. The law prohibited slavery in the territories and also guaranteed in them such basic rights as trial by jury and freedom of religion.

We the People...

Despite the boldness of the Northwest Ordinance, the weakness of Congress under the Articles of Confederation was demonstrated almost daily. For example, the federal government could do nothing to help Massachusetts, which was faced with its own minor insurrection when a farmer named Daniel Shays led an attack on the state judicial system. Nor could the government intervene when Rhode Island issued a mountain of absolutely worthless paper money. In 1786, a convention was held in Annapolis, Maryland, to discuss problems of interstate commerce. The delegates soon recognized that these issues were only part of a much larger issue that could be addressed by nothing less than a revision of the Articles. The Annapolis delegates called for a constitutional convention, which met in Philadelphia in May 1787. The task of revision grew into a project of building anew. By the end of May, the delegates agreed that what was required was a genuine national government, not a mere hopeful confederation of states.

Main Event

In August 1786, armed mobs of beleaguered farmers began forcing the closure of courts in Massachusetts's frontier counties. A charismatic Revolutionary War veteran, Daniel Shays (ca. 1747–1825), emerged as the leader of what came to be called Shays's Rebellion. It was not until January 25, 1787, that a state militia force was able to disperse rebels in Springfield.

Constitutional Convention

Fifty-five delegates convened in Philadelphia and elected George Washington as president of the convention. Just as Washington had held the Continental Army together during the long trial of revolution, so now he managed the disputatious delegates with dignity and fairness.

The Virginia Plan

While some delegates held out for a simple revision of the Articles of Confederation, the Virginia delegation, led by Edmund Randolph, introduced the Virginia Plan, which proposed the creation of a central federal government consisting of a bicameral legislature, an executive branch, and a judicial branch. The executive was to be elected by the members of the legislature, who, in turn, were elected by the citizens. The Virginia Plan further specified that representation in the bicameral legislature would be proportionate to state population—a provision that worried and angered representatives of the smaller states.

Word for the Day

Bicameral literally means "two-chambered" and refers to a type of legislature consisting of two groups of representatives. In the case of the British Parliament, the two houses are the House of Lords and the House of Commons; in the case of the U.S. Congress, they are the Senate and the House of Representatives.

The New Jersey Plan

As debate raged over the Virginia Plan, William Paterson of New Jersey introduced a plan labeled with the name of his state. The New Jersey Plan retained most of the Articles of Confederation, and it gave all the states equal representation in the legislature, but it added a separate and independent Supreme Court. Now the debate became even more lengthy, tangled, and heated.

Connecticut Compromise

At last, Roger Sherman, delegate from Connecticut, proposed a compromise between the two plans. This so-called Great Compromise called for a bicameral legislature; however, the "upper house" of this body, the Senate, would provide each state with equal representation, whereas representation in the "lower house," the House of Representatives, would provide representation proportionate to each state's population. Moreover, the chief executive—the president—would not be elected by the representatives in the legislature, but by an Electoral College.

Three-Fifths of a Person

Any number of additional compromises remained to be made, but the stickiest involved apportioning representation in the House of Representatives. The more representatives a state could claim, the more influential it would be in the federal government. If representation was to be proportional to population, the South wanted its slaves counted as population. The North objected, arguing that the slaves should be excluded entirely from the calculation.

A peculiar-sounding solution was reached. Embodied in the Constitution as Article I, Section 2, the "Three-Fifths Compromise" manages delicately to avoid the word *slave* altogether: "Representation and direct taxes will be apportioned among the several states according to respective numbers determined by adding to the whole number of free persons including those bound to service for a set number of years and excluding Indians not taxed three-fifths of all other persons." For purposes of levying taxes and apportioning representatives, slaves were counted as three-fifths of a person.

Federalist Papers

With the compromises in place, William Johnson (secretary of the Convention), Alexander Hamilton, James Madison, Rufus King, and Gouverneur Morris wrote the actual Constitution document, the product of three and a half months of debate. When 38 of the 55 Convention delegates approved the document, it was sent to Congress, which submitted it to the states for ratification.

Thus began an uphill battle. Those who supported the proposed Constitution were called Federalists; those opposed, Anti-Federalists. Although Delaware, Pennsylvania, and New

Jersey instantly ratified the document, a total of nine states had to ratify in order for the Constitution to become law. The process was hotly contested in many states and nowhere more so than in the key states of Virginia and New York. To convince New York voters to ratify, Alexander Hamilton, James Madison, and John Jay collaborated on a series of essays collectively called *The Federalist Papers*, published during 1787–88 in various New York newspapers under the name "Publius."

The Federalist Papers is a brilliant defense of the Constitution. The tenth essay penetrated to the very heart of the principal Anti-Federalist argument that the nation was simply too big to be regulated by a central government. Madison argued that precisely *because* the nation was so large, it would be most effectively governed by a strong central government, which would prevent any single special interest from taking control. Essays 15 through 22 deftly analyzed the weaknesses of the Articles of Confederation.

Stats

Of the 85 *Federalist* essays, most scholars agree that Hamilton wrote 52, Madison 28, and Jay 5.

Virginia ratified the Constitution by a close vote of 89 to 79, but only after the framers promised to add a "Bill of Rights" to satisfy the Anti-Federalist argument that the Constitution failed to address the rights of individuals. In the meantime, *The Federalist Papers* tipped the balance in New York—though just barely. The vote was 30 to 27.

Father of His Country

When New Hampshire became the ninth state to ratify the Constitution on June 21, 1788, the document became law, but it was not put into effect officially until March 4, 1789. The next month, the U.S. Senate convened to count ballots cast by members of the Electoral College for the first president of the United States. The result surprised no one. George Washington had been unanimously elected, and John Adams became his vice president. It was, in fact, with the understanding that Washington would be elected that the framers of the Constitution entrusted so much power to the chief executive. Washington had amply demonstrated not only a genius for leadership in commanding the Continental Army, but his skill as a statesman in presiding over the Constitutional Convention. Equally important, Washington had made manifest the character of a true republican. Too often, revolutions are followed by new tyrants and tyrannies. It was clear to Congress and the people of the United States that Washington was no tyrant.

The new president was inaugurated in New York City on April 30, 1789. Even with a Constitution in place, it was up to Washington to create much of the American government and in particular to shape the office of president. He quickly created key executive departments, naming Thomas Jefferson as Secretary of State, Henry Knox as Secretary of War, Alexander Hamilton as Secretary of the Treasury, Samuel Osgood as head of the Post Office, and Edmund Randolph as Attorney General.

Washington became the model for the presidency, and the chief quality he introduced into the office was restraint. He avoided conflict with Congress, believing it was not the chief executive's duty to propose legislation. He also opposed the formation of political parties—although, by the time of his second term, two opposing parties had, indeed, been formed: the conservative Federalists, headed by John Adams and Alexander Hamilton, and the more liberal Democratic-Republicans, headed by Thomas Jefferson. In a measure of Washington's steadfast refusal to become a post-revolutionary tyrant, he declined to stand for a third term of office. The two-term presidency thereafter became an inviolate tradition until the twin crises of the Depression and World War II prompted the nation to elect Franklin Delano Roosevelt to a third and a fourth term. (Although the nation was grateful to FDR, it also approved the 22nd amendment to the Constitution on February 26, 1951, restricting future presidents to no more than two elected terms.)

Real Life

George Washington (1732–99) was born in Westmoreland County, Virginia, to a prosperous planter. After his father died in 1743, he was raised by his half-brother Lawrence at Mount Vernon, Lawrence's Potomac River plantation. Washington became a surveyor—a powerful profession in colonial America—and helped lay out Belhaven, Virginia (now Alexandria). Following the death of his half-brother, Washington inherited Mount Vernon.

He left that beloved home to serve in the French and Indian War, returning afterward to Mount Vernon and service in Virginia's House of Burgesses.

Washington made a happy—and opportune—marriage to a young and wealthy widow, Martha Dandridge Custis and by 1769 was a prominent leader of Virginia's opposition to Britain's oppressive colonial policies. During 1774–75, Washington was a delegate to the First and Second Continental Congress, and in June 1775 was unanimously chosen as commander in chief of the Continental forces, which he led brilliantly.

After the war, Washington headed the Virginia delegation to the Constitutional Convention and was unanimously elected presiding officer. Upon ratification of the Constitution, he was unanimously elected president in 1789 and was reelected in 1792. In March 1797, when Washington left office, he left a well-established government and a stable financial system.

Unfortunately, the Father of His Country had little time to enjoy retirement at his beloved Mount Vernon. In mid-December 1799, he fell ill with acute laryngitis, which rapidly worsened. He died on December 14.

Washington not only created the office of president, he signed key treaties with England and Spain and approved the creation of a national bank. He also proclaimed neutrality in what would become a long series of wars between England and France, and he successfully quelled a spasm of internal rebellion. More than anything else, this able executive possessed a character that helped establish the United States among the other nations of the world. The classical Romans reserved one title for their greatest leaders—*Pater Patriae*, Father of His Country—and almost immediately, a grateful nation accorded this epithet to George Washington.

Glorious Afterthought: The Bill of Rights

The framers of the Constitution had no desire to deny individual rights, but they believed it unnecessary to provide a special, separate guarantee of those rights because the Constitution states that the government is one of "enumerated powers" only. That is, the government can take no action or assume any authority except those explicitly provided for in the Constitution. This assumption, however, was not a sufficient safeguard for the Anti-Federalists—those who feared too strong a central government. In 1789, Congress began to consider amending the new Constitution to guarantee, in specific terms, a set of inalienable individual rights. James Madison spearheaded the effort, carefully examining, weighing, and synthesizing the rights already included in several state constitutions, especially the Virginia Declaration of Rights, which had been adopted in 1776.

Ultimately ratified on December 15, 1791, the Bill of Rights is a set of the first ten amendments to the Constitution.

The first protects freedom of religion, freedom of speech, freedom of the press, and the right of popular assembly for the purpose of petition for redress of grievances.

The second amendment guarantees the right to bear arms, and the third severely limits the quartering of soldiers in private homes.

The fourth amendment forbids unreasonable searches and seizures and requires warrants to be specific (not blanket documents) and to be issued only upon probable cause.

The fifth amendment mandates grand jury indictments in major criminal prosecutions, prohibits "double jeopardy" (being tried more than once on the same charge), and guarantees that no one need testify against himself or herself. The amendment also forbids taking private property for public use without just compensation and prohibits deprivation of life, liberty, or property without due process of law.

The sixth amendment guarantees a speedy public trial by jury. It specifies that the accused shall be fully informed of the accusation, shall be confronted with the witnesses against him or her, shall have the power to subpoena witnesses for his or her defense, and shall have access to legal counsel.

The seventh amendment guarantees jury trials in civil cases, and the eighth prohibits excessive bail, unreasonable fines, and "cruel and unusual punishments."

The ninth and tenth amendments are special: The ninth explicitly provides that the enumeration of rights in the Constitution does not deny others retained by the people. The tenth expresses the "doctrine of reserved powers": all powers not delegated to the United States are reserved to the states or the people.

Distilled within the Bill of Rights is what most people would consider the very essence of all that is most valuable in the idea of the United States of America.

Secretary Hamilton

Among the most influential members of Washington's cabinet was Secretary of the Treasury Alexander Hamilton. He not only developed a strong financial program for the infant nation but also used finance to unify the United States and to elevate federal authority over that of the states. He proposed a plan whereby the federal government would assume all debts incurred by the several states during the Revolution and pay them at par value rather than at the reduced rates some states had already negotiated on their own. Hamilton reasoned that this policy would demonstrate the nation's financial responsibility and ultimately improve its standing among other nations and its ability to conduct commerce. Even more important, the plan would demonstrate to the world that the *federal* government, not the individual states, was the responsible contracting party in all international commerce and foreign affairs. Despite great resistance from the Southern states, Hamilton's plan was enacted by Congress.

Equally controversial was Hamilton's proposal to create the Bank of the United States. Fearing that this plan would concentrate far too much power in the central government, Thomas Jefferson led the opposition against the proposal within Washington's cabinet. He argued that the bank was unconstitutional, because the tenth amendment granted to the states and the people rights and powers not explicitly given to the United States. If this provision was breached by the creation of the bank, what other powers would the federal government usurp?

Jefferson's view of the Constitution became known as "strict construction." Hamilton, in contrast, supported the constitutional view that became known as "loose construction," arguing in support of it the doctrine of "implied powers." Hamilton declared that the framers of the Constitution could not possibly have anticipated all eventualities and contingencies; therefore, it is impossible to list all the powers the federal government may assume. In the case of the Bank of the United States, Hamilton held, the Constitution does grant the federal government the power to tax, and taxation *implies* the creation of a place to keep the revenue collected—namely, a bank.

Main Event

In 1791, Congress levied a federal tax on corn liquor. In frontier Pennsylvania, farmers distilled whiskey to use up surplus corn, and the product became for them a form of currency. Farmers protested and often refused to pay the tax. In 1794, President Washington sent collectors, who were met by armed resistance in what constituted the first serious test of the new U.S. government's ability to enforce a federal law. Secretary of the Treasury Alexander Hamilton advised the president to call out the militia. In a bold exercise of federal authority, Washington did just that, and the Whiskey Rebellion collapsed.

The disagreement between Jefferson and Hamilton formed the foundation of the American two-party political system, with either party more or less defined and distinguished by its view of the nature of the federal government. Jefferson's Democratic-Republican party believed in a restrained central government that allowed a great measure of power to individuals and states; Hamilton's Federalist party stood for a relatively powerful and active central government, which claimed for itself the lion's share of authority. The dynamic, shifting balance between these two poles of opinion has defined the lively American political scene ever since the days of the first president. Over the years, the running dialogue has sometimes erupted into ugly argument and even terrible violence— as in the Civil War. Yet the two-party system has also insured a government and society that is never stagnant and always open to change and challenge.

The Least You Need to Know

➤ The key to the Constitution is a strong central government that is itself governed by a system of checks and balances.

➤ In addition to the nation's first president, George Washington, the defining personalities of the early republic were Thomas Jefferson (who favored the forces of liberal democracy) and Alexander Hamilton (who favored a powerful central government).

Chapter 12

1812 Overture (1798–1812)

In This Chapter

➤ The XYZ Affair and the Alien and Sedition Acts

➤ *Marbury v. Madison*

➤ The Louisiana Purchase

➤ Neutralization of the Barbary pirates

➤ The Embargo and its consequences

➤ War in the West

When George Washington delivered his Farewell Address in March 1797, the United States was recognized by the world's powers as a nation. That single fact was, in large part, *his* greatest accomplishment. In his speech, the outgoing president advised his fellow Americans to avoid "foreign entanglements," to preserve the financial credit of the nation, and to beware of the dangers of political parties, which might fragment the nation.

Everyone agreed that the advice was good, but the second presidential election, in 1796, had already shown that political parties were dividing the nation. John Adams, a Federalist, was elected with 71 votes in the Electoral College. In those days, the runner-up became vice president, and that was Thomas Jefferson, leader of the Democratic-Republican party, with 68 electoral votes. Thus the president and vice president were of different parties and significantly different philosophies of government. Adams would have been called a conservative in his day, a believer in a strong central government. Jefferson, a liberal, wanted more authority entrusted to states and individuals. That these sharply different views did *not* tear the country apart was a measure of the essential strength of the new nation; yet its recently won liberty was put to severe tests as the 18th century yielded to the 19th.

Foreign Affairs

During Washington's second term of office, intense friction developed between Britain and the United States. The British government refused to evacuate the frontier forts in the Old Northwest, despite having agreed to do so in signing the Treaty of Paris. Worse, many Americans were convinced that British traders as well as crown officials were encouraging the Indians to attack settlers. Finally, English naval vessels had begun seizing American merchant ships and impressing American sailors into the British service to fight its war against France. The British also complained that Americans had breached the terms of the Paris treaty by failing to pay pre-Revolutionary debts owed British creditors and by refusing to compensate Loyalists for confiscated property during the Revolution.

Anxious to avert a new war with Britain, Washington commissioned Chief Justice John Jay to conclude a treaty, signed on November 19, 1794, to secure the British evacuation of the frontier forts and refer debt and boundary disputes to settlement by joint U.S.–British commissions. This amicable solution greatly alarmed the French, who feared that their former ally, the United States, would now unite with Britain against them. Certainly it was true that most Americans, especially the Federalists, recoiled in horror from the excesses of the French Revolution (1789–99). Just a year before the Jay Treaty was concluded, Washington rebuffed the overtures of Edmond Charles Edouard Genêt (1763–1834), a French diplomat sent to the United States to secure American aid for France in its war with England. "Citizen Genêt" (as French revolutionary etiquette dictated he be addressed) defied Washington by plotting with American privateers to prey on British vessels in U.S. coastal waters. The president warned Genêt that he was violating U.S. sovereignty. When Citizen Genêt responded with a threat to make a direct appeal to the American people, Washington asked the French government to recall him.

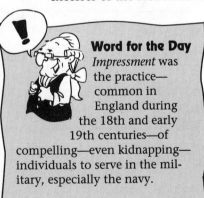

Word for the Day
Impressment was the practice—common in England during the 18th and early 19th centuries—of compelling—even kidnapping—individuals to serve in the military, especially the navy.

In France, however, a new revolutionary party, the Jacobins, had replaced the Girondists, the party to which Genêt belonged. In contrast to the United States, where political parties could "disagree without being disagreeable," rival factions in revolutionary France settled their differences with the guillotine. The Jacobin government asked Washington to extradite Genêt, but the president refused to compel Genêt to return to France, where-upon Citizen Genêt chose to become a citizen of the United States.

As Easy as XYZ

The Genêt episode, combined with the Jay Treaty, brought Franco-American relations to the verge of war. After the French Directory high-handedly refused to receive U.S. minis-ter Charles Cotesworth Pinckney, the new president, Adams, sent a commission consist-ing of Pinckney, John Marshall, and Elbridge Gerry to attempt to heal the breach by concluding a new treaty of commerce. Incredibly, French prime minister Charles Maurice de Talleyrand-Perigord (1754–1838) sent three agents to greet the American commission-ers in Paris in October 1797. The agents told the commissioners that before they could even discuss a treaty, the United States would have to loan France $12 million *and* pay Talleyrand a personal bribe of $250,000.

On April 3, 1798, an indignant President Adams submitted to Congress the correspon-dence from the commission, which designated the French agents as "X," "Y," and "Z." Congress, equally indignant, published the entire portfolio, and the public learned of the "XYZ Affair." Americans of all political stripes united in outrage, the nation mobilized for war with its erstwhile ally, and, in fact, an undeclared naval war was sporadically fought from 1798 to 1800. Fortunately, that conflict was limited, and international tempers cooled as the French Revolution came to an end.

Overreaction

Yet something far more sinister than another war was brewing. In the summer of 1798, in response to the Genêt episode, the XYZ Affair, and the escalating war fever, the Federalist-dominated Congress passed the Alien and Sedition Acts, which included the Naturaliza-tion Act (June 18, 1798), raising the residence prerequisite for citizenship from 5 to 14 years; the Alien Act (June 25), authorizing the president to deport all aliens regarded as dangerous; and the Alien Enemies Act (July 6), authorizing the president, in time of war, to arrest, imprison, or deport subjects of an enemy power. Most tyrannical of all, the Sedition Act (July 14) prohibited assembly "with intent to oppose any measure...of the government" and forbade printing, uttering, or publishing anything "false, scandalous, and malicious" against the government. What made the dangerous Alien and Sedition Acts even more insidious in the fledgling democracy was the fact that many of the leading Anti-Federalists were recent refugees from Europe. The acts were aimed directly at neutralizing their power.

In 1798–99, Virginia and Kentucky published resolutions (written by James Madison and Jefferson) opposing the acts as unconstitutional and, therefore, not binding on the states. Jefferson maintained that a state had the right to judge the constitutionality of acts of Congress and to "nullify" any acts that it determined to be unconstitutional. Because to the resolutions, the Alien and Sedition Acts were (for the most part) short-lived.

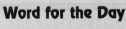

Word for the Day

Nullification would become a major issue in the decade before the Civil War, when South Carolina's John C. Calhoun echoed Jefferson and asserted that the states could override ("nullify") any federal laws they judged unconstitutional. Nullification attacked the foundation of American nationhood.

The Age of Jefferson

Public disgust with the Alien and Sedition Acts helped oust the Federalist Adams in the elections of 1800, but the Electoral College voted a tie between the two Democratic-Republican candidates, Thomas Jefferson and Aaron Burr. As prescribed by the Constitution, the tied election was sent to the House of Representatives for resolution. Hamilton, the implacable enemy of Burr, convinced fellow Federalists to support Jefferson, who was elected on the *36th* ballot. Runner-up Burr became vice president.

Real Life

Born in Newark, New Jersey, Aaron Burr distinguished himself in the Revolution, made a prosperous marriage (1782) to the widow of a former British officer, and set up a successful law practice in New York City. He entered the U.S. Senate in 1791 and served as U.S. vice president from 1801 to 1805.

Jefferson distrusted Burr and dropped him from the Democratic-Republican ticket in the 1804 race. Thus rejected, Burr ran for New York governor, garnering support (in part) by suggesting that he would aid certain Federalist radicals in their effort to break New York free of the Union. Burr was attacked in print by Alexander Hamilton, and when Burr lost the election, he challenged his enemy to a duel on July 11, 1804. Hamilton was mortally wounded, and Burr received the dubious distinction of becoming the first (and thus far only) U.S. vice president charged with murder.

Burr ultimately was acquitted, completed his vice presidential term with dignity, but then entered into a conspiracy of bewildering proportions. Even now, it is impossible to determine just what Burr intended to do, but he seems to have envisioned creating an empire stretching from the Ohio River to Mexico—an empire over which he would rule. Burr conspired with U.S. army general James Wilkinson to incite the West to a rebellion supported by Mexico. Before Burr could take significant action, however, Wilkinson betrayed him to President Jefferson. Chief Justice John Marshall presided over Burr's trial for treason, pointing out to the jury that Burr had not committed any *acts* of treason, but had been shown only to have *intended* to commit such acts. Marshall declared that one could not be found guilty on account of one's intentions. After 25 minutes of deliberation, the jury acquitted Burr, who fled to Europe and did not return to the United States until May 1812. He lived out the remainder of his life in retirement.

Historians speak of an "Age of Jefferson," but not of an Age of Adams. Perhaps the reason is that, despite Federalist objections to most of Jefferson's policies, the people embraced them, and they became key elements of the popular American agenda. Internal taxes were reduced, the military budget was cut, the Alien and Sedition Acts were repealed or died. The climactic triumph of Jefferson's first term was the momentous expansion of the nation through the Louisiana Purchase.

Supreme Court Reigns Supreme

Although Jefferson commenced his first term as president by proposing to the Federalists that they bury the hatchet, he was not above manipulating the law to prevent a group of Federalist judges, appointed by John Adams, from assuming office. After his inauguration, Jefferson discovered that, during Adams' final days as president, the former president had signed a number of judicial appointments but had not distributed them. Not wanting to place Federalists in important circuit court and federal court positions, Jefferson decided not to distribute the signed appointments.

When one of the appointees, William Marbury, failed to receive his commission as justice of the peace for Washington, D.C., he petitioned the Supreme Court for a writ of mandamus—an order to Secretary of State James Madison to distribute the commissions. This order created a critical dilemma for Chief Justice John Marshall; if he issued the writ, he would put the court in direct opposition to the president. If Marshall denied the writ, he would dilute the power of the Supreme Court by appearing to bow to the president's wishes. Refusing to be impaled on the horns of the dilemma, Marshall found that Marbury had been wrongfully deprived of his commission, but he also declared that

Section 13 of the Judiciary Act of 1789, under which Marbury had filed his suit, was unconstitutional. Section 13 added to the Supreme Court's "original jurisdiction" by improperly allowing into the Supreme Court a case that should be heard by a lower court. Marbury's suit was thrown out, a political crisis averted, and—most important of all—the right of the Supreme Court to "judicial review" was established.

Ever since the case of *Marbury v. Madison*, the Supreme Court has functioned to set aside statutes of Congress the Court judged unconstitutional. The case represented the birth of an extraordinary federal power, which made complete the definition of the system of "checks and balances" the framers of the Constitution had created among the executive, legislative, and judicial branches of government.

A Purchase and a Journey

Jefferson's first term was crowned by an action that added a vast new territory to the United States. This triumph began with a crisis. Following the French and Indian War, France ceded the Louisiana Territory to Spain. However, in 1800, Napoleon Bonaparte reacquired the territory by secret treaty in exchange for parts of Tuscany, which Napoleon pledged to conquer on behalf of Spain. Napoleon also promised to maintain Louisiana as a buffer between Spain's North American settlements and the United States. After the secret treaty was concluded, Napoleon promptly abandoned his Tuscan campaign, and the two nations fell to disputing. During this period, beginning in 1802, Spain closed the Mississippi to American trade.

Jefferson could not tolerate an end to western trade, but neither did he relish the notion of Napoleon at his back door. To resolve the crisis, the president dispatched James Monroe to France with orders to make an offer for the purchase of the port city of New Orleans and Florida.

Stats

The Louisiana Purchase added 90,000 square miles of trans-Mississippi territory to the United States. Purchased at a cost of 60 million francs (about $15 million), it was a great real estate bargain at four cents an acre.

Monroe, it turned out, was in the right place at the right time. One of Napoleon's armies was bogged down in the disease-infested West Indies. Rather than lose his forces to illness, Napoleon decided to withdraw from the hemisphere and focus his conquests on Europe. Even as Monroe was crossing the Atlantic, Napoleon's minister Talleyrand asked U.S. foreign minister to France Robert R. Livingston how much Jefferson would offer not just for New Orleans and Florida, but for the *entire* Louisiana Territory. Negotiations proceeded after Monroe arrived, and the bargain was concluded for 60 million francs.

The Louisiana Purchase was an overwhelmingly popular move, and it catapulted Jefferson to a second term. In contrast to the tie contest of 1800, Jefferson swept every state except two—Connecticut and Delaware—in the election of 1804.

Main Event

Jefferson, fascinated like so many others with the idea of finding a Northwest Passage connecting the Mississippi with the Pacific, planned an expedition to Louisiana Territory long *before* the purchase, choosing his trusted secretary Meriwether Lewis (1774–1809) to lead the expedition. Lewis asked his close friend William Clark (1770–1838) to serve as co-captain.

The expedition left Saint Louis on May 14, 1804, and reached central North Dakota in November. Accompanied by a remarkable Shoshoni woman Sacajawea (ca. 1784–1812), who served as translator and guide, the group explored the Rockies and reached the Continental Divide on August 12, 1805. Lewis and Clark were now convinced that the Northwest Passage did not exist. However, they pressed on, reaching the Columbia River and the Pacific in November 1805. They returned to Saint Louis on September 23, 1806.

If the expedition failed to find the nonexistent Northwest Passage, it did supply a wealth of information about what had been a great blank space on the map of North America.

Pirates and Embargo

Jefferson's second term began with great promise as his administration negotiated a favorable peace in the Tripolitan War, putting an end to intimidation by the Barbary pirates of Tripoli, Algiers, Morocco, and Tunis, who had been extorting protection money in return for safe passage of U.S. merchant vessels through the Mediterranean. Alas, the rest of Jefferson's second administration was marked by an economic crisis resulting from a failure of foreign policy.

In Europe, the Wars of the French Revolution had dissolved into the Napoleonic Wars. When neither the English nor the French could score a decisive victory, they turned to attacks on the commerce of noncombatant nations, including the United States. The English resumed the practice of impressing American sailors and also seized American vessels attempting to enter French ports. Jefferson retaliated with the Non-Importation Act, which prohibited the importation of many English goods.

The simmering crisis came to a head on June 22, 1807, when the British man-of-war *Leopard*, off Norfolk Roads, Virginia, fired on the U.S. frigate *Chesapeake*. The British boarded the frigate and seized four men they claimed to be deserters from His Majesty's navy. The incident fanned the flames of war fever throughout the nation, but President Jefferson resisted. Instead of resorting to war, he pushed through Congress the Embargo Act of December 22, 1807, prohibiting all exports to Europe and restricting imports from Great Britain.

The embargo was a self-inflicted wound, severely crippling the American economy and provoking outrage from American farmers and merchants. Smuggling became rampant, national unity was threatened, and Jefferson's popularity plummeted while that of the Federalists rose.

Tecumseh Rises

While Jefferson was dealing with England and France, the West that he had done so much to "open" with the Louisiana Purchase was erupting in violence. In 1794, the major tribes of the Old Northwest (the region from the Ohio River to the Great Lakes) were defeated by General "Mad Anthony" Wayne at the watershed Battle of Fallen Timbers (August 20). After almost a decade of relative peace on that frontier region, President Jefferson in 1803 directed the territorial governor of Indiana, William Henry Harrison (1773–1841), to obtain "legal" title to as much Indian land as possible. Over the next three years, Harrison acquired 70 million acres by negotiating with whatever chiefs and tribal leaders were willing to sign deeds. The trouble was that for every Indian leader who claimed authority to sell land, another rose up to repudiate that authority and that sale.

The most prominent, brilliant, and charismatic of those who resisted the transfer of Indian lands to the whites was the Shawnee Tecumseh (ca. 1768–1813), who organized a united resistance against white invasion while cultivating an alliance with British interests. Westerners were fearful of Tecumseh and other British-backed Indians, and they were also angry. Not only did the Indians need a good whipping, but so did the British, who became the focus of concentrated hatred in the new American West, not only for inciting Indians to war, but for disrupting American shipping and commerce. What was bad for the coastal economy was disastrous for the West, which, during this critical phase of its development, was being prevented from shipping out its abundant exports. The West was spoiling for a war, and William Henry Harrison and Tecumseh would give it one.

The Least You Need to Know

➤ The liberal "Age of Jefferson" swept away the repressive Alien and Sedition Acts and expanded the United States with the Louisiana Purchase.

➤ Chief Justice John Marshall defined the function and power of the Supreme Court through his decision in the case of *Marbury v. Madison*.

➤ Jefferson's second term was marred by the Embargo Act and a breakdown in relations with Great Britain.

Chapter 13

Washington Burns, a Nation Is Reborn (1812–1814)

In This Chapter

➤ Early disasters and the near-collapse of the West

➤ Naval triumphs and Western victories

➤ The burning of Washington and the defense of Baltimore

➤ The Battle of Lake Champlain and the Treaty of Ghent

➤ Jackson as the "Hero of New Orleans"

Late in the summer of 1811, Tecumseh left the Ohio country for the South to expand his alliances to the Chickasaws, Choctaws, and Creeks. Except for a militant Creek faction known as the Red Sticks, these groups wanted no part of Tecumseh's enterprise. Worse, William Henry Harrison used Tecumseh's absence to move against Tecumseh's headquarters at Tippecanoe. Having assembled a ragtag army of 1,000 men—including 350 U.S. regulars, raw Kentucky and Indiana militiamen, and a handful of Delaware and Miami Indian scouts—Harrison attacked outside of Tippecanoe on November 7, 1811. Losses were equally heavy on both sides—about 50 whites and 50 Indians slain, but the battle cost Tecumseh's followers their headquarters and prompted many of them to desert Tecumseh. Thus the settlers of the West had their first taste of a major fight and a significant victory. Of fighting, they were about to get more than their fill during the next three years. Victories, however, would be very few.

War Hawks Triumphant

The War of 1812 is one of those historical events nobody thinks much about nowadays. But earlier generations of American schoolchildren were taught that it was nothing less than the "second War of Independence," righteous conflict fought because the British, at war with Napoleon and in need of sailors for the Royal Navy, insisted on boarding U.S. vessels to impress American sailors into His Majesty's service. Actually, the U.S. declared war on Britain on June 19, 1812, three days after the British had agreed to stop impressing seamen. The real cause of the war was not to be found on the ocean, but in the trans-Appalachian West. In Congress, the region was represented by a group of land-hungry "War Hawks," spearheaded by Representative Henry Clay of Kentucky.

The War Hawks saw war with Britain as an opportunity to gain relief from British-backed hostile Indians and as a chance to gain what was then called Spanish Florida—a "parcel" of land extending from Florida west to the Mississippi River. Spain, which held this land, was allied with Britain against Napoleon. War with Britain, therefore, would mean war with Spain, and victory would mean the acquisition of Spanish Florida, which would complete an unbroken territorial link from the Atlantic, through the recently purchased Louisiana Territory, clear to the Pacific.

The trouble was that President James Madison, elected to his first term in 1808, did not want war. He renewed the diplomatic and economic initiatives Jefferson had introduced, but, facing a tough reelection battle in 1812, he at last yielded to Clay and the other leading War Hawks, John C. Calhoun of South Carolina and Kentucky's Richard Mentor Johnson. President Madison asked a willing Congress for a declaration of war.

Three-Pronged Flop

Since colonial times, Americans shunned large standing armies. Now, having *declared* war, the country had to *fight* it—with an army of only 12,000 regular troops scattered over a vast territory. The troops were led by generals, most of whom had achieved their rank not through military prowess but through political connections. As to the nation's navy, its officers were generally of a higher caliber, but it was a very puny force, especially in comparison with the magnificent fleets of the British. Despite these terrible handicaps,

U.S. planners developed a three-pronged invasion of Canada: a penetration from Lake Champlain to Montreal; another across the Niagara frontier; and a third into Upper Canada from Detroit.

The sad fact was that the attacks, thoroughly uncoordinated, all failed.

The Fall of Detroit

The governor of Michigan Territory, William Hull (1753–1825) was nominated to command the American forces north of the Ohio River. A minor hero of the Revolution, Hull was almost 60 years old when he led his forces across the Detroit River into Canada on July 12, 1812. His objective was to take Fort Malden, which guarded the entrance to Lake Erie, but Hull believed himself outnumbered and delayed his assault, thereby providing enough time for the highly capable British commander, Major General Isaac Brock, to bring his regulars into position. While this maneuvering was going on, the American garrison at Fort Michilimackinac, guarding the Mackinac Straits between Lake Huron and Lake Michigan, was overrun and surrendered without a fight on July 17. On August 2, Tecumseh chased Hull out of Canada and back to Fort Detroit. Now Brock united his men with Tecumseh's warriors, and Hull surrendered Fort Detroit and some 1,500 men, without firing a shot, on August 16.

Farther south, just the day before Hull surrendered Detroit, Fort Dearborn (at the site of present-day Chicago) surrendered. As troops and settlers evacuated the fort, Potawatomi Indians attacked, killing 35 men, women, and children, mainly by torture.

Defeat on the Niagara Frontier

New York militia general Stephen Van Rensselaer led 2,270 militiamen and 900 regulars in an assault on Queenston Heights, Canada, just across the Niagara River. Part of the force, mostly the regulars, got across the river before General Brock, having rushed to Queenston from Detroit, and pinned them down on October 13. The balance of the militia contingent refused to cross the international boundary and stood by as 600 British regulars and 400 Canadian militiamen overwhelmed their comrades.

Stats

The Battle of Queenston was a terrible American defeat: 250 U.S. soldiers lost their lives and 700 became prisoners of war. The British lost 14 men, with 96 wounded. However, the brilliant General Isaac Brock was among the slain.

A No-Show in Canada

The principal U.S. force had yet to attack. Major General Henry Dearborn led 5,000 troops, mostly militia, down Lake Champlain and on November 19, was about to cross into Canada. At that point, the militia contingent, asserting its "constitutional rights," refused to fight in a foreign country. Dearborn had no choice but to withdraw without seriously engaging the enemy.

The West in Flames

The collapse of Detroit, Fort Dearborn, and the Canadian campaign laid the West open to Indian assault and British invasion. Suffering along the frontier was acute, yet neither the British nor their Indian allies were able to capitalize decisively on their advantages. Although most of the Old Northwest soon fell under Indian control, a coordinated British assault on the region, which might have brought the war to a quick and crashing end, never materialized. Tecumseh was eager to push the fight, but Colonel Henry Proctor, the British commander who had taken over from the slain Brock, was as dull and hesitant as Brock had been brilliant and aggressive. Proctor failed to support Tecumseh.

Proctor's hesitation bought U.S. general William Henry Harrison time to mount counter-attacks. As 1812 drew to a close, Harrison destroyed villages of the Miami Indians near Fort Wayne (despite the fact that Miamis were noncombatants), and he raided what amounted to Indian refugee camps near present-day Peru, Indiana. In January, Harrison moved against Fort Malden, advancing across a frozen Lake Erie. But he suffered a stunning defeat on January 21 at the hands of Procter and a contingent of Red Stick Creeks. Yet, Procter was unable to score a final, decisive victory.

British Blockade

In frankly miraculous contrast to the dismal American performance on land was the activity of the U.S. Navy. The British brought to bear 1,048 vessels to blockade U.S. naval and commercial shipping in an effort to choke off the nation's war effort. Opposed to this vast armada were the 14 seaworthy vessels of the United States Navy and a ragtag fleet of privateers. The U.S. frigates emerged victorious in a series of single-ship engagements, the most famous of which were the battles between the *U.S.S. Constitution* ("Old Ironsides") and the British frigates *Guerriere,* off the coast of Massachusetts on August 19, 1812, and the *Java,* off the Brazilian coast on December 29, 1812. Despite such American triumphs, the British were able to tighten their blockade into a veritable stranglehold that wiped out American trade, bringing the U.S. economy to the verge of collapse.

We Have Met the Enemy and They Are Ours

During 1813, renewed American attempts to invade Canada were again unsuccessful. In the West, however, the situation brightened. William Henry Harrison managed to rebuild—and even enlarge—his army, so that by late summer of 1813, he fielded 8,000 men. In the meantime, a dashing young naval officer named Oliver Hazard Perry (1785–1819) cobbled together an inland navy. Beginning in March 1813, he directed construction of an armed flotilla at Presque Isle (present-day Erie), Pennsylvania, while drilling his sailors in artillery technique. By August, he was ready to move his vessels onto Lake Erie. On September 10, Perry engaged the British fleet in a battle so fierce that he had to transfer his flag from the severely damaged brig *Lawrence* to the *Niagara,* from which he commanded nothing less than the destruction of the entire British squadron. He sent to General Harrison a message that instantly entered into American history: "We have met the enemy and they are ours."

Perry's triumph cut off British supply lines and forced the abandonment of Fort Malden, as well as a general retreat eastward from the Detroit region. On October 5, 1813, Harrison overtook the retreating British and their Indian allies at the Battle of the Thames. The great Indian leader Tecumseh fell in this battle. Although no one knows who killed him, it is certain that, with the death of Tecumseh, the Indians' last real hope of halting the northwestward rush of white settlement likewise died.

O Say Can You See

The American victories in the West, so long in coming, might have turned the tide of the war had it not been for the defeat of Napoleon in Europe and his first exile to St. Elbe. With Napoleon out of the way, the British could now turn their attention to what had become (from their point of view) a very nasty little war in North America. Soon, more ships and more troops—including experienced veterans of the campaigns against Napoleon—sailed across the Atlantic.

The British plan was to attack in three principal areas: in New York, along Lake Champlain and the Hudson River, which would sever New England from the rest of the union; in New Orleans, which would block the vital Mississippi artery; and in Chesapeake Bay, a diversionary maneuver tactic that would draw off U.S. manpower. The British objective was to bring America to its knees and thereby extort major territorial concessions in return for peace. By the fall of 1814, the situation looked very bleak for the United States. The nation was flat broke, and in New England, opponents of the war had begun talking about leaving the Union.

Main Event

The Hartford Convention met in Hartford, Connecticut, from December 15, 1814, to January 5, 1815. Twenty-six delegates from five New England states gathered to protest the disastrous Democratic-Republican conduct of the war. The secret convention raised alarms that the delegates were plotting secession; however, the resolutions they actually formulated were quite tame—principally a call for amending the Constitution to weaken the influence of the South on the federal government. Indeed, some recent historians suggest that the Hartford Convention was actually a (successful) attempt by moderate Federalists to head off radical Federalist attempts to bring about a secession movement. Whatever its intention, the Hartford Convention turned out to be a bad public relations move for the Federalists. They were generally regarded with deepening suspicion and, outside of New England, the party rapidly collapsed.

Late in the summer of 1814, American resistance to the attack in Chesapeake Bay folded. The British, under Major General Robert Ross, triumphed in Maryland at the Battle of Bladensburg (August 24), when inexperienced Maryland militiamen commanded by the thoroughly incompetent General William H. Winder broke and ran in panic. Ross invaded Washington, D.C., and burned most of the public buildings, including the Capitol and the White House, as President Madison and most of the government fled into the countryside.

Ross next set his sights on Baltimore, but at last met stiffer resistance. His forces bombarded Fort McHenry, in Baltimore Harbor, on September 13–14, 1814. The event was witnessed by a young Baltimore lawyer, Francis Scott Key (1779–1843), while he was detained on a British warship. Peering anxiously through the long night, Key saw at dawn that the "Star-Spangled Banner" yet waved; the fort had not fallen to the British, who ultimately withdrew. Key was moved to write a poem that eventually became our national anthem.

Main Event

Key penned "The Star-Spangled Banner" on September 14, 1814, but the music for it had been written in 1777 by the Englishman John Stafford Smith. The music was a setting for another poem, "To Anacreon in Heaven," which was a favorite of a London drinking club called the

Anacreontic Society. Smith's original is a celebration of the pleasures of music, love, and wine. The melody soon became popular in the United States—both before and after Key made up the new words for it. In fact, by 1820, at least 84 different poems were being sung to the "Anacreontic melody."

"The Star-Spangled Banner" instantly became a popular patriotic air and was the informal anthem of the Union Army during the Civil War. The U.S. Army adopted the song officially during World War I, but it did not become truly the national anthem until March 3, 1931, when President Herbert Hoover signed it into law.

Salvation on Lake Champlain

Even while Washington burned and Baltimore fell under attack, a grim band of 10,000 British veterans of the Napoleonic wars was advancing into the United States from Montreal. On land, nothing more than an inferior American force stood between them and New York City. But on September 11, 1814, American naval captain Thomas MacDonough (1783–1825) defeated and destroyed the British fleet on Lake Champlain. This event was sufficient to send into retreat the British army, which feared losing its lines of communication and supply.

The failure of the British offensive along Lake Champlain added some high cards to the hand of American peace negotiators meeting with their British counterparts across the ocean in the Flemish city of Ghent. The war-weary British decided to forego territorial demands, and the United States, relieved to escape without major losses, let up on its demand that Britain recognize American neutral rights. The Treaty of Ghent, signed on December 24, 1814, restored the *"status quo antebellum,"* and the document was unanimously ratified by the U.S. Senate on February 17, 1815.

Word for the Day
The Latin phrase *status quo antebellum* is common in treaties and underscores the utter futility of much combat. The phrase means literally "the way things were before the war."

Hero of New Orleans

The official outcome of the Treaty of Ghent is misleading; for America was not the same after the war as it was before. To begin, the nation suffered a crippling economic depression—though it would, in time, recover. More important, withdrawal of British support for its wartime Indian allies greatly weakened the hostile tribes, making the West that much riper for white expansion. Finally, in the world of 1814, trans-Atlantic communication was anything but instantaneous. Word of the Treaty of Ghent did not reach General Andrew Jackson, who, fresh from victory against the "Red Stick" Creek Indians in the South, had moved on to New Orleans to engage 7,500 British veterans under Major General Edward Pakenham sailing from Jamaica to attack the city.

Jackson's forces consisted of 3,100 Tennessee and Kentucky volunteers, in addition to New Orleans militiamen and a ragtag mob of locals, which Jackson wisely kept well to the rear. Jackson's inferior forces withstood a fierce artillery bombardment and repulsed two British assaults on their defensive positions. On January 8, 1815, the British, having suffered terrible losses (including the death of Pakenham and his two senior subordinates), withdrew. Although the War of 1812 had actually ended in December 1814, Jackson gave his countrymen their most glorious victory of the war.

Stats
The British lost 2,100 men at the Battle of New Orleans, including commanding general Edward Pakenham. Jackson's badly outnumbered troops suffered fewer than 100 casualties.

To most Americans, it now mattered little that the War of 1812 had been mostly a misery and a disaster. The victory at New Orleans, which made Americans feel like they had won the war, greatly strengthened the bonds of nationhood and made the economic and physical hardships seem worthwhile. This last battle also gave to America a new hero, a "westerner" born and bred far from the traditional seaboard seats of power. As Jefferson had before him, Andrew Jackson would lend his name to an entire era.

The Least You Need to Know

➤ The War of 1812 was provoked by Westerners, who were eager to expand the territory of the United States.

➤ Although the war brought great hardship to the United States, it ultimately reinforced the bonds of national unity.

Chapter 14

Fanfare for the Common Man (1814–1836)

> **In This Chapter**
>
> ➤ President Monroe's misnamed "Era of Good Feelings"
>
> ➤ The Monroe Doctrine
>
> ➤ Economic crisis: the Panic of 1819
>
> ➤ The Missouri Compromise
>
> ➤ Jacksonian Democracy

Casualties of the War of 1812 included many soldiers, settlers, and Indians. Casualties also included the U.S. economy, which declined sharply during the war, bottoming out in the Panic of 1819. Also slain in battle was the British desire to fight any more wars with its erstwhile colonies. No, Great Britain certainly didn't *lose* the War of 1812, but it didn't win it, either. Britain came away convinced that fighting the United States just wasn't worth doing. A final casualty was the Federalist party. Federalists, all of whom bitterly questioned the wisdom of the war and some of whom even advocated dissolution of the union because of it, were seen as unpatriotic and lacking in resolve. In 1816, Democratic-Republican James Monroe, presented to the electorate as the heir apparent of James Madison, handily won election to the presidency.

Good Feelings

The history of the American democracy is filled with contradictions, and one of the great misnomers that describes this nation in the years following the War of 1812 is the "Era of Good Feelings." The famous phrase was coined sarcastically by a Federalist newspaper following the reelection of Monroe in 1820, when he stood unopposed and was ushered into office by an electoral vote of 231 to 1. Monroe himself was popular, revered by the people as the last of the "cocked hats"—an affectionate name for the Founding Fathers. However, Monroe presided over a country that, although proud of its nationhood after the war, was seriously torn by bitter sectional rivalries and disputes over the interpretation of the Constitution.

Monroe tried to salve sectionalism by appointing a stellar cabinet that included the best political minds of the day, among them John Quincy Adams (Secretary of State), John C. Calhoun (Secretary of War), and William H. Crawford (Secretary of the Treasury). But these leading lights soon disputed with one another, not only over philosophical and sectional issues, but over who would succeed Monroe as president.

A Democratic-Republican, Monroe nevertheless broke with Thomas Jefferson and supported the rechartering of the Bank of the United States, which had been the brainchild of Federalist Alexander Hamilton. The bank was popular with the East Coast "establishment," because it effectively gave them control of the nation's purse strings. The bank was bitterly opposed by Westerners, however, who needed easy credit to expand and establish themselves.

Those Westerners also argued for a loose interpretation of the Constitution, particularly the phrase in the Preamble, "to promote the general welfare." These words, Calhoun and Henry Clay (powerful Congressman from Kentucky) argued, mandated the federal government to build the roads the West badly needed to develop its commerce and economy. Monroe consistently vetoed road-building bills, but did support a high tariff on imports, which aided the industrialized Northeast. This tariff heightened sectional strife.

Word for the Day

A *tariff*, as the word was used during the era of Monroe, is a tax on imported goods. Tariffs produce significant revenues for the government, and they "protect" certain domestic industries by giving their goods an artificial price advantage over imports. However, tariffs also result in higher prices to domestic purchasers because the higher costs are ultimately passed on to them.

Erie Canal

Monroe's opposition to federally built roads for the West did not stop—and may even have spurred—development of the nation's first great commercial link between the East Coast and the vast inland realm. Gouverneur Morris, U.S. Senator from New York, proposed in 1800 the construction of a great canal from New York City to Buffalo on Lake Erie. The project was approved by the New York legislature in 1817, and it was completed in 1825. Running 363 miles, the Erie Canal was a spectacular engineering achievement and a testament to American labor. The project was also a stunning commercial triumph, which quickly repaid the $7 million it had cost to build and soon returned an average of $3 million in annual profits—all without the assistance of the federal government.

The success of the Erie Canal, which truly inaugurated the *commercial* opening of the West, touched off a canal-building boom, linking the Northeast with the western system of natural waterways. By 1840, the United States boasted 3,326 miles of canals. The result was a trend toward commercial strength that helped pull the nation out of its postwar economic funk. The canals also tied the Northeast more securely to the West, thereby making deeper the growing division between the North and South, which had few east–west connections.

Among the Family of Nations

The completion and success of the Erie Canal justifiably puffed the nation's pride, even if its economy was still shaky and the jarring demands of sectionalism increasingly strident. The United States under Monroe could at least point to growing prestige among the family of the world's nations. Secretary of State John Quincy Adams negotiated the Rush-Bagot Agreement and the Convention of 1818 with Britain. The first document established the U.S. border with Quebec, hitherto a bone of contention, and established the precedent of a nonfortified, open border between the United States and Canada.

The second document, the Convention of 1818, addressed the issue of the disputed Oregon Territory (that is, the land west of the Rocky Mountains, north of the 42nd parallel to the 54° 42' line). The convention specified joint U.S. and British occupation of the area—a temporary solution to a hot dispute, but also a demonstration that England now took American sovereignty seriously.

On February 12, 1819, Adams concluded a treaty with Luis de Onis, Spain's minister to Washington, that secured both western and eastern Florida for the United States. With the acquisition of Florida, a prime objective of the War of 1812 was realized—albeit belatedly. A thornier problem was the establishment of the border between the United States and Mexico, at the time a colonial possession of Spain. Adams wanted a border that would pull Texas into American territory. However, to get Florida, he ultimately sacrificed

Texas and agreed on a boundary at the Sabine River, the western boundary of the present-day state of Louisiana. The United States renounced all claims to Texas. That renunciation was destined to endure during the handful of years before the revolutions by which Mexico won its independence from Spain. After the Texan War for Independence in 1836, U.S. rights to the territory would become a cause of war.

Yet one more treaty was concluded, this one with the czar of Russia, who had asserted a claim to the California coast as far south as San Francisco Bay. Adams managed to talk Czar Alexander I into a position north of the 54° 42' line, so that Russia would no longer be a contender for the Oregon Territory. The czar did retain his claim to Alaska, which at the time, nobody in the United States wanted anyway.

Monroe Doctrine

Although these foreign agreements were of great importance to establishing American sovereignty, the cornerstone of Monroe's foreign policy came in 1823 and has been stamped with the president's name. The origin of the Monroe Doctrine is found in the turbulent years of the Napoleonic Wars. These wars touched South America, sparking widespread revolution. After peace was re-established in Europe in 1815, Spain began making noises about reclaiming its colonies. President Monroe responded in his 1823 message to Congress with the four principles now known as the Monroe Doctrine:

1. The Americas were no longer available for colonization by any power.

2. The political system of the Americas was essentially different from that of Europe.

3. The United States would consider any interference by European powers in the Americas a direct threat to U.S. security.

4. The United States would not interfere with existing colonies or with the internal affairs of European nations, nor would the U.S. participate in European wars.

Bad Feelings

The so-called Era of Good Feelings was filled with plenty of distinctly *bad* feelings, a mixture of present financial hardships and an anxiety-filled foreboding of political and civil calamity just over the horizon.

American System

Monroe and Calhoun were driven by a vision of what came to be called the "American System," a way of harnessing the full power of the federal government to nurture struggling American industry through a protective tariff to ward off competition from imports; the creation of the Bank of the United States to provide a reliable source of credit to industry; and federal financing of road, canal, and harbor construction. Unfortunately, Monroe and Calhoun were never able to agree on all three of these components. While both supported the bank, Monroe repeatedly vetoed bills to fund "internal improvements"—roads and the like—while he endorsed heavy tariffs. Without adequate transport, Calhoun noted with bitterness, the West could not compete commercially with the East. He also said that the tariff, instead of protecting all American industry, fostered eastern development while operating to keep the isolated West financially strapped. A three-legged stool can stand; a two-legged one cannot. The American economy tottered.

Panic of 1819

Economic conditions in the wake of the War of 1812 read like a recipe for disaster:

➤ Start with a grinding war debt.

➤ Add high tariffs to create commodity inflation.

➤ Stir in wild speculation on western lands opened by the war.

➤ Overextend manufacturing investments.

➤ Pour the whole thing down the drain.

From 1811, when constitutional challenges prevented the rechartering of the Bank of the United States, until 1816, when it was revived under Monroe, a host of shabby state banks rushed to provide credit to practically all comers. Then, when the war broke out, all the state banks (except for those in New England) suspended the practice of converting paper bank notes to gold or silver ("specie") on demand. The value of all that paper money so recklessly loaned now plummeted. Banks failed, investors collapsed, businesses went belly up.

Monroe's Second Bank of the United States stepped in with a plan to stabilize the economy by sharply curtailing credit and insisting on the repayment of existing debts in specie. This plan preserved the Bank of the United States, but it hit the nation hard. "The Bank was saved," one pundit of the day observed, "but the people were ruined." In the West and South, individuals were particularly hard hit, and these states passed laws to provide debt relief, but not before 1819, when the panic peaked.

The nation ultimately weathered the Panic of 1819, but it created lasting resentment against the Bank of the United States (called "The Monster" by Missouri Senator Thomas Hart Benton). The panic deepened sectional rivalries, chipping away at the solidarity of the Union. The West and the South mightily resented the economic stranglehold of the Northeast.

Word for the Day
Specie payments are payments in gold and silver rather than paper money.

Compromise

The deepening gulf between the northern and southern states gaped its widest in 1818–19. At that point, the United States Senate consisted of 22 Senators from northern states and 22 from southern states. Since the era of the Revolution, the balance between the nonslaveholding North and the slaveholding South had been carefully and precariously preserved with the addition of each state. Now, the territory of Missouri petitioned Congress for admission to the Union as a slaveholding state. The balance threatened suddenly to shift, like a heavy burden on the back of a weary laborer.

Representative James Tallmadge of New York responded to Missouri's petition by introducing an amendment to the statehood bill calling for a ban on the further introduction of slavery into the state (but persons who were slaves in the present territory would remain slaves after the transition to statehood). The amendment also called for the emancipation of all slaves born in the state when they reached 25 years of age. Thus, gradually, slavery would be eliminated from Missouri. The House passed the Tallmadge amendment, but the Senate rejected it—and then adjourned without reaching a decision on Missouri statehood.

When the Senate reconvened, a long and tortured debate began. Northern Senators held that Congress had the right to ban slavery in new states, whereas the Southerners asserted that new states had the same right as the original 13, to determine whether they would allow slavery or not. Not until March 1820 was a complex compromise reached on this issue, which, in reality, could admit of no satisfactory compromise. Missouri, it was agreed, would be allowed to join the Union as a slave state, but simultaneously, Maine (hitherto a part of Massachusetts) would be admitted as a free state. By this means, the slave state/free state balance was maintained.

Voice from the Past

John Quincy Adams, recoiling from the bitter debate, called the Missouri Compromise the "title page to a great tragic volume," and the aged Thomas Jefferson said that the clamor over Missouri, "like a fire bell in the night, awakened and filled me with terror."

Then, looking toward the future, the Missouri Compromise provided that a line would be drawn across the Louisiana Territory at a latitude of 36° 30'. North of this line, slavery would be forever banned, except in the case of Missouri. Nobody was really pleased with the Missouri Compromise, but it did manage to hold together the increasingly fragile Union for another three decades.

Age of Jackson

The single strongest candidate in the presidential election of 1824 was Andrew Jackson (1767–1845), "Old Hickory," "The Hero of New Orleans," the candidate of the people. However, Jackson did not win the election.

As the facade of the Era of Good Feelings crumbled away, no party had replaced the Federalists to oppose the Democratic-Republicans. Within the Democratic-Republican camp, however, a host of candidates emerged, each reflecting deep regional divisions. The Tennessee and Pennsylvania state legislatures nominated Jackson, Kentucky nominated Henry Clay, Massachusetts nominated John Quincy Adams, and Congress presented William H. Crawford.

In the subsequent election, Jackson received 99 electoral votes, Adams 84, Crawford 41, and Clay 37. Because none of the candidates had a majority, the election was sent to the House of Representatives to choose from among the top three. Illness forced Crawford out of the running, and the choice was between Adams and Jackson. Because Adams had supported the American System, Henry Clay threw his support in Congress behind him. The House voted Adams into office over Jackson, who had received the greater number of electoral votes. Charging that a corrupt bargain had been made, Jackson's supporters split from the Democratic-Republican party and became Democrats. Supporters who remained loyal to Clay were known as National Republicans.

Adams had a tough time as a "minority president," but he nevertheless boldly submitted a nationally based program to a Congress and a public that had become increasingly splintered into regional and other special interests. Adams's support of canals and other internal improvements, his call for the establishment of a national university, and his advocacy of scientific explorations—all for the common, *national* good—were largely rejected by Congress. Instead, Congress focused on laissez-faire expansionism and frontier individualism. This attitude, which prevailed through the nation, swept Jackson into office in 1828.

Word for the Day

Laissez-faire, French for "let it happen," describes both a general political attitude of not interfering or intervening in the actions of others and, more specifically, an economic doctrine opposed to government regulation of commerce beyond the bare minimum.

Common Man or King Andrew?

Jackson, seventh president of the United States, was the first who had not been born in patrician Virginia or New England. Although he was, in fact, a wealthy man who lived in a magnificent mansion, the Hermitage, outside of Nashville, Tennessee, Jackson was also a self-made son of the Carolina back country. By the political geography of the day, he was a "westerner."

There can be no doubt that Andrew Jackson's two terms as president—from 1829 to 1837—brought a greater degree of democracy to American government. Jackson's contemporaries, as well as subsequent generations of historians, have debated whether the *kind* of democracy his administration fostered was always a good thing. During the Jackson years, most states abandoned property ownership as a prerequisite for the right to vote. This move broadened the electorate and made elected officials act in a way that was more fully representative of the people who had put them in office. While this transformation nurtured democracy, it also encouraged demagoguery.

Although Jackson introduced a policy of equitable rotation in federal jobs—the forerunner of the modern civil service system—he also brought with him the so-called "spoils system," boldly rewarding his supporters with lucrative and secure government jobs (known today as political patronage). Jackson also engineered the defeat of a program of internal improvements that was sponsored by Henry Clay and John Quincy Adams. Jackson argued that the plan favored the wealthy; yet, in defeating it, he retarded the development of commerce in the West—the very territory of his constituency. A believer in the paramount importance of preserving the Union, Jackson worked vigorously to silence the growing abolitionist movement, fearing that those who wanted to end slavery would tear the nation apart.

The Monster

Jackson reserved his strongest venom for the Second Bank of the United States. Never persuaded of the bank's constitutionality, Jackson was also acutely aware that his supporters hated the institution. When the bank's charter came up for renewal, Jackson opposed it, vetoing a recharter bill. After winning reelection in 1832, he issued an executive order withdrawing all federal deposits from the bank. That was a fatal blow, and the bank fizzled, finally closing its doors when its charter expired in 1836. With the demise of the Second Bank of the United States, credit became more plentiful, and westward settlement proceeded more rapidly. But for the rest of the 19th century, the American economy—especially in the rough-and-tumble West—was doomed to a punishing roller-coaster ride, repeatedly rising to "boom" only to plummet to "bust."

The Least You Need to Know

➤ Monroe was a popular leader, who nevertheless presided over a period of great economic hardship and bitter sectional rivalries.

➤ The "Age of Jackson" brought with it a vast expansion of the concept of democracy. However, this period also sacrificed some of the reason and restraint that had characterized the nation under the "Founding Fathers."

Trails of Tears (1817-1842)

Democracy seems logical and sounds simple—a matter of giving the people what they want. But just who are the American people? In Andrew Jackson's time, they were rich, poor, easterners, westerners, northerners, southerners, whites and blacks, slaves and masters, Indians, and everyone else. All, of course, are people, but most of them wanted entirely different things.

The "Age of Jackson," like Jackson the man, was full of contradiction and paradox. Bringing to the United States its first full measure of true democracy, "Old Hickory" was also derided as "King Andrew," a tyrant. A believer in individual rights, Jackson made the federal government more powerful than ever. A frontier southerner, he didn't want to disturb the institution of slavery, yet he turned against the South when that region threatened the authority of his government. A military hero who had built his reputation in large part by killing Indians, he espoused what was considered, in his day, the most enlightened approach to the so-called "Indian problem"—relocation from the East ("removal") to new lands in the West. *Enlightened?* The great "removal" opened the darkest chapter of Indian–white relations in the United States and forever stained the administration of Andrew Jackson.

Liberty and Union, Now and Forever

In 1828, as the administration of John Quincy Adams drew to a close, Congress passed the latest in a long series of tariff laws designed to foster American manufacturing industries by levying a hefty duty on manufactured goods imported from abroad. These laws were warmly embraced by the rapidly industrializing Northeast, but they were deeply resented in the South. The southern economy thrived on trade in raw materials, such as rice, indigo, and cotton. Among the South's best customers were the nations of Europe, especially England, which would buy the raw goods, turn them into manufactured products (such as fine fabric), and export them to the United States. If tariffs made it too costly for Americans to buy European goods, then Europe would have reduced need for the South's raw materials, and the region's export business would dry up.

Southerners called the 1828 measure the "Tariff of Abominations." Led by John C. Calhoun, U.S. Senator from South Carolina, Southerners charged that the act was both discriminatory in economic terms *and* unconstitutional. Calhoun wrote the *South Carolina Exposition and Protest* in 1828, arguing that the federal tariff could be declared "null and void" by any state that deemed it unconstitutional.

Calhoun could point to an impressive precedent for his bold position. Two founding fathers, Thomas Jefferson and James Madison, had introduced the concept of nullification when they wrote the Kentucky and Virginia Resolutions of 1798, which declared that the Alien and Sedition Acts violated the Bill of Rights. But a major showdown over the Tariff of Abominations was temporarily deferred by the 1828 election of Andrew Jackson, who pledged tariff reform. Southerners, however, were soon disappointed by the limited scope of Jackson's reforms, and when the Tariff Act of 1832 was signed into law, South Carolina called a convention. On November 24, 1832, the convention passed an Ordinance of Nullification forbidding collection of tariff duties in the state.

Calhoun gambled that Jackson's loyalty as a "son of the South" would prompt him to back down on the tariff. But Jackson responded on December 10 with a declaration upholding the constitutionality of the tariff, denying the power of any state to block enforcement of a federal law, and threatening armed intervention to collect duties. To show that he meant business, Jackson secured from Congress passage of a Force Act, which might well have ignited a civil war right then and there. However, the same year that the Force Act was passed, 1833, also saw passage of a compromise tariff. Although Calhoun's South Carolina stubbornly nullified the Force Act, it did accept the new tariff, which rendered nullification moot. Civil war was averted—for the time being—but the theory of nullification remained a profound influence on Southern political thought and provided a key rationale for the breakup of the Union less than three decades later.

War with the Seminoles

The political fabric was not the only aspect of the Union showing signs of wear during the Age of Jackson. Violence between settlers and Indians had reached epidemic proportions during the War of 1812 and never really subsided thereafter. During the war, General Jackson had scored a major triumph against the "Red Stick" Creeks in the lower Southeast, extorting from them the cession of vast tracts of tribal lands. Closely allied with the Creeks were the Seminoles, who lived in Florida and Alabama. The Creek land cessions made the Seminoles all the more determined to hold their own homelands. When the British withdrew in 1815 from the fort they had built at Prospect Bluff, Florida, it was taken over by a band of Seminoles and a group of fugitive slaves. Now known as "Negro Fort," it posed a military threat to navigation on key water routes in Florida, Georgia, and Alabama. Moreover, slaveholders were angered that the fort sheltered their escaped "property."

Word for the Day

To *cede* land is to give it up, usually as a condition of surrender or in exchange for something of value (money or other land). *Cession* is the noun form of the word and is not to be confused with *secession*, which refers specifically to the breakaway of 11 Southern states that precipitated the Civil War.

In 1816, General Jackson ordered Brigadier General Edmund P. Gaines to build Fort Scott on the Flint River fork of the Apalachicola in Georgia. In July of that year, Jackson dispatched Lieutenant Colonel Duncan Lamont Clinch, with 116 army regulars and 150 white-allied Coweta Creeks, to attack Negro Fort. Ordered to recover as many fugitive slaves as possible, Clinch attacked the fort on July 27 and was supported by a pair of riverborne gunboats. The skipper of one of these vessels decided that bombardment would be most effective if he heated the cannonballs red hot and fired them with an extra-heavy charge. The first projectile launched in this way landed in the fort's powder magazine, setting off a spectacular explosion that has been described as the biggest bang produced on the North American continent to that date. Three hundred fugitive slaves and 30 Seminoles were blown to bits, and the Indian tribe was propelled to the brink of war.

Late in 1817, a Seminole chief named Neamathla warned General Gaines to keep whites out of his village, Fowl Town. In response, Gaines sent a force of 250 to arrest Neamathla. The chief escaped, but the troops attacked the town, and the First Seminole War was underway.

Andrew Jackson led 800 regulars, 900 Georgia militiamen, and a large contingent of friendly Creeks through northern Florida, bringing destruction to the Seminole villages he encountered and high-handedly capturing Spanish outposts in the process. The taking of Pensacola on May 26, 1818, created a diplomatic crisis, which was resolved, however, when Spain decided to abandon Florida and cede the territory to the United States. With that, many more settlers rushed into the region, overwhelming the battered Seminoles and their remaining Creek allies. A minority of these tribes signed treaties in 1821, 1823, and 1825, turning over 25 million acres to the United States. The Seminoles were ordered to a reservation inland from Tampa Bay; few actually went to it. A majority of the Creeks repudiated the land cessions but were mercilessly persecuted under the policies of Georgia governor George Troup. When the Creeks appealed to Andrew Jackson (now president) for help, he advised them to move to "Indian Territory" west of the Mississippi. Ultimately, they did just that.

The Rise and Fall of Black Hawk

In the meantime, the so-called Old Northwest was racked with violence as well. The end of the War of 1812 and the death of Tecumseh failed to bring peace as white settlement pushed farther and farther west, through present-day Ohio and Indiana, and into Illinois. A group of determined Indian militants rallied behind Black Hawk (1767–1838), charismatic chief of the closely allied Sac and Fox tribes.

Black Hawk had fought at the side of Tecumseh during the War of 1812, after a minority of Sac and Fox warriors signed away tribal lands in Illinois to William Henry Harrison. After the war, a flood of settlers rushed onto the now-disputed Sac and Fox lands. Tensions mounted, but the government managed to persuade Black Hawk to move to Iowa, across the Mississippi. However, the winter hunt proved meager, and in desperation, Black Hawk and the British Band moved back into Illinois, where officials responded with militia and army regulars. Black Hawk bested the troops during the early encounters but was soon betrayed by English traders in the region and by the Winnebagos, both of which failed to deliver promised aid. Worse, a Sac and Fox chief named Keokuk, believing that the Indians' best hope for the future lay in cooperating with the whites, tipped off an Indian agent to Black Hawk's whereabouts. Keokuk also dissuaded a large number of Sac and Fox from participating in what had come to be called Black Hawk's War.

Voice from the Past

As was true of all white–Indian wars, much time was consumed in fruitless pursuit without encountering the enemy. A young Abraham Lincoln was a member of the Illinois militia in 1832. He later recalled: "If General Cass [Michigan's territorial governor, who later became Andrew Jackson's secretary of war] went in advance of me in picking whortleberries, I guess I surpassed him in charges upon wild onions. If he saw any live fighting Indians, it was more than I did, but I had a good many bloody experiences with the mosquitoes; and although I never fainted from loss of blood, I can truly say I was often very hungry."

On August 1, 1832, Black Hawk tried to persuade his band to travel up the Mississippi to seek refuge among the Winnebagos. Only a minority agreed; the rest started cobbling together makeshift rafts and canoes for a dash westward across the river. A few had made it across when the steamboat *Warrior* hove into sight, bearing troops and a six-pounder cannon. The boat anchored, and the British Band raised a white flag of truce, but a nervous commander opened fire with the six-pounder. Twenty-three of the British Band were slain, and the others were stranded on the east bank of the river. Black Hawk himself, together with his closest followers, had escaped northward and were on their way to Wisconsin.

On August 3, 1,300 more troops arrived and began slaughtering men, women, and children indiscriminately. The *Warrior* returned as well and again opened fire. About 200 Sac and Fox Indians made it through the general chaos to the west bank of the Mississippi, only to be intercepted and killed there by white-allied Sioux.

Black Hawk did find the Winnebagos in Wisconsin, but in exchange for a $100 reward and 20 horses, they betrayed the chief to the authorities. He was captured and imprisoned. The surviving Sac and Foxes signed a new treaty, ceding many more millions of acres to the United States, and they agreed to "remove" to lands west of the Mississippi River. In the meantime, Black Hawk was paroled to be taken on a tour of the nation as a kind of battle trophy. To the surprise and dismay of his keepers, the chief was honored in most places as a noble adversary.

The Indian Removal Act

As seen by later generations, Andrew Jackson is one of our most controversial chief executives. However, even his most enthusiastic admirers have difficulty justifying his role in the passage of the Indian Removal Act of 1830. This law effectively evicted the major Indian tribes from land east of the Mississippi and consigned them to "Indian Territory" in the West. In fairness to Jackson and Congress, it was reasonably enlightened legislation by the standards of the time. The act, passed on May 28, 1830, did not propose to rob the Indians of their land, but to exchange western for eastern territory and to make additional compensation, including payment of tribal annuities.

A Hollow Victory in the Supreme Court

In theory, and by law, Indian "removal" was a voluntary exchange of eastern lands for western lands. In practice, however, Indians were most often coerced or duped into making the exchange. Typically, government officials would secure the agreement of some Indian leaders deemed—by the government—to speak for the tribe, make the exchange, and declare that exchange binding to all members of tribe. Whether or not a majority of the tribe acknowledged the authority of these leaders hardly mattered. After an agreement was concluded, the government claimed the right to move all the Indians off the land, by force if necessary.

Some individuals and tribes went quietly; others, such as the Seminoles, fought. Still others, including numbers of Cherokees, holed up in the mountains to evade removal. The Cherokees, a politically sophisticated tribe, also took legal action. The tribe's majority party, called the Nationalist party, appealed to the U.S. Supreme Court in 1832 to protest state-sanctioned seizures of property and prejudicial treatment in state and local courts, all intended to pressure the Indians into accepting the "exchanges" mandated by the Removal Act. In *Worcester v. Georgia* (1832), Chief Justice John Marshall declared Georgia's persecution of the Indians unconstitutional. But this judgment proved a hollow victory, because President Jackson refused to use federal power to enforce the high court's decision. The chief executive, who had shown himself quite capable of threatening South Carolina with armed intervention during the Nullification Crisis, now claimed that the federal government was powerless to interfere in the affairs of a state. Jackson advised the Indians to resolve their difficulties by accepting removal.

In the meantime, Jackson's officials were directed to negotiate a removal treaty with the compliant minority faction of the Cherokees (called the Treaty party), representing perhaps 1,000 out of 17,000 Cherokees living in the South. On December 29, 1835, the Jackson administration concluded the Treaty of New Echota, binding *all* of the Cherokees to remove. To crush resistance, Jackson barred the Cherokee National party from holding meetings to discuss the treaty or alternative courses of action. Nevertheless, under the leadership of John Ross, the Nationalists managed to delay the major phase of the removal operation until the fall and winter of 1838–39.

A Man Called Osceola

While the Cherokees were being subdued and removed, federal authorities turned their attention to the always troublesome Seminoles. Like the Cherokees, the Seminoles suffered abuse from state and local governments; their suffering was compounded in 1831 by a devastating drought. Faced with annihilation, Seminole leaders signed a provisional treaty on May 9, 1832, agreeing to removal pending tribal approval of the site designated for resettlement. Accordingly, a party of seven Seminoles traveled westward. But before they returned, an Indian agent named John Phagan coerced tribal representatives into signing a final treaty, binding the Seminoles to leave Florida by 1837. Not only did the tribe rescind the signatures as fraudulent, but even the government acknowledged the wrongdoing by removing Phagan from office. Nevertheless—and despite the fact that the Seminoles' report on the proposed new homeland was negative—President Jackson sent the treaty to the Senate for ratification. With the treaty secured, troops were sent into Florida to begin organizing the removal.

By early in the winter of 1835, the increasing troop strength made it clear to Seminole leaders that war was in the offing. During this period, Osceola (1803–1838)—called Billy Powell by the whites—emerged as a charismatic Seminole leader. He negotiated with federal Indian agents to put off removal until January 15, 1836, hoping to buy sufficient time to prepare for the coming combat. Osceola set about organizing Seminole and "Red Stick" Creek resistance.

Beginning in December 1835, Osceola initiated guerrilla warfare, taking special pains to attack bridges critical for transporting troops and artillery. In every respect, Osceola proved a formidable adversary, a brilliant tactician who made extensive use of effective reconnaissance, and a fierce warrior. Generals Edmund Gaines, Duncan Clinch, Winfield Scott, Robert Call, Thomas Jesup, and Zachary Taylor all failed to bring the Second Seminole War to a conclusion. Osceola himself was finally captured, on October 21, 1837, not through the military skill of the federal troops, but by deception. General Jesup requested a "truce" conference in Osceola's camp; Osceola complied—and was treacherously taken captive. Consigned to a prison cell at Fort Moultrie, South Carolina, Osceola contracted "acute quinsy" and died on January 30, 1838.

Despite Osceola's capture and death, the war continued from 1835 to 1842, a period during which 3,000 Seminoles did submit to removal, but at the average cost of one soldier killed for every two Indians "removed." The Second Seminole War never really ended, but petered out, only to become reactivated during 1855-58 as the Third Seminole War. The last Seminole holdouts refused to sign treaties with the United States until 1934.

"The Cruelest Work I Ever Knew"

During the summer of 1838, Major General Winfield Scott began a massive roundup of Cherokees. In accordance with the terms of the fraudulent Treaty of New Echota, the Cherokees were to be removed to "Indian Territory," an area encompassing present-day Oklahoma and parts of Nebraska, Kansas, and the Dakotas. Those few Indians who did not successfully find refuge in the Blue Ridge Mountains were herded into concentration camps, where they endured the misery of a long, hot, disease-plagued summer.

During the fall and winter of 1838–39, the Indians were marched under armed escort along the 1,200-mile route to Indian Territory. Cold, short of food, subject to the abuse of their military guards (including theft, rape, and murder), 4,000 of the 15,000 who made the journey perished. Many years later, a Georgia soldier recalled: "I fought through the Civil War and have seen men shot to pieces and slaughtered by thousands, but the Cherokee removal was the cruelest work I ever saw." The Cherokees forever afterward called the experience the "Trail of Tears."

Indian Territory

What awaited the Cherokees and other Native peoples removed from the East was a vast tract of relatively barren western land. Whereas their eastern homelands had been lush and green, the Oklahoma, Kansas, Nebraska, and Dakota region was arid. Much of the stubborn soil was resistant to cultivation and certainly unsuited to the type of agriculture the Indians had pursued in the East. The hardships of soil and climate, combined with the callous inefficiency and general corruption of the federal system that was obligated by treaty to aid and support the "resettled" Indians, killed many. Others, certainly, died of nothing more or less than broken hearts. Yet, over time, many among the removed tribes made the best of their grim situation and, in varying degrees, even prospered.

Contrary to treaty agreements, the Kansas–Nebraska Act of 1854 reduced the area of Indian Territory. During the Civil War, many Cherokee, Creeks, and others allied themselves with the Confederates. The victorious Union forces punished these Indians in 1866 by further reducing the size of Indian Territory, confining it to the area encompassed by present-day Oklahoma.

The Least You Need to Know

➤ In the Nullification Crisis, "states' rights" confronted federal authority in a prelude to civil war.

➤ The Indian Removal Act was an attempt to separate Indians and whites by means of land exchanges. In practice, the act authorized the brutal exile of Cherokee, Seminole, Chickasaw, Choctaw, and Creek Indians (the "Five Civilized Tribes") to arid Indian Territory concentrated in present-day Oklahoma.

Part 4
A House Divided

Just as you can find people to tell you that the Revolution had little or nothing to do with liberty, there are still plenty of folks who'll argue that the Civil War was about states' rights or about the North wanting to achieve economic domination over the South. These things are important and partly true, but if it hadn't been for slavery in the South and the opposition to it in the North, there would have been no Civil War. This section tells the story of how the "peculiar institution" of slavery divided a nation, and how, finally, the question of whether a "nation conceived in liberty and dedicated to the proposition that all men are created equal can long endure" was answered by the bloodiest, costliest, most destructive war in American history.

Chapter 16

Chains, Whips, and Heartbreak (1724–1857)

In This Chapter

➤ A nation divided over the slavery issue

➤ Abolition movements, the Underground Railroad, and rebellion

➤ Compromises on the slavery issue

➤ Bleeding Kansas and the Dred Scott decision

By the early 1700s, slavery had caught on in a big way throughout the Southern colonies. In places like South Carolina, slavery became essential to the economy, and slaves soon outnumbered whites in that colony. The Declaration of Independence declared no slave free, and the Constitution mostly avoided the issue, except for the purposes of levying taxes, determining representation in Congress (for purposes of such enumeration, slaves were deemed three-fifths of a human being), and specifying that the slave trade (that is, importation) was to end within 20 years.

The irony was most bitter. The sweet land of liberty persisted in maintaining an institution that the rest of the world's nations were quickly abandoning. The British Parliament outlawed the slave trade in 1807 and all slavery in 1833. The emerging nations of South America made slavery illegal, and Spain and Portugal officially abolished slave trading in 1840. But America remained a slave nation, and this fact was tearing the country apart.

Against the American Grain

From the beginning, a great many Americans were opposed to slavery. The first organized opposition came from the Quakers, who issued a statement against the institution as early as 1724.

During the colonial periods, slave markets were active in the North as well as the South. However, the agricultural economy of the northern colonies was built upon small farms rather than vast plantations. Although many people in the North were passionately opposed to slavery on moral grounds, it is also true that the region lacked the economic motives for it. Therefore, an increasing number of colonists regarded slavery as unnecessary and undesirable; following independence, various states outlawed slavery. Rhode Island, traditionally a seat of tolerance, abolished the institution as early as 1774. Another bright spot existed in this early era: The Northwest Ordinance of 1787 excluded slavery from the vast Northwest Territory.

Cotton Gin

Just six years after passage of the Northwest Ordinance, however, a New Englander working as a tutor in Georgia invented a brilliantly simple machine that revolutionized the cotton industry; in so doing, he ensured the continuance of slavery. Eli Whitney (1765–1825), fascinated by operations on the large Southern plantations, saw that planters were vexed by a problem with the short-staple cotton raised in the lower South. The plants' seeds required extensive handwork to remove. Even done by slaves, the labor was so time-consuming that profits were sharply curtailed. By April 1793, Whitney had fashioned a machine that used a toothed cylinder to separate the cottonseed from the cotton fiber. Each "cotton gin" could turn out 50 pounds of cleaned cotton a day—far more than what manual labor could produce.

Word for the Day

Cotton gin sounds to us like a peculiar form of booze, but late 18th-century ears would have immediately recognized "gin" as a shortened from of "engine." Two hundred years ago, a gin—or engine—was any labor-saving device, particularly one intended to help move heavy objects.

With cotton production suddenly becoming extremely profitable, farmers all over the South turned to it, and "King Cotton" soon displaced tobacco, rice, and indigo as the primary Southern export crop. With increased production also came a greatly increased demand for slave labor to pick the cotton.

Underground Railroad

As an earlier generation had been fascinated by inventions like the cotton gin, so now Americans were enthralled by another innovation, railroads, which began appearing in the United States during the late 1820s. If the railroad seemed a technological miracle, abolitionists (those who wanted to *abolish* slavery) were aware that they needed a spiritual and moral miracle. By 1830, the highly organized abolitionists developed a network they called the Underground Railroad.

The system was a loose network of individuals—whites and free blacks, called "conductors"—and safe houses ("stations") dedicated to nothing less than the secret delivery—and deliverance—of slaves ("passengers") from slave states to free ones. In the years prior to the Civil War, 50,000 to 100,000 slaves found freedom via the Underground Railroad.

Southern slaveholders did not suffer the Underground Railroad gladly. "Conductors" were menaced, assaulted, and even killed. Fugitive slaves, once retaken, were often severely punished as an example to others. When the Supreme Court ruled in 1842 (*Prigg v. Pennsylvania*) that states were not required to enforce the Fugitive Slave Law of 1793 (which provided for the return of slaves who escaped to free states), opposition to the Underground Railroad became rabid.

Real Life

The most famous "conductor" on the Underground Railroad was Harriet Tubman, a courageous, self-taught, charismatic escaped slave, single-minded in her dedication to freeing others. Born in Dorchester County, Maryland, about 1821, she escaped to freedom about 1849 by following the North Star. Not content with having achieved her own freedom, she repeatedly risked recapture throughout the 1850s by journeying into slave territory to lead some 300 other fugitives, including her parents, to freedom.

With the outbreak of the Civil War, Tubman volunteered her services as a Union army cook and nurse, then undertook hazardous duty as a spy and guide for Union forces in Maryland and Virginia. Capture would surely have meant death.

Following the war, Tubman operated a home in Auburn, New York, for aged and indigent African-Americans. She ran the facility until her death on March 10, 1913, when she was buried with full military honors.

Nat Turner's Rebellion

Resistance to slavery was not always nonviolent, and the fear of slave rebellion was never far from the thoughts of Southern slave holders. Nat Turner was a slave on the Southhampton County, Virginia, plantation of Joseph Travis. A fiery lay preacher, Turner gathered about him a band of rebellious fellow slaves, and just before dawn on August 22, 1831, he and his followers killed every white member of the Travis household. The band then swept through the countryside, killing every white they encountered during the next 24 hours—perhaps 60 whites in all. Reaction, in turn, was swift and terrible. Turner and 50 of his band were apprehended and quickly tried. Twenty were summarily hanged. The enflamed white avengers went beyond this measure, however, indulging in their own rampage of killing and torture, directed indiscriminately at whatever blacks they happened to run across.

Although slave rebellions were hardly new in 1831, in an atmosphere of organized opposition to slavery, Nat Turner's Rebellion created unprecedented panic in the South and hardened Southern antagonism to abolitionist efforts.

The Liberator and the Narrative

The year that saw Nat Turner's Rebellion also witnessed the emergence of a new newspaper in the North. William Lloyd Garrison (1805–1879) was a genteel New England abolitionist—a native of Newburyport, Massachusetts—who became coeditor of a moderate periodical called *The Genius of Universal Emancipation*. But the injustice of slavery soon ignited a fiercer fire in Garrison's belly, and on January 1, 1831, he published the first issue of *The Liberator*. This was a radical and eloquent abolitionist periodical that declared slavery an abomination in the sight of God and that demanded the immediate emancipation of all slaves, without compromise. *The Liberator* galvanized the abolitionist movement. Three years after the first number was printed, Garrison presided over the founding of the American Anti-Slavery Society. Using *The Liberator* and the society, Garrison embarked on a massive campaign of what he called "moral suasion." He believed that slavery would be abolished when a majority of white Americans experienced a "revolution in conscience."

Garrison grew increasingly strident in his views, and by the late 1830s, some abolitionists broke with him. In 1842, he made his most radical stand, declaring that Northerners should disavow all allegiance to the Union because the Constitution protected slavery. A pacifist, Garrison nevertheless hailed John Brown's bloody 1859 raid on Harper's Ferry for the purpose of stealing guns to arm slaves for a general uprising.

If *The Liberator* was the most powerful white voice in support of abolition, a gripping account of slavery and liberation by an escaped Maryland slave named Frederick Douglass was the most compelling African-American voice. Published in 1845, *Narrative of the Life of Frederick Douglass* was widely read and discussed. Not only did the *Narrative* vividly portray the inhumanity of slavery, it simultaneously made manifest the intense humanity of the slaves, especially of the brilliant, self-educated Douglass himself. Active as a lecturer in the Massachusetts Anti-Slavery Society, Douglass parted company with Garrison over the issue of breaking with the Union. Douglass wanted to work within the Constitution.

The Tortured Course of Compromise

The awkward Missouri Compromise hammered out in 1820 began to buckle in 1848–49 when gold was discovered in California. The territory was officially transferred to the United States by the Treaty of Guadalupe Hidalgo, which ended the Mexican War on February 2, 1848. On January 24, 1848, just a few days before the treaty was signed, gold was found at a sawmill on the South Fork of the American River. During the height of the gold rush, in 1849, more than 80,000 fortune seekers poured into the territory. This event suddenly made statehood for the territory an urgent issue. But would California be admitted as a slave state or free?

In 1846, Congress, seeking a means of bringing the Mexican War to a speedy conclusion, had debated a bill to appropriate $2 million to compensate Mexico for "territorial adjustments." Pennsylvania congressman David Wilmot introduced an amendment to the bill, called the Wilmot Proviso, that would have barred the introduction of slavery into any land acquired by the United States as a result of the war. As usual, Southern opposition to the limitation of slavery was articulated by South Carolina's John C. Calhoun. He proposed four resolutions:

1. Territories, including those acquired as a result of the war, were the common and joint property of the states.

2. Congress, acting as agent for the states, could make no law discriminating between the states and depriving any state of its rights with regard to any territory.

3. The enactment of any national law regarding slavery would violate the Constitution and the doctrine of states' rights.

4. The people have the right to form their state government as they wish, provided that its government is republican.

As if Calhoun's resolutions were not enough, he dropped another bombshell, warning that failure to maintain a balance between the demands of the North and the South would lead to "civil war."

1850

Congress labored over the next three years to bolster the 1820 compromise. Thanks to abolitionists such as Garrison and Douglass, most Northerners were no longer willing to allow slavery to extend into any new territory, whether it lay above or below the line drawn by the Missouri Compromise. To break the dangerous stalemate, Senator Lewis Cass of Michigan advanced the doctrine of "popular sovereignty," proposing that new territories would be organized without any mention of slavery one way or the other. When the territory wrote its own constitution and applied for admission as a state, the people of the territory would vote to be slave or free. As to California, it would be admitted to the Union directly instead of going through an interim of territorial status.

Southerners cringed. They assumed that California would vote itself free, as would New Mexico down the line. Senators Henry Clay and Daniel Webster worked out a new compromise. California would indeed be admitted to the Union as a free state. The other territories acquired as a result of the Mexican War would be subject to "popular sovereignty." In addition, the slave trade in the District of Columbia would be discontinued. To appease the South, however, a strong Fugitive Slave Law was passed, strictly forbidding Northerners to grant refuge to escaped slaves. Finally, the federal government agreed to assume debts Texas (admitted as a slave state in 1845) incurred before it was annexed to the United States.

As with the Missouri Compromise, the Compromise of 1850 pleased no one completely. Abolitionists were outraged by the Fugitive Slave Law, while states' rights supporters saw the slave–free balance in Congress as shifting inexorably northward.

Main Event

Harriet Beecher Stowe (1811–96) was the daughter of a celebrated Congregationalist minister, Lyman Beecher, and the wife of biblical scholar Calvin Ellis Stowe. In 1843, she wrote her first book, *The Mayflower; or, Sketches of Scenes and Characters among the Descendants of the Pilgrims*, which revealed her familiarity with New England. However, living near Kentucky for a time acquainted her with the South. After Stowe and her husband moved to Brunswick, Maine, in 1850, the passage of the Fugitive Slave Law stirred memories of what she had seen of slavery.

Stowe began to write a book called *Uncle Tom's Cabin, or Life Among the Lowly*, which was published serially in the *National Era* during 1852. The following year, the work came out in book form and created a tremendous popular sensation. With its vivid—and sentimental—scenes dramatizing the cruelty of slavery, the book shook the apathy out of many Northerners and enraged slaveholding Southerners. So powerful was the effect of the novel in the years preceding the Civil War that, when Abraham Lincoln met Mrs. Stowe during the conflict, he reportedly referred to her as "the little lady who wrote the book that made this big war."

Kansas-Nebraska Act

In the Compromise of 1850, many observers saw the handwriting on the wall: the Union was coming apart at the seams. In 1854, the territories of Nebraska and Kansas applied for statehood. In response, Congress repealed the Missouri Compromise and passed the Kansas-Nebraska Act, which left the question of slavery to "popular sovereignty." There was never any doubt that Nebraskans would vote themselves a free state, but Kansas was very much up for grabs. Pro-slavery Missourians suddenly flooded across the border, elected a pro-slavery territorial legislature, then, mission accomplished, returned to Missouri. Anti-slavery Iowans likewise poured in, but they decided to settle. Soon a chronic state of civil warfare developed between pro- and anti-slavery factions in Kansas. The situation became so ugly that the territory was soon called "Bleeding Kansas."

The anti-slavery faction set up its headquarters at the town of Lawrence. In 1856, pro-slavery "border ruffians" raided Lawrence, setting fire to a hotel and a number of houses, and destroying a printing press. In the process, several townspeople were killed. During the night of May 24, John Brown, a radical abolitionist who had taken command of the territory's so-called Free Soil Militia, led four of his sons and two other followers in an assault on pro-slavery settlers along the Pottawatomie River. Five defenseless settlers were hacked to death with sabers. Claiming responsibility for the act, Brown pronounced it payback for the sack of Lawrence. The incident was just one jarring passage in a grim overture to the great Civil War.

The Dred Scott Disgrace

In 1857, at the height of the Kansas bloodshed, the U.S. Supreme Court weighed in with a decision concerning the case of one Dred Scott, a fugitive slave. Scott had belonged to John Emerson of Saint Louis. An army surgeon, Emerson had been transferred first to Illinois and then to Wisconsin Territory, with his slave in tow. When Emerson died in 1846, Scott returned to Saint Louis and sued Emerson's widow for his freedom, arguing that he was a citizen of Missouri, now free by virtue of having lived in Illinois, where slavery was banned by the Northwest Ordinance, and in Wisconsin Territory, where the terms of the Missouri Compromise made slavery illegal. The Missouri state court decided against Scott, but his lawyers appealed to the Supreme Court.

The high court was divided along regional lines. The anti-slavery Northern justices sided with Scott, while the pro-slavery Southerners upheld the Missouri state court decision. Chief Justice Roger B. Taney had the final word. He ruled, in the first place, that neither free blacks nor enslaved blacks were citizens of the Untied States and, therefore, could not sue in federal court. That ruling would have been enough to settle the case, but Taney went on. He held that the Illinois law banning slavery had no force on Scott after he returned to Missouri, a slave state. The law that obtained in Wisconsin was likewise null and void, Taney argued, because the Missouri Compromise was (he said) unconstitutional. According to Taney, the law violated the fifth amendment to the Constitution, which bars the government from depriving an individual of "life, liberty, or property" without due process of law.

The decision outraged abolitionists and galvanized their cause. Here was the spectacle of the United States Supreme Court using the Bill of Rights to deny freedom to a human being! Here was the federal government saying to slave owners that their ownership of human beings would be honored and protected everywhere in the nation! No longer was the slavery issue a question of how the nation could expand westward while maintaining a balance in Congress. It was now an issue of property. Justice Taney's decision had put slavery beyond compromise. If, as his decision implied, the rights of slaveholders were to be universally respected as long as slavery existed, then, universally, slavery had to be abolished so that the rights of slaveowners could be abolished. And that, inevitably, meant war.

The Least You Need to Know

➤ The labor-intensive cultivation of cotton made the Southern economy dependent on slavery.

➤ A series of compromises staved off civil war for three decades, as Northern opposition to slavery grew stronger and Southern advocacy of it became increasingly strident.

➤ The Dred Scott decision made slavery an issue transcending individual states; therefore, it made compromise impossible—and civil war inevitable.

Chapter 17

Looking West (1834–1846)

In This Chapter

➤ Land: the great American asset

➤ McCormick's reaper and Deere's plow

➤ Independence for Texas

➤ Development of the western trails and the telegraph

White–Indian warfare continued as a seemingly chronic pastime, and the slavery issue was cracking the country's foundation faster and more deeply than any number of flimsy compromises could patch. The United States during the first half of the 19th century seemed a violent place—especially when you add into the picture two major wars with foreign powers: the War of 1812 and the Mexican War.

Yet, as the old saw goes, everything's relative. Between 1800 and the 1850s, Europe was in an almost continual state of war, and despite their own problems, Americans, looking across the sea, counted themselves lucky. For America had one powerful peace-keeping asset Europe lacked: space. Seemingly endless space stretched beyond the Appalachian Mountains and the Mississippi River, across plains and desert, over more mountains, to the Pacific Ocean itself. Surely, America had room enough for everybody.

The Plow and the Reaper

Of course, land aplenty was one thing; actually *living* on it and *using* it could be quite another matter. In the Northeast, the American farm of the early 19th century was a family affair, providing enough food to feed the family, with something left over for market. Farm life wasn't easy, but it was manageable. In the South, farms often expanded into vast plantations, which grew rice, indigo, tobacco, and cotton. These crops were all commercial, and slaves were the cheap source of labor to produce them profitably.

The West also offered the prospect of large-scale farming, but most of the western territories and states barred slavery. Plus, the "emigrants" who settled on the western lands were culturally and morally disinclined to keep slaves. A big piece of land wasn't worth much if you couldn't work it.

There was worse. Typically, prairie soil was hard and clumpy. It did not yield to the plow, but clogged it, making cultivation all but impossible. Was the nation destined to cling to its east coast, leaving vast western tracts desolate and empty? As would happen time and again in American history, technology changed everything.

> **Word for the Day**
> The dictionary will tell you that an *emigrant* is one who emigrates— that is, leaves one place to settle in another— whereas an *immigrant* immigrates: he or she comes *into* a place. The emphasis is on arrival rather than departure. Be that as it may, those who made the westward trek were almost always called emigrants by their contemporaries.

Cyrus McCormick

Cyrus McCormick (1809–1884) was born and raised on a Rockbridge County, Virginia, farm where his father, Robert, gave him the run of his well-equipped workshop. There, Cyrus began to redesign a mechanical reaper the elder McCormick had been tinkering with. By the time he was 22, Cyrus McCormick had come up with a practical prototype of a horse-drawn reaper. It was equipped with a cutting bar, a reel, divider, guards over reciprocating knives, and a platform on which the grain was deposited after having been cut. Everything was driven and synchronized by a gear wheel. Perfected and patented in 1834, the device was an important step toward making large-scale farming possible with a minimal labor force.

> **Stats**
> Before the advent of the reaper, it took 20 hours to harvest an acre of wheat. By the time the McCormick device was fully perfected, about 1895, the same task consumed less than an hour.

John Deere

The reaper solved only half the problem of large-scale farming on the stubborn prairies of the Midwest and West. John Deere (1804–1886) was a young man who left his native Rutland, Vermont, for Grand Detour, Illinois, in 1837 to set up as a blacksmith. While McCormick was perfecting his reaper, Deere hammered out a new kind of plow. Made of stout steel, the plow was beautifully shaped, calling to mind the prow of a graceful clipper ship. And it was sturdy, much stronger than a conventional plow. The combination of shiplike design and stout strength made the plow ideal for breaking and turning the tough prairie soil.

The McCormick reaper and John Deere plow came in the nick of time to open the West to agriculture. Each year, more and more emigrants pushed the frontier farther west.

Martyrdom at the Alamo

As the prairie voids of the northern Midwest and West began to fill in, the Southwest, still the territory of the Republic of Mexico, was being settled by an increasing number of American colonists. In 1820, Moses Austin secured a grant from the Spanish government to establish an American colony in Texas, but fell ill and died in 1821 before he could begin the project of settlement. On his deathbed, Austin asked his son, Stephen F. Austin, to carry out his plans. Mexico, in the meantime, had won independence from Spain in the revolution of 1821. Under terms established by a special act of the new Mexican government in 1824 (as well as additional agreements negotiated in 1825, 1827, and 1828), Austin brought more than 1,200 American families to Texas. Colonization was so successful that by 1836 the American population of Texas was 50,000, while that of the Mexicans was a mere 3,500.

Throughout the 1830s, the American majority chafed under Mexican rule—especially Mexican laws forbidding slavery. Violent conflicts between settlers and military garrisons became frequent. Feeling that his colony was not ready for a full-scale war of independence, Austin repeatedly negotiated peace with the tumultuous Mexican government. He drew up a proposed constitution to make Texas a Mexican state, and in 1833, traveled to Mexico City to seek an audience with Antonio López de Santa Anna, the country's new president. For five months, Austin tried in vain to see the president; at last, he gained an audience, only to have Santa Anna reject the statehood demand—although Santa Anna did agree to address a list of Texas grievances. However, as Austin was riding back to Texas, he was arrested, returned to Mexico City, and imprisoned there on a flimsy pretext for the next two years.

When Austin was finally released in 1835, he returned to Texas embittered and broken in health. He urged Texans to support a Mexican revolt against Santa Anna, and this effort triggered the Texas Revolution. Santa Anna led troops into Texas during January 1836 and reached San Antonio in February. There, against the advice of independence leader

Sam Houston (1793–1863), a force of 187 Texans under militia colonel William B. Travis took a defensive stand behind the walls of a decayed Spanish mission formally called San Antonio de Valero but nicknamed "the Alamo" because it was close to a grove of cotton-woods (*alamos* in Spanish).

The tiny Texas band, which included such renowned frontier figures as Jim Bowie and Davy Crockett, held off 5,000 of Santa Anna's troops for 10 days. The band hoped desperately that the American nation somehow would rally and rush to its aid. But that didn't happen. On March 6, the Mexican troops breached the mission's wall and slaughtered everyone inside.

This Mexican "victory" turned out to be a disaster for Santa Anna. Sam Houston united Texans under the battle cry "Remember the Alamo!" and brilliantly led his ragtag army against Santa Anna at the Battle of San Jacinto on April 21. The result was decisive, and Texas became an independent republic.

Trails West

During the 1830s and well into the 1840s, before the McCormick reaper and the Deere plow had worked their act of transformation, the western plains were known as the Great Desert, and they remained largely unsettled. Instead, settlers first set their sights on the Far West. By the early 1830s, Americans were beginning to settle in California, many of them "mountain men"—fur trappers—who turned from that profession to ranching and mercantile pursuits.

These pioneers made their way into the territory by way of the southwestern deserts until 1833, when Joe Walker, a mountain man from Tennessee, marched due west from Missouri. Walker took the so-called South Pass through the Great Divide, went east to west across the Great Basin, climbed the Sierra Nevada Mountains, and entered California. This path became the California fork of what would be called the Overland Trail. Walker had opened California to the rest of the nation. By 1840, 117 mountain men were settled in Mexican California, bringing the American population to about 400.

Overland Trail

The mountain men and other explorers carried back to the East tales of the wondrous and potentially bountiful lands that lay toward the sunset. Through the decade of the 1830s, America's westering dreams simmered. At last, on February 1, 1841, 58 men—settlers living in Jackson County, Missouri—met at the town of Independence to plan the first fully organized emigrant wagon train to California. Assembling across the Missouri River, at Sapling Grove, the party had grown to 69—including more than 20 women and children—under the leadership of John Bartleson. The prominent Catholic missionary

Father Pierre-Jean deSmet and the mountain man Thomas Fitzpatrick also joined the train of 15 wagons and four carts.

The trek consumed five months, three weeks, and four days. It was marked by a single death, a single birth, and a single marriage. The following year, some 20 wagons carrying well over 100 persons made the trip. Other journeys followed each year thereafter until the completion of the transcontinental railroad in 1869 made the Overland Trail and the other trans-West routes obsolete.

Surviving the three- to seven-month journey across an often brutal and always unforgiving landscape took discipline, strength, and luck. Yet most who undertook the trek survived—albeit transformed by the ordeal: haggard, even reduced to skin and bones. Such hardship was sufficient to convince many emigrants to make an expensive and often stormy journey by sea—either all the way around Cape Horn at the tip of South America or to the Isthmus of Panama. No such thing as a Panama Canal existed in the 19th century (the canal would not be completed and opened to traffic until 1914). Therefore, travelers bound for the West Coast had to disembark on the Atlantic side, make a disease-ridden overland journey across the steaming jungles of the Isthmus, then board a California-bound ship on the Pacific side.

Oregon Fever

Until gold was discovered in California in 1848–49, Oregon was the strongest of the magnets drawing emigrants westward. In 1843, a zealous missionary named Marcus Whitman led 120 wagons with 200 families in what was called the Great Migration to Oregon. Soon, stories of a lush agricultural paradise touched off "Oregon fever," which brought many more settlers into the Northwest.

Oregon was a hard "paradise." The elements could be brutal, and disease ranged from endemic to epidemic. Whitman worked tirelessly as a missionary and physician to the Cayuse Indians in the vicinity of Walla Walla (in present-day Washington state). An overbearing man who insisted that the Indians accept none other but the Christian God (and *his* version of that God), Whitman fell afoul of the Cayuse during a measles epidemic that killed half their number. Blamed for the epidemic, he and his pretty blonde wife, Narcissa, were massacred on November 29, 1847.

"What Hath God Wrought?"

Historians often refer to the emigrant trails as "avenues" of civilization—as if they were neatly constructed highways. In fact, the trails were often nothing more than a pair of wheel ruts worn by one wagon after another. Yet, even as ox hooves and iron-rimmed wheels crunched through the dust of rudimentary trails, a very different, very modern means of linking the continent emerged.

In 1819, the Danish scientist Hans C. Oersted (1777–1851) discovered the principle of "induction" when he noticed that a wire carrying an electric current deflected a magnetic needle. After this discovery, a number of scientists and inventors began experimenting with deflecting needle telegraphs. Two scientists, William F. Cooke and Charles Wheatstone, installed a practical deflecting needle telegraph along a railway line in England in 1837. In 1825, William Sturgeon invented the electromagnet, and the experiments of Michael Faraday and Joseph Henry on electromagnetic phenomena in 1831 excited an American painter, Samuel F. B. Morse, to begin working on a telegraph receiver.

Morse developed a device in which an electromagnet, when energized by a pulse of current from the line—that is, when the remote operator pressed a switch ("telegraph key")—attracted a soft iron armature. The armature was designed to inscribe, on a piece of moving paper, dot and dash symbols, depending on the duration of the impulse. Morse developed "Morse Code" to translate the alphabet into combinations of dots and dashes. On March 4, 1844, Morse demonstrated his magnetic telegraph by sending the message "What hath God wrought?" from Baltimore to Washington.

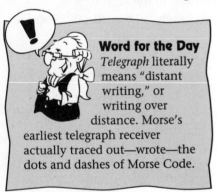

Word for the Day
Telegraph literally means "distant writing," or writing over distance. Morse's earliest telegraph receiver actually traced out—wrote—the dots and dashes of Morse Code.

Morse's receiver, as well as his code system, were widely adopted—although the cumbersome graphic device was soon abandoned. The difference between the dot and dash signals was quite audible, and a well-trained operator could translate them more quickly and reliably than any mechanical printing device. Within the span of only ten years, the single line from Baltimore to Washington had multiplied into 23,000 miles of line connecting the far-flung corners of the nation. In a burst of keystrokes, Morse compressed vast distance and gave the nation a technology that would help bind East to West.

The Least You Need to Know

➤ Vast spaces were always America's greatest resource as well as heaviest burden; a large nation was difficult to unify and govern.

➤ Technology played a key role in westward expansion. The McCormick reaper and Deere plow made farming the plains practical, and Morse's telegraph made the vastness of the West less daunting.

Chapter 18

Destiny (1846–1860)

SHUCKA SHUCKA

In This Chapter

➤ War with Mexico

➤ The Mormon Trek

➤ The Gold Rush of 1849

Phrases enter and exit the American language as if it were a revolving door. But one phrase, used in 1845 by *New York Post* editor John L. O'Sullivan to describe America's passion for the new lands of the West, rang out loudly and in tones that echoed through-out the entire century. "It is our *manifest destiny*," O'Sullivan wrote, "to overspread and to possess the whole of the continent which Providence has given us for the development of the great experiment of liberty and federated self-government entrusted to us." Under the banner of "manifest destiny," the American West would be won—the obstinacy of prairie soil, the harshness of the elements, the lives and life-ways of the Indians, and the rights of Mexico notwithstanding.

After Texas gained its independence, the United States was reluctant to accept the new-born republic's bid for annexation. Not only would the Union be adding a slave state, but it would surely ignite war with Mexico. However, when France and England made overtures of alliance to Texas, outgoing President John Tyler urged Congress to adopt an annexation resolution. Tyler's successor, James K. Polk, admitted Texas to the Union on December 29, 1845. In the meantime, England and France also seemed to be eyeing California, held so feebly by Mexico that it looked to be ripe and ready to fall into the hands of whomever was there to catch it.

"Mr. Polk's War"

Polk was moved to action. He offered Mexico $40 million for the California territory. The Mexican president not only turned down the offer, but he refused even to see President Polk's emissary. Thus rudely rebuffed, Polk commissioned the U.S. consul at Monterey (California), Thomas O. Larkin, to organize California's small but powerful American community into a separatist movement sympathetic to annexation by the U.S. In the meantime, John Charles Frémont, an intrepid western explorer surveying potential transcontinental railroad routes for the U.S. Bureau of Topographical Engineers, marched onto the stage with the so-called Bear Flag Rebellion. California's independence from Mexico was proclaimed.

As far as Mexico was concerned, the independence of California merely added insult to injury. Mexico disputed with the United States the boundary of the new state of Texas. President Polk dispatched troops to Texas and, on May 13, 1846, declared war on Mexico. But even before the official declaration, Mexican forces laid siege against Fort Texas—present-day Brownsville—on May 1.

General Zachary Taylor, marching to the relief of the fort, faced 6,000 Mexican troops with a mere 2,000 Americans, but he nevertheless emerged victorious in the May 8 Battle of Palo Alto. The battle set the pattern for the rest of the conflict. Usually outnumbered, the Americans almost always outmatched the poorly led Mexican forces.

In the meantime, early in June, official U.S. action commenced against the Mexicans in California as Stephen Watts Kearny led the "Army of the West" from Fort Leavenworth, Kansas, to California via New Mexico. Near Santa Fe, at steep-walled Apache Canyon, New Mexico's Governor Manuel Armijo set up an ambush to destroy Kearny's column, but the governor's ill-disciplined and ill-equipped troops panicked and dispersed. Kearny passed through the canyon unopposed, Santa Fe was taken, and on August 15, New Mexico was annexed to the United States, all without firing a shot.

General Taylor attacked Monterrey (Mexico) on September 20, 1846, taking the city after a four-day siege. Taylor declined to capitalize on what he had gained and allowed Mexican forces to withdraw. In the meantime, the remarkably resilient Antonio López de Santa Anna, who had been living as an exile in Cuba after a rebellion had ended his dictatorship of Mexico, made a proposal to the government of the United States. He pledged to help the U.S. win the war, to secure a Rio Grande boundary for Texas, and to secure a California boundary through San Francisco Bay. In return, Santa Anna asked for $30 million and safe passage to Mexico. American officials were prudent enough not to pay him, but Santa Anna was allowed to return to his homeland—whereupon he began assembling an army to defeat Zachary Taylor.

By January 1847, Santa Anna had gathered 18,000 men, about 15,000 of whom he hurled against Taylor's 4,800-man force at Buena Vista. After two days of bloody battle, Taylor—incredibly—forced Santa Anna's withdrawal on February 23. Despite this signal victory,

President Polk was distressed by Taylor's repeated reluctance to capitalize on his victories and also worried lest he make a military celebrity out of a potential political rival. So Polk replaced Taylor with General Winfield Scott, hero of the War of 1812. On March 9, Scott launched an invasion of Veracruz, beginning with the first amphibious assault in U.S. military history. He laid siege against the fortress at Veracruz for 18 days, forcing Santa Anna to withdraw to the steep Cerro Gordo canyon with 8,000 of his best troops.

Scott declined the frontal attack the Mexicans expected. Instead, he sent part of his force to cut paths up either side of Cerro Gordo and attacked in a pincers movement, sending Santa Anna's troops into headlong retreat all the way to Mexico City. Scott took the kind of gamble Taylor would not have taken and boldly severed his rapidly pursuing army from its slower-moving supply lines. On September 13, Chapultepec Palace, the seemingly impregnable fortress guarding Mexico City, fell to Scott. (The Palace had been defended by a force that included teenage cadets from the Mexican Military College. These cadets are celebrated in Mexican history as "Los Niños," the children.) On September 17, Santa Anna surrendered.

The Mexican War ended with the Treaty of Guadalupe Hidalgo, which was ratified by the Senate on March 10, 1848. Mexico ceded to the United States New Mexico (which also included parts of the present states of Utah, Nevada, Arizona, and Colorado) and California. The Mexicans also renounced claims to Texas above the Rio Grande.

God and Gold

The Mexican War was controversial. Citizens in the Northeast, especially in New England, saw the war as an unfair—somehow un-American—war of aggression, and they protested it. Southerners and Westerners, however, thrilled to the cause, volunteering to fight in such numbers that recruiting offices were overwhelmed and had to turn eager men away. Right, wrong, or somewhere in between, the war vastly expanded the territory of the United States.

A Trek

The force of war was not the only engine that drove "manifest destiny." The West likewise lured seekers of God and those who lusted after gold. In March 1830, a young Joseph Smith, Jr. published something he called *The Book of Mormon*. One month later, he started a religion based on the book, which relates how, in 1820, the 15-year-old Smith was visited by God the Father and Jesus Christ near his family's farm in upstate New York. Three years after this, young Smith was visited by an angel named Moroni, who instructed him to dig in a certain place on a nearby hill. There Smith unearthed a book consisting of beaten gold plates engraved with the words of Moroni's father, Mormon. The book told of a struggle between two tribes, one good, the other evil, which took place in the New World long before the arrival of Columbus. Moroni emerged as the sole survivor of the tribe of the good. Whoever dug up *The Book of Mormon* would be charged with restoring to the world the true Church of Christ.

The church Smith founded in April 1830 consisted of six members. By 1844, 15,000 members of the Church of Jesus Christ of Latter Day Saints—popularly called Mormons—were settled in Nauvoo, Illinois, the separatist community they had built. Persecuted wherever they went, the Mormons always lived apart. Particularly distasteful to "gentiles" (as Mormons called those outside of the faith) was the Mormon practice of polygamy (multiple wives).

Opposition to the Mormons often grew violent. On June 27, 1844, a "gentile" mob murdered Joseph Smith and his brother. Smith's second-in-command, the dynamic Brigham Young, realized that the Mormons would have to move somewhere so remote that no one would ever bother them again. Over the next two years, under his direction, a great migration was organized. The destination, which Young had read about in an account by John C. Frémont, was near the Great Salt Lake in the present-day state of Utah.

Young planned and executed the Mormon Trek with the precision and genius of a great general in time of war. Hundreds of wagons were built, and a staging area, called Camp of Israel, was set up in Iowa. Emigrant parties were deployed in groups of a few hundred at a time and sent 1,400 miles across some of the most inhospitable land on the face of the planet. During the 1840s and 1850s, Saints—as Mormons called themselves—poured into the Salt Lake region. Young oversaw the planning and construction of a magnificent town, replete with public squares, broad boulevards, and well-constructed houses, all centered around a great Temple Square. In addition, Young and his followers introduced into the arid Salt Lake Valley irrigation on a scale unprecedented in American agriculture. By 1865, 277 irrigation canals watered 154,000 square miles of what had been desert.

Main Event

The Mormon Trek was accomplished with great efficiency and very little loss of life. The church established a Perpetual Emigrating Fund to lend money to those lacking the means to finance their own way west. By 1855, the church realized that outfitting fully equipped wagon trains would soon break the fund. Brigham Young hit on a solution. He directed Mormon carpenters in Iowa to build *handcarts* as cheap substitutes for the horse-drawn prairie schooners. The emigrants would walk to Salt Lake City.

The small, boxlike carts looked like miniature covered wagons. They were equipped with only two oversize wheels, designed to roll easily over rough terrain. Approximately 500 handcart "Saints" left Iowa City on June 9 and 11, 1856. Although the trek took longer than anticipated (the emigrants did not arrive in Salt Lake City until late in September), the emigrants arrived safely, and Young was encouraged.

Departure of the next two "Handcart Brigades" was delayed until July and August because of a shortage of carts. Faced with a scarcity of seasoned lumber, the carpenters had to use green wood, which shrunk in the hot, arid air of the plains. Filled to overflowing, the carts broke down or simply fell apart, supplies ran short, and, worse still, the delayed departure from Iowa put the emigrants in Wyoming during the first snows. Of the 1,000 emigrants in the second Handcart Brigade, 225 died.

All That Glitters

Johann Augustus Sutter had bad luck with money. Born in Kandern, Germany, in 1803, he went bankrupt there and, to escape his many creditors, fled to the Mexican Southwest, where he tried his fortune in the Santa Fe trade. Twice more Sutter went bust, before finally settling in Mexican California in 1838, where he managed to build a vast ranch in the region's central valley.

Presumably, January 24, 1848, started like any other day on the ranch. James Wilson Marshall, an employee of Sutter's, went out to inspect the race of a new mill on the property. He was attracted by something shiny in the sediment collected at the bottom of the mill race. It was gold.

Within a month and a half of the discovery, all of Sutter's employees had deserted him, in search of gold. Without a staff, Sutter's ranch faltered. Worse, his claims to the land around the mill were ultimately judged invalid. While everyone around Sutter (it seemed) grew instantly rich, Sutter himself was, yet again, financially ruined and would die, bitter and bankrupt, in 1880.

It was not Marshall or Sutter, but a Mormon entrepreneur who did the most to stir up the great Gold Rush of 1849. Sam Brannon was one of a very few Mormon men brash enough to challenge the authority of Brigham Young. In defiance of Young, Brannon had set up his own Mormon community in the vicinity of San Francisco—then called Yerba Buena (*good herb*). Brannon saw in the discovery of gold a chance to profit from serving the needs of hopeful prospectors and other settlers. Fresh from a trip to Salt Lake City, where Young had excommunicated him from the church, Brannon took a quinine bottle, filled it with gold dust, and ran out into the streets of his town. "Gold!" he yelled. "Gold! Gold from the American River!" For good measure, he covered the gold story in *The California Star*, a newspaper he owned. Within two weeks, the population of Yerba Buena plummeted from a few thousand to a few dozen, as men dropped their tools and left their jobs to prospect on the south fork of the American River.

From the West Coast, word of gold spread east. The scene played out in San Francisco was repeated in city after city. Employment was unceremoniously terminated, wives and children were left behind, and seekers set out on the long trek to California. The journey was characteristically filled with hardship and heartbreak, whether the traveler chose the tedious overland route, the treacherous sea passage around stormy Cape Horn, or the boat to Panama (and a trek across the disease-ridden Isthmus to meet another ship for the voyage to the California coast). For some, the trip was worthwhile; great fortunes were made. Most prospectors, however, found only hard lives, mean spirits, and barely enough gold to pay for meals, shelter, and clothing. Many didn't even find that much.

> **Word for the Day**
> People who participated in the great California Gold Rush of 1849 earned the name *'49er* or *Forty-niner*. The 1849 rush was not the country's first, however; nor would it be the last. Western Georgia was the scene of the first rush in the late 1830s, and gold rushes would occur elsewhere in California and throughout the West during much of the 19th century. In 1896, the Klondike drew thousands of prospectors, and two years later, more came to Alaska in search of the yellow ore.

The fact was that most men made the mistake of looking for their fortune on the ground, while the real money was made by those, like Brannon, who sold groceries, hardware, real estate, liquor, and other necessities to the '49ers. Collis Huntington and Mark Hopkins made a fortune in miner's supplies. Charles Crocker used the profits from his dry goods operation to start a bank. Leland Stanford parlayed his mercantile pursuits into a political career culminating in the governorship of California and the founding of the university that bears his name. Together—as the "Big Four"—Huntington, Hopkins, Crocker, and Stanford provided the major financing for the Central Pacific Railroad—the western leg of the great transcontinental railroad completed in 1869.

The California Gold Rush lasted through the eve of the Civil War. The rush populated much of California, and then, as gold was discovered farther inland in Nevada, Colorado, and the Dakotas, yet more of the frontier West was settled. But as the bonds of union grew stronger between East and West, those uniting North and South steadily dissolved. Still basking in the reflected glory of western gold, the American nation was about to enter its darkest hours.

The Least You Need to Know

➤ While controversial, the war with Mexico greatly expanded the western territory of the United States.

➤ In addition to agriculture, the promise of religious freedom and the promise of gold lured many thousands out west in the years between the Mexican War and the Civil War.

Chapter 19

Strange Flag Over Sumter (1859–1862)

In This Chapter

➤ Lincoln's rise

➤ John Brown's raid on Harpers Ferry

➤ The fall of Fort Sumter and the early battles

➤ Union military failures

➤ Antietam and the Emancipation Proclamation

Abraham Lincoln was born on February 12, 1809, in a log cabin in Hardin (now Larue) County, Kentucky. In 1816, the family moved to Indiana and, finally, to Illinois in 1830. Largely self-taught, Lincoln tried various occupations and served as a militiaman in the Black Hawk War (1832). Although he had little appetite for military life, Lincoln took "much satisfaction" in having been elected captain of his militia company. That position opened new horizons for the young backwoodsman. Lincoln ran for the Illinois state legislature, losing his first bid but subsequently gaining election to four consecutive terms (1832–41). After setting up a successful law practice in Springfield, the state capital, he served a term (1847–49) in the U.S. House of Representatives but then returned to his law practice.

At this point, by his own admission, Lincoln "was losing interest in politics." Then came the Kansas-Nebraska Act in 1854. Its doctrine of popular sovereignty potentially opened new territories to slavery, and Lincoln saw the provisions of the act as immoral. Although he believed that the Constitution protected slavery in states where it already existed, he also thought that the Founding Fathers had put slavery on the way to extinction by legislating against its spread to new territories. Lincoln ran unsuccessfully for the U.S. Senate in 1855, then, the following year, left the Whig party to join the newly formed Republicans.

In 1858, Lincoln ran for the Senate against the Illinois incumbent, Stephen A. Douglas. Lincoln accepted his party's nomination (June 16, 1858) with a powerful speech suggesting that Douglas, Chief Justice Roger B. Taney, and Democratic presidents Franklin Pierce and James Buchanan had actually conspired to nationalize slavery. Declaring that compromise was doomed to fail and that the nation would become either all slave or all free, he paraphrased the Bible: "A house divided against itself cannot stand." For the fate of the country, it was as if he spoke prophecy.

John Brown's Body

Lincoln, a highly principled moderate on the issue of slavery, soon found himself transformed from an obscure Illinois politician to the standard bearer of his party. He challenged Douglas to a series of debates that captured the attention of the national press. Although Lincoln failed to win a seat in the Senate, he emerged as an eloquent, morally upright, yet thoroughly balanced embodiment of prevailing sentiment in the North. Radical Southerners warned that the election of any Republican, even Lincoln, would mean civil war.

While Lincoln and other politicians chose the stump and the rostrum as forums suited to decide the fate of the nation, others took more radical action. John Brown was born on May 9, 1800, in Torrington, Connecticut, but he grew to undistinguished adulthood in Ohio, drifting from job to job, always dogged by bad luck and bad business decisions. By the 1850s, however, Brown's life began to take direction, as he became profoundly involved in the slavery question.

Brown and his five sons settled in "Bleeding Kansas," where they became embroiled in the violence between pro-slavery and anti-slavery forces for control of the territorial government. Brown assumed command of the local Free-Soil militia, and after pro-slavery forces sacked the Free-Soil town of Lawrence, Brown, four of his sons, and two other followers retaliated by hacking to death, with sabers, five unarmed settlers along the Pottawatomie River during the night of May 24, 1856.

Although he was not apprehended, Brown claimed full responsibility for the act and became increasingly obsessed with the idea of emancipating the slaves by inciting a massive slave revolt. The charismatic Brown persuaded a group of Northern abolitionists to back his scheme financially. He chose Harpers Ferry, Virginia (present-day West Virginia), as his target, planning to capture the federal small-arms arsenal there. Then Brown planned to establish a base of operations in the mountains, from which he would direct the slave rebellion as well as offer refuge to fugitives. On October 16, 1859, with 21 men, Brown seized the town and broke into the arsenal. Local militia responded, and within a day, federal troops under the command of Robert E. Lee arrived, attacked, and killed 10 of Brown's band. The wounded Brown was taken prisoner.

Yet the battle was hardly over. Arrested and tried for treason, Brown conducted himself with impressive dignity and courage. It was, in fact, his finest hour, and he succeeded in arousing Northern sympathy, eliciting statements of support from the likes of William Lloyd Garrison and Ralph Waldo Emerson. Brown's execution by hanging, on December 2, 1859, elevated him to the status of martyr. To many, the raid on Harpers Ferry seemed a harbinger of the great contest to come.

Bleak Transition

The brand-new Republican Party, with Lincoln as its presidential candidate, united remnants of the essentially defunct Free-Soil Party and the Liberty party, as well as the old Whigs and other anti-slavery moderates and radicals. Stephen A. Douglas, who had defeated Lincoln in the race for the Senate, sought the Democratic nomination in 1860. But having denounced the pro-slavery constitution adopted by Kansas, Douglas had alienated the pro-Democratic South. Although Douglas was finally nominated, he was the candidate of a splintered party; a breakaway Southern Democratic party emerged, with outgoing vice president John C. Breckinridge as its candidate. Yet another splinter group, the Constitutional Union party, fielded a candidate, further dividing the party and propelling Lincoln to victory with 180 electoral votes against 123 for his combined opponents.

News of the victory of a "black Republican" (as radical Southerners called Lincoln) pushed the South to secession. First to leave the Union was South Carolina, on December 20, 1860; Mississippi followed on January 9, 1861, Florida on January 10, Alabama on January 11, Georgia on January 19, Louisiana on January 26, and Texas on February 1. Four days later, delegates from these states met in Montgomery, Alabama, where they wrote a constitution for the

Stats
The popular vote was much closer than the electoral vote. Lincoln received only 1,866,452 votes against 2,815,617 votes for his combined opponents.

Confederate States of America and named Mississippi's Jefferson Davis provisional president. As the Union crumbled about him, lame duck President James Buchanan temporized, unwilling to take action.

Prior to his inauguration, President-elect Lincoln discovered that Jefferson Davis was not spoiling for war but offered to negotiate peaceful relations with the United States. And Senator John J. Crittenden (1787–1863) of Kentucky proposed, as a last-ditch alternative to bloodshed, the Crittenden Compromise—constitutional amendments to protect slavery while absolutely limiting its spread. Lincoln, determined to avoid committing himself to any stance before actually taking office, nevertheless let others attribute positions to him. The fact was that Lincoln's prime objective was to preserve the Union, and he was actually willing to consider protecting slavery where it existed, even by constitutional amendment. Lincoln also thought the Fugitive Slave Act should be enforced. Yet, by remaining silent during the period between his election and inauguration, he conveyed the impression that he fully shared the radical Republican opposition to compromise.

April 12, 1861, 4:30 A.M.

With Lincoln in office and all hope of compromise extinguished, the Confederate president and Confederate Congress authorized an army and navy and set about taking control of federal civil and military installations in the South. Fort Sumter, which guarded Charleston harbor, was especially important. If the Confederacy could not control the key international port on the coast of South Carolina, it could not effectively claim sovereignty. Throughout March 1861, the Confederate government attempted to negotiate the peaceful evacuation of the Union garrison at Fort Sumter, but Lincoln remained adamant that the United States would not give up the fort. Yet, not wanting to provoke the Southerners, Lincoln delayed sending reinforcements.

Faced with South Carolina "fire-eaters" (ardent secessionists) who threatened to seize the fort on their own, Jefferson Davis decided that he had to take action. He assigned the mission of capturing the fort to Brigadier General Pierre Gustave Toutant Beauregard, who laid siege to the fort, hoping to starve out post commandant Major Robert Anderson and his men. In the meantime, Lincoln and the rest of the federal government seemed to be sleepwalking. With great deliberation and delay, a ship was loaded with reinforcements and supply. But it was too late now. Just before he was prepared to open fire, Beauregard offered Anderson, his former West Point instructor, generous surrender terms: "All proper facilities will be afforded for the removal of yourself and command, together with company arms and property, and all private property, to any post in the United States which you may select. The flag which you have upheld so long and with so much fortitude, under the most trying circumstances, may be saluted by you on taking it down."

Anderson refused, and the first shot of the Civil War was fired at 4:30 a.m. on April 12, 1861. Edmund Ruffin (1794–1865), a 67-year-old "fire-eater," claimed credit for having pulled the lanyard on that initial volley—although the truth is that Captain George S. James fired a signal gun first. The ensuing bombardment lasted 34 hours before Anderson surrendered. Incredibly, this first engagement of the war resulted in no casualties. It would be the last bloodless battle of the war.

From Bull Run to Antietam

During the spring of 1861, Virginia, North Carolina, Tennessee, and Arkansas joined the seven original Confederate States. Yet even that number put the odds at 11 versus 23 Northern states. The North had a far more extensive industrial base than the South and more than twice as many miles of railroad. As far as the production of foodstuffs was concerned, Northern agriculture was also better organized. Although the North was just recovering from an economic depression, the entire South could scrape together no more than $27 million in specie (gold and silver). The North not only commanded far more wealth, but it also had diplomatic relations with foreign powers and, therefore, could secure extensive credit.

Yet the South did have more of the army's best officers, who, at the outbreak of hostilities, had resigned their commissions in the U.S. Army and joined the army of the Confederate States. Confederate leaders knew that their only chance was to score swift military victories that would sap the North's will to fight.

The first major engagement of the war, after the fall of Fort Sumter, proved just how effective the Confederate officers and men were. When it began, the battle the South would call First Manassas and the North would call First Bull Run was a picnic. On July 21, 1861, Washington's fashionable folk rode out to nearby Centreville, Virginia, in carriages filled with baskets of food and bottles of wine. Through spy glasses, they viewed the action three miles distant. The Union troops seemed similarly carefree; as they marched to battle, they frequently broke ranks to pick blackberries. Remarkably lax, too, was military

Stats
The population of the South in 1861 was about 9 million people, including 3 million slaves (who were not military assets). The North had 22 million people.

security. Newspapers published the Union army's plan of action, and what information the papers didn't supply, rebel sympathizers, such as the seductive Rose O'Neal Greenhow, volunteered to spy for the cause. Thus General Beauregard was prepared for the Union advance and had erected defenses near a railroad crossing called Manassas Junction. There, across Bull Run Creek, his 20,000 rebels (later augmented by reinforcements) faced the 37,000 Yankees under the command of the thoroughly mediocre General Irvin McDowell.

The battle began well for the North, as McDowell managed to push the rebels out of their positions. But then the Southern forces rallied when they beheld a Virginia brigade led by General Thomas J. Jackson. Like a "stone wall" the brigade held its ground, and thereafter, Thomas Jackson was best known by the name his soldiers gave him: Stonewall. The entire Confederate force now rallied and, ultimately, broke through the Union lines. Suddenly, panicked Northern troops retreated all the way to Washington. The First Battle of Bull Run stunned the capital—which trembled in anticipation of a Confederate invasion that never came—and it stunned Union loyalists all across the nation. The picnickers ran for their lives. It would be a long, hard war.

Real Life

Rose O'Neal Greenhow was born in Port Tobacco, Maryland, in 1817, and moved to Washington, D.C., where, from early womanhood, she cast a powerful spell on men. She married a State Department official, through whom she met a circle of highly influential Washingtonians, including James Buchanan. Widowed in 1854, Greenhow became particularly intimate with the bachelor president. Although this relationship was probably platonic, Greenhow had many others that were anything but. Among her "gentleman callers" was a host of military and government officials, perhaps including a U.S. Senator.

Greenhow was a highly intelligent woman who had nursed John C. Calhoun through his final illness when he was a resident at her aunt's fashionable Capitol Hill boardinghouse. She imbibed Calhoun's states' rights theories and became a passionate partisan of the South. When the Civil War broke out, Greenhow was recruited by Confederate spy master Thomas Jordan to obtain Union military secrets. Using her many charms, she procured information that proved highly valuable to the Confederacy at First Bull Run.

Arrested on August 23, 1861, by Alan J. Pinkerton, the man who virtually invented the profession of private detective, Greenhow was later paroled to the South, and on August 5, 1863, sailed to Europe on a mission to revive French and British support for the Confederate cause. There she met Napoleon III and Queen Victoria, and she published a best-selling memoir.

Rose O'Neal Greenhow drowned in 1864 when the blockade-runner on which she was returning from abroad ran aground off Wilmington, North Carolina.

Seven Days

Justifiably dismayed by McDowell's performance at Bull Run, President Lincoln called General George B. McClellan to command the main Union force. Jefferson Davis combined Beauregard's troops with those of General Joseph E. Johnston, who was given senior command of the Confederate forces in Virginia. Now the major action centered in Virginia as McClellan set about building a large army with which to invade Richmond, which became the Confederate capital in May 1861.

Despite the triumph at First Bull Run, the outlook seemed grim for the Confederates. Richmond could not withstand a massive assault. Yet McClellan, a popular commander who succeeded in transforming the Union army from an undisciplined rabble into a cohesive body of credible soldiers, suffered from a Hamlet-like tendency to ponder and delay. Eventually exasperated, Lincoln would peg him with homely accuracy: McClellan has a "bad case of the slows," the president pronounced.

McClellan repeatedly delayed his assault on Richmond, finally losing the initiative, so that he had to settle into an arduous campaign on the Virginia peninsula. In that campaign's principal series of battles, called the Seven Days (June 26–July 2, 1862), more men were killed or wounded than in all the Civil War battles fought elsewhere during the first half of 1862, including another encounter that became a byword for slaughter, Shiloh (April 6–7, 1862). Shiloh pitted General Ulysses S. Grant's 42,000-man Union against a 40,000-man Confederate force under General Albert S. Johnston. Grant lost 13,000 men, and the Confederates lost more than 10,000 in a battle that resulted in strategic stalemate on the war's western front.

Back in Virginia, the Seven Days saw the placement of Robert E. Lee at the head of the South's major army, which he renamed the Army of Northern Virginia. Lee led his forces in a brilliant offensive against the always-cautious McClellan, launching daring attacks at Mechanicsville, Gaines Mill, Savage's Station, Frayser's Farm, and Malvern Hill. In fact, Lee lost twice as many men as his adversary, but he won a profound psychological victory. McClellan backed down the peninsula all the way to the James River.

Real Life

No military figure in American history is more universally admired than Robert E. Lee, who not only served the Confederate cause as a brilliant commander but, in defeat, became an enduring example of courage and dignity.

Lee was born on January 19, 1807, in Westmoreland County, Virginia, the son of Henry "Light Horse Harry" Lee, a fine cavalry officer during the American Revolution. Appointed to West Point in 1825, Robert E. Lee graduated at the top of

continues

continued

his class in 1829 and, two years later, married Mary Ann Randolph Custis, great-granddaughter of Martha Washington by her first marriage. Lee served as an engineering officer under General Winfield Scott during the Mexican War (1846–48) and, from 1852–1855, was superintendent of West Point. In 1859, Lee led the force that suppressed John Brown's raid on Harpers Ferry.

Robert E. Lee was anything but a Southern "fire-eater." He deplored the extremism—on both sides—that led to the Civil War. But Lee felt intense loyalty to Virginia, and when war came, he declined an offer to command the Union army, resigned his commission, and offered his services to Virginia.

Lee repeatedly took the offensive against the North—and repeatedly attained victory against superior forces, achieving his greatest triumph at Chancellorsville (May 1863). But as the South ran short of men and money, the tide turned in favor of the North. Falling back into Virginia, Lee continued to wage war brilliantly. Finally trapped at Appomattox Court House, he surrendered the Army of Northern Virginia on April 9, 1865, in what is considered the symbolic end of the Civil War.

After the war, Lee became president of Washington College (now Washington and Lee University) in Lexington, Virginia. He died on October 12, 1870, a universally admired figure.

Back to Bull Run

Appalled and heartbroken by McClellan's repeated failure to seize the initiative, Lincoln desperately cast about for a general to replace him. On July 11, Lincoln appointed Henry W. Halleck. It was not a good choice. Halleck dispatched a regrouped army into Virginia under John Pope, but Lee met him with more than half the Army of Northern Virginia. At Cedar Mountain on August 9, "Stonewall" Jackson drove Pope back toward Manassas Junction, then Lee sent the "Stonewall Brigade" to flank Pope and outmarch him to Manassas. After destroying the Union supply depot, Jackson took a position near the old Bull Run battlefield. Pope lumbered into position to attack Jackson on August 29, just as Lee sent a wing of his army, under James Longstreet, against Pope's left on August 30.

The action was devastating. Pope reeled back across the Potomac. At this point, the "invading" Union army had been effectively swept out of Virginia, and the Confederates went on the offensive. For the North, it was the low point of the war.

Perryville and Antietam

Lee was a keen student of Napoleon Bonaparte's strategy and tactics, the key to which was the principle of always acting from boldness. Thus Lee boldly conceived a double offensive: in the West, an invasion of Kentucky; in the East, an invasion of Maryland. Neither of these so-called "border states" had seceded, yet both were slave states, and capturing them would significantly expand the Confederacy. Moreover, if Louisville, Kentucky, fell to the Confederates, Indiana and Ohio would be open to invasion, and control of the Great Lakes might pass to the rebels. For the Union, the war could be lost.

But things didn't happen this way. Confederate general Braxton Bragg delayed, lost the initiative, and was defeated at Perryville, Kentucky, on October 8, 1862. In Maryland, Lee's invasion went well—until a copy of his orders detailing troop placement fell into the hands of George McClellan (restored to command of the Army of the Potomac after Halleck's disastrous performance at Second Bull Run). The Union general was able to mass 70,000 troops in front of Lee at Sharpsburg, Maryland, along Antietam Creek. On September 17, in the bloodiest day of fighting up to that time, McClellan drove Lee back to Virginia. Indeed, only the belated, last-minute arrival of a division under A.P. Hill saved Lee's forces from total annihilation.

Stats
Although Antietam was a Union victory, McClellan lost more troops than Lee: 12,000 troops versus 10,000.

Emancipation Proclaimed—More or Less

Antietam was not the turning point of the war, but it was nevertheless a momentous battle. It provided the platform from which Abraham Lincoln issued the so-called "preliminary" Emancipation Proclamation.

The fact is that Lincoln was no enthusiastic advocate of emancipation. To be sure, he personally hated slavery, but as president, he was sworn to uphold the Constitution, which clearly protected slavery in the slave states. More immediately, Lincoln feared that universally declaring the slaves free would propel the four slaveholding border states into the Confederate fold. For many Northerners, the moral basis of the Civil War *was* the issue of emancipation. But Lincoln moved cautiously.

In August 1861, Lincoln prevailed on Congress to declare slaves in the rebellious states "contraband" property. As such, slaves could be seized by the federal government, which could then refuse to return them. In March 1862, Congress passed a law *forbidding* army officers from returning fugitive slaves. In July 1862, Congress passed legislation freeing slaves confiscated from owners "engaged in rebellion." In addition, a militia act authorized the president to use freed slaves in the army. With these acts, Lincoln's government edged closer to emancipation.

Secretary of State William H. Seward warned that a proclamation of emancipation would ring hollow down the depressingly long corridor of Union defeats. It was not until Antietam, a Union victory—albeit a costly one—that Lincoln felt confident in issuing the preliminary proclamation on September 23, 1862. This document did not free the slaves, but rather, warned slave owners living in states "still in rebellion on January 1, 1863" that their slaves would be declared "forever free." When that deadline came and passed, Lincoln issued the "final" Emancipation Proclamation—which set free only those slaves in areas of the Confederacy that were not under the control of the Union army (areas under Union control were no longer, technically, in rebellion); slaves in the border states were not liberated.

Timid, even disappointing as the Emancipation Proclamation may seem from our perspective, it served to galvanize the North by explicitly and officially elevating the war to a higher moral plane: slavery was now the central issue of the great Civil War.

The Least You Need to Know

➤ The Confederacy attempted to negotiate independence from the Union before commencing hostilities by firing on Fort Sumter in Charleston harbor.

➤ Plagued by cautious or inept commanders, the Union Army performed poorly in the first months of the war.

➤ The Emancipation Proclamation was a fairly timid document, which reflected Lincoln's first priority: to preserve the Union, not necessarily to free the slaves.

Bloody Road to Appomattox and Beyond (1863–1876)

No face in American history is more familiar, better loved, or more terrible than that of Abraham Lincoln. Fortunately for us, famed Civil War photographer Mathew Brady was there to photograph it. In the 16th president's face, we see his character: the hard life of the backwoods, an infinite gentleness, an infinite sorrow. Lincoln's burden is unimaginable; he had a mission to save the Union, even if doing so cost more than half a million lives.

Through the long, terrible summer of 1862, the president despaired. Lincoln was no military man, but he had a sound and simple grasp of strategy, and he saw that Generals

Don Carlos Buell and George B. McClellan failed to press their gains toward decisive victories. Frustrated, Lincoln removed Buell from command of the Army of the Ohio and replaced him with William S. Rosecrans in late October 1862. The next month, he put Ambrose E. Burnside in McClellan's place as commander of the Army of the Potomac. Rosecrans scored a very costly victory at Murfreesboro, Tennessee (December 31, 1862–January 3, 1863), forcing Braxton Bragg out of Tennessee, but Burnside suffered a terrible defeat at Fredericksburg, Virginia. He tried to regain the initiative for the Union forces by renewing a drive on Richmond, but faltered at the Rappahannock River and was checked by Lee's army. On December 13, Burnside hurled a series of assaults against the Confederate trenches. He not only failed to penetrate the Confederate lines but lost more than 12,000 men in the process.

A month after Fredericksburg, Lincoln replaced Burnside with "Fighting Joe" Hooker, who led the Army of the Potomac at Chancellorsville (May 1–3, 1863) in the wilderness of northern Virginia, again aiming to take Richmond. Hooker was defeated—brilliantly—by Stonewall Jackson (who, however, lost his life in the battle, accidentally shot by one of his own troops). Lincoln replaced Hooker with George Gordon Meade on June 29, 1863—just two days before Union and Confederate forces would clash at an obscure Pennsylvania hamlet called Gettysburg.

Four Score and Seven

Anxious to move the war into Union territory, Lee invaded Pennsylvania with an army of about 75,000. He did not aim to do battle with the forces of the North in the vicinity of Gettysburg, a village distinguished only in that it was positioned at important crossroads, but the fact is that Lieutenant General A.P. Hill's corps of Confederates needed shoes. Short of manufacturing capability, the South always had a difficult time keeping its soldiers shod. On June 30, while marching toward Gettysburg in search of shoes, Hill was engaged by cavalry under Union Brigadier General John Buford. The battle began in earnest on the next day, July 1.

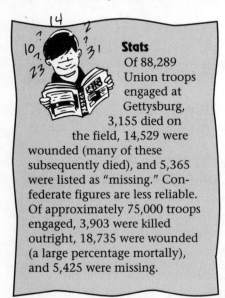

Stats
Of 88,289 Union troops engaged at Gettysburg, 3,155 died on the field, 14,529 were wounded (many of these subsequently died), and 5,365 were listed as "missing." Confederate figures are less reliable. Of approximately 75,000 troops engaged, 3,903 were killed outright, 18,735 were wounded (a large percentage mortally), and 5,425 were missing.

The encounter did not go well for the Union. Hill's troops killed Major General John F. Reynolds, commander of the Union I Corps, almost as soon as he came onto the field. Despite shock and confusion, his troops held their ground until reinforcements arrived. But in the afternoon, Hill and Lieutenant General R.S. Ewell joined forces in an attack that routed the Federals through the town of

Gettysburg. The forces regrouped and rallied on Cemetery Ridge, where they were joined by fresh troops from the south and east. The Confederates arrayed their forces in an encircling position, encompassing Seminary Ridge, parallel to Cemetery Ridge.

Thus the field was set for the second day. Robert E. Lee attacked on July 2 but was unable to achieve a double envelopment of the Union forces—though he did inflict heavy casualties. On July 3, still holding the initiative, Lee committed what was for him a rare tactical error. Believing that a victory here and now, at Gettysburg, in Northern territory, might turn the war decisively in favor of the Confederacy, he ordered a direct attack— across open country—on the Union's center.

Voice from the Past

On November 19, 1863, President Abraham Lincoln traveled to Gettysburg to dedicate a national cemetery on the battlefield. Some did not find his brief speech adequate to the solemn occasion. Others were moved by its straightforward eloquence as a definition of what was at stake in the Civil War. Today the speech is universally regarded as one the greatest public utterances in history:

"Fourscore and seven years ago our fathers brought forth on this continent a new nation, conceived in liberty and dedicated to the proposition that all men are created equal. Now we are engaged in a great civil war, testing whether that nation or any nation so conceived and so dedicated can long endure. We are met on a great battlefield of that war. We have come to dedicate a portion of that field as a final resting-place for those who here gave their lives that that nation might live. It is altogether fitting and proper that we should do this. But in a larger sense, we cannot dedicate, we cannot consecrate, we cannot hallow this ground. The brave men, living and dead who struggled here have consecrated it far above our poor power to add or detract. The world will little note nor long remember what we say here, but it can never forget what they did here. It is for us the living rather to be dedicated here to the unfinished work which they who fought here have thus far so nobly advanced. It is rather for us to be here dedicated to the great task remaining before us—that from these honored dead we take increased devotion to that cause for which they gave the last full measure of devotion—that we here highly resolve that these dead shall not have died in vain, that this nation under God shall have a new birth of freedom, and that government of the people, by the people, for the people shall not perish from the earth."

Fifteen thousand Confederate troops advanced against the Union position on Cemetery Ridge. Exploiting the advantages of high ground, the Union pounded the advancing rebels with heavy artillery and musket fire. Major General George Pickett's division pressed the attack up to the Ridge. The division was decimated: two brigadiers fell, the third was severely wounded, and all 15 of Pickett's regimental commanders were killed or wounded. Briefly, 150 men from the division, led by Brigadier General Lewis Armistead (who perished in the effort), raised the Confederate banner above Cemetery Ridge—only to be cut down or captured. In the end, "Pickett's Charge," perhaps the single most famous military action in American history, resulted in the death or wounding of 10,000 of the 15,000 men in Pickett's division.

Watching the survivors return from the failed assault that third awful day, Lee said to a subordinate: "It is all my fault." Hoping, in effect, to win the war at Gettysburg, Lee had suffered a terrible defeat. Although the losses on both sides were staggering, they were hardest on the Confederates. One very simple fact was at the base of this very complex war: The North, with more men as well as more hardware than the South, could lose more of both and still go on fighting. Lee was right. The Battle of Gettysburg *was* a turning point—but it did not turn the war in his favor. From here to the end, despite more Union defeats to come, it became increasingly clear that the North would ultimately prevail.

Vicksburg and Chattanooga

Northern attention focused most sharply on Gettysburg as the battle that foiled the Confederate invasion of the North. However, while that battle was being fought, Union forces under General Ulysses S. Grant were bringing to a conclusion a long and frustrating campaign against Vicksburg, Mississippi, the Confederacy's seemingly impregnable stronghold on the Mississippi River. The prize here was not just a fortress, but control of the great river. Once the South lost the Mississippi, the Confederacy was split in two, the western states unable to communicate with the East or to supply reinforcements to it. Grant had campaigned—in vain—against Vicksburg during the fall and winter of 1862–63, finally taking it on July 4, 1863.

Grant next turned his attention to Chattanooga, which occupied a critical position in a bend of the great Tennessee River. Union forces under William S. Rosecrans had ousted Braxton Bragg from Chattanooga in early September 1863, but, reinforced, Bragg returned to engage Rosecrans at the Battle of Chickamauga on September 19–20. Bragg fielded 66,000 men against Rosecrans's 58,000. By the second day of this bloody struggle along Chickamauga Creek in northwestern Georgia, the Confederates had driven much of the Union army from the field in disarray.

Complete disaster was averted by General George H. Thomas, in command of the Union left flank. Moreover, Bragg failed to press his advantage, laying incomplete siege around Chattanooga while also detaching troops to attack Knoxville. By failing to act with greater focus, Bragg allowed Grant sufficient time to arrive, on October 23, and reinforce the Army of the Cumberland (now under Thomas's command). Sixty thousand Union troops now faced Bragg's reduced forces—about 40,000 men—in two battles set in the rugged terrain overlooking Chattanooga. The Battle of Lookout Mountain (November 24) was called the "Battle Above the Clouds," because it was fought at an elevation of 1,100 feet above the Tennessee River—and above a dense line of fog. The Battle of Missionary Ridge followed (November 25). In these two engagements, Thomas and Grant decisively defeated Bragg, with the result that Tennessee and the Tennessee River fell into Union hands.

Back to Richmond

To many Americans, George Meade was the hero of Gettysburg—the great turning-point battle of the war. However, President Lincoln observed that Meade, like so many of his other generals, failed to capitalize on victory. In contrast, Ulysses S. Grant had demonstrated a willingness to fight and then fight some more. Thus, with the war entering its fourth year, Lincoln finally found his general. In March 1864, the president named Grant general in chief of all the Union armies. Grant's strategy was simple: exploit the North's superiority in industrial strength and in population. This meant that Grant and his subordinate commanders could not afford to be fearful of sacrificing men and material. Grant was so single-minded in pursuing this strategy that some men within his own ranks cursed him as "The Butcher."

Grant put the Union's fiercest warrior, William Tecumseh Sherman, in command of the so-called western armies (which actually fought in the middle South). Meade retained command of the Army of the Potomac—albeit under Grant's watchful eye. Using these two principal forces, he relentlessly kept pressure on the South's Army of Tennessee and the Army of Northern Virginia.

The Wilderness Campaign (May–June 1864) was the first test of the strategy of attrition. Grant directed Meade, leading a force of 100,000, to attack 70,000 men of Lee's Army of Northern Virginia in the tangled woodlands just 50 miles northwest of Richmond. The Battle of the Wilderness (May 5–6) cost some 18,000 Union lives. Undaunted, "The Butcher" then ordered Meade southeast to Spotsylvania Court House, where more than 14,000 Union soldiers were killed between May 8 and 18. Still Grant pushed, attacking Lee's right at Cold Harbor, just north of Richmond. Thirteen thousand Union troops fell between June 3 and June 12.

Following Cold Harbor, Grant marched south of the James River and began the Petersburg Campaign, laying siege to this important rail center just south of Richmond. The siege consumed nearly a year, from June 1864 to April 1865, and it succeeded in hemming in Lee, who was put on the defensive, trying to stave off the assault on Richmond.

Word for the Day
A *war of attrition* is waged by a numerically stronger force against one that is numerically weaker. The assumption is that, by the application of constant stress, the weaker force will crumble, while the stronger force, despite losses, will endure. This theory was the foundation of Grant's strategy.

In order to restore maneuverability to his army, Lee attempted to draw off some of Grant's strength by detaching Jubal Early, with Stonewall Jackson's old corps, in an assault against Washington in mid-June. Although the capital was briefly bombarded, Union General Philip Sheridan pursued Early into the Shenandoah Valley and defeated him at Cedar Creek on October 19.

Just three weeks later, Lincoln was elected to a second term by a comfortable margin. Clearly, the North was prepared to continue the fight, and the defenders of Petersburg, starving, sick, and exhausted, at last broke in March 1865. On April 2, Lee evacuated Richmond. Jefferson Davis and the entire Confederate government fled the Southern capital.

The March to the Sea

While Grant concentrated on taking Richmond, William Tecumseh Sherman, after leaving Chattanooga in early May 1864, invaded Georgia with 100,000 men. Sherman was opposed by Joseph P. Johnston's army of 60,000, which repeatedly fell back during the onslaught—although Johnston scored a victory at Kennesaw Mountain on June 27. By early July, Johnston had assumed a position defending the key rail center of Atlanta. However, President Jefferson Davis, enraged by Johnston's many retreats, brashly replaced him with General John B. Hood. A heroic but utterly reckless commander, Hood attacked Sherman and lost. By September, Hood abandoned Atlanta, and the Northern army's occupation of this major city greatly boosted Union morale.

After the fall of Atlanta, Hood played a desperate gambit by invading Tennessee, hoping that Sherman would pursue him. But Sherman had his own strategy. Later generations would call it "total war"—war waged against not only an enemy army, but against "enemy" civilians. Instead of pursuing Hood himself, Sherman detached General George H. Thomas to do that. With the main force of his army, Sherman then marched from Atlanta to the Atlantic coast. The "March to the Sea" burned a broad, bitter swath of destruction all the way to Savannah.

In the meantime, General Hood did win a battle at Franklin, Tennessee, on November 30, but General Thomas triumphed at Nashville on December 15–16, 1864, sending the ragged remnants of Hood's army back toward Georgia. Confederate General Joseph P. Johnston, now in command of the greatly reduced Army of Tennessee, engaged Sherman several times as the Union army stormed through the Carolinas in the spring of 1865. On April 13, 1865, Sherman occupied Raleigh, North Carolina, and on April 26 at Durham Station, Johnston formally surrendered his army.

The Country Courthouse

Although sporadic fighting would continue west of the Mississippi until the end of May, the principal land campaign of the Civil War ended at Durham Station on April 26. However, an earlier event is traditionally considered the symbolic end of the Civil War. Following the collapse of Petersburg and the evacuation of Richmond, Robert E. Lee's Army of Northern Virginia desperately foraged for food and arrived at Appomattox Court House, about 25 miles east of Lynchburg, Virginia. Lee's forces, which now stood at perhaps 9,000 effective troops, were surrounded by the Army of the Potomac under General George Meade.

After heavy skirmishing on the morning of April 9, Lee concluded that his was a lost cause. He met Ulysses S. Grant, who pressed him to surrender all the Confederate armies, which were nominally under his command. Lee refused to do that, but his surrender of the Army of Northern Virginia, over which he had direct command, signaled the inevitable end of the war.

Voice from the Past

Shortly before he died, Grant described in his *Personal Memoirs* the scene in the McLean house, at Appomattox, where Lee surrendered to him:

"What General Lee's feelings were I do not know. As he was a man of much dignity, with an impassible face...his feelings...were entirely concealed from my observation; but my own feelings...were sad and depressed. I felt like anything rather than rejoicing at the downfall of a foe who had fought so long and valiantly and had suffered so much...

General Lee was dressed in a full uniform which was entirely new, and was wearing a sword of considerable value...In my rough traveling suit...I must have contrasted very strangely with a man so handsomely dressed, six feet high and of faultless form...

We soon fell into a conversation about old army times...Our conversation grew so pleasant that I almost forgot the object of our meeting."

With Malice Toward Some

Confident of ultimate victory, President Lincoln delivered a gentle, healing message in his second inaugural address on March 4, 1865, calling for a consummation of the war with "malice toward none" and "charity for all" in an effort to "bind up the nation's wounds." Weary, careworn beyond imagining, Lincoln nevertheless looked forward to the end of the war. On the evening of Good Friday, April 14, 1865, he and his wife, Mary Todd, sought a few hours' diversion in a popular comedy called *Our American Cousin*. The play was being presented at Ford's Theatre, a short distance from the White House.

An Evening at Ford's Theatre

John Wilkes Booth was a popular young scion of America's foremost theatrical family. While he had no part in *Our American Cousin*, Booth was desperate to play a role in the drama of the great Civil War, which was now rushing to conclusion. Back in 1864, the Maryland-born racist had concocted a plot to kidnap Lincoln and ransom him in exchange for Confederate prisoners of war. That plan came to nothing, and now, with surrender in the air, there was no point in simply kidnapping Lincoln. Booth wanted raw vengeance. He conspired with a small band of followers, George A. Atzerodt, David Herold, and a former Confederate soldier called Lewis Paine (real name Louis Thornton Powell). They plotted to murder Lincoln and also kill Vice President Andrew Johnson and Secretary of State William H. Seward.

On April 14, Atzerodt backed out of his assignment to kill Johnson. In the meantime, Herold held Paine's horse while Paine broke into Seward's residence. He stabbed and clubbed Seward, an aged man who was recuperating from injuries suffered in a carriage accident. It was a bloody scene: Seward, his son Augustus, and his daughter Fanny were all injured, as were a State Department messenger and a male nurse. Yet none of them died.

Booth was more efficient. Booth simply walked into the theater, entered the president's box, raised his derringer, and pointed it between Abraham Lincoln's left ear and spine. He squeezed off a single shot. Booth leaped from the box onto the stage, shouting "Sic semper tyrannis!"—Thus ever to tyrants. But Booth's right spur had caught on the Treasury Regiment banner festooning the box, and he landed, full force, on his left foot, which broke just above the instep. Booth limped across the stage and made a clean getaway into Maryland and then Virginia. He was not found until April 26, when he was cornered in a barn near Fredericksburg. Union soldiers set fire to the barn, then, seeing the actor's form silhouetted by the flames, one of the soldiers (a sergeant named Boston Corbett claimed credit) fired a shot that fatally wounded Booth.

Reconstruction Abuses

The mortally wounded president had been carried to a house across the street from the theater. There Lincoln died at 7:22 the next morning. With him died any hope of "malice toward none" and "charity for all." Booth murdered Lincoln to avenge the South. In fact, the South became the most thoroughly brutalized victim of the assassination.

As the war was winding down, President Lincoln had formulated plans to set up loyal governments in the Southern states as quickly as possible. New governments were, in fact, formed in Louisiana, Tennessee, and Arkansas, but Congress refused to recognize them. Radical Republicans, wishing to delay the restoration in part to keep Democrats out of Washington, passed the Wade-Davis Reconstruction Bill. This bill would have delayed the process of readmission to the Union pending the signature of loyalty oaths. Lincoln vetoed the measure.

After Lincoln was assassinated, his vice president, Andrew Johnson, modified the Wade-Davis plan by issuing amnesty to anyone who took an oath to be loyal to the Union in the future. Johnson required that the states ratify the 13th Amendment (which freed the slaves), abolish slavery in their own state constitutions, repudiate debts incurred while in rebellion, and declare secession null and void. By the end of 1865, all of the secessionist states, except for Texas, had complied.

Congress, however, was not satisfied with Johnson's program, which, Congress feared, restored power to the very individuals who had brought rebellion. Moreover, the readmitted states persisted in keeping former slaves in subservience. To correct this problem, Congress passed in 1866 the Freedman's Bureau Act and the Civil Rights Act, both intended to ensure African-American equality before the law. When Johnson vetoed these acts, Republicans responded by refusing to recognize the legitimacy of the Southern states and overrode the veto.

Republicans also introduced the 14th Amendment, declaring African-Americans to be citizens and prohibiting states from discriminating against any class of citizen. When the Southern state governments created under Johnson's plan refused to ratify the 14th Amendment, Congress passed a series of Reconstruction Acts in 1867, effectively placing the South under military occupation. African-Americans were quickly enfranchised, and Congress forced acceptance of the 14th Amendment by refusing to recognize new state governments until those governments had ratified it. Recognized Confederate leaders were specifically barred from participating in the creation of the new governments.

Articles of Impeachment

In defiance of Congress, Johnson deliberately interfered with the enforcement of the reconstruction laws. When, at last, in 1868, Johnson dismissed Secretary of War Edwin M. Stanton in a bid to gain complete control of the army, House Republicans charged a violation of the Tenure of Office Act. Passed in 1867, this act barred a president from removing, without the Senate's approval, any officeholder appointed with the Senate's consent. The House impeached Johnson, but after a trial spanning March through May 1868, the Senate acquitted him by a single vote.

His Fraudulency

With Andrew Johnson neutralized, the radical Republicans visited a harsh reconstruction program on the South. African-Americans were given equal rights, state-supported free public school systems were established, labor laws were made fairer to employees, and tax laws were more generally equitable; however, radical reconstruction also exacted a heavy tax burden and led to widespread, ruinous corruption. In many places, uneducated former slaves were thrust into high-level government positions for which they were inadequately prepared. In response, whites set up shadow governments and established the Ku Klux Klan and other vigilante-type groups.

Radical reconstruction was born of mixed motives—a desire to bring equality to African-Americans and to establish governments loyal to the Union, but also to keep Democrats out of Congress and punish the South. These efforts created much bitterness, crippled the Southern economy for generations, and ultimately deepened the gulf of understanding separating the races.

During the early 1870s, white resistance to reconstruction often turned violent. In this tumultuous atmosphere, the presidential election of 1876 resulted in a majority of popular votes going to Democrat Samuel J. Tilden. However, the Republicans reversed the *electoral* vote tally in the three Southern states they still controlled under Reconstruction legislation. The Republicans effectively stole the election from Tilden and gave it to Republican Rutherford B. Hayes. After months of wrangling, both sides agreed to send the votes to a special commission. It ruled Hayes the winner—though only after he secretly agreed to stop using federal troops to enforce Reconstruction. In effect, this agreement ended Reconstruction, in its positive as well as negative aspects. Dubbed "Your Fraudulency," Hayes served a single term as best he could but remained one of the nation's least popular presidents.

The Least You Need to Know

➤ Victory in the Civil War was the result of numbers: The North had more men, money, and manufacturing capacity than the South.

➤ Lincoln's assassination deprived the South—as well as the North—of a wise and compassionate leader. Without Lincoln, the process of reconstruction was bitter, divisive, and deeply damaging to the nation.

Part 5
The House Rebuilt

The years following the Civil War saw the full-scale settlement of the American West, and increased pressure on the Indians, whose tribes were broadcast across the plains and mountains. War between settlers and Native Americans, more or less chronic since the days of Columbus, now became acute, and the U.S. Army was called upon to fight three decades of "Indian Wars." Against this background, the West produced real-life legends: cattle barons, cowboys, outlaws, and fortune seekers as well as fortune makers. The late 19th century was an era marked by technological triumphs, by the creation of financial empires, and by the corruption of crooked politics. Good and bad, all seemed bigger than life as the century drew to a close, as we see in the chapters that follow.

Chapter 21

Sea to Shining Sea (1862–1878)

In This Chapter

➤ The homesteaders and sodbusters

➤ Expansion of overland mail and freight operations

➤ The transcontinental railroad

Armies, money, and the will to continue the fight won the Civil War and restored the Union. There was something else as well. Call it the "American Dream."

To some modern ears, perhaps this phrase rings hollow. But in the mid-19th century, the American Dream had a foundation as solid as it was vast. Even amid the bitter carnage of a war that tore them apart, Americans looked west. There, it seemed, was refuge from the war. There was a place for new beginnings. There was the future. And what is the future, if it is not a dream?

Homesteaders

At least as early as the 1830s, various groups clamored for free distribution of the vast public lands of the West. In 1848, the Free-Soil party was organized to oppose the extension of slavery into the territories newly acquired as a result of the Mexican War. The party failed to carry a single state in the presidential election that year, but it did give a unified voice. The party's idea of regulating federal distribution of public lands was one means of stopping the spread of slavery into the territories.

When the Republican Party was founded in 1854, most of the "Free-Soilers" abandoned their dead-end party and joined the new one, which adopted distribution of federal lands as a plank of its 1860 platform. This issue fanned the flames of Southern secession; the slave states were always opposed to any policy that would bring more free states into the Union. But when the Civil War broke out, Southern opposition became a moot point.

On May 20, 1862, President Lincoln signed into law the Homestead Act, which granted 160 acres of public land in the West as a homestead to "any person who is the head of a family, or who has arrived at the age of 21 years, and is a citizen of the United States, or who shall have filed his declaration of intention to become such."

This was no *free* gift. Although the homesteader had only to pay a modest filing fee, he did have to live on the land for five years and make certain improvements—the most important of which was the construction of a dwelling. After these conditions were satisfied, the homesteader received clear title to the land. Alternatively, a homesteader could "preempt" the land after only six months' residence by purchasing it at the rate of $1.25 per acre. If the settler could scrape together $50—a very substantial sum in the 1860s and beyond the means of many homesteaders—he could augment his original grant with an additional 40 acres, up to a maximum of 160.

Stats

By the end of the 19th century, some 600,000 farmers had received clear title under the Homestead Act to approximately 80 million acres of formerly public land.

The Homestead Act was a bold experiment in public policy and was shaped by years of hard experience with the distribution of unsettled land. Traditionally, such territories had drawn unscrupulous speculators, who figured out ways to come into control of vast acreages and make quick fortunes. The new law sought to avoid such abuses and aspired to a high degree of democracy. For the most part, it succeeded, although there were plenty of sharpers eager to burrow through legal loopholes. The greatest culprits in fraud were big railroads and big mining companies seeking large tracts of land at the public expense.

Despite the abuses, the Homestead Act opened the West to hundreds of thousands. The new settlers were different from the first waves of westerners. The solitary trapper and mountain man, the bachelor soldier, the grizzled prospector now made way for the farmer and the family, and with the family came stable, permanent communities.

The Sod Frontier

Timber was a scarce commodity on the treeless plains, but sod was abundant. The very soil that posed such a formidable obstacle to farming—at least until the manufacture of John Deere's "Grand Detour Plow"—was a durable, dense, and (quite literally) dirt-cheap building material.

The work of the sod frontier was back breaking. Even with the Deere plow, "busting" the sod into viable crop rows was no easy task. For the many homesteaders who had the misfortune to stake claims at a distance from creeks and streams, there was the added burden of digging a well. Few sodbusters could afford to hire a drilling rig, so this work, like most of the work on the prairie farm, had to be done by hand. With nothing more than pick and spade, homesteaders dug to depths up to 300 feet, where they were exposed to the dangers of cave-in as well as asphyxiation from subterranean gases such as methane and carbon monoxide. Not only that, but breaking your back and risking your life did not guarantee you'd find water. If, by the time you hit bedrock or shale, you came up dry, you had to start digging somewhere else.

> **Word for the Day**
> Plains homesteaders who built sod houses were called *sodbusters*. The houses themselves were often referred to as *soddies*.

Water in a well goes nowhere unless you take it there. As the prairie earth yielded an abundance of natural building material, so the winds that fiercely scoured the prairie afforded a natural source of energy. In 1854, a Connecticut tool-shop tinkerer named David Halladay invented a windmill with a vane that allowed it to pivot into the wind; moreover, the centrifugal force of the turning blades adjusted the pitch of the mill blades so that the gusty, often violent winds would not tear them apart. A crankshaft transformed the rotary motion of the mill into the up-and-down action needed to operate a pump. Using wind power, hundreds of gallons of water could be moved each day to irrigate crops and quench the thirst of livestock.

The sodbusters turned stubborn soil and fierce winds into assets. They also found strength in another, less tangible, but no less harsh, reality of prairie life. Limitless spaces and driving winds were a trial for the spirit. The emotional demands of the wide-open spaces served to reinforce the solidarity of the family as a bulwark against loneliness, despair, and danger. Beyond the family, these uncompromising conditions helped bond neighbor with distant neighbor, gradually forging communities where there had been none before. Neighbors were a new phenomenon in the West; for the trapper, the prospector, and the soldier had no need for community.

Ruts and Rails

Transportation and westward movement have always been a chicken-and-egg proposition in this country. Farmers and others clamored for better and cheaper transportation, while freight carriers did what they could to promote a level of settlement that would make service to the outlying regions profitable. The earliest western transportation was river-borne, with shallow-draft flatboats abounding on the Missouri and its tributaries. Then, spurred by the discovery of gold in California, stagecoach and freight entrepreneurs took the plunge, investing in coaches, livestock, and road improvements.

By the 1850s, Adams Express Company and Wells, Fargo & Company were engaged in cutthroat competition for California freighting. The success of California overland operations prompted others to establish routes elsewhere in the West, often with government subsidy in the form of postal contracts. By 1854, William H. Russell and William B. Waddell merged with their principal competitor, Alexander Majors, to create a freighting empire that endured until the Civil War.

Russell and Waddell were financial men, and Majors was the practical manager. Majors, more than any other single individual, developed western freighting to a peak of efficiency. His company's wagons were designed and built to his exacting specifications, using carefully seasoned wood to make wagon boxes that flared outward to prevent as much as 5,000 pounds of cargo from shifting. The wagons resembled ships, their forward ends curved like prows, their aft ends squared off to facilitate loading and unloading. Majors had a genius for organizing men and material. He divided his forces into *outfits* of 26 wagons under the absolute command of a wagon master and an assistant. Each wagon was pulled by a team of 12 oxen driven by a *bullwhacker* at an average rate of 15 miles a day. Each outfit also included a *herder*, who drove 40 to 50 oxen for use as replacements, and a *night herder*, who tended the animals at night. Each day's routine was strictly regulated, including an absolute requirement to "observe the Sabbath."

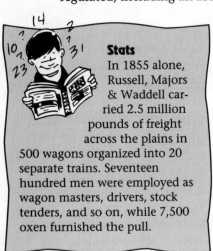

Stats
In 1855 alone, Russell, Majors & Waddell carried 2.5 million pounds of freight across the plains in 500 wagons organized into 20 separate trains. Seventeen hundred men were employed as wagon masters, drivers, stock tenders, and so on, while 7,500 oxen furnished the pull.

The other giants of freighting in the West included George Chorpenning, John Butterfield, John M. Hockaday, and Ben Holladay (who was so successful that he was dubbed the "Napoleon of the Plains"). Yet, if the opportunity for profit was great, the overhead—in livestock, personnel, and maintenance of routes—was staggering. Moreover, stage and freight lines were preyed upon by robbers (popularly called *road agents*), including the likes of Henry Plummer, Black Bart, the James Gang, and many others who entered into western legend and lore. Sooner or later, most overland entrepreneurs went belly up. Those who survived were either wiped out by the advancing railroads or learned to coordinate their service with the new rail lines, serving the widely dispersed stations as relatively short *feeder routes*.

Main Event

In 1857, Russell, Majors & Waddell secured a big government contract to supply the army in what threatened to become a war against rebellious Mormons in Utah. The firm paid top dollar to buy additional wagons and hire additional crews, but the operation became the target of Mormon guerrilla attacks, a devastating winter, and ultimately, federal default on contracts. Facing financial collapse, William H. Russell saw his company's salvation in making a rapid transition from slow freighting to express mail service.

To make a dramatic demonstration of the speed and efficiency of his company, Russell invented what he called the Pony Express. He promised to deliver mail from St. Joseph, Missouri, to Sacramento, California—a distance just 44 miles shy of an even 2,000—in 10 days.

The unit would have no passengers and no coaches. Instead, the Express would achieve speed by a relay of ponies and riders stretched across the continent.

Russell had purchased 500 semiwild *outlaw* horses and had 80 riders continuously en route, 40 westbound, 40 east, who had answered his ads calling for "daring young men, preferably orphans."

Financially, the Pony Express was a failure, charging a staggering $5 per half ounce (soon lowered to $2) of mail that actually cost the company an even more staggering $16 to deliver. Within 19 months, the Pony Express was out of business, rendered obsolete by the completion of transcontinental telegraph lines. But in 650,000 miles of travel, the company lost only one consignment—and managed to capture the nation's imagination.

Iron Road

After the success of the Erie Canal, completed in 1825 and linking New York City with the Great Lakes, other eastern seaport cities rushed to build systems of canals. Baltimore was an exception and chose to invest not in a canal, but in a brand new technology: the railroad. Begun in 1828, the Baltimore and Ohio Railroad reached the Ohio River, principal artery to the West, by 1852. At about this time, railroads were also being built in the Midwest. The Chicago and Rock Island (*The Rock Island Line*) became the first rail route to the Mississippi River in 1854. By 1856, the route bridged the river and penetrated the fertile farmlands of Iowa. Other midwestern roads followed.

Practically from the start of all this rail activity, in 1832, a Dr. Hartwell Carver published articles in the *New York Courier & Enquirer* proposing a transcontinental railroad to be built on eight million acres of government land from Lake Michigan to Oregon (then the only coastal territory to which the United States had any claim). Carver's scheme came to nothing, and 10 years later, Asa Whitney, a New Yorker engaged in the China trade, proposed to Congress that the United States sell him nearly 80 million acres, from Lake Michigan to the Columbia River, at 16 cents per acre. Whitney planned to sell parcels of the land to settlers and farmers, using the proceeds to push a railroad farther and farther West in pay-as-you-go fashion.

Whitney butted up against Missouri Senator Thomas Hart Benton, who wanted a transcontinental railroad with an eastern terminus at St. Louis rather than Chicago, as Whitney proposed. Benton got Whitney's plan permanently tabled and, in 1848, persuaded Congress to fund a railroad survey led by his son-in-law, John C. Frémont. The recklessly conducted survey resulted in the deaths of ten of Frémont's party, frozen or starved in a Rocky Mountain blizzard, and ultimately proved inconclusive.

While arguments over routes raged, the means of financing a transcontinental railroad were being hammered out. Railroad lobbyists proposed a system of government land grants alternating checkerboard fashion north and south of the proposed right-of-way. The railroads would sell their land to finance construction, and the presence of the railroad would greatly increase the value not only of the purchasers' land, but of the alternate sections retained by the government. A series of such grants was immediately apportioned to a number of western rail lines.

In 1853, Congress authorized Secretary of War Jefferson Davis to conduct detailed surveys of potential transcontinental rail routes. The result of the hasty surveys was, again, inconclusive (though they added significantly to general knowledge of the West). It soon became apparent that Davis—the Mississippian who would become president of the Confederacy with the outbreak of civil war—stacked the deck in favor of a southerly route.

The wrangling might have gone on forever had it not been for one remarkable man. Theodore Dehone Judah (1826–63), son of an Episcopal clergyman in Bridgeport, Connecticut, was a civil engineer with a genius for building railroads. In 1854, Colonel Charles Wilson, president of California's Sacramento Valley Railroad, commissioned Judah to survey a right-of-way from Sacramento to the gold-mining town of Folsom. Judah reported to Wilson that this stretch of track could serve as something far more significant than a link to Folsom. The track was ideally suited to be the Pacific end of a transcontinental railroad. Wilson and other backers were excited, but then the gold petered out at Folsom, and the rail line went no farther.

Judah did not stop. He lobbied Washington, even as he continued searching for a viable pass across the Sierra Mountains. A frontier pharmacist, Daniel "Doc" Strong, pointed out a likely route, and right then and there, he and Judah quickly concluded an agreement to incorporate a Pacific railroad association. All that was lacking now was money. Lots of money. Judah did not stop. He found seven backers, including four whose fortunes were destined to be made by the railroad: Collis P. Huntington and Mark Hopkins, partners in a hardware store; Leland Stanford, wholesale grocer; and Charles Crocker, dry goods merchant. Returning to Washington, D.C., Judah successfully lobbied for passage of the Pacific Railway Act of 1862, authorizing the Central Pacific and the Union Pacific railroads to begin construction of a transcontinental railroad. The Central Pacific would build from the West Coast eastward, and the Union Pacific would build westward from Omaha, Nebraska.

With the North and South torn apart by war, President Lincoln and Congress were anxious to bind the nation together East and West. The Railway Act granted huge tracts of land to the railroad, along with massive construction loans, and, at the behest of Abraham Lincoln, multimillionaire congressman Oakes Ames and his brother Oliver created a corporation to build the railroad and another corporation to finance construction. The latter was named Credit Mobilier, after the company that had successfully financed the French railway system 10 years earlier. The Ames brothers made investors an offer they couldn't refuse: Credit Mobilier, run by the directors (principal investors) of the Union Pacific, was paid by the Union Pacific to build the Union Pacific. The directors made a profit on the railroad as well as on the cost of building it. The scheme was an open door to fraud, and construction bills were routinely padded.

In the end, scandal and greed could take nothing away from the heroism and wonder of what it meant actually to build a transcontinental railroad—especially in an age when earth was moved and iron rails laid not by machines, but by human muscle.

Under the leadership of Grenville Mellon Dodge and another ex-army general, John Stephen Casement, the Union Pacific began laying prodigious lengths of track—266 miles in 1866 alone. The tracks were set into place mostly by unskilled Irish immigrants, who received, in addition to their pay, room and board. On the Central Pacific, the bulk of the work force was Chinese, who were paid about the same rate but had to furnish their own tent accommodations and their own food.

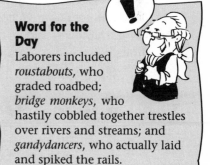

Word for the Day
Laborers included *roustabouts*, who graded roadbed; *bridge monkeys*, who hastily cobbled together trestles over rivers and streams; and *gandydancers*, who actually laid and spiked the rails.

Laying and spiking 500-pound rail sections was difficult enough, but these men—some 25,000 in all— faced other perils as well. They encountered harsh weather on the prairies and in the mountains, including summer floods, winter blizzards, and the ever-present danger of avalanche; attack from Sioux and Cheyenne, as the rails penetrated Indian hunting grounds in western Nebraska and southeastern Wyoming; and unceasing pressure from bosses, who had little love for Irish immigrants and even less for Chinese "coolies."

Taskmasters drove the laborers relentlessly, heedless of life and limb, for the Central Pacific and Union Pacific, though they would be joined, were actually in fierce competition. The volume of their government land grants were directly proportional to the amount of track laid. In fact, in the absence of an officially predetermined meeting point for the converging tracks, survey parties laid out some 200 miles of overlapping, parallel, entirely redundant right-of-way. After roustabout parties passed each other—blasting away at hard rocks and almost at one another—U.S. Secretary of the Interior Orville H. Browning intervened and named Promontory Summit, 56 miles west of Ogden, Utah, as the meeting point. (Many histories of the West confuse Promontory Summit with nearby Promontory Point.)

Golden Spike at Promontory

The ceremonial union of the two lines at Promontory Summit was set for May 8, 1869. Leland Stanford of the Central Pacific almost failed to arrive because of a train wreck. Thomas C. Durant of the Union Pacific was kidnapped en route by tie cutters his company had not paid for months. Durant telegraphed for money and was released, delaying the ceremony by two days.

On May 10, 1869, workers and executives alike were prepared to savor their finest moment. The event did not go quite as planned. Chinese laborers, acutely aware of how Caucasians felt about them, were lowering the last rail into place when a photographer hollered, "Shoot!" The laborers dropped the quarter-ton rail and ran.

Leland Stanford himself stepped up to join the last eastbound and westbound rails. He poised himself to drive home a commemorative Golden Spike, wired to the telegraph, so that each blow would be transmitted across the nation. Stanford raised the heavy sledge, brought it on down—and clean missed. Laborers assisted him, and the deed was done. From sea to shining sea, the United States was bound by bands of iron.

The Least You Need to Know

➤ The Homestead Act of 1862 filled in the space between the Mississippi and the Pacific and brought to the West an unprecedented degree of family-based, community-based settlement.

➤ Technology, in the form of the transcontinental railroad, did more than politics to bind East and West into a single nation.

Chapter 22

"The Only Good Indian..." (1862–1891)

In This Chapter

➤ Indian roles in the Civil War

➤ The Santee Sioux uprising

➤ The victory of Red Cloud

➤ Futile campaigns, the War for the Black Hills, and Custer's Last Stand

➤ Defeat of the Nez Percé and Geronimo

➤ Massacre at Wounded Knee

The West was a land of many dreams, but what we seem to remember most vividly are the nightmares. On the vast stage of prairie and mountain, the last act of a four-century tragedy was played out. The curtain had been raised by the crew of Christopher Columbus, who clashed with the people they called Indians on an island they called Hispaniola. From then on, warfare between Native Americans and European Americans was chronic and continual. When whites and Indians did not start wars between themselves, Indians became embroiled in wars between whites: the French and Indian War, the Revolutionary War, the War of 1812, and finally, the Civil War.

Read any standard history of the Civil War, and you will learn that this epic struggle was mainly an eastern conflict. In the West, battles were smaller and less frequent, yet often, they were uglier.

Blue, Gray—and Red

Union loyalists in the West feared that the Confederates would acquire Indian allies. The Confederacy recruited some members of some eastern tribes, and both the North and South recruited troops from among tribes that had been "removed" to Indian Territory: the Cherokees, Chickasaws, Choctaws, Creeks, and Seminoles. But the more significant impact Indians had on the Civil War was to draw off some Union troops who otherwise would have been used against Confederates. Most important, the demands of the war meant that fewer troops occupied western posts, which provided Indians ample opportunity to raid settlers with relative impunity.

A Man Called Cochise

On the eve of the Civil War, Cochise (1812–74) emerged as leader of the Apaches. Feared throughout the Southwest by whites as well as other Indian tribes (*Apache* is a Hopi word for *enemy*), the Apaches had been fierce warriors and raiders for centuries. However, Cochise was actually inclined to like the American whites who settled in Arizona, and he even secured a contract with the Butterfield Overland Mail to supply fuel wood to the station at Apache Pass.

In 1861, Cochise was falsely accused of raiding a local rancher (a thoroughly disreputable drunk named John Ward), rustling his cattle, and abducting his son. Second Lieutenant George N. Bascom asked Cochise for a parley on February 4, 1861; Cochise came voluntarily, only to be taken captive with five others. The chief managed to escape by slitting a tent with his knife, and, enraged, he raided the Butterfield station, killing one employee and taking another prisoner. Cochise then ambushed a small wagon train and seized eight Mexicans and two Americans. He burned the Mexicans alive but offered to exchange the Americans for the Apache prisoners Bascom still held. When Bascom refused, Cochise murdered his remaining captives, and Bascom retaliated by summarily executing his hostages.

This scenario was the way of white–Indian war in the West: a crescendo of eye for eye, usually escalating into a full-scale war. In this case, war with the Apaches would consume the next quarter century.

Southwestern Terror

The entire Southwest was racked by violence. The outbreak of the Civil War stripped the U.S. Army's western outposts of 313 officers—one-third of the *entire* officer corps—who resigned their commissions to fight on the side of the Confederacy. Confederate Lieutenant Colonel John Robert Baylor exploited the Union's weakened position to take possession of Arizona Territory for the Confederacy. Baylor was able to roll over the greatly diminished Union presence, but he didn't count on the hostility of the Chiricahua and Mimbreño Apaches, who terrorized the region. Baylor hastily formed the Arizona Rangers in August 1861 and ordered them to "exterminate all hostile Indians."

In the meantime, hoping to retain New Mexico, Union General Edward R.S. Canby negotiated a treaty with the Navajo, pledging to distribute rations to the Indians. At Fort Fauntleroy, designated site of the distribution, a friendly series of horse races was run between Navajos and a regiment of New Mexico volunteers. The featured event was a race between an army lieutenant and Chief Manuelito (ca. 1818–94). Heavy wagers were laid, and from the beginning, it was apparent that Manuelito—an expert horseman—was not in control of his mount. After he came in a poor second, Manuelito protested that his bridle had been slashed, and he demanded a rematch. The soldiers refused, a fight broke out, and the troops began firing indiscriminately. "The Navahos, squaws, and children ran in all directions and were shot and bayoneted," according to a white civilian eyewitness who testified before Congress. Forty Indians were killed, and the Navajo retaliated. Through August and September, the already legendary Kit Carson, leading the First New Mexico Volunteer Cavalry, relentlessly counterattacked.

Real Life

Christopher Houston Carson, better known as Kit Carson, was born near Richmond, Kentucky, on December 24, 1809, and grew up in Missouri. He joined a Santa Fe trading caravan when he was 16 and, from 1827 to 1842, lived in the Rocky Mountains as a fur trapper and mountain man. In 1842, Carson served John C. Frémont as a guide in Oregon and California and, during the Mexican War, carried dispatches for him. After the war, Carson settled in Taos, New Mexico, where he served from 1853 to 1861 as Indian agent to the Utes, earning a reputation as one of very few genuinely competent, honest, and compassionate officials.

With the outbreak of the Civil War, Carson became colonel of the First New Mexico Volunteer Cavalry, where he distinguished himself in repelling the Confederate invasion of New Mexico and in combat against the Apache and Navajo. Although he became—in the popular phrase—a legend in his own time, especially for his role as an Indian fighter, Carson was deeply moved by the plight of the Indians, with whom he had a strong fellow feeling. Carson died on May 23, 1868, at Fort Lyon, Colorado.

The result, by the end of 1863, was total defeat of the Navajo, who were exiled to a desolate reservation called the Bosque Redondo. Eventually, 8,000 Navajo jammed the reservation, under conditions so intolerable that, after the Civil War, in an all-too-rare act of humanity, a U.S. peace commission granted Navajo pleas to be returned to their homelands.

The Great Santee Sioux Massacre

While the Southwest erupted, storm clouds also gathered far to the north. Unlike the Navajo, the Santee Sioux of Minnesota seemed willing to accept "concentration" on a reservation. But as increasing numbers of German and Scandinavian immigrants moved into the region, the Santee found themselves confined to a narrow strip of land along the Minnesota River. Worse, provisions and annuity money guaranteed them by treaty were routinely withheld. In June 1862, Little Crow led the Santee to the Yellow Medicine Indian Agency to demand release of provisions and funds. When these items were not forthcoming by August, warriors broke into the agency warehouse but were temporarily repelled.

Desperate and hungry, the Santee appealed to a local trader, Andrew J. Myrick, on August 5–6. His heartless reply—"let them eat grass"—enraged the warriors, and on August 18, they ambushed Myrick in his store, killed him, and stuffed *his* mouth with grass. From this point on, raiding became general in and around the town of New Ulm. By the end of August, 2,000 Minnesotans were refugees, and the Sioux had killed between 350 and 800 others. Governor Alexander Ramsey telegraphed Abraham Lincoln, requesting an extension of a federal deadline for fulfilling his state's military draft quota. The president replied: "Attend to the Indians. If the draft cannot proceed of course it will not proceed. Necessity knows no law."

Through the balance of August and most of September, fighting in Minnesota was brutal. On September 26, 2,000 Santee hostiles surrendered to General Henry Hopkins Sibley, and the deadliest Indian uprising in the history of the West was at an end. In November, a military tribunal sentenced 303 warriors to hang. Doubting the justice of these proceedings, President Lincoln personally reviewed the convictions and reprieved all but 39. In the end, 38 were hanged (another Indian received a last-minute reprieve), but administrative error resulted in the hanging of two Indians who were not on Lincoln's list. As for Chief Little Crow, he fled the final battle, was refused refuge in Canada, and was ambushed and killed in Minnesota on July 3, 1863, while picking raspberries with his 16-year-old son.

War for the Bozeman Trail

Throughout the Civil War, warfare with the Apaches continued. Wars also broke out with the Shoshoni, Bannock, Utes, and Northern Paiutes—also called the Snakes—in parts of Wyoming, Nevada, Utah, and Idaho. Wars erupted with the Navajo in the Southwest and with the combined forces of the Cheyenne and Arapaho tribes in Colorado. All of these wars ended badly for the Indians, although, as one official observed, "Ten good soldiers are required to wage successful war against one Indian."

One of the few conflicts from which the Indians emerged victorious broke out just after the end of the Civil War. Military authorities had anticipated that the collapse of the Confederacy would free up many troops for service in the West. What actually happened is that the Union army rushed to demobilize, and the army of the West shrunk rather than expanded. A modest force under Colonel Henry B. Carrington was sent to protect the Bozeman Trail, a major route of western migration through Wyoming and Montana. The trail was being menaced by Oglala Sioux led by Red Cloud, who was determined to resist white invasion of his people's land. Carrington was not popular with his officers, who felt that he devoted too much time to building forts and not enough to fighting Indians.

One subordinate, Captain William J. Fetterman, boasted that with 80 men, he could ride through the entire Sioux nation. On December 21, 1866, Fetterman was given his chance to make good on the boast. Sent with a detachment of 80, his mission was to relieve a wood-hauling wagon train that was being harassed by Indians. Fetterman found himself up against 1,500 to 2,000 warriors led by Crazy Horse, and his command was wiped out in what came to be called the Fetterman Massacre.

A peace commission concluded a treaty with Red Cloud on April 29, 1868, promising (among other things) to abandon the Bozeman Trail—which (the commissioners well knew) was about to be rendered obsolete by the transcontinental railroad.

The Campaigns of Hancock and Sheridan

General William Tecumseh Sherman, in charge of western operations, found the peace with Red Cloud humiliating. Sherman advised army General-in-Chief Grant that "we must act with vindictive earnestness against the Sioux, even to their extermination, men, women, and children." But the mood in Washington drifted toward conciliation, and Sherman continued to prosecute "punitive campaigns" in the West with little support and, ultimately, to little purpose.

From April through July 1867, one of Sherman's best commanders, Winfield Scott Hancock, fruitlessly pursued the Cheyenne and Sioux through Kansas. The following year, Sherman's most able lieutenant, General Philip Sheridan, conducted a brutal winter campaign against the Sioux and Cheyenne. This campaign proved almost as punishing to the pursuers as to the pursued, all of whom suffered in snows and bitter cold.

The colorful colonel of the 7th Cavalry, George Armstrong Custer, laid claim to the biggest victory of "Sheridan's Campaign," when he attacked a peaceful Cheyenne camp on the Washita River. Among the 103 Indians he and his men killed were 93 women, old men, and children. Chief Black Kettle, actually a leading advocate of peace, was slain along with his wife.

War for the Black Hills

The futility and tragedy of Hancock's and Sheridan's campaigns were the hallmarks of the so-called Indian Wars. Weeks and months of fruitless pursuit characteristically culminated in wanton spasms of violence in which innocent victims perished alongside "hostiles." In 1873, the brief but intense Modoc War broke out in California because a tiny tribe stubbornly refused to leave an utterly worthless volcanic wasteland. In 1874, the Red River War was launched to punish the Comanches and Cheyennes for attacking a group of white hunters at Adobe Walls, Texas. Then, in 1874, an expedition led by George A. Custer discovered gold in the Black Hills, the land most sacred to the Sioux. When government attempts to persuade the Indians to sell or lease the land failed, they were ordered to vacate. They refused, and war erupted.

The army never had an easy time fighting the Indian Wars, but now they found themselves up against an enemy equipped with formidable riding and warrior skills, motivated by religious fervor in defense of a sacred land, and led by the charismatic Tatanka Iyotake, better known as Sitting Bull. On June 17, Sitting Bull led a pounding attack against General George Crook's column at the Rosebud Creek in southern Montana. This event made George Armstrong Custer more determined to pursue and destroy the "hostiles."

Voice from the Past

Fortunately, genocidal phrases rarely enter folklore, but everybody knows the expression "The only good Indian is a dead Indian." It originated with General Philip Sheridan, when a Comanche named Tosawi came to him to sign a treaty after Custer's "victory" at Washita. "Tosawi, good Indian," said Tosawi. Sheridan replied: "The only good Indians I ever saw were dead." The phrase was subsequently transformed through repetition.

Real Life

Sitting Bull (Tatanka Iyotake, 1831–90) made an early reputation as a warrior and was revered for his great bravery, strength, generosity, and wisdom. His fame and influence spread far beyond his own Hunkpapa Sioux tribe. With chiefs Crazy Horse and Gall, Sitting Bull led resistance against the white invasion of the sacred Black Hills after gold was discovered there in 1874. Following the annihilation of Custer at the Little Bighorn in 1876, Sitting Bull and his closest followers fled to Canada. Upon his return to the United States in 1881, Sitting Bull was imprisoned for two years and then sent to Standing Rock Reservation. In 1883, he traveled as a performer with Buffalo Bill Cody's Wild West Show. Buffalo Bill was perhaps the only white man Sitting Bull ever trusted.

In 1890, Sitting Bull was identified with the antiwhite religious movement known as the Ghost Dance. He was killed during a scuffle when reservation police (who were Indians) attempted to arrest him on December 15, 1890.

Defeat of Custer

On the morning of June 22, 1876, to the strains of its regimental tune, "Garry Owen," the 7th Cavalry passed in review before Generals Alfred Terry and John Gibbon. They were embarking on what the commanders conceived as a final pincers campaign against the Sioux. As Colonel Custer rode off to join his men, Gibbon called after him: "Now, Custer, don't be greedy, but wait for us." Custer answered, "No, I will not."

Frustrated by long, fruitless pursuits, Custer was determined to fight it out whenever and wherever he could. That is why, on June 25, when his scouts discovered a Sioux camp and warriors near the Little Bighorn River, Custer decided not to wait until the next day, when he was supposed to rendezvous with the others. He decided to attack now. First, Custer sent Captain Frederick Benteen with 125 men south, to make sure the Sioux had not moved to the upper valley of the Little Bighorn. Then he sent another 112 men under Major Marcus A. Reno in pursuit of a small body of warriors he had sighted. With his remaining troops, Custer planned to charge the Sioux village. But it was soon apparent that Reno and his men were being overwhelmed, and Custer dispatched his bugler to recall Benteen. Custer then charged, only to be engulfed himself by massive numbers of Sioux warriors, who killed the colonel and 250 cavalrymen. Reno, joined by Benteen— 368 officers and men total—held off a relentless siege for the next two days.

"I Will Fight No More Forever"

The Battle of the Little Bighorn was the last major Indian victory of the Indian Wars. In subsequent engagements, the Sioux were defeated by the army's two most successful Indian fighters, Ranald Mackenzie and Nelson A. Miles. It was Miles who finally defeated the Nez Percé at the five-day Battle of Bear Paw Mountain (September 30–October 5, 1877) in Montana, bringing to an end an epic pursuit that had begun in June.

Led by Chief Joseph the Younger, a faction of the Nez Percé refused to leave their homeland in the Wallowa Valley of Oregon. Troops under the command of General Oliver O. Howard and Colonel Miles pursued and battled some 800 Indians over 1,700 miles of the most inhospitable terrain on the continent. When it was over, Joseph and his people had earned the respect of their pursuers. Both Howard and Miles joined in Joseph's petition to the White House to return to the Wallowa Valley. The petition was nevertheless denied—for the valley was rich in minerals—and Joseph lived out the remainder of his long life with his people on a reservation near Colville, Washington.

Voice from the Past

Joseph surrendered to Nelson A. Miles with words that have come to symbolize the poignant dignity with which Native Americans ultimately bowed to the inevitable:

"I am tired of fighting. Our chiefs are killed. Looking Glass [a war chief] *is dead. Toohoolhoolzote is dead. The old men are all dead. It is the young men who say yes or no. He who led on the young men* [Joseph's brother, Ollikut] *is dead. It is cold and we have no blankets. The little children are freezing to death. My people, some of them, have run away to the hills, and have no blankets, no food; no one knows where they are—perhaps freezing to death. I want to have time to look for my children and see how many of them I can find. Maybe I shall find them among the dead. Hear me, my chiefs! I am tired; my heart is sick and sad. From where the sun now stands I will fight no more forever."*

The Geronimo Campaign

The pursuit of the Nez Percé involved a concerted military operation focused on a small band of fugitives. Down in the Mexican border region, an entire army task force was devoted to the pursuit of a single Indian. His Apache name was Goyathlay (*one who yawns*), but he was better known by the name the Mexicans gave him: Geronimo (1829–1909). In 1850, Mexican settlers ambushed and killed Geronimo's first wife and his children, after which Geronimo devoted much of his life to ruthlessly raiding the border-lands along with his brother-in-law, Juh, a Chiricahua chief.

In 1875, U.S. authorities branded Geronimo a troublemaker, who opposed military plans to "concentrate" all the Apaches at the desolate San Carlos reservation in eastern Arizona. Geronimo fled with a band of followers into Mexico but was soon arrested and returned to the reservation. Not to be contained, Geronimo used the reservation as a base from which he staged raids throughout the remainder of the decade.

In 1881, authorities killed another "troublemaker," Nakaidoklini, revered by the Apaches as a prophet. His death incited Geronimo to abandon the reservation altogether for a secret stronghold in the Sierra Madre Mountains, from which he terrorized the border region.

In May 1882, Apache scouts working for the army discovered Geronimo's sanctuary and persuaded him and his followers to return to the reservation. He fled again on May 17, 1885, with 35 warriors and 109 women and children. In January 1886, a small army unit, together with Apache scouts, penetrated deep into Mexico, where they found Geronimo, who surrendered to General George Crook. Geronimo escaped one more time but ultimately surrendered to Nelson Miles on September 4, 1886. Geronimo and some 450 other Apaches were sent to Florida for confinement in Forts Marion and Pickens. In 1894, the Apaches were removed to Fort Sill, Indian Territory (present-day Oklahoma), and Geronimo became a rancher.

Wounded Knee

In 1886, when Geronimo surrendered to General Miles, 243,000 Native Americans were confined to 187 reservations. With Geronimo's last resistance extinguished, the Indian Wars were practically at an end. Yet, if the body of defiance was dead, its spirit lingered. Wovoka was the son of a Paiute shaman, but he had spent part of his youth with a white ranch family, who leavened his Paiute religious heritage with the teachings of their own Christianity. By the 1880s, Wovoka began to preach to the reservation Indians, foretelling a new world in which only Indians dwelled, generations of slain braves would come back to life, and the buffalo (nearly hunted to extinction during the first two-thirds of the 19th century) would again be plentiful. To hasten this deliverance, Wovoka counseled, all Indians must dance the Ghost Dance and follow the paths of peace.

Among a people who had lost all hope, the Ghost Dance religion spread rapidly. Soon, many western reservations were alive with what white overseers regarded as frenzied dancing. Leaders among the Teton Sioux at Pine Ridge, South Dakota, called for armed rebellion against the whites. Reservation agent Daniel F. Royer frantically telegraphed Washington, D.C., in November 1890: "Indians are dancing in the snow and are wild and crazy. We need protection and we need it now." But the arrival of troops under Nelson A. Miles seemed only to enflame the Indians. As a precaution, Indian reservation police were sent on December 15, 1890, to arrest Sitting Bull, domiciled at Standing Rock Reservation. A scuffle broke out, and the most revered chief of the Plains tribes was slain.

In the meantime, another chief, Big Foot of the Miniconjou Sioux, was making his way to Pine Ridge. Miles assumed that his purpose was to bring to a boil the simmering rebellion, and he dispatched the 7th Cavalry to intercept Big Foot and his followers. The troops caught up with the Indians on December 28, 1890, at a place called Wounded Knee Creek, on the Pine Ridge Reservation.

Big Foot did not, in fact, have hostile intentions. On the contrary, although he was desperately ill with pneumonia, Big Foot was traveling to Pine Ridge to try to persuade the rebellion leaders to surrender. Neither Miles nor Colonel James W. Forsyth, commander of the 7th, knew Big Foot's intention, and Forsyth quietly surrounded Big Foot's camp, deploying four Hotchkiss guns (deadly rapid-fire howitzers) on the surrounding hills. On the 29th, the soldiers entered the camp and began to confiscate the Indians' weapons. A hand-to-hand fight developed, shots were fired—it is unclear whether these came from the Indians or the soldiers—and then the Hotchkiss guns opened up, firing almost a round a second at men, women, and children.

Nobody knows just how many died at Wounded Knee. The bodies of Big Foot and 153 other Miniconjous were found, but it is likely that the 300 or 350 camped beside the creek ultimately lost their lives. After a brief fight with the 7th Cavalry on December 30, the Indians withdrew. Two weeks later, on January 15, 1891, the Sioux formally surrendered to U.S. Army officials. It was a miserable end to 400 years of racial warfare on the American continent.

The Least You Need to Know

➤ Few Indians participated directly in the Civil War, but some did take advantage of a reduced military presence in the West to raid and plunder.

➤ The Indian Wars in the West, spanning the Civil War years to 1891, consisted mainly of long, exhausting pursuits and relatively few battles. The strategy was to fight a "total war" against women, children, and old men as well as warriors, in order to force the Indians onto reservations.

Chapter 23

From Panic to Empire (1869-1908)

In This Chapter

➤ Western agriculture and the day of the cowboy

➤ The triumph of capitalism and the rise of philanthropy

➤ Technological revolution

The phrase *Wild West* has become so worn with use that it's hard to say the second word *without* adding the first to it. The spirit that marked the West pervaded national life during the years following the Civil War. If the West had its cowboys and its outlaws, so did the world of big business and power politics in such cities as New York and Washington. Fortunes were made and lost, it seemed, overnight. A wealth of new inventions suddenly materialized, accelerating American life to a pace many found increasingly frenzied. And if tycoons and inventors were pulling the strings, working men and women were often the ones being jerked around.

Empire of Cows

If the West equaled space, the equation came out differently for different people. To the homesteader, space meant a place to live. To the cattleman, space meant grass and water to fuel the beef herds that made his fortune.

Before the Mexican War, even Texas ranches were relatively modest in size, but the war brought a tremendous demand for beef to feed the U.S. Army. After the cattle industry geared up for this need, it never pulled back. Texans started to drive cattle beyond the confines of the ranch, pushing herds northward to fatten on the grass of public lands before being shipped east. This period was the start of the range cattle industry, which the Civil War threatened to bring to an untimely end. Union blockades kept Texans from shipping their beeves to market, and the cattle were left to run wild on the Texas plains, the ranchers and ranch hands having gone off to fight the war. When the sons of Texas returned after Appomattox, the only visible assets left to many of them were some five million free-ranging animals. Ex-Confederate soldier boys now set up as cowboys, rounding up and branding as many cattle as they could, then "trailing" the herds to grazing lands, marketplaces, and railheads.

American Cowboy

The range cattle industry didn't just make beef; it also created the single most beloved, celebrated, talked about, and *sung* about worker in American history. If generations of little boys and girls across the Atlantic grow up on tales of knights in shining armor, American children have long been raised on tales, songs, and images of the noble riders of the range. Cowboys embody a very powerful—very American—myth of freedom and self-sufficiency. But from the cold, hard perspective of economic reality, cowboys were the poorest of the poor. Dirty, dangerous, lonely, and poorly paid, *cowboy* was a job for desperate men: down-and-out ex-Confederates who had lost all they owned; liberated black slaves who, suddenly masterless, found themselves at loose ends; Indians, struggling at the bottom of the socioeconomic ladder; and Mexicans, sharing that bottom rung.

Word for the Day

The *cowboy*'s ancestors are the *vaqueros* (from the Spanish *vaca*, "cow"), originally Indians attached to the old Spanish missions and employed by them to handle their beef herds. The cowboys roped steers with a loop of braided rawhide rope known as *la reata*—a lariat. They wore *chaparreras*, leather trousers designed to protect their legs from brush and chaparral; later, American cowboys wore *chaps*. The word *vaquero* found its American counterpart in *buckaroo*, a synonym for cowboy.

On the ranch, the cowboy's principal job was to ride over an assigned stretch of range and tend the cattle, doing whatever needed to be done. The most demanding labor was the trail drive, in which cowboys moved a herd of cattle—perhaps as small as 500 head or as large as 15,000—to northern ranges for maturing or to market at railhead cattle towns like Abilene, Ellsworth, and Dodge City, Kansas; Pueblo and Denver, Colorado; and

Cheyenne, Wyoming. Distances were often in excess of 1,000 miles over four principal cattle trails. Hazards of the trails were almost as numerous as the herds themselves: storms, floods, drought, stampede, rustlers, hostile Indians. Pay was about $100 for three or four months' work.

Law and Disorder

It was not unusual for a cowboy to blow his whole $100 stake during a few nights in the cattle town that lay at the end of the trail. The towns served as points of transfer from the trail to the rails. Here beef brokers shook hands on deals, and the cattle were loaded into rail cars bound for the cities of the East. For the cowboy, a stay in town meant a bath, a shave, a woman (300 prostitutes plied their trade in the small town of Wichita), and plenty to drink (in many towns, saloons outnumbered other buildings two to one). Such towns were also home to professional gamblers who were ready, willing, and able to part a cowboy from his cash. Like the mining camps of California in the 1850s, the cattle towns of the latter part of the century were rowdy, violent places. Gunfights became commonplace—though, alas, neither so frequent nor so violent as they are on the streets of many American cities today.

Jesse, Billy, and the Rest

Arising from the welter of casually violent men in the West were more than a handful of determined and deliberate criminals. A few have entered into American legend. Jesse James was born in Clay County, Missouri, on September 5, 1847, and, with his older brother Frank (born 1843), was caught up in the brutality of the Civil War in Missouri. The brothers joined the fierce Confederate guerrilla band of William Quantrill and his lieutenant, "Bloody Bill" Anderson. In the guise of carrying out military operations, these guerrillas were no better than vicious gangsters, and their units became the schools of a generation of accomplished criminals. Cole Younger and Arch Clement, who would become principal members of the James Gang after the war, were also Quantrill–Anderson alumni.

The gang robbed its first bank in February 1866 and continued to prey upon banks, stagecoaches, and trains until 1876. At that time, determined citizens ambushed and decimated the gang during a robbery attempt in Northfield, Minnesota. The James brothers escaped and formed a new gang, which included one Robert Ford. On April 3, 1882, eager to claim a bundle of reward money, Ford shot and killed Jesse, who was living in St. Joseph, Missouri, under the alias of Thomas Howard. Ford's deed was greeted as anything but a public service. Although they were clearly cold-blooded armed robbers, the "James boys" had acquired a popular reputation as latter-day Robin Hoods. People now sang of the "dirty little coward who shot Mr. Howard and laid poor Jesse in his grave." Frank James later surrendered, was twice tried and twice acquitted by friendly juries; he died of natural causes in 1915.

Contemporary legend, dime novels, and later, movies and television transformed another outlaw into a latter-day Robin Hood. Billy the Kid was born Henry McCarty in 1859 (either in Marion County, Indiana, or possibly New York City). Raised in Kansas, the Kid was orphaned early and embarked on a life of petty crime that escalated to murder when, aged 17, he killed a man in a saloon brawl. A year later, in 1878, the Kid became embroiled in the so-called Lincoln County War, a New Mexico range war between one set of cattlemen and another. During the conflict, on April 1, 1878, he ambushed and murdered the Lincoln County sheriff and his deputy. As a fugitive, Billy the Kid supported himself with robbery, all the while pursued by the new sheriff, Pat Garrett, to whom he finally surrendered in December 1880. Four months later, the Kid escaped the noose by killing his two jailors and taking flight. When the Kid stopped at Fort Sumner, New Mexico (some say it was to see his sweetheart), Garrett again caught up with him and, this time, gunned him down.

Stats

For all their notoriety, neither Jesse James nor Billy the Kid holds any Wild West record for gunfighting. In terms of number of men slain, Billy the Kid comes in at 10th place (4 murders), behind Jim Miller (12), Wes Hardin (11), Bill Longley (11), Harvey Logan (9), Wild Bill Hickok (7), John Selman (6), Dallas Stoudenmire (5), Cullen Baker (5), and King Fisher (5). Jesse James doesn't even come close to the top 10. In nine gunfights, only one killing is confirmed, though James may have assisted in the slaying of three more.

Cornering the Market

Jesse James, Billy the Kid, and a host of lesser figures were unquestionably criminals. But who were their victims? As many Americans saw it at the time, Jesse, Billy, and the rest did not victimize innocent citizens but attacked big banks, big railroads, big money—the very forces that were daily robbing the "common man." If you wanted to talk about victims, well, the *real* victims were those who weren't lucky enough to have been born a Gould or a Rockefeller. In the popular logic of the day, capitalists such as these were the robber barons, whereas the western outlaws were the Robin Hoods.

And what about government? In the popular view, lawmakers and police were counted on to go with the money, making and enforcing laws to serve the Goulds, the Rockefellers, and their kind. People who lived during the years following the Civil War took to calling their era the Gilded Age—glittering with showy wealth but corrupt to the core. The railroads boomed, transporting the raw ores of the West to the industrial machines of the East. With hundreds of thousands of discharged veterans flooding the job market, labor was dirt cheap, and the government was—well—pliant. Andrew Johnson, having narrowly escaped removal from office, was succeeded in the White House by Ulysses Simpson Grant in 1869. Grant had proven to be one of the nation's greatest generals, but in two terms as president, he presided over the most thoroughly corrupt administration in American history. He was personally above reproach, but, naively, he surrounded himself with scoundrels who administrated, legislated, and operated hand in hand with the interests of big business—and (in the infamous phrase of railroad magnate William H. Vanderbilt) "The public be damned!"

Gould and Gold

Jay Gould was born in Roxbury, New York, on May 27, 1836, the son of a poor farmer. By 21, Gould had saved up $5,000, which he invested in the leather business and railroad stocks. Within a decade, Gould was a director of the Erie Railroad and, by means of illegal stock and bribery, clawed his way to a controlling interest in a number of railroads. With fellow tycoon James Fisk (1834–72), Gould hatched a scheme to corner the U.S. gold market. He persuaded President Grant to suspend government gold sales, thereby driving up the price of gold—which Gould and Fisk held in great quantity. Rousing momentarily from naive stupor, Grant realized what was going on and ordered the Treasury to release $4 million of its own gold to checkmate Gould. The result was Black Friday, September 24, 1869, which precipitated a major financial panic followed by severe economic depression as the inflated price of gold tumbled.

Many of the nation's railroads, already reeling from cutthroat competition, now tottered on the verge of bankruptcy. John Pierpont Morgan (1837–1913), who had multiplied his family's already mighty fortune by loaning money to France during the Franco-Prussian War of 1871, now rushed in to pick up the pieces. By 1900, Morgan had acquired *half* the rail trackage in the nation. Most of the rest of the railroads were owned by Morgan's friends, and together, they fixed freight prices at exorbitant levels. There was little shippers could do but pay.

Rockefeller and Oil

The years immediately following the Civil War ran on rails and were fueled by gold. People who controlled either or both interests drove the nation, regardless of who was in the White House, the Congress, or the courts.

There was gold, and then there was *black* gold. In 1859, oil was struck in western Pennsylvania. This event gave a thin-lipped, ascetic-looking young Ohioan an idea. John Davison Rockefeller (1839–1937) decided that oil would become a big business and that his hometown of Cleveland was ideally situated to refine and distribute it to the nation.

Rockefeller built a refinery there in 1862, then put together the Standard Oil Trust, an amalgam of companies by which he came to control all phases of the oil industry, from extraction, through refining, through distribution. Standard Oil was the first of many almighty trusts formed in various industries during the post-Civil War period.

The Gospel of Wealth

The Gilded Age was an epoch of naked greed. Those few capitalists who bothered to defend their motives turned to the science of the day. In 1859, the great British naturalist Charles Darwin (1809–82) published *On the Origin of Species by Means of Natural Selection*. This book set forth the theory of evolution, arguing that in nature, only the fittest—the strongest, the most cunning, the ablest—creatures ultimately survive to reproduce their kind. Capitalists translated nature into economics, arguing that the state should not interfere in economic life because people at the top of the socioeconomic heap were there because they were the fittest, having survived the battles of the marketplace. This concept was Social Darwinism.

Yet the era was not entirely heedless or heartless. Andrew Carnegie (1835–1919) came to the United States with his impoverished family from Scotland in 1848. As a youth, Carnegie worked in a cotton factory, then in a telegraph office, and finally for the Pennsylvania Railroad, rising quickly through the executive ranks until he became head of the western division in 1859. Carnegie resigned from the railroad in 1865 to form the Keystone Bridge Company, the first in a series of iron and steel concerns he owned. He consolidated his holdings in 1899 as the Carnegie Steel Company, then sold it to J.P. Morgan's United States Steel Company in 1901 for $492 million—roughly the equivalent of five billion of today's dollars. (And income tax didn't exist in 1901!)

Carnegie was as ruthless as any of his fellow robber barons, wielding his steel company like a club, knocking out all competition and (for a time) knocking out the American industrial union movement as well. But in 1889, Carnegie delivered a speech titled "The Gospel of Wealth," in which he reeled out the Social Darwinist line that wealth was essential for civilization and that the natural law of competition dictated that only a few would achieve wealth. Yet Carnegie added a unique twist. The rich, he proclaimed, had a responsibility to use their money for the clear benefit of society.

From 1901 until his death, Carnegie dedicated himself to philanthropy, donating more than $350 million to a wide spectrum of causes. He founded more than 2,500 public libraries throughout the United States; he established the Carnegie Institute of Pittsburgh, the Carnegie Institution at Washington, the Carnegie Foundation for the Advancement of Teaching, the Carnegie Endowment for International Peace, and the Carnegie Corporation of New York. The truly remarkable thing is that many other robber barons took the Gospel of Wealth to heart. Rail magnate Leland Stanford founded and endowed Stanford University. Rockefeller endowed the University of Chicago, created the Rockefeller Institute of Medical Research, established the Rockefeller Foundation, and bought vast tracts of land that became national parks. Many other wealthy individuals did similar deeds and continue to do so today.

An Age of Invention

If, blooming among the uncut weeds of wild greed, the Gospel of Wealth seemed miraculous, so did the incredible series of inventions that burst forth during what otherwise might have been a dull, hard Age of the Machine. Americans of the post-Civil War era were extraordinarily industrious and inventive.

"Mr. Watson, Come Here..."

Alexander Graham Bell was born in 1847 in Scotland and grew up in England. His grandfather and father earned famed as teachers of the deaf, and Alexander likewise followed this career, continuing in it after the family immigrated to Canada in 1870. In 1872, Alexander Graham Bell became a professor of vocal physiology at Boston University. His profound interest in the nature of speech and sound was combined with a knack for things mechanical, and he began working on a device to record sound waves graphically in order to *show* his deaf students what they could not hear. Simultaneously, Bell was also trying to develop what he called the harmonic telegraph, a device capable of transmitting multiple telegraph messages simultaneously over a single line.

About 1874, the two inventions suddenly merged in his mind. Bell wrote in his notebook that if he could "make a current of electricity vary in intensity precisely as the air varies in density during the production of sound," he could "transmit speech telegraphically."

The insight was staggering: Convert one form of intelligible energy (sound) into another (modulated electric current). With his tireless assistant, Thomas Watson, Bell worked on the device for the next two frustrating years. One day, in 1876, while Watson maintained what he thought would be another fruitless vigil by the receiver unit in the next room, Bell made adjustments to the transmitter. In the process, Bell upset a container of battery acid, which spilled on his lap. Burned by the acid, he inadvertently made the world's first phone call—a call for help: "Mr. Watson, come here, I want you." The telephone caught on quickly, and the Bell Telephone Company, founded by Alexander's father-in-law, Gardner G. Hubbard, became a utility of vast proportions and incalculable importance.

Let There Be Light

Bell was a teacher of the deaf who taught the world to hear over unlimited distances. Thomas Alva Edison, almost totally deaf because of a childhood accident, helped the world to see. Born in Milan, Ohio, in 1847, Edison had little education and less money when he started selling candy and newspapers on trains of the Grand Trunk Railroad. What Edison did have was a passion for tinkering and a fascination with an invisible force called electricity. His first commercially successful invention was an electric stock ticker, which delivered stock quotations almost instantaneously and which J.P. Morgan eagerly snatched up. Edison plowed his profits into creating a state-of-the-art laboratory/workshop first in Newark, then in Menlo Park, New Jersey. By the end of his long creative life, Edison had some 3,000 patents to his name, covering more than 1,000 separate inventions.

Edison's greatest single invention was undoubtedly the incandescent electric lamp, which he publicly demonstrated on December 31, 1879, after many tortured months of trial and error. By 1881, Edison had built the world's first central generating plant, on Pearl Street in lower Manhattan. Within a very short time, electricity became a fixture not only of American life, but of life throughout the world. The incandescent lamp spawned many industries dedicated to producing an array of electrical devices. It is hardly necessary to point out how much our civilization now depends on what Edison began, but it is significant that, after he died on October 18, 1931, plans to dim the lights of the nation for a full minute as a memorial gesture had to be scrapped. Electric lighting was just too important.

Recorded Sound, Recorded Light

Although the incandescent lamp was Edison's single greatest invention, it was not his favorite. Two years before he demonstrated his lamp, he designed a device intended to raise some quick cash for his still-fledgling laboratory. Edison drew a crude sketch of the device he wanted built and then turned it over to an assistant, John Kruesi, to build. The man dutifully followed his employer's instructions, without any idea of what the device was supposed to do. A grooved metal cylinder was turned by a hand crank; a sheet of tinfoil was stretched over the cylinder; the point of a stylus rested against the tinfoil, and the other end of the stylus was affixed to a flexible diaphragm. Kruesi presented the finished model to Edison, who took it, turned the crank, and spoke into the diaphragm. The stylus, moving with the vibration of his voice, embossed the tinfoil. Then Edison stopped cranking and speaking, reapplied the stylus to the cylinder, and turned the crank. From the diaphragm, the machine recited "Mary Had a Little Lamb." Thomas Edison had invented the phonograph.

After recording sound and producing light, the Wizard of Menlo Park (as the press soon dubbed the inventor) *recorded* light. Edison became interested in motion photography after he attended a lecture by Eadweard Muybridge (1830–1904) on his experiments with recording motion on film using multiple cameras. In 1882, a French scientist, E.J. Marey, invented a means of shooting multiple images with a single camera, and Edison patented his own motion picture camera in 1887. Edison then worked with William Kennedy Laurie Dickson to create a practical means of recording the images, using flexible celluloid film, created by George Eastman (1854–1932). (Eastman's Kodak box camera would bring photography to the masses in 1888.) By the 1890s, Dickson had shot many 15-second movies using Eastman's film in Edison's Kinetograph camera.

> ## Main Event
>
> Strangely enough, the usually canny Edison saw little future in motion pictures. He even decided against projecting the films for audiences, because he didn't think there would be much demand. Instead, Edison developed an electrically driven peephole viewing machine—the Kinetoscope—which displayed moving images to one viewer at a time for the price of a nickel. Not until 1903 did the Edison Company began to exploit *projected* motion pictures. In this year, Edwin S. Porter, an Edison employee, directed "The Great Train Robbery," generally considered the first movie—the filming of a genuine story, complete with beginning, middle, and end. If the origins of the American film industry can be traced to any single event, it is the creation of "The Great Train Robbery."

Bridge and Skyscraper, Kitty Hawk and Detroit

The end of the Civil War brought many monuments—statues, arches, and tombs—but more significant than these were the monuments to American civilization itself. In 1857, a German immigrant named John Augustus Roebling (1806–69), a master bridge builder who had constructed suspension bridges over the Monongahela River and at Niagara Falls, proposed a spectacular span over the East River to unite Manhattan and Brooklyn. Roebling completed his plans in 1869 but suffered a severe leg injury at the construction site and died of tetanus. His son, Washington Augustus Roebling (1837–1926), took over the epic task—which very nearly killed him as well; he spent too much time in an underwater caisson, supervising construction of the bridge towers. As a result, Roebling developed a permanently crippling, excruciatingly painful case of the bends caused by nitrogen bubbles in the blood. The bridge, finally completed in 1883, was and remains a magnificent combination of timeless architecture and cutting-edge 19th-century technology.

If the Roeblings' masterpiece brought to its grandest expression the union of 19th-century art and science, the American skyscraper looked forward to the next century. William LeBaron Jenny's Home Insurance Company Building in Chicago (1883–85) is generally considered the first skyscraper, but it was Louis Sullivan (1856–1924), one of the nation's greatest architects, who became the most important master of the new building form. With his partner Dankmar Adler, Sullivan based his practice in Chicago, a city he helped to raise, phoenix-like, from the disastrous fire of 1871. Thanks to Sullivan and those who followed him, American cities became vertical, aspiring dramatically heavenward, bristling with the spires of new cathedrals founded not on religious faith, but on the wealth and raw energy of the age.

The very name *skyscraper* seemed to proclaim that nothing could contain the spirit of a nation that, like Chicago, had been reborn from the ashes. In 1903, the sons of Milton Wright, bishop of the United Brethren in Christ Church in Dayton, Ohio, transported to a beach at Kitty Hawk, North Carolina, a spindly, gossamer machine that resembled an oversized box kite. While his brother Wilbur (1867–1912) observed, Orville Wright (1871–1948) made history's first piloted, powered, sustained, and controlled flight in a heavier-than-air craft on December 17. Orville flew a distance of 120 feet over a span of 12 seconds. Within two years, the Wright brothers achieved a flight of 38 minutes over 24 miles and, by 1909, were manufacturing and selling their airplanes.

Of course, in 1909, flight was still out of the reach of most "ordinary" people. But the year before, a farm boy from Dearborn, Michigan, gave the masses wings of a different sort. True, Henry Ford (1863–1947) did not actually lift purchasers of his Model T off the ground, but he did give them unprecedented physical freedom.

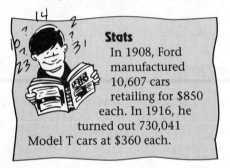

Stats

In 1908, Ford manufactured 10,607 cars retailing for $850 each. In 1916, he turned out 730,041 Model T cars at $360 each.

Ford did not invent the automobile—a gasoline-fueled automobile first appeared in Germany, and commercial production began in France about 1890—but he did make it practical and affordable. In 1908, he designed the simple, sturdy Model T and began to develop assembly line techniques to build it. The price of the car plummeted, and demand increased; with increased demand, Ford further perfected his assembly line, turning out more and more cars at lower and lower prices.

The Model T, a landmark achievement in mass production, transformed the way Americans lived. The car created a mobile society and it created a skyrocketing demand for mass-produced consumer goods of all kinds. The Model T also changed the American landscape, veining it with a network of roads. Where the nation had been sharply divided into city and farm, suburbs now sprouted. Even more than the transcontinental railroad had done in 1869, the automobile unified the United States, connecting city to city, village to village. Yet, for all this, there was a cost well beyond the $360 price tag of a 1916 Model T. It often seemed as if the automobile was an invader rather than a liberator. Worse, American labor lost a certain degree of humanity, compelled now to take its pace from the relentless rhythms of the assembly line. The gulf between management and labor, always wide, broadened into a bitter chasm, and if the moneyed classes welcomed the technological revolution, they now had reason to fear a political one.

The Least You Need to Know

➤ The kind of raw energy that animated the "Wild West" seemed to drive the rest of the country as well during the latter half of the 19th century.

➤ After the Civil War, big business grew largely unchecked, even at the expense of the public welfare, creating a roller-coaster boom-and-bust economy.

➤ Big business generated investment in innovation, and the post-Civil War period was an era of great inventions.

Chapter 24

Octopus and Jungle (1877–1906)

In This Chapter

➤ Immigration and opposition to immigration

➤ Oklahoma land rush

➤ Labor organization to fight oppression

➤ Corruption and reform

"History," said the English writer Thomas Carlyle, "is the biographies of great men." For a long time, most historians thought of their craft in this way. Thus the tale of the last quarter of the 19th century might be told exclusively through the lives of Carnegie, Gould, Rockefeller, Ford, and the rest. However, more recent historians have come to realize that these biographies relate only part of the story. History is also an account of ordinary people, the working men and women whose lives were influenced, even shaped, by the actions of politicians, robber barons, and (to use another phrase of Carlyle) the "captains of industry." While the moneyed elite fought one another for control of more and more capital, the nation's working people were tossed on the brutal seas of an economic tempest. Fortunes were being made and great inventions created, but for plain folk, the waning century presented plenty of hard times.

The Golden Door

America is a nation of immigrants. During the 17th century, colonial entrepreneurs actively recruited new settlers. Most of the early immigrants spoke English, but by the 18th century, waves of German immigrants arrived as well, causing alarm and resentment among the English-speakers, especially those who had been born on these shores. Yet, gradually, the German immigrants and those of the Anglo-American mainstream came to terms.

The next great wave of immigration began in 1841, when Ireland suffered a great potato famine, which caused untold hardship and even starvation. Millions left the country, most of them bound for the United States. The influx of Irish-Catholics into what was principally an Anglo-Protestant nation prompted many to worry that "their" American culture would crumble. The Irish immigrants were subjected to abuse and prejudice, some of it even backed by local legislation.

Beginning around 1880, the clamoring demands of American industry began to drown out the anti-immigrant chorus. Immigrant labor was cheap labor, and employers looked for unskilled and semiskilled workers to feed newly emerging assembly lines and do the heavy lifting required to build bridges and raise skyscrapers. American employers called not only on the German states and Ireland, but also on southern and eastern Europe, encouraging the immigration of Italians, Greeks, Turks, Russians, and Slavs. For the first time, substantial numbers of Jews came to the United States, adding a new element to the nation's blend of ethnic identities and religious faiths.

While the cities of the East and the Midwest tended to assimilate the new immigrants readily, resistance to immigration remained strong in the West and Southwest. Not that employers in these regions scrupled against hiring foreigners; they just didn't want the workers to enjoy citizenship. Asians, prized as hard workers, were barred from attaining U.S. citizenship by naturalization laws. In the Southwest, migrant labor from Mexico provided a scandalously cheap source of temporary farm workers. By 1882, prejudice against Asians resulted in passage of the first of a series of Chinese Exclusion Acts, which blocked the importation of Chinese laborers. However, authorities winked at the continued influx of Mexican migrants, some of whom came lawfully and others not.

By the second decade of the 20th century, most Americans were eager to close the golden door. In 1917, would-be immigrants were required to pass a literacy test, and in 1924, Congress set a strict limit on immigration—154,000 persons annually. Congress also established quotas aimed at reducing immigration from southern and eastern European countries.

Voice from the Past

Were immigrants welcome in the United States? Not always. Were they exploited and discriminated against? Sometimes. Yet, despite this treatment, America offered the best hope for peoples oppressed, starved, and made desperate in the nations of their birth. The poet Emma Lazarus (1849–87) expressed these sentiments in the poem she composed for inscription at the base of the Statue of Liberty. The statue was created by the sculptor Frederic August Bartholdi and presented to the United States as a gift from the French people. The coolly majestic 151-foot-high female figure (modeled after the artist's mother), holding aloft a torch and carrying a tablet inscribed with the date of American independence, was unveiled in New York Harbor in 1886. Here are the closing lines of the Lazarus sonnet:

Give me your tired, your poor,

Your huddled masses yearning to breathe free,

The wretched refuse of your teeming shore,

Send these, the homeless, tempest-tost, to me,

I lift my lamp beside the golden door!

Stats

In 1892, the United States Immigration Bureau opened a major central facility for handling the flood of immigration. Ellis Island, within sight of the Statue of Liberty in New York Harbor, was a place where immigrants could be examined for disease, evaluated as fit or unfit for entry, and either admitted to the mainland, quarantined, or deported. During the 62 years of its operation, from 1892 to 1943, Ellis Island processed immigrants at rates as high as a million people a year.

How the Other Half Lived

At the end of the 19th century, most large American cities were deeply divided places. Established citizens lived in varying degrees of prosperity, decently clothed, fed, and housed, while many of the newer arrivals languished in overcrowded, dilapidated, and

213

ultimately crime-plagued slums. The middle-class reaction to this "other half" of America was to ignore it—at least until Jacob August Riis (1849–1914), a New York journalist, published an eye-opening study in text and photographs of his city's slum life. *How the Other Half Lives* (1890), Theodore Roosevelt declared, came as "an enlightenment and an inspiration." The book heralded reform movements not only in New York, but across the nation.

Land Rush

If, to easterners, the United States seemed to be turning into a nation of crowded cities with teeming slums, the dream of wide-open western spaces had by no means died. At noon on April 22, 1889, government officials fired signal guns, sending hundreds of homesteaders racing across the border of Indian Territory to stake claims. It was the greatest mass settlement of the West since the Homestead Act of 1862, and the event kindled or rekindled the American dream not only in those who rushed to new lands, but in other Americans who experienced the excitement vicariously.

The kindling of one dream meant that another was extinguished. The government rescinded its agreements to protect and preserve Indian Territory for the Native Americans who were forcibly removed to it by the Indian Removal Act of 1830 and subsequent legislation. The great land rush led to statehood for Indian Territory, which became Oklahoma on November 16, 1907, and tribal lands were drastically reduced in the process.

Knights of Labor

The Indians, victimized by U.S. land policy, could do little but appeal (mostly in vain) to the American conscience. The laboring man, victimized by big business operating in the absence of government regulation, began to fight back by organizing unions. The Knights of Labor was founded in 1878 as a national union of skilled as well as unskilled workers. The Knights agitated for the universal adoption of the eight-hour day, and targeting the railroads (the "octopus," as novelist Frank Norris had called them), the union struck against several lines in 1877. The strike brought rail traffic to a halt and won certain concessions. However, in 1886, after a general strike failed in Chicago and the Haymarket Riot ensued, the Knights of Labor also dissolved.

Main Event

On May 3, 1886, laborers scuffled with police at the McCormick Reaper Company in Chicago after the company had hired nonunion workers during a strike. In the course of the melee, a laborer was killed, and the strikers—among them avowed anarchists—accused the police of brutality. A protest rally was called at the city's Haymarket Square the next day, May 4. A contingent of 180 police marched in to disperse the rally, and a bomb exploded in their ranks, wounding 66 officers, seven fatally. A riot broke out, and the police fired into the crowd, killing four persons and wounding at least 200.

Travesty followed tragedy, when eight anarchist leaders were convicted as accessories to murder—despite the fact that the actual bomber was never identified. Four of the anarchists were hanged, one committed suicide, and three were jailed. In an act of great moral heroism that destroyed his political career, Illinois Governor John Peter Altgeld (1847–1902) pardoned the three survivors in 1893.

The Great Strikes

While the courts generally eased restrictions on labor strikes during the 19th century, legislators did not act to protect strikers. As a result, violence between employers and unions was frequent. In 1892, workers struck the Carnegie Steel Company plant in Homestead, Pennsylvania, after company manager Henry Clay Frick imposed a wage cut. On June 29, Frick hired some 300 Pinkerton detectives to run the plant, and on July 6, an armed confrontation occurred, resulting in several deaths. The state militia was called in to protect nonunion laborers, who worked the mills from July 12 to November 20, at which point the strike collapsed.

As a result of the Homestead Strike, the nation's union movement suffered a severe setback, which was compounded two years later during the Pullman Strike of 1894. This violent confrontation between railroad workers and the Pullman Palace Car Company of Illinois tied up rail traffic across the United States from May to July. Workers, who lived in the company-owned town of Pullman (today a part of Chicago's south side) were protesting wage cuts that had been made without corresponding reductions in company-levied rents and other employee charges. Laborers belonging to the American Railway Union protested—and were summarily fired. Railway union head Eugene V. Debs (1855–1926) called a boycott of all Pullman cars, an action to which Pullman lawyers responded by using the newly enacted Sherman anti-trust legislation against the strikers. On July 2, a court injunction was issued to halt the strike. Federal troops were dispatched to enforce the injunction, and a riot broke out, during which several strikers were killed. The strike was crushed by July 10.

AFL

Although the labor movement would not fully recover from these early blows until the 1930s, an enduring union did emerge in 1886. The American Federation of Labor was led by a former cigar maker named Samuel Gompers (1850–1924). What set this union apart from the Knights of Labor was that it did not attempt to lump together all trades, skilled and unskilled. Recognizing that working people had certain common interests, but also had differing needs, the AFL existed as a coordinating group for separate trades. The union, which agitated for an eight-hour day, workmen's compensation, controls on immigrant labor, and protection from "technological unemployment" created by automation, exists today as the AFL-CIO.

I Won't Work

Although reasonably successful, the AFL did little to address the needs of unskilled labor. So in 1905, the Industrial Workers of the World (IWW) was formed by the Western Federation of Miners and a number of other labor organizations. Eugene Debs was an early force in this, the most radical of American labor unions, but leadership soon passed to William "Big Bill" Haywood (1869–1928). The "Wobblies," as IWW members were disparagingly called, vowed permanent class warfare against employers and looked forward to nothing less than a revolution, which would replace capitalism with an "industrial democracy." The Wobblies' many opponents simply swore that IWW stood for "I Won't Work."

Tweed of Tammany

Where unions fell short of looking after the needs, wishes, and demands of the masses, American city governments spawned "bosses" who operated "political machines." The big-city boss was characteristically a demagogue, who presented himself as a common man looking out for the interests of the common man. In reality, bosses were corrupt politicians, enriching themselves and their cronies at the expense of their constituents.

Typical of the big-city bosses was William Marcy Tweed (1823–78) of New York, who worked his way up through the city's political machine (known as Tammany Hall, after the name of a powerful Democratic club). Tweed eventually came to dominate municipal and then state politics. In 1861, Tweed had scarcely a dollar to his name; by 1871, he had amassed a fortune in excess of $2.5 million—all built on influence peddling and kickbacks from the sale of city contracts and franchises. Tweed gathered about himself a band of cronies, called the Tweed Ring, who collectively siphoned off anywhere from $40 million to $200 million in public funds. Tweed was convicted of fraud in 1873, but he fled to Spain. During his heyday, he had been ruthlessly caricatured by the great political cartoonist Thomas Nast (1840–1902), and in 1876, Tweed was recognized through a Nast cartoon. As a result, Tweed was arrested and returned to New York, where he died after serving two years in prison.

Word for the Day
A *political machine* is a group, usually dominated by a political party, that dictates the political life of a city. At the "controls" of the "machine" is the *boss*, who may or may not be an elected official.

Urban Reform

The flight and subsequent imprisonment of Boss Tweed did not bring down Tammany Hall; Thomas Croker and "Honest John" Kelly soon took Tweed's place. Nor was New York unique in being run by a machine and a boss. During the later 19th century, Pittsburgh had its Chris Magee and Bill Finn, Philadelphia its "King Jim" McMahon, Boston its "Czar" Martin Lomansey, and St. Louis its "Colonel" Ed Butler.

The Age of the Machine soon gave rise to an Age of Reform in response to it. *The Shame of the Cities*, written in 1904 by freelance journalist and passionate reformer Lincoln Steffens, exposed the corruption of St. Louis and showed that it was typical of big-city America. Public outrage flared, making way for such crusading politicians as Theodore Roosevelt and Robert M. La Follette.

Chicago Meat

Talk of corruption and reform was all well and good, but to many, the subject seemed rather abstract and remote. It took a novel, *The Jungle*, written in 1906 by a socialist writer named Upton Sinclair (1878–1968), to bring corruption and reform—quite literally—to the gut level. Sinclair described the plight of one Jurgis Rudkus, a Lithuanian immigrant who worked in a Chicago meat-packing plant. Through the eyes of this downtrodden and exploited worker, Sinclair described in sickening detail the horrors of modern meat packing. To fatten the bottom line, packers did not hesitate to use decayed meat, tubercular meat, offal, even rat meat in the manufacture of meat products. Comfortable middle-class Americans may or may not care about the exploitation of a blue-collar Lithuanian immigrant, but the idea of big business poisoning *them* and *their* families was truly nauseating. As a result of the indignation stirred by *The Jungle*, Congress enacted the landmark Pure Food and Drug Act a mere six months after the novel was published.

Muckrakers and Progressivism

Sinclair was one of a group of writers President Theodore Roosevelt, himself a progressive reformer, dubbed "muckrakers." Sinclair, Lincoln Steffens, Ida Tarbell (author of a landmark exposé of Standard Oil), and other journalists, caught up in the Progressive movement sweeping the nation, reported on the corruption and exploitation that seemed rampant in Gilded Age America. The muckrakers exposed child labor practices, slum life, racial persecution, prostitution, sweatshop labor, and the general sins of big business and machine politics.

Word for the Day

Muckraker was a reference to *Pilgrim's Progress*, a Christian allegorical novel by the 17th-century British writer John Bunyan. One of Bunyan's allegorical characters, used a "muckrake" to clean up the (moral) filth around him, even as he remained oblivious of the celestial beauty above.

Government Takes a Hand

The muckrakers succeeded in galvanizing popular opinion and motivating government action. Under President Theodore Roosevelt, antitrust laws were used to break up certain monopolies or trusts. After a long government assault, Standard Oil, most notorious of the trusts, was broken up into 34 companies in 1911. Under Roosevelt, too, public lands were protected from private exploitation, and he is considered a pioneer of the environmental movement. During the Roosevelt era, government also stepped in to establish and enforce standards of purity in food and drugs. The government created safeguards to curb unfair exploitation of workers and restricted child labor. On a local level, cities embarked on programs to clean up slum districts and to educate immigrants and youth.

Real Life

Theodore Roosevelt feared that Republican party bosses had consigned him to a secondary political role when he was nominated as William McKinley's running mate in the 1900 presidential election. However, Roosevelt became the nation's 26th president on September 14, 1901, after McKinley died of a gunshot wound inflicted on September 6 by an anarchist named Leon Czolgosz. Roosevelt proved so dynamic a leader that he was elected to the office in his own right in 1904, serving until 1909.

Roosevelt had been born into a moneyed old New York family on October 27, 1858. Weak and asthmatic as a child, Roosevelt was determined to build up his body and engaged in a regimen of exercise, sport, and outdoor activity he proudly dubbed "the strenuous life." He was, by turns and sometimes simultaneously, an author, politician, and rancher. Appointed assistant secretary of the navy under McKinley in 1897, he advocated preparation for war with Spain over its colonial policies in Cuba. With the outbreak of the Spanish-American War the following year, Roosevelt helped organize a volunteer cavalry unit called the Rough Riders, serving in Cuba as its dashing colonel.

His war record and reform reputation propelled Roosevelt to election as governor of New York in 1898. His crusading soon cramped the style of Republican party boss Thomas Collier Platt, who decided to "kick him upstairs" by arranging for his nomination as McKinley's vice-presidential running mate in 1900.

If the nation mourned McKinley's assassination the following year, none did so more than Republican conservatives, who had little stomach for Roosevelt's "Progressivism." The new president took aim at the big corporate trusts, wielding the Sherman Anti-Trust Act of 1890 as a club.

With election to a second term, Roosevelt became even more zealous in his Progressive reforms, doing battle against what he called the "malefactors of wealth." He strengthened the Interstate Commerce Commission's power to regulate railroads, and he supported the Meat Inspection and the Pure Food and Drug bills. In foreign policy, Roosevelt was equally vigorous and (as many saw it) radical. In 1903, when Colombia rejected a treaty giving the United States the right to dig a canal across the isthmus of Panama, "TR" supported the revolution that created an independent Panama. He then struck a canal treaty with the new nation and supervised construction of the Panama Canal.

For better or worse, Roosevelt was an American imperialist, who advocated extending the nation's sphere of influence—by force, if necessary. "Speak softly and carry a big stick," Roosevelt remarked in a September 2, 1901, speech at the Minnesota State Fair. Criticized by some contemporaries and historians alike as a war monger, Roosevelt stepped between Russia and Japan in 1905 to mediate peace in the Russo-Japanese War, an action that earned him the Nobel Peace Prize.

After he left office in 1909, Roosevelt embarked on various adventures (including African big game hunting), then helped Robert M. La Follette found the Progressive Party—popularly called the Bull Moose Party. As third-party candidate, Roosevelt outpolled Republican William Howard Taft in the 1912 elections, but he lost to Democrat Woodrow Wilson. Falling ill in 1918, TR died on January 6, 1919.

Three years after Roosevelt left office, Robert M. La Follette, U.S. Senator from Wisconsin, led a faction of the most reform-minded Republicans to form a third party, the Progressive Party. The new party drafted an enthusiastic Roosevelt as its standard bearer in the 1912 presidential elections. The Progressives sought a middle road between traditional conservatism on the one hand and populism on the other, without veering toward socialist radicalism. The Progressives advocated programs of moral uplift, such as Chicago's Hull House, founded in 1889 by social activist Jane Addams. Hull House became a model for providing recreational facilities to slum children, advocating child labor laws, and "Americanizing" immigrants. The Progressives also supported clean government, women's suffrage, and prohibition. Although many people, contemporaries and historians alike, criticized Progressivism as narrow-minded and ultimately supportive of the status quo, its spirit changed American government, bringing it more intimately and thoroughly into the everyday lives of everyday Americans.

Word for the Day

Populism is a political philosophy that supports the rights and power of the people versus the privileged, moneyed elite. It was the philosophy of the Populist Party that polled more than a million votes in the presidential election of 1892.

The Least You Need to Know

➤ In 19th-century America, the great fortunes were made on the backs of working men and women, but the labor movement gradually brought a greater degree of democracy to U.S. society.

➤ The greed and corruption rampant after the Civil War triggered a sweeping reform movement, Progressivism, which encompassed politics, social justice, and general moral "uplift."

Part 6
World Power

A "splendid little war" is what Secretary of State John Hay called America's brief combat with Spain over the independence of Cuba. Although controversial at home, the Spanish-American War demonstrated to the world that the United States was a power to be reckoned with. It was followed by a period of isolationist retreat, shattered by the United States' entry into World War I.

Following the Armistice, the nation was swept by simultaneous waves of a devil-may-care morality and a contrasting mania for sobriety, resulting in an amendment to the Constitution outlawing liquor. Drunk or sober, the country spent money like mad, made unwise investments it couldn't cover, and went broke one dismal Tuesday in 1929. A Great Depression swept the nation and the world, bringing desperation and the rise of dictators to Europe, and a new leader, Franklin Delano Roosevelt, to the United States. Here is the story of the century's most frantic and frightening years.

Chapter 25

Over There (1898–1918)

In This Chapter

➤ Jingoism, imperialism, and "yellow journalism"

➤ The Spanish-American War

➤ The Wilson administration and entry into World War I

In his Farewell Address of 1797, George Washington cautioned his fellow Americans to avoid "foreign entanglements"; for a century thereafter, the nation did just that. The United States, insulated from the European and Eastern powers by great oceans, maintained a foreign policy of strict isolation. The one chink in this isolationist armor was Central and South America. President James Monroe promulgated his Monroe Doctrine in 1823, essentially declaring the entire Western Hemisphere off-limits to European powers with designs on creating new colonies. In the course of the 19th century, the United States became the de facto major power of the hemisphere. During the century, too, while other nations amassed far-flung empires throughout the world, the United States expanded exclusively across its vast continent.

By the end of the century, the nation extended from "sea to shining sea," and a significant number of Americans (some called them "patriots," others "imperialists," and still others "jingoists") started thinking that it should extend even farther. Not content with the United States as a force in this hemisphere, these individuals wanted to see it on an equal footing with the great European powers of the world.

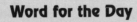

> **Word for the Day**
>
> Americans who, in characteristically loud tones, voiced support for a
> warlike, imperialist foreign policy were called *jingoes*. The word *jingo*
> apparently came from "by jingo," an expression in the refrain of a
> bellicose 19th-century English music-hall song. "By jingo" also entered
> into American popular speech as a socially acceptable alternative expletive
> to "by Jesus."

Color It Yellow

Strange as it may seem, the birth of U.S. imperialism was related to a newspaper comic. In 1895, Richard Felton Outcault, a cartoonist for the *New York World*, introduced a single-panel comic that featured as its main character a slum child costumed in a garment that was tinted yellow by a brand-new color process, of which the paper was very proud. The *World*'s publisher, Joseph Pulitzer (1847–1911), was delighted with "The Yellow Kid of Hogan's Alley," the popularity of which allowed him to close the gap in his circulation race with *The New York Journal*, published by rival news magnate William Randolph Hearst (1863–1951). Not to be outdone, Hearst lured Outcault to the ranks of the *Journal*, whereupon Pulitzer hired George Luks (who would go on to become a major American painter) to continue the original comic as simply "The Yellow Kid."

> **Word for the Day**
> *Yellow journalism*: sensational, usually nonobjective, even distorted or outright untrue journalistic practices aimed directly at readers' emotions and meant to boost newspaper circulation.

The battle over the comic was but one episode in an ongoing, high-stakes circulation war between Pulitzer and Hearst, both of whom were intent on building great publishing empires. The papers continually strove with one another to publish sensational news stories that would attract readers. But it was the yellow ink of the slum kid comics that gave this style of newspaper publishing its name when newspaperman Ervin Wardman made reference to the "yellow press of New York."

"I'll Furnish the War..."

Sometimes the quest for sensational news led the likes of Pulitzer and Hearst to publish muckraker material that exposed social injustice, corruption, and public fraud. Indeed, for all its faults, the age of yellow journalism contributed greatly to the cause of reform and introduced onto the American scene the tradition of the crusading journalist. But, noble motives aside, the circulation war kept escalating. Both Hearst and Pulitzer, hoping to bag the Big Story, dispatched reporters to cover a developing situation in Cuba, a colony of Spain that was a mere 90 miles off the Florida coast. At considerable expense, Hearst hired the great painter of life in the American West, Frederic Remington (1861–1909), and dispatched him to Cuba. When combat failed to materialize, Remington cabled Hearst: "Everything quiet. There is no trouble. There will be no war. I wish to return." The newspaper tycoon cabled in reply: "Please remain. You furnish the pictures and I'll furnish the war."

It was true that Cuban hostilities were slow to brew. The island had long been rebellious, and in February 1896, Spain sent General Valeriano Weyler (dubbed "Butcher Weyler" by Hearst) as governor. He created outrage not only in Cuba, but in the United States, when he summarily placed into "reconcentration camps" Cubans identified as sympathizing with or supporting the rebels. Although both President McKinley and his predecessor, Grover Cleveland, stoutly resisted intervening in Cuba, U.S. popular sentiment, whipped up by atrocity stories published in the papers of Pulitzer and Hearst, at last moved McKinley to order the battleship *Maine* into Havana Harbor to protect American citizens and property there.

Remember the Maine!

The temperature of America's war fever was not raised by sentiment alone. United States companies had made major investments in the island, especially in sugar plantations. Not only did revolution threaten those investments, but, to put the situation in more positive terms, a pliant puppet "independent" government in Cuba (or better yet, a Cuba annexed to the United States) would be very good for business. On February 9, Hearst scored a journalistic coup by publishing a purloined private letter in which the Spanish minister to the United States insulted President McKinley. Having for so long avoided "foreign entanglements," America was now propelled to the brink of war.

On February 15, 1898, the nation held hands and leaped over that brink. An explosion rocked Havana Harbor, and the U.S.S. *Maine* blew up, killing 266 crewmen. The Hearst and Pulitzer papers vied with one another to affix blame on Spain, and cries of "Remember the *Maine*...to hell with Spain!" echoed throughout the nation.

President McKinley, himself still reluctant, waited until April to ask Congress to authorize an invasion of Cuba. Congress not only complied but voted a resolution recognizing Cuban independence from Spain. In response, Spain declared war on the United States on April 24. However, the first action took place in the Spanish-occupied Philippine Islands, not Cuba. U.S. Admiral George Dewey (1837–1917) sailed the Asiatic Squadron from Hong Kong to Manila Bay, where, on May 1, he attacked the Spanish fleet, sinking all 10 ships in the bay. This action was followed by a landing of 11,000 U.S. troops, who, acting in concert with the guerrilla forces of Filipino rebel leader Emilio Aguinaldo, quickly defeated the Spanish army in the islands. In July, Spanish Guam also fell, and the U.S.

gathered up previously unclaimed Wake Island. Most importantly, Congress passed a resolution annexing Hawaii.

Action on Cuba was equally swift and decisive. On May 29, the U.S. fleet blockaded the Spanish fleet at Santiago Harbor, and in June, 17,000 U.S. troops landed at Daiquiri and assaulted Santiago. The war's make-or-break land battle, at San Juan Hill on July 1, included a magnificent charge by the volunteer Rough Riders, led by Lieutenant Colonel Theodore Roosevelt. In the meantime, Admiral Pasqual Cervera sailed into the harbor of Santiago de Cuba, where he was blockaded by the U.S. fleet. On July 3, after the U.S. victory at San Juan Hill, Cervera decided to run the blockade. Within four hours, his fleet was almost completely destroyed. The battle claimed 474 Spanish sailors and only two U.S. sailors. On July 17, 24,000 Spanish troops surrendered, and Madrid sued for peace nine days later. U.S. Secretary of State John Hay (1838–1905) summed it all up by dubbing the ten-week conflict a "splendid little war."

Spain withdrew from Cuba and ceded to the United States Puerto Rico and Guam; it sold the Philippines to the U.S. for $20 million. The U.S. established a territorial government in Puerto Rico but temporized on Cuba, first establishing a military government there and then allowing Cuba to draft its own constitution, albeit with U.S. supervision and with provisos. The provisos included the right to establish American military bases on the island and to intervene in Cuban affairs "in order to preserve [Cuban] independence." Until the revolution spearheaded by Fidel Castro in 1959, Cuba would exist as the often less than willing puppet of the United States.

Theodore Roosevelt, who assumed office after the September 5, 1901, assassination of McKinley and who was subsequently elected to a presidential term in his own right, promulgated the so-called "Roosevelt Corollary" to the Monroe Doctrine. In effect, this policy made the United States a kind of international police force in the Western Hemisphere. The policy was a major step toward establishing the nation as a *world* power.

He Kept Us Out of War

After taking that step, however, Americans had second thoughts. Roosevelt handpicked his old friend William Howard Taft to succeed him as president, and Taft won handily. However, Taft soon proved far more conservative than Roosevelt—although he did continue some of TR's Progressive reforms, including anti-trust prosecution and, most significantly, support for the proposed income-tax amendment to the U.S. Constitution. However, Taft did not pursue Roosevelt's aggressive foreign policy, for it was clear that most Americans wanted to return to a comfortable degree of isolationism. Taft failed to win reelection in 1912, finishing a poor third to Democrat Woodrow Wilson and TR himself (running as a third-party Progressive—"Bull Moose"—candidate).

Main Event

The 16th Amendment to the Constitution was ratified by the required two-thirds of the states in February 1913, and the federal government was henceforth authorized to collect income taxes. Initially, rates were set at 1 percent of taxable income above $3,000 for individuals and $4,000 for married couples. The highest rate was 7 percent, imposed on those with incomes in excess of $500,000. The century's two world wars would temporarily send income tax rates sky high—as high as 77 percent during World War I and 91 percent during World War II. In the middle of the second war, in 1943, Congress enacted an automatic payroll withholding system, thereby greatly increasing taxpayer "compliance" (as the IRS politely terms it) and doubling tax revenues by 1944.

Democrat Woodrow Wilson (1856–1924), president of Princeton University and, afterward, zealously reform-minded governor of New Jersey, was elected U.S. president on a Progressive platform. During his first term, the income tax was introduced, protectionist tariffs were lowered, the Federal Reserve Act (1913) reformed currency and banking laws, and antitrust legislation was strengthened in 1914 by the Federal Trade Commission Act and the Clayton Anti-Trust Act. In 1915, Wilson supported legislation that federally regulated working conditions of sailors, and in 1916, he signed the Federal Farm Loan Act into law, providing low-interest credit to farmers. Labor reform came with the Adamson Act, granting an eight-hour day to interstate railroad workers, and the Child Labor Act, curtailing children's working hours.

But Wilson faced staggering problems in foreign relations. He unsuccessfully attempted to negotiate a Pan-American pact to guarantee the mutual integrity of the Western Hemisphere. Wilson also wrestled with revolutionary Mexico, at first seeking to promote self-government by refusing to recognize the military dictatorship of General Victoriano Huerta and instead supporting constitutionalist Venustiano Carranza. But in 1916, Wilson intervened against revolutionary guerrilla leader Pancho Villa after Villa raided the border town of Columbus, New Mexico, killing several American citizens. In 1915 and 1916, Wilson also sent troops to rebellion-racked Haiti and Santo Domingo, where he established U.S. protectorates.

Despite these problems and conflicts, the majority of Americans were highly relieved that, under Wilson, the United States remained safely aloof from the cataclysm that had begun in Europe on June 28, 1914. On that pretty day in early summer, the Austro-Hungarian Archduke Franz Ferdinand and his wife, the Grand Duchess Sophie, paid a state visit to what was then the remote and obscure Balkan capital city of Sarajevo. The couple was gunned down by a young Serbian nationalist named Gavrilo Princeps. Austria-Hungary responded by accusing Serbia of having plotted the assassination. A tangled series of threats, ultimatums, and alliances was suddenly set into motion—mindlessly—as if some terrible machine had come to life. And between the great gears of that mindless machine, the people of Europe would be mangled.

At first, it looked as if the war would be a short one. The German armies made a spectacular drive through France, sweeping all resistance before them. Then, in a moment of strategic uncertainty, the German column turned and, about 30 miles outside Paris, dug in. For the next four years, Europe was doomed to the fruitless horrors of trench warfare. To the grinding tattoo of machine-gun fire, the ceaseless pounding of artillery, and the strangled moans of asphyxiation by poison gas, the nations of Europe fought one another to a standstill. France, Britain, Russia, and lesser allies were on one side; Germany, Austria-Hungary, and their lesser allies were on the other.

Lusitania Lost

President Wilson adroitly managed to keep the American nation out of this charnel house. Anxious to preserve the rights of American neutrality, he sternly warned Germany in February 1915, that the United States would hold it strictly accountable for the loss of American lives in the sinking of neutral or passenger ships. Just four months later, on May 7, 1915, a German U-boat torpedoed the British passenger liner *Lusitania,* killing 1,200 people, including 128 Americans.

Many in the United States—among them Theodore Roosevelt—clamored for immediate entry into the war. Wilson demurred, but he issued a strong protest to Germany, demanding reparations and the cessation of unrestricted submarine warfare. Although Germany protested that the *Lusitania* carried munitions (a truth that was vigorously denied by the British), officials were anxious to avoid having to face yet another enemy. Germany ordered its U-boats to give passenger ships ample warning before firing upon them. Wilson's firmness with Germany so deeply disturbed isolationist Secretary of State William Jennings Bryan that he resigned in protest. But popular sentiment was on the side of Wilson, who had retained American honor without shedding American blood. He ran successfully for a second term, propelled by the slogan "He kept us out of war."

Word for the Day

American David Bushnell (ca. 1742–1824) invented a submarine that was used during the Revolution in 1776. Then in 1864, the Confederate navy operated the submarine *Hunley* with disastrous results—for the crew of the *Hunley.* By the early 20th century, all the major European powers built submarines. By far the best were the German vessels, which were called *Unterseebooten,* or *U-booten* for short: U-boats.

Zimmermann Note

Although the Germans had backed down on unrestricted submarine warfare, relations between the United States and Germany deteriorated steadily after the *Lusitania* sinking. In February 1917, Germany announced the resumption of unrestricted submarine warfare, and on February 3, the U.S.S. *Housatonic* was torpedoed and sunk without warning. In response, President Wilson severed diplomatic relations with Germany. In the meantime, evidence of German espionage in the U.S. mounted, and on March 1, the American public learned of the "Zimmermann Note" or "Zimmermann Telegram." It was a coded message, sent on January 19, 1917, from German foreign secretary Alfred Zimmermann to his nation's ambassador to Mexico outlining the terms of a proposed German-Mexican alliance against the United States. Public sentiment left Woodrow Wilson little choice. On April 2, 1917, he asked Congress for a declaration of war. The declaration was issued on April 6.

Voice from the Past

From Woodrow Wilson's war message to Congress, April 2, 1917:

"…The present German submarine warfare against commerce is a warfare against mankind. It is a war against all nations. American ships have been sunk, American lives taken in ways which it has stirred us very deeply to learn of, but the ships and people of other neutral and friendly nations have been sunk and overwhelmed in the waters in the same way. There has been no discrimination. The challenge is to all mankind. Each nation must decide for itself how it will meet it. The choice we make for ourselves must be made with a moderation of poise and a temperateness of judgment befitting our character and our motives as a nation.

"…We have no selfish ends to serve. We desire no conquest, no dominion. We seek no indemnities for ourselves, no material compensation for the sacrifices we shall freely make. We are but one of the champions of the rights of mankind. We shall be satisfied when those rights have been made as secure as the faith and the freedom of the nations can make them…."

…Safe for Democracy

Wilson told Congress that America must go to war in order "to make the world safe for democracy." With this statement, the nation's role as guardian of the Western Hemisphere expanded to an assertion of the United States as a true world power.

The puny U.S. Army numbered only about 200,000 men in 1917; by the end of the war, it would swell to 4 million. President Wilson led a spectacular mobilization, creating a welter of special war agencies, effectively placing private industry entirely under federal control. In May 1917, Wilson pushed through Congress a Selective Service bill, by authority of which 2.8 million men were drafted. About half the army—some 2 million men—served in the AEF (Allied Expeditionary Forces) led by the very able General John J. Pershing. Naval forces sailed under the command of Admiral William S. Sims.

Pershing arrived in Paris on June 14, 1917, at a low point in the fortunes of the Allies. Every major French offensive had failed, and the demoralized French army was plagued by mutinies. The British had made a major push in Flanders, which ended in a costly stalemate. The Russians, fighting on the Eastern Front, had collapsed and were rushing headlong toward a revolution that would end centuries of czarist rule and introduce communism into the world. This revolution would also result in a "separate peace" between Russia and Germany, freeing up masses of German troops for service on the Western Front. Although the first AEF troops followed Pershing on June 26, it was October 21, 1917, before units were committed to battle and the spring of 1918 before masses of Americans actually made a difference in the fighting.

Patriots and Slackers

Pershing's first battle was not with the Germans, but with his French and British allies, who demanded that U.S. forces be placed under their control. Backed by Wilson, Pershing resisted this demand and at last prevailed, retaining full authority over U.S. troops.

There was yet another war to fight. Although a majority of Americans supported the war effort, many objected to spilling blood in a "foreign war." Wilson built a powerful propaganda machine, which produced hundreds of films, posters, pamphlets, and public presentations to portray the "Great War" as a titanic contest between the forces of good and evil, of civilization versus the omnivorous "Hun." And wherever propaganda failed, the government used emergency war powers to censor the press and to silence critics of the war. Little was done to protect the rights of U.S. citizens of German ancestry, many of whom were threatened and persecuted.

As to America's young manhood, the noblest thing one could do was to enlist. And if waiting to be drafted was considered less than patriotic, protesting or attempting to evade the draft was downright treasonous. Those who were suspected of avoiding service were branded as "slackers" and publicly humiliated.

Over the Top

Between June 6 and July 1, 1918, the "Yanks" recaptured for the Allies Vaux, Bouresches, and—after a particularly bitter battle—Belleau Wood. The Americans also managed to hold the critically important Allied position at Cantigny against a great German offensive during June 9–15. If ever the cliché about a "baptism by fire" was appropriate, it was now. American troops quickly came to know what the soldiers of Europe had experienced for the past four years: the results of humanity gone mad.

Marne

Between July 18 and August 6, 85,000 American troops broke the seemingly endless stalemate of the long war by decisively defeating the German's last major offensive at the Second Battle of the Marne. Here, at last, was a battle that could be deemed a genuine turning point. The victory was followed by Allied offensives—at the Somme, Oise-Aisne, and Ypres-Lys during August.

St. Mihiel

Although Americans fought in each of the major August offensives, they acted independently—and brilliantly—against the St. Mihiel salient during September 12–16. This battle initiated a campaign involving a massive number of U.S. troops—some 1.2 million of them—who pounded then cut German supply lines between the Meuse River and the Argonne Forest. The campaign, which continued until the very day of armistice, November 11, 1918, was highly successful, but terribly costly. American units suffered, on average, a casualty rate of 10 percent.

Word for the Day

In a military context, a *salient* is a line of battle, especially a concentrated area of defense.

Armistice

It became apparent to Germany that American soldiers were not only willing and able to fight (a matter of doubt among optimistic German strategists the year before), but that their numbers were inexhaustible, as was the American capacity for military-industrial production. The German government agreed to an *armistice*—a cessation of hostilities—to be concluded at the 11th hour of the 11th day of the 11th month of 1918.

Stats

A total of 65 million men and women served in the armies and navies of combatant nations during World War I. Of this number, at least 10 million were killed and 20 million wounded. Of the 2,000,000 U.S. troops who fought, 112,432 died, and 230,074 were wounded. The monetary cost of the war to the United States was the equivalent of $32,700,000,000 in current dollars.

As deadly as bullets, shells, and poison gas were, an influenza epidemic produced by the filthy living conditions of the war proved even more terrible. About half the number of American troop deaths were caused by "flu." The epidemic would grow to pandemic proportions after the war, killing some 21.64 million people worldwide—1 percent of the world's population. In the United States, 25 percent of the nation fell ill, and 500,000 died.

The Least You Need to Know

➤ The end of the 19th century saw the end of America's long tradition of isolation from world affairs.

➤ The United States emerged from World War I, the most terrible war the world had seen up to that time, as the champion of world democracy; although some politicians held out for a return to the nation's old isolationist ways, turning back was not possible.

Chapter 26

Jazzed, Boozed, and Busted Flat (1918–1929)

In This Chapter

➤ Wilson's "Fourteen Points"

➤ Rejection of the League of Nations

➤ The "Lost Generation" and the "Roaring Twenties"

➤ Women's right to vote and advancement of African-Americans

➤ Prohibition and the birth of organized crime

➤ Crash of the stock market

The United States had entered World War I late, but in time for the American Expeditionary Force to suffer a ghastly 10 percent casualty rate—even higher if deaths from the influenza epidemic are included. President Wilson was determined that these deaths in a "foreign war" would not be in vain. He had told the American people that the "Great War" was a "war to end all war," and he meant it. On January 8, 1918, almost a year before the war ended, Wilson announced to Congress "Fourteen Points," which he called "the only possible program" for peace. After a complex of treaty obligations had escalated an obscure Balkan conflict into a worldwide conflagration, Wilson's dream was that his Fourteen Points would create a single international alliance, making armed conflict among nations impossible. The alliance would be called the League of Nations.

A League of Nations

As vigorously as Wilson had worked to mobilize his nation for war, he now struggled to bring about a peace meant to spell the end of war. Wilson personally headed the American delegation to the Paris Peace Conference, which was charged with creating a final treaty. Driven by his intense and intensely idealistic vision of a world league and a world of perpetual peace, Wilson did not deign to develop strong bipartisan support for his peace plans. Fearing Republican isolationists would be hostile to the League of Nations, he chose not to appoint a prominent Republican to the delegation. Worse, Wilson made peace a political issue by appealing to voters to reelect a Democratic Congress in 1918. In fact, the 1918 contest went to the Republicans, who won majorities in both houses. To many, this election seemed a no-confidence vote against Wilson and his crusade for world peace.

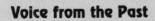

Voice from the Past

Woodrow Wilson addressed Congress on January 8, 1918, and promulgated his "Fourteen Points":

"I. Open covenants of peace, openly arrived at...

"II. Absolute freedom of navigation upon the seas...

"III. The removal...of [international] economic barriers...

"IV. Adequate guarantees...that...armaments will be reduced...

"V. ...impartial adjustment of all colonial claims...

"VI. The evacuation of all Russian territory...

"VII. Belgium...must be evacuated and restored...

"VIII. All French territory should be freed and the invaded portions restored...

"IX. A readjustment of the frontiers of Italy should be effected along clearly recognizable lines of nationality.

"X. The peoples of Austria-Hungary...should be accorded the freest opportunity of autonomous development.

"XI. Rumania, Serbia, and Montenegro should be evacuated...

"XII. The Turkish portions of the present Ottoman Empire should be assured a secure sovereignty...

"XIII. An independent Polish state should be erected...

"XIV. A general association [league] of nations must be formed..."

In Europe, Wilson was at first greeted with nothing but confidence in his leadership. However, it soon became apparent that the other major Allied leaders—Georges Clemenceau of France, David Lloyd George of Great Britain, and Vittorio Orlando of Italy—wanted to conclude a settlement that simply and severely penalized Germany. Wilson nevertheless hammered away at his Fourteen Points, ultimately seeing them embodied in the Treaty of Versailles, which, however, also imposed crippling terms on Germany. Gratified that he had won inclusion of the League of Nations as part of the treaty, Wilson presented the Versailles document to his fellow Americans as the best obtainable compromise. He felt that the League of Nations itself would eventually rectify some of the injustices presently imposed upon Germany.

Red Scare

While Wilson was trying to engineer world harmony, popular American sentiment was already retreating toward isolationism. The Russian Revolution of 1917, which toppled the long regime of the czars, was not greeted by most Americans as a victory over autocracy, but was regarded with terror as an assault on established order. A "Red Scare" swept western Europe and the United States.

At the beginning of 1919, U.S. Attorney General Mitchell Palmer ordered a series of raids on the headquarters of radical organizations in a dozen cities, indiscriminately rounding up 6,000 U.S. citizens *believed* to be "sympathetic to Communism." Palmer and others lumped Communist, radicals, and "free thinkers" together with out-and-out anarchists, who, in the wake of the Russian Revolution, were committing acts of terrorism. Anarchists mailed bombs to Palmer, Rockefeller, J.P. Morgan, and more than 30 other wealthy, prominent conservatives. Ironically, many of the bombs failed to reach their destinations—due to insufficient postage!

In a climate of intense fear, outrage, and confusion, Palmer created the General Intelligence Division, headed by an eager young Justice Department investigator named J. Edgar Hoover. With meticulous zeal, Hoover (in those precomputer days) created by hand a massive card index of 150,000 radical leaders, organizations, and publications. As all too often happened in American history, beginning with the Alien and Sedition Acts passed at the end of the 18th century, legislators and administrators did not hesitate to take totalitarian measures to defend American liberty.

End of the Dream

Fear of Communism was not the only thing that chipped away at Wilson's dream. Although the president tried to convince the American people—and himself—that the Treaty of Versailles was the best compromise possible, it was actually one of the most tragic documents in history. Although Wilson succeeded in persuading France to concede its key demand—that the left bank of the Rhine be severed from Germany and put under

235

French military control—the treaty dictated humiliating, economically devastating terms. Germany was forced to accept full guilt for the war, to cede huge sections of territory, and to disarm almost completely.

The Allies hoped that, by weakening Germany, the nation could never again threaten Europe's peace. However, the punitive terms of Versailles so destabilized Germany that the nation became ripe for the dark promises of Adolf Hitler, who came into prominence during the 1920s and 1930s. Instead of preventing another war, the Treaty of Versailles *guaranteed* one—a war that would prove even more devastating that the 1914–18 conflict.

At home, Wilson's lapse of political savvy was taking its toll as Henry Cabot Lodge (1850–1924) led Senate Republican opposition to the U.S. commitment to the League of Nations. Believing the League to be above politics, Wilson accepted little compromise and decided to bring popular pressure on the Senate by taking his case directly to the people. He embarked on a rigorous 9,500-mile transcontinental whistle-stop speaking tour. On September 25, 1919, exhausted by war, by the heartbreaking labors of making peace, and by his battle on behalf of the League of Nations, Woodrow Wilson collapsed following a speech in Pueblo, Colorado. He was rushed back to Washington, but his condition deteriorated and, a week later, he suffered a devastating stroke that left him partially paralyzed. Ill, desperate, frustrated, and embittered, Wilson instructed his followers to accept absolutely no compromise on the League.

American politics has always thrived on compromise; and now, without it, the Senate rejected the Treaty of Versailles and the League of Nations. Woodrow Wilson, his health continuing to decline, could only watch as the "war to end all war" came to look more and more like just another war fought in vain. Warren G. Harding (1865–1923), the Republican who succeeded Wilson in the White House, ran on a pledge of a "return to normalcy." Harding told Congress that "we seek no part in directing the destinies of the world...[the League] is not for us."

A Generation Lost and Found

Woodrow Wilson was not the only embittered individual in postwar America. Four years of European carnage had shown the worst of which humanity was capable. The war broke the spirit of some people; in others, it created a combination of restlessness, desperation, boredom, and thrill-seeking that earned the decade its nickname: the Roaring Twenties. Some Americans, mostly young intellectuals, found that after the war, they could not settle back into life at home. A colony of expatriate artists and writers gathered in Paris. Many of these individuals congregated in the apartment of a remarkable medical school dropout named Gertrude Stein—writer, art collector, and cultivator of creative talent. One day, she remarked to one of these young people, Ernest Hemingway, "You are all a lost generation." That phrase stuck as a description of those individuals cast adrift after the war, their former ideals shattered by battle, yet unable to find new values to replace the old.

Stein, Fitzgerald, Hemingway & Co.

The United States, land of liberty and opportunity, had much to be proud of. The nation touted its superiority to Europe, whose masses often suffered under conditions of political enslavement and spiritual and physical want. Yet, in matters of art and culture, America never quite outgrew its "colonial" status. True, the United States did produce a number of remarkable world-class writers during the 19th century—including Washington Irving, Edgar Allan Poe, Ralph Waldo Emerson, Henry David Thoreau, Nathaniel Hawthorne, Walt Whitman, Herman Melville, Emily Dickinson, Mark Twain, and others. And America had some extraordinary visual artists—such as the unparalleled group of landscape painters dubbed the Hudson River School, who emerged under the leadership of Thomas Cole and Frederick Edwin Church. Despite this prominent talent, the United States entered the 20th century still bowing to the aesthetic culture of Europe, as if Americans could never quite measure up.

During the 1920s, however, a group of American writers made an unmistakable impact on the cultural life of the world. Two of the most important, Ernest Hemingway (1899–1961) and F. Scott Fitzgerald (1896–1940), were frequent guests at Gertrude Stein's *salon*, where they discussed how they would write "the great American novel." Francis Scott Key Fitzgerald (named for the ancestor who wrote "The Star-Spangled Banner") burst onto the literary scene with *This Side of Paradise,* a 1920 novel that ushered in the "Jazz Age" with a vivid portrait of the youth of the Lost Generation. Two years later came *The Beautiful and Damned* and, in 1925, *The Great Gatsby.* This story of the enigmatic Jay Gatsby explored the American dream in poetic, satirical, and ultimately tragic detail. The theme was again plumbed a decade later in *Tender Is the Night* (1934).

While Fitzgerald probed the American psyche by dissecting the desperate denizens of the Jazz Age, Hemingway created character after character who turned away from the roar of the Roaring Twenties to worlds of elemental dangers and basic pleasures. His stories portrayed driven efforts to recover the meaning that, through a combination of war and postwar spiritual exhaustion, had evaporated from life. The work of Fitzgerald and Hemingway, as well as the novelist Theodore Dreiser (1871–1945), the poet Hart Crane (1899–1932), and the playwright Eugene O'Neill (1888–1953), at last allowed Americans to see themselves as the cultural equals of Europeans. Through the despair and desperation that lay behind the wild music and loose morality of the 1920s, American art and literature came of age.

Women Get the Vote

The American woman also came of age in the 1920s, emerging from subjugation to straitlaced Victorian ideals of decorum and femininity. Women joined the work force in increasing numbers, and they became lively participants in the intellectual life of the nation. The most profound step toward the liberation of American women was the ratification of the 19th Amendment to the U.S. Constitution, which gave women the right to vote.

A Renaissance in Harlem

There was growing liberation, too, for another long-oppressed group: African-Americans. Slavery had ended with the Civil War, but blacks hardly enjoyed the same opportunities and privileges as most other Americans. In the North as well as the South, blacks were discriminated against in education, employment, housing, and in just about every other phase of life. Segregation was *de facto* in the North—unofficial, but nonetheless real—and *de jure* in the South—actually mandated by law. African-Americans had served with distinction during World War I but were put into segregated units. The French did not discriminate against blacks, and for some African-American soldiers, the overseas experience was an eye-opener. They returned to the States no longer willing to accept second-class citizenship.

Many white Americans did not so much discriminate against blacks, as they failed to *see* them, as if they were invisible. Excluded from positions of power and influence, African-Americans simply did not much matter—as far as mainstream white society was concerned.

The humble peanut helped to change this attitude. In 1921, George Washington Carver, who had been born a Missouri slave in 1864, testified before Congress on behalf of the National Association of Peanut Growers to extol and explain the wonders of what had been a minor crop. Against all odds, Carver had worked his way through college, earning a master's degree in agriculture in 1896 and accepting a teaching position at Tuskegee Institute. Tuskegee had been founded in Alabama by African-American educator Booker T. Washington (1856–1915) as a source of higher education for blacks. At Tuskegee, Carver concentrated on developing new products from crops—including the peanut and the sweet potato—that could replace cotton as the staple of southern farmers. Cotton was a money maker, but it quickly depleted soil, and farmers solely dependent on cotton soon were ruined. Carver transformed peanuts and sweet potatoes into plastic materials, lubricants, dyes, drugs, inks, wood stains, cosmetics, tapioca, molasses, and most famously, peanut butter. His contribution to revitalizing the perpetually beleaguered agricultural economy of the South was significant; but even more, Carver showed both white and black America that an African-American could accomplish great things. For blacks, he was a source of pride; for white Americans, he was the first culturally *visible* black man.

Indeed, while oppression was still a fact of African-American life during the 1920s, white intellectuals became intensely interested in the intellectual and artistic creations of blacks. African-American artists and writers were drawn to New York City's Harlem neighborhood, where they produced works that drew widespread attention and admiration. This literary and artistic movement was called the Harlem Renaissance and drew inspiration from the black political leader W.E.B. Du Bois (1868–1963). Du Bois edited *The Crisis*, the magazine of the National Association for the Advancement of Colored People (NAACP), an important organization founded in 1909 by a group of black as well as white social thinkers. Du Bois argued that blacks could not achieve social equality by merely emulating whites, but that they had to awaken black racial pride by discovering their own African cultural heritage. Some significant American writers associated with the movement Du Bois was instrumental in launching were poet Countee Cullen (1903–46), novelist Rudolph Fisher (1897–1934), poet-essayist Langston Hughes (1902–67), folklorist Zora Neale Hurston (1901–60), poet James Weldon Johnson(1871–1938), and novelist Jean Toomer (1894–1967).

Harlem became a popular spot for white nightclubbers seeking first-class jazz from great African-American musicians like Fletcher Henderson (1898–1952), Louis Armstrong (1900–1971), and the young Duke Ellington (1899–1974). The neighborhood also developed into a gathering place for avant-garde white intellectuals who did what would have been unthinkable just a decade before: they spoke and mingled with African-American writers, artists, and thinkers.

America Dries Up

The general liberalization of morals that accompanied America's entry into World War I fueled a temperance movement that culminated in the 18th Amendment to the Constitution, prohibiting the sale, importation, or consumption of alcoholic beverages anywhere in the United States. The Volstead Act, passed after ratification, provided for federal enforcement of Prohibition.

Gangster Culture

Greeted by some as a "noble experiment," Prohibition was for a majority of Americans an invitation to violate the law. The 1920s, therefore, became by definition a lawless decade. Otherwise law-abiding citizens made bathtub gin, brewed homemade beer, fermented wine in their cellars, and frequented "blind pigs" and "speakeasies"—covert saloons that served booze in coffee mugs and teacups. Police raids on such establishments were common enough, but mostly, officials looked the other way—especially if they were paid to do so.

Corruption hardly stopped with the cop on the street. City and state governments were receptive to payoffs, and indeed, the presidential administration of Warren G. Harding rivaled that of Ulysses S. Grant for scandals. In this national atmosphere, mobsterism came to birth and flourished. Underlying the violence was the idea of crime as a business, and by the end of the decade, a quasi-corporate entity called the Syndicate would be formed to "organize" crime.

Countdown to Black Tuesday

If morals, mores, and ideas were freewheeling in the 1920s, so was spending. For most— except farmers and unskilled laborers—the decade was prosperous, sometimes wildly so. Americans speculated on stocks in unprecedented numbers, often overextending themselves by purchasing securities "on margin," putting down as little as 10 cents on the dollar in the hope that the stock would rise fast and far enough to cover what amounted to very substantial loans.

Joy Ride

The fact was that so much stock had been bought on margin—backed by dimes rather than dollars—that much of it amounted to little more than paper. Even worse, although production in well-financed factories soared, the buying power of consumers failed to keep pace. Soon, industry was making more than people were buying. As goods piled up and prices fell, industry began laying off workers. People without jobs do not buy goods. As more workers were laid off, the marketplace shrunk smaller and smaller. Companies do not make new hires in a shrinking marketplace. And so the cycle went.

Crash

Despite this cycle, stock prices continued to spiral upward. But the market showed warning signs of instability. During the autumn of 1929, stock prices fluctuated wildly, then, on October 24, the stock market was seized by a selling spree. Five days later, on October 29, "Black Tuesday," the bottom fell out and stock prices plummeted. With prices falling, brokers "called" their margin loans, demanding immediate payment in full on stocks that were now worthless. Many investors were wiped out in an instant. A rash of suicides swept the business community; some investors actually leapt from Wall Street high-rise windows.

Stats

Stocks lost an average of 40 points on Black Tuesday. In 1930, 1,300 banks failed. By 1933, another 3,700 would fail, and 1 of 4 workers would be jobless.

President Calvin Coolidge had declared during the booming mid-decade years that "The business of America is business." Herbert Hoover, elected president in 1928, found himself nervously assuring his stunned and fearful fellow Americans that "prosperity was just around the corner." As it so happened, that corner would not be turned for an entire decade.

The Least You Need to Know

➤ The failure of the United States to join the League of Nations doomed that precursor of the United Nations to ultimate failure.

➤ The climate of the 1920s, at once wildly creative, liberating, desperate, and reckless, was in large part the result of the aftereffects of World War I.

➤ The stock market crash of 1929 was the culmination of a cycle of careless, credit-based investment and increased industrial output versus a shrinking market for industrial goods.

Chapter 27

A New Deal and a New War (1930–1941)

In This Chapter

➤ The Hoover administration during the Great Depression

➤ FDR's New Deal

➤ An era of "organized crime"

➤ Approach and outbreak of World War II

Herbert Clark Hoover was born on August 10, 1874, the son of a West Branch, Iowa, blacksmith. He learned the meaning of hard work practically from the cradle, and at age 8, he also came to know the tragedy of loss. Orphaned, Hoover was sent to live with an uncle in Oregon and enrolled in the mining engineering program at Stanford University, graduating in 1895. For some 20 years, Hoover traveled the world, earning a fortune as a mining engineer. The Quaker ideals acquired from his uncle prompted him to aid in relief efforts during World War I, and Hoover earned a reputation as an effective humanitarian. During the period of U.S. participation in the war, Hoover served as food administrator, charged with promoting agricultural production and food conservation. At the end of the war, President Wilson sent Hoover to Europe to direct the American Relief Administration. Hoover served as U.S. secretary of commerce in the cabinets of Warren G. Harding and Calvin Coolidge.

When Coolidge declined to seek a second term (privately observing that an economic disaster was on the way, and he didn't want any part of it), Hoover easily won election as the nation's 31st president. He ran on the optimistic platform that, if everyone would just put their heads together, poverty would be eliminated in America. The future looked bright. And who should know this better than a man justly hailed as "the great humanitarian"?

Brother, Can You Spare a Dime?

When the Wall Street crash came, Hoover was slow to react and merely assured the public that "prosperity was just around the corner." As each month brought worse financial news and lengthened the lines of the jobless, the homeless, and the desperate, Hoover proposed a number of relief programs, but insisted that the state and local governments were responsible for financing them. In principle, this arrangement was prudent. Who better knew the needs of the people than their local government? In practice, however, the policy was doomed for a very simple reason: state and local governments had no money.

Most significantly, Hoover steadfastly refused to make federal aid available directly to individuals. He feared that big-government intervention would compromise the liberty, integrity, and initiative of the individual citizen.

In the meantime, shanty towns constructed of boxes and crates bloomed like evil flowers across the American landscape to house the homeless. "Hoovervilles" they were called, and the "great humanitarian's" reputation was forever tarnished. Unjustly—but understandably—blame for the Great Depression was laid entirely at the doorstep of the White House.

The Verge of Revolution

America had had its share of boom and bust before. But the Great Depression of the 1930s was unparalleled in magnitude, scope, and duration. Fifteen to 25 percent of the work force was jobless. Families lost their savings, their homes, and even their lives—to disease and sometimes starvation. The Depression was not confined to the United States. It gripped the world, especially those citadels of democracy, the Western capitalist nations. Worst of all, the Depression showed no signs of letup. As the unrelieved years went by, want and misery became a way of life.

Discontent and despair bred revolution. The nations of Europe seethed—especially Germany, already economically crippled by the punitive Treaty of Versailles, now brought to its knees by the Depression. First in Italy, then in Germany—and to a lesser extent, elsewhere in Europe—two major ideologies came into violent opposition: Fascism versus Communism. To most Americans, both of these totalitarian ideologies seemed clearly repugnant to democracy.

Word for the Day

Fascism, a system of government marked by centralization of authority under an absolute dictator, was masterminded in Italy by Benito Mussolini (1883–1945). The name comes from the Latin word *fasces,* a bundle or rods bound together around an ax, which was the ancient Roman symbol of authority. *Communism,* as proposed by Karl Marx (1818–83), is a system of collective ownership of property and the collective administration of power for the common good. In practice, Communism is a system of government characterized by state ownership of property and the centralization of authority in a single political party or dictator. *Totalitarianism* describes any system of government in which the individual is wholly subordinate to the state.

Democracy was not putting beans on the table, however. Among intellectuals and even some radical workers, Communism seemed to offer a viable alternative to what was apparently the nation's failed capitalism. Slowly but surely, the gunpowder scent of revolution tainted American air.

The Epoch of FDR

Born to wealth in Hyde Park, New York, in 1882, Franklin Delano Roosevelt never experienced poverty firsthand. The product of Groton School, Harvard University, and Columbia University Law School, young Roosevelt became a Wall Street lawyer. He devoted some of his time to free legal work for the poor and by this means came to know and sympathize with the plight of the so-called common man. FDR worked his way to prominence in Dutchess County (New York) politics and was appointed assistant secretary of the Navy in the Wilson administration. In 1920, FDR was running mate to James M. Cox, the democratic presidential hopeful who lost to Republican Warren G. Harding.

Then came Roosevelt's darkest—and finest—hour. In the summer of 1921, while resident at his summer home on Campobello Island (New Brunswick, Canada), Roosevelt was felled by polio. Desperately ill, he recovered, but was left paralyzed from the waist down.

His mother urged him to retire to the family's Hyde Park estate. His wife, the remarkable Eleanor Roosevelt—FDR's distant cousin and the niece of Theodore Roosevelt—persuaded FDR to return to public life. With great personal strength and courage, Roosevelt underwent intensive physical therapy, learned to stand using iron leg braces, to walk with the aid of crutches, and even to drive his own car. He ran for governor of New York and won, bringing to the state such progressive measures as the development of public power utilities, civil-service reform, and social-welfare programs.

When he decided to run for president, Roosevelt faced opponents who objected that he was neither intellectually nor (obviously!) physically fit for the White House.

FDR proved his opponents dead wrong. Having overcome the odds in his personal fight against polio, Roosevelt set about proving himself capable of overcoming the even grimmer odds in the national fight to lift America out of Depression. FDR flew to Chicago and addressed the 1932 Democratic National Convention, pledging to deliver to the American people a "New Deal," a *federally* funded, *federally* administered program of relief and recovery.

Government Redefined

When he accepted the 1932 Democratic presidential nomination, Franklin D. Roosevelt declared: "I pledge you, I pledge myself, to a new deal for the American people." Following Roosevelt's inauguration, the phrase "New Deal" caught on in a way that transformed the federal government. Within the first three months of the new administration—dubbed with Napoleonic grandeur by the press the "Hundred Days"—FDR introduced to Congress his relief legislation. The legislation promised to stimulate industrial recovery, assist individual victims of the Depression (something Hoover and all previous presidents had refused to do), guarantee minimum living standards, and help avert future crises.

Most of the actual legislation of the Hundred Days was aimed at providing immediate relief. The Federal Deposit Insurance Corporation (FDIC) was established to protect depositors from losing their savings in the event of bank failure. The measure did much to restore confidence in the nation's faltering banking system. The Federal Reserve Board, which regulates the nation's money supply, was strengthened. The Home Owners Loan Corporation was established to supply funds to help beleaguered home owners avoid foreclosure. A Federal Securities Act reformed the regulation of stock offering and trading—an effort to avert the kind of wild speculation that helped bring about the crash of 1929.

Next, the Civilian Conservation Corps—the CCC—put thousands of men to work on projects in national forests, parks, and public lands; the National Recovery Act (NRA), most sweeping and controversial of the early New Deal legislation, established the Public Works Administration (PWA) and imposed upon industry a strict code of fair practice.

The act set minimum wages and maximum working hours and gave employees the right to collective bargaining. Private industry fought FDR tooth and nail on the NRA, but such was the depth of the Depression crisis and the personal charisma of Roosevelt that the administration prevailed.

In sharp contrast to the world's communist regimes, the Roosevelt administration showed equal concern for the industrial worker and the agricultural worker. Farmers were in a desperate plight during the Depression, and in May 1933, FDR prevailed on Congress to create the Agricultural Adjustment Administration, a program of production limits and federal subsidies. Perhaps the single most visible manifestation of the New Deal program of agricultural reform was the establishment of the Tennessee Valley Authority (TVA), which built roads, great dams, and hydroelectric plants in seven of the nation's poorest states.

More programs followed the Hundred Days. In 1935, the Works Progress Administration (WPA) was formed, which put 8.5 million people to work between 1935 and 1943—when the program ended. The employees built public projects out of concrete and steel, and they also created cultural works through the Federal Theater Project, the Federal Writers' Program, and the Federal Art Project. The most enduring of the New Deal programs was Social Security, introduced in 1935, which created old-age pension funds through payroll and wage taxes. None of the New Deal programs brought full recovery, but they helped restore confidence in the American government and propelled Roosevelt to a landslide second-term victory over Republican Alf Landon in 1936. A "Second New Deal" went into effect, which concentrated on labor reforms.

Stats
Despite the New Deal, 9.5 million people remained unemployed by 1939.

Urban War

In the end, it would take the approach of World War II, with its demand for the materials of strife, to end the Great Depression. But years before the United States entered that war, another, different kind of combat was being waged on the streets of the nation's cities. Prohibition had spawned a gangster culture in the 1920s, which many Americans found colorful, almost romantic. After all, the urban outlaws supplied the public with the good times that government denied them.

Then came St. Valentine's Day, 1929, the day Al Capone decided to eliminate rival Chicago gangland leader "Bugs" Moran. Capone dispatched gunmen, disguised as policemen, who rounded up seven members of the gang, stood them up against the wall of Moran's commercial garage, and brutally executed them with Tommy guns. (Moran himself wasn't present and escaped assassination.) Mobsters had been rubbing one another out for years, but the blatant butchery of the St. Valentine's Day Massacre finally outraged the public. Capone and other gangsters were no longer viewed as Robin Hoods, but as cold-blooded murderers. Yet, as gangsters became more viciously violent, they also became increasingly organized.

In the same year as the St. Valentine's Day Massacre, Capone proposed to the gang leaders of New York and other cities that they meet to *organize* crime throughout the United States. The meeting took place in Atlantic City and included such underworld luminaries as Lucky Luciano, Joe Adonis, Alberto Anastasia, Frank Costello, and Meyer Lansky. The national crime Syndicate was born, consolidating nationwide gambling, prostitution, extortion, and liquor trafficking. After 1933, when the 18th Amendment was repealed, thereby ending Prohibition, the Syndicate began to enter the trade in narcotics, hoping it would replace booze as the public's illicit substance of choice.

The economic conditions of the 1930s produced at least two durable legacies into American life: one, a federal government that takes an active role in the welfare of its citizens (even today, when many conservative politicians clamor to slash "welfare budgets," few are foolhardy enough to suggest reducing the Social Security program) and two, organized crime.

Main Event

The Depression-born longing for a bright future was summed up in two great World's Fairs. The Century of Progress Exhibition of 1933–34, held in Chicago, did much to popularize modern architecture. And the New York World's Fair of 1939–40 was built around the theme of "The World of Tomorrow"—even as the nightmare of total war broke once again upon Europe.

A New War

The Great Depression brought the United States close to the brink of revolution, but a deeply ingrained tradition of democratic capitalism, combined with FDR's ability to restore and maintain faith in the government, averted a violent breakdown. In Europe, also hard hit by the Depression, the people of Italy and Germany hungered not for democracy, but for the strongman leadership promised by a journalist named Benito Mussolini (1883–1945) and a failed artist, sometimes house painter, and full-time political agitator named Adolf Hitler (1889–1945). Exhausted humanity had assumed that the horrors of World War I, combined with the peaceful prosperity of the 1920s, guaranteed the permanent rise of international stability and liberal constitutionalism. But Germany, crippled by the harsh conditions of the Versailles treaty, was robbed of postwar prosperity. Then the Depression drove its people to desperation. In Germany and Italy, militaristic authoritarianism burst into iron blossom with promises of a return to national glory and national prosperity.

Europe Darkens, Then Dies

In Germany, Hitler and his Nazi party won a popular following that propelled him to the position of chancellor under the aged and infirm President Paul von Hindenberg and into absolute dictatorship after Hindenberg's death in 1934. Hitler took Germany out of the League of Nations in 1933 and, in defiance of the Treaty of Versailles, initiated a massive rearmament program. In 1936, the dictator sent troops into the Rhineland, which had been demilitarized by the Versailles treaty. The League of Nations stood by helplessly, as did the Allies of World War I. Indeed, one of those erstwhile Allies, Italy, openly sided with Nazi Germany. Seeking an easy foreign conquest to solidify popular support, Benito Mussolini, like some monstrous incarnation of a schoolyard bully, sent Italy's modern army into Africa against Ethiopians who were armed chiefly with spears. Ethiopia collapsed by 1936, and although the nation's emperor, Haile Salassie (1892–1975), appealed to the League of Nations with great dignity and eloquence, the world body, once again, proved impotent.

Hard on the heels of the Italian conquest of Ethiopia came the Spanish Civil War (1936–39), a complex struggle between factions allied with the nation's liberal–leftist republican government and Fascist-sympathizing rightists led primarily by General Francisco Franco (1892–1975). Hitler and Mussolini eagerly sent military aid to Franco, and Hitler's *Luftwaffe* (air force) in particular used Spanish towns as practice targets in preparation for the greater conflict looming on the dark horizon. While Soviet dictator Joseph Stalin (1879–1953) gave military equipment to the Spanish republicans, the United States, Britain, and France—fearing the outbreak of a general war—remained neutral.

Their reluctance was as understandable as it was tragic. After all, in 1914, a tangle of alliances had escalated a local Balkans war into a conflagration that engulfed the world. Yet while the former Allies waffled and waited, Germany and Italy forged the Rome–Berlin Axis in 1936. That same year, in Asia, the Empire of Japan concluded the Anti-Comintern Pact (an alliance against Communism) with Germany; in 1937, Italy signed on to the pact as well. The following year, 1938, Hitler invaded Austria and annexed it to his Third Reich. The year 1938 also saw Hitler's demand that the Sudetenland—western Czechoslovakia, where many ethnic Germans lived—be joined to the Reich. France and Britain were bound by treaty to defend the territorial integrity of Czechoslovakia, but they nevertheless yielded the Sudetenland to Germany in an effort to "appease" Hitler. British prime minister Neville Chamberlain told the world that the cession of the Sudetenland (the Munich Agreement) insured "peace in our time."

He was wrong. In 1939, Hitler seized the rest of Czechoslovakia, then took a part of Lithuania and prepared to gobble up the so-called Polish Corridor, a narrow strip of land that separated East Prussia from the rest of Germany. At this time, Mussolini's Italy annexed Albania. Finally, on September 1, 1939, Germany invaded—and crushed—Poland. France and Britain could no longer stand by. World War II had begun.

Infamy at Pearl

While American eyes focused nervously on Europe, Asia was heating to the point of crisis. Despite a 1922 pledge to respect China's territorial integrity, Japan invaded Manchuria in 1931 and established the puppet state of Manchuko the following year. The League of Nations protested, resulting in nothing more than Japan's withdrawal from the organization in 1933. By 1937, Japan and China were engaged in full-scale war. On September 27, 1940, Japan signed the Tripartite Pact with Italy and Germany, thereby creating the Berlin–Rome–Tokyo Axis.

Although it remained officially neutral, the United States, guided by Roosevelt, edged closer to war. The sale of military supplies was authorized, and then, in March 1941, Congress passed the Lend-Lease Act, permitting the shipment of material to nations whose defense was considered vital to U.S. security—Great Britain and, later, China and the U.S.S.R. In September 1940, the first peacetime draft law in U.S. history had been passed, authorizing the registration of 17 million men. In August and September 1941, U.S. merchant vessels were armed for self-defense. The powder was packed in the keg. All it took was a flame for the war to explode upon America.

It came on December 7, 1941. At 7:50 on that quiet Sunday morning, Japanese aircraft struck without warning at Pearl Harbor, Hawaii, where some 75 major U.S. Navy ships were moored. By 10 am, the attack was over.

The next day, President Roosevelt asked Congress for a declaration of war, calling December 7, 1941, a "day which will live in infamy." Suddenly, the Great Depression ended in a headlong rush of young men into the armed forces and of others, men as well as women, into the nation's factories. Industries now tooled up—for the second time in the century—to serve as the "arsenal of democracy."

The Least You Need to Know

➤ Although unjust, Herbert Hoover is often blamed for having caused the Depression; however, the federal government did not take major steps to bring economic relief until Roosevelt assumed office.

➤ The massive programs of the New Deal probably averted social breakdown and revolution in the U.S., but it was the economic demands of World War II that finally ended the Great Depression.

Chapter 28

The "Good War" (1941–1945)

In This Chapter

➤ Early defeats

➤ Turning points: victory in North Africa and at Midway

➤ Collapse of Germany

➤ Use of the atomic bomb against Japan

When America had entered World War I, it rushed to mobilize forces for a *European* war. Now, even as Europe was being overrun by Nazi Germany, Japan had struck directly at United States territory (Hawaii did not become a *state* until 1959). Preparations for war were even more urgent in 1941 than they had been in 1917, and the blow at Pearl Harbor was just one of many Japanese assaults. Japanese forces attacked Wake Island and Guam (both U.S. possessions), British Malaya, Singapore, the Dutch East Indies, Burma, Thailand, and the Philippines (at the time a U.S. commonwealth territory). The U.S. garrison on Guam was overwhelmed and surrendered. On Wake Island, Marines repelled a first Japanese attack but yielded to a second. Britain's crown colony of Hong Kong collapsed, soon followed by Singapore (another British possession), and then the Dutch East Indies.

Burma likewise fell, despite the efforts of Claire L. Chennault (1890–1958), a former U.S. Army Air Service officer and now air adviser to China's premier Chiang Kai-Shek. Chennault led his famous Flying Tigers—a small force of U.S.-made Curtiss P-40 fighter planes—in crippling action against the enemy's aircraft.

For the United States, as for the rest of the formerly "free" world, the opening years of World War II were humiliating, dismal, and terrifying.

I Shall Return

The hardest blow in the Pacific came in the Philippines, where General Douglas MacArthur (1880–1964), commanding 55,000 Filipinos and Americans, made a heroic stand on the Bataan Peninsula, but at last, in February 1942, was ordered to escape to Australia to assume command of the Allied forces in the southwestern Pacific. Regretfully, MacArthur left his troops to their fate. "I shall return," he pledged—but it would take until 1944 for the Allies to put him into a position to redeem that pledge.

Under Lieutenant General Jonathan M. Wainwright, the Filipino-American forces held out until May 6, 1942, when they surrendered and were subject to unspeakable brutality at the hands of Japanese captors.

Main Event

The Japanese military was guided by the code of the Samurai warrior, as ancient as it was harsh. To be killed in battle was an honor, but to be taken prisoner, a disgrace. Accordingly, the Japanese treated its prisoners of war as dishonored men. America learned this fact the hard way when U.S. and Filipino soldiers who surrendered at Corregidor on April 9, 1942, were sent on a forced march to captivity in Bataan. The infamous Bataan Death March resulted in the deaths of 10,000 P.O.W.s because of abuse and starvation.

Thirty Seconds Over Tokyo

Desperate for a counterstrike against Japan, the Army Air Force approved the plan of Lieutenant Colonel James Doolittle (1896–1993) to take 16 B-25s aboard the aircraft carrier *Hornet* and launch, on April 18, 1942, a surprise bombing raid on Tokyo. This attack was the closest thing to a deliberate suicide mission American military personnel ever undertook during the war. Everyone well knew that the twin-engine bombers could not carry sufficient fuel to return to any American base. Even if they had had enough fuel capacity to return to the *Hornet*, the bombers, not designed for carrier flight, would have been unable to land. The plan was to ditch the planes in China, find safe haven among Chinese resistance fighters, and somehow, find a way to return home. Miraculously, most of the bomber crews were, in fact, rescued, and while the damage to Tokyo was minor, the psychological effect was great. The attack shocked the Japanese, who were forced to tie up more fighter aircraft at home, and American morale was given a terrific boost.

Home Front

For all its horror, World War II is recalled by many Americans as an almost magical time, when the nation united with single-minded purpose in a cause both desperate and just— a struggle, quite literally, of good against evil. Everyone pitched in to produce the materials of war, and women joined the work force in unprecedented numbers as the men were inducted into the armed forces.

Activity on the home front also had an ugly side. On February 19, 1942, responding to pressure from West Coast politicians, FDR signed Executive Order 9066. The order required all Japanese-Americans living within 200 miles of the Pacific shores—citizens and resident aliens alike—to report for relocation in internment camps located in California, Idaho, Utah, Arizona, Wyoming, Colorado, and Arkansas. Military officials feared sabotage, but non-Japanese farmers in the region feared competition even more and were eager to get rid of their Japanese-American neighbors.

Afrika Korps

In 1941, Northern Africa was held by Field Marshal Erwin Rommel (1891–1944), known as the "Desert Fox," whose Afrika Korps was seemingly invincible. The British and Americans agreed to conduct a North African campaign, defeat the Germans there, and then attack what Britain's great wartime prime minister Winston Churchill called the "soft underbelly of Europe." Forces under British Field Marshal Bernard Law Montgomery and American generals Dwight D. Eisenhower and George S. Patton decisively defeated the Germans and Italians in North Africa by May 1943, and an Italian invasion was launched.

Voice from the Past

For many Americans, the most stirring voice of the war was that of a Britisher, Prime Minister Winston Churchill. The man was so greatly admired in this country that, in 1963, Churchill was made an honorary citizen by act of Congress—a unique event in American history. His first address as prime minister was delivered on May 13, 1940:

continues

"…I say to the House as I said to Ministers who have joined this government, I have nothing to offer but blood, toil, tears, and sweat. We have before us an ordeal of the most grievous kind. We have before us many, many months of struggle and suffering.

"You ask, what is our policy? I say it is to wage war by land, sea, and air. War with all our might and with all the strength God has given us, and to wage war against a monstrous tyranny never surpassed in the dark and lamentable catalogue of human crime. That is our policy.

"You ask, what is our aim? I can answer in one word. It is victory. Victory at all costs—victory in spite of all terrors—victory, however long and hard the road may be, for without victory there is no survival…"

Coral Sea and Midway

While the Germans began to lose to their grip on Africa, U.S. forces also started to turn the tide in the Pacific. During May 3–9, 1942, the navy sunk or disabled more than 25 Japanese ships, blocking Japan's extension to the south and preventing the Japanese from severing supply lines to Australia. However, the Japanese soon returned to the offensive by attacking the island of Midway, some 1,100 miles northwest of Hawaii. Marshalling a task force of 200 ships and 600 planes, the Japanese counted on the element of surprise to achieve a rapid victory. But, unknown to them, American intelligence officers had broken Japanese codes, and the navy had advance warning of the task force.

The battle commenced on June 3, 1942, and U.S. aircraft, launched from the *Hornet*, *Yorktown*, and *Enterprise*, sank four Japanese carriers. Reeling from this blow, the Imperial Navy withdrew their fleet, but the Americans gave chase, sinking or disabling two heavy cruisers and three destroyers, as well as destroying 322 planes. Although the U.S. Navy took heavy losses—the carrier *Yorktown*, a destroyer, and 147 aircraft—Midway Island remained in American hands, and the Japanese were never able to resume the offensive in the Pacific.

Island Hopping

After suffering defeat at Midway, the Japanese turned their attention to mounting a full-scale assault on Australia. They began by constructing an airstrip on Guadalcanal in the southern Solomon Islands. In response, on August 7, 1942, a U.S. task force landed Marines at Guadalcanal, where the Japanese resisted for six months. Guadalcanal was the beginning of a U.S. strategy of "island hopping": a plan to take or retake all Japanese-held islands, thereby gradually closing in on the Japanese mainland itself. The campaign promised to be a very long haul. Guadalcanal, having taken six hellish months to conquer, was fully 3,000 miles from Tokyo.

The next step was to neutralize the major Japanese air and naval base at Rabaul, on the eastern tip of New Britain Island, just east of New Guinea. Under General MacArthur, U.S. and Australian troops attacked through the Solomons and New Guinea. When the Japanese rushed to reinforce their position on the islands of Lae and Salamaua, on March 3–4, 1943, U.S. B-24 Liberators and B-17 Flying Fortresses attacked troop transports and their naval escorts with devastating results. The Battle of the Bismarck Sea cost the Japanese 3,500 men; the Allies lost only five planes. The defeat was a severe blow to the Japanese presence in the southwest Pacific. By the end of 1943, Rabaul had been neutralized, severing some 100,000 Japanese from any hope of supply, support, or reinforcement.

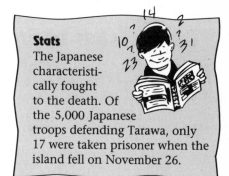

Stats

The Japanese characteristically fought to the death. Of the 5,000 Japanese troops defending Tarawa, only 17 were taken prisoner when the island fell on November 26.

In the central Pacific, U.S. forces moved against Tarawa and Makin islands. Makin quickly fell, but Tarawa was defended by veteran Japanese jungle fighters, and the battle, begun on November 20, 1943, was extraordinarily costly to both sides.

Mediterranean Shores

By mid-May 1943, Roosevelt and Churchill agreed to postpone crossing the English Channel to invade France until the "soft underbelly" of Europe had been penetrated via an invasion of Sicily from North Africa. On July 9–10, 1943, British and American forces landed in Sicily, and the Italian army crumbled before them. German resistance was a different matter, however, and costly fighting ensued. The invasion of Sicily culminated in the fall of Messina to the Allies on August 17, 1943.

By this time, Benito Mussolini had been overthrown (July 25, 1943) and was saved from arrest only by a German rescue mission. The Italian government, now under Marshal Pietro Badoglio (1871–1956), made secret peace overtures to the Allies while the Germans dug in on the Italian peninsula and awaited an invasion.

On September 3, 1943, British and U.S. forces left Messina and landed on the toe of the Italian boot. The Fifth U.S. Army, under General Mark W. Clark (1896–1984), landed at Salerno, and within a month southern Italy fell to the Allies. The Germans evacuated the key city of Naples on October 1 but then greatly stiffened their resistance, struggling to hold Rome. After Badoglio's government signed an armistice with the Allies and, on October 13, declared war on Germany, Hitler installed Mussolini as head of a puppet regime in northern Italy.

For the balance of 1943, the Allied armies in Italy were stalemated. On January 22, 1944, 50,000 U.S. troops landed at Anzio, just 33 miles south of Rome, but were pinned down by German forces. Not until June 4, 1944, did Rome fall to the Allies. From this point on, the Germans steadily retreated northward. On April 28, 1945, Mussolini and his mistress, Claretta Petacci, were captured by Italian anti-Fascists, then shot and hung by the heels in a Milanese public square.

The Beaches of France

Although U.S. forces entered Europe through Italy, fighting on the continent was more widespread. The Soviets, who suffered the heaviest casualties of the war and who had been devastated by a surprise German invasion begun on June 22, 1941, were fighting back with a vengeance. The Battle of Stalingrad (present-day Volgograd), fought from July 17 to November 18, 1942, resulted in the loss of 750,000 Soviet troops, but also 850,000 Nazis. This battle turned the grim tide of warfare on the Eastern Front. In the meantime, British Royal Air Force (RAF) bombers and U.S. Army Air Corps bombers pummeled industrial targets throughout Germany. At sea, the Battle of the Atlantic had raged since early 1942. From January to June, German U-boats sunk three million tons of U.S. shipping. However, the development of longer-range aircraft and more advanced radar systems led to effective defenses against U-boats, and by the spring of 1943, the U-boat threat had been greatly reduced.

With pressure applied from the south, from the east, from the air, and at sea, the time was at last right for a major Allied thrust from the west: a full-scale assault on what Hitler liked to call "Fortress Europe." For this offensive, the Allies mounted in Britain the largest and most powerful invasion force in history. Officially christened Operation Overlord, the invasion of Normandy became popularly known by the military designation of the day of its commencement: D-Day, June 6, 1944.

Stats
Approximately 5,000 Allied ships, 11,000 Allied aircraft, and more than 150,000 troops participated in the June 6 D-Day landing.

U.S. General Dwight David Eisenhower was in command of the high-stakes operation, which—astoundingly—caught the Germans off guard. True, the Germans expected an invasion—but not at Normandy. Through an elaborate program of deception and disinformation, the Allies had led the Germans to believe that the invasion would come at Calais. Nevertheless, German resistance was stiff, but the Allies prevailed and on August 15, 1944, launched a second invasion of France, this time in the South between Toulon and Cannes. The objective was to trap German forces within the jaws of a giant pincers. On August 25, Paris—beloved capital of France, in German hands since 1940—fell to the Allies.

Real Life

Dwight David Eisenhower, as Supreme Allied Commander, was the single most powerful military figure in World War II.

After World War II, Eisenhower served briefly as army chief of staff, wrote a memoir of the war (the 1948 *Crusade in Europe*), and served as president of Columbia University. In December 1950, President Harry S Truman named him military commander of NATO. Two years later, Eisenhower was tapped by the Republican party as its presidential candidate. He served two terms as, quite possibly, the most popular president in American history. Retiring to his farm in Gettysburg, Pennsylvania, in 1961, Eisenhower wrote a series of books. He died in 1969.

To Berlin and Victory in Europe

From France, the Allies launched an invasion into the German homeland itself. By early September, British forces liberated Brussels, Belgium, and American troops crossed the German frontier at Eupen. On October 21, the U.S. First Army captured Aachen—the first German city to fall to the Allies.

The Germans had lost the war. At least, that is how any rational leader would have viewed it. But Adolf Hitler was no longer rational—if he ever had been. Hitler ordered his soldiers to fight to the last man, and he reinforced his thinning lines with underage boys and overage men. Although the Germans continued to retreat, resistance was always fierce. Then, on December 16, 1944, General Gerd von Rundstedt (1875–1953) led a desperate counteroffensive, driving a wedge into Allied lines through the Ardennes on the Franco-Belgian frontier. With German forces distending the Allied line westward, the ensuing combat was called the Battle of the Bulge. The U.S. First and Third armies—the latter led brilliantly by General George S. Patton (1885–1945)—pushed back the bulge, which was wholly contained by January 1945. The battle was the last great German offensive, and it was Germany's last chance to stop the Allies' advance into its homeland.

Toward V-E Day

During February 1945, General Patton sped his armored units to the Rhine River and, after clearing the west bank, captured the bridge at Remagen, near Cologne, on March 7. Allied forces crossed this bridge and at other points along the Rhine, and were now poised to make a run for Berlin. However, General Eisenhower, believing Hitler would make his last stand in the German south, chose to head for Leipzig. With U.S. troops just 96 miles west of Berlin, the Supreme Allied Commander sent a message to Soviet dictator Josef Stalin, telling him that he was leaving the German capital to the Red Army.

Main Event

World War II was conducted with an unprecedented degree of cooperation among the Allies, whose leaders held several key strategic and political conferences during the conflict. One of the most important was the Yalta Conference, held from February 4 to February 11, 1945, in the Crimea. Here Roosevelt, Churchill, and Stalin planned the end of the war and laid a foundation for the postwar world. Stalin promised to establish provisional governments in the nations of eastern Europe now occupied by the Soviets, and he pledged to hold free, democratic elections as soon as possible.

The group agreed that the Soviet Union would annex eastern Poland and that Poland would be compensated by German war reparations. The conquered Germany would be divided into four zones of occupation, to be administered by the U.S., U.S.S.R., Britain, and France. Reluctant to enter the war against Japan, Stalin agreed that his nation would do so within three months of Germany's surrender. In exchange, the U.S.S.R. would receive the southern half of Sakhalin Island, the Kuril Islands, and special rights in certain ports.

While the British and Americans had been closing in from the West, the Soviets had executed a massive assault on the German's Eastern Front. By the end of January, the Red Army had pushed through Poland into Germany itself. In truth, little was left of Berlin. A combination of U.S. and British air power and Soviet artillery had razed the capital of Hitler's vaunted "Thousand-Year Reich." On April 16, 1945, Soviet Marshal Georgy Zhukov moved his troops into Berlin. Many German soldiers and civilians, terrified of the vengeance the Soviets might exact, fled westward to surrender to the Americans and the British.

Indeed, Germans could have found few places of refuge in the spring of 1945, for the entire world was learning of war crimes committed on an unimaginably vast scale. In their drive toward Berlin, the Allies liberated one Nazi concentration camp after another—centers of extermination to which Jews, Gypsies, Slavs, homosexuals, and others deemed by the Reich as "undesirable" had been sent for extermination. Such names as Auschwitz, Buchenwald, Belsen, and Dachau seared themselves into history. The Nazis had not been content with conquest; they intended nothing less than genocide.

Westbound Soviet and eastbound American troops met at the river Elbe on April 25, 1945. Five days later, Adolf Hitler, holed up in a bunker beneath the shattered streets of Berlin, shot himself. On May 7, 1945, senior representatives of Germany's armed forces surrendered to the Allies at General Eisenhower's headquarters in Reims. The very next day came a formal unconditional surrender. From the pages of American newspapers, headlines shouted the arrival of V-E—Victory in Europe—Day.

Stats
Civilian deaths in World War II exceeded 25 million, of whom 6 million were Jews systematically murdered by order of Adolf Hitler.

Main Event

Franklin Delano Roosevelt, elected to an unprecedented four terms as president of the United States and having seen his nation through the Depression and the blackest days of World War II, succumbed to a cerebral hemorrhage on April 12, 1945. Roosevelt was succeeded by his vice president, Harry S Truman (1884–1972). Truman attended the last wartime Allied conference at Potsdam, Germany, during July 17–August 2 with Churchill (who was replaced by his successor, Clement Attlee, during the conference) and Stalin.

The conference crystallized plans for the postwar world, confirming the four-zone division of Germany, establishing plans for de-Nazification and demilitarization, and establishing a tribunal to prosecute those guilty of war crimes and atrocities. The group resolved that nothing less than unconditional surrender would end the war against Japan. Truman also revealed at Potsdam that the United States had successfully tested an atomic bomb, which could be used against Japan.

Fat Man and Little Boy

German scientists discovered the possibility of nuclear fission—a process whereby the tremendous energy of the atom might be liberated—in 1938. Fortunately for the world, Hitler's tyranny drove many of Germany's best thinkers out of the country, and the nation's efforts to exploit fission in a weapon came to nothing. Three Hungarian-born American physicists—Leo Szilard, Eugene Wigner, and Edward Teller—were all intimately familiar with what a man like Hitler could do. They asked America's single most prestigious physicist, Albert Einstein (a fugitive from Nazi persecution), to write a letter to President Roosevelt, warning him of Germany's nuclear weapons research.

Late in 1939, FDR authorized the atomic bomb development program that became known as the Manhattan Project. Under the military management of General Leslie R. Groves (1896–1970) and the scientific direction of J. Robert Oppenheimer (1904–1967), the program grew to vast proportions and employed the nation's foremost scientific minds. A prototype bomb—called "the gadget" by the scientists—was completed in the summer of 1945 and was successfully detonated at Alamogordo, New Mexico, on July 16, 1945.

At this time, the Allies were planning the final invasion of Japan, which, based on the bloody experience of "island hopping," was expected to add perhaps a million more deaths to the Allied toll. President Truman therefore authorized the use of the terrible new weapon against Japan. On August 6, 1945, a lone B-29 bomber dropped "Little Boy" on Hiroshima, obliterating the city in three-fifths of a second. Three days later, "Fat Man" was dropped on Nagasaki, destroying about half the city.

Stats

Dropped on Hiroshima, with a population of about 300,000, "Little Boy" killed 78,000 people instantly; 10,000 more were never found; more than 70,000 were injured; and many subsequently died of radiation-related causes. Nagasaki, with a population of 250,000, instantly lost some 40,000 people when "Fat Man" was dropped. Another 40,000 were wounded.

On August 10, the day after the attack on Nagasaki, Japan sued for peace on condition that the emperor be allowed to remain as sovereign ruler. On August 11, the Allies replied that they and they alone would determine the future of Emperor Hirohito. At last, on August 14, the emperor personally accepted the Allied terms. A cease-fire was declared on August 15, and on September 2, 1945, General MacArthur presided over the Japanese signing of the formal surrender document on the deck of the U.S. battleship *Missouri*, anchored in Tokyo Bay.

The Least You Need to Know

➤ Never before or since World War II have Americans fought with such unanimity and singleness of purpose.

➤ If ever a war was a contest of good versus evil, such was World War II, and America's role in achieving victory elevated the nation to "superpower" status in the postwar political order.

Part 7
Superpower

World War II was a contest between fascist powers on one side and an alliance of democratic and communist powers on the other. Following the defeat of fascism, democracy and communism squared off as the great opposing ideologies of the postwar world. The World War II alliance shattered in a long contest of diplomatic maneuvering and military posturing called the Cold War. This period saw two costly shooting wars as well, one in Korea and one in Vietnam. In the meantime, the home front after World War II was both a booming and turbulent place. The economy soared, the civil rights movement went into full swing beginning in the late 1950s, and the Vietnam War proved the catalyst for a general social protest movement during the 1960s. The chapters in this section cover what poet W. H. Auden called "the Age of Anxiety."

IRON CURTAIN — GET IT?

Chapter 29

A Cold War and a Korean War (1944–1954)

In This Chapter

➤ The U.N. and other postwar peace programs

➤ Descent of the "Iron Curtain" and start of the Cold War

➤ The CIA and McCarthyism

➤ The Korean War

Rejoicing at the end of World War II was intense, but brief. The Soviet Union, portrayed by U.S. politicians and press alike as a valiant ally during the war, once again became an ideological and political enemy. The eastern European nations occupied by the Red Army became satellites of the U.S.S.R., and the postwar world found itself divided between the western democracies, led by the United States, and the eastern communist "bloc," dominated by the Soviets. It seemed as if the seeds of yet another war—World War III?—had been sown. At least Americans could take comfort in their sole possession of the atomic bomb...but that, too, would soon change.

Winning the Peace

It was clear to America's leaders that the Allies had won World War I, only later to "lose the peace." They were determined to not make the same mistake again.

The Birth of the United Nations

During World War II, the powers aligned against the Axis called themselves the "United Nations." The concept that label conveyed held great promise; after all, had the League of Nations been a more effective body, World War II might have been averted altogether. From August to October 1944, the United States, Great Britain, the U.S.S.R., and China met at a Washington, D.C., estate called Dumbarton Oaks to sketch out plans for a new world body. The wartime allies—plus France—would constitute a peacekeeping ("security") council, while the other nations of the world, though represented, would play secondary roles.

The Dumbarton Oaks Conference was remarkably successful, except in regard to two major issues: the principle of unanimity among the security council members (Should action require unanimous consent?) and the Soviet demand for separate membership for each of its 16 republics. Meeting at Yalta in the Crimea, February 4–11, 1945, the Big Three—Roosevelt, Stalin, and Churchill—resolved their differences. The principle of unanimity was upheld, but Stalin reduced his separate membership demand from 16 to three: Russia, Ukraine, and Byelorussia. Later in the year, a formal United Nations Charter was drawn up and adopted by 50 nations at the San Francisco Conference. The charter became effective after a majority of the signatory nations ratified it on October 24, 1945. The United Nations, the most significant world body in history, had become a reality.

Germany Divided

Another element vital to winning the peace was the postwar treatment of Germany. American, British, and French leaders, mindful of how the punitive Treaty of Versailles had created the conditions that brought Hitler to power and plunged the world into the second great war of the century, did not clamor for revenge. On the other hand, the Soviet Union wanted more than revenge; it demanded the utter subjugation of Germany. For the present, Germany was carved up into four "zones of occupation," each under the control of a different ally: the United States, Britain, the U.S.S.R., and France. All the Allies agreed on instituting programs to "de-Nazify" Germany, purging it of individuals who might seek to resurrect the National Socialist party. The Allies further agreed to establish a tribunal for the trial and prosecution of those who committed war crimes.

Main Event

The major German war criminals were prosecuted in the Nuremberg Trials, which took place in that German city from November 1945 to October 1946, presided over by jurists from the Allied nations. The principal trial brought 22 German Nazi leaders to justice, of whom 12 were sentenced to death, including Wilhelm Keitel (Hitler's closest military adviser), Joachim von Ribbentrop (German foreign minister), Alfred Rosenberg (a principal architect of Nazi genocide programs), and Martin Bormann (Hitler's secretary). Bormann vanished after Hitler's suicide on April 30, 1945, and was tried in absentia; in 1972, a skeleton identified as his was discovered in West Berlin. Hermann Goering, second only to Hitler in authority, committed suicide before he could be executed. Three other war criminals were given life sentences, and four received 20-year terms. Three of the first 22 tried were acquitted. Over the succeeding months, lesser criminals were tried in a series of 12 proceedings.

Secretary Marshall's Plan

The single boldest step toward winning the peace was proposed on June 5, 1947, by George C. Marshall. The former army chief of staff, now secretary of state, described in an address at Harvard University a plan whereby the nations of Europe would draw up a unified scheme for economic reconstruction *to be funded by the United States*. Although the Soviet Union and its satellite nations were invited to join, in the growing chill of the Cold War, they declined. Sixteen western European nations formed the Organization for European Economic Cooperation to coordinate the program formally known as the European Recovery Program, but more familiarly called the Marshall Plan.

Winston Churchill called the Marshall Plan the "most unsordid" political act in history, but it was, above all, a *political* act. Although Marshall assured the Soviets that the plan was not directed "against any country or doctrine but against hunger, poverty, desperation, and chaos," it was a powerful economic salvo fired against communism. Having witnessed totalitarian regimes rush to fill the void of postwar economic catastrophe, Marshall and other U.S. leaders were eager to restore the war-ravaged economies of the West and even to stimulate growth. Economic well-being, they felt, was the strongest ally of democracy.

The United States poured some $13 billion into Europe and also established a massive Displaced Persons Plan, whereby almost 300,000 homeless Europeans (including many Jewish survivors of the Holocaust) immigrated to the United States and became citizens.

Curtain of Iron

On March 5, 1946, Winston Churchill addressed tiny Westminster College in Fulton, Missouri. "From Stettin in the Baltic to Trieste in the Adriatic," he declared, "an iron curtain has descended across the continent." The former prime minister's eloquent phrase took root, and *Iron Curtain* was used for more than 50 years to describe the economic, social, and military barriers created against the West by the Soviet Union and the communist countries of Eastern Europe.

"Containing" Communism

In 1823, President James Monroe issued his famous "Monroe Doctrine," warning European powers that the United States would act to halt any new attempts to colonize the Americas. In 1947, President Harry S Truman promulgated the "Truman Doctrine," warning the Soviet Union—which supported a threatened communist takeover of Greece and Turkey—that the United States would act to halt the spread of communism wherever in the world it threatened democracy.

The Truman Doctrine had its basis in a proposal by State Department official George F. Kennan (b. 1904). The proposal stated that the most effective way to combat communism was to *contain* it, confronting the Soviet Union whenever and wherever it sought to expand its ideological influence. Thus the "Cold War" began in earnest, and with it, a National Security Act, passed in 1947. The act reorganized the War Department into the Department of Defense and also created the Central Intelligence Agency—perhaps the most controversial federal agency ever established. The CIA had as its mission covert intelligence gathering, which meant that the CIA sometimes functioned with neither executive nor legislative knowledge, let alone approval. In the name of fighting communism, the National Security Act had created the closest thing to a secret police (long a mainstay of oppressive eastern European regimes) this nation ever had.

Word for the Day

Coined in 1947 by journalist Herbert Bayard Swope in a speech he wrote for financier Bernard Baruch, *cold war* refers to the postwar strategic and political struggle between the United States (and its western European allies) and the Soviet Union (and communist countries). A chronic state of hostility, the Cold War was associated with two major "hot wars" (in Korea and Vietnam) and spawned various "brushfire wars" (small-scale armed conflicts, usually in Third World nations), but it was not itself a shooting war. The end of the Cold War was heralded in 1989 by the fall of the Berlin Wall.

Airlift to Berlin

Truman's policy of containment prompted the United States and its western allies to take a strong stand in Germany after the Soviet Union began detaining troop trains bound for West Berlin in March 1948. (Although Berlin was deep inside the Soviet sector of occupied Germany, the city, too, was divided into zones of Allied occupation.) In response, on June 7, the western allies announced their intention to create the separate, permanent capitalist state of West Germany. Two weeks later, the Soviet Union blockaded West Berlin, protesting that because of its location in Soviet-controlled territory, West Berlin could not serve as the capital of West Germany.

Would the West back down? Would this be the start of World War III?

President Truman did not take armed action against the Soviets. Instead, he ordered an airlift, a spectacular chain of round-the-clock supply flights into West Berlin—272,000 flights over 321 days, carrying tons of supplies. The airlift was a political as well as logistical triumph, which caused the Soviet Union to lift the blockade. The event was also a vindication of the policy of containment, and in April 1949, it led to the creation of the North Atlantic Treaty Organization—NATO—a key defensive alliance of the western nations against the communist East.

> **Voice from the Past**
>
> The crux of the North Atlantic Treaty, which created NATO, is Article 5: "The parties agree that an armed attack against one or more of them in Europe or North America shall be considered an attack against them all."

Witch Hunts

While national leaders and the military were scrambling to "contain" communism abroad, certain Americans looked homeward. Joseph R. McCarthy (1908–1957) was a thoroughly mediocre senator from Wisconsin whose popularity was flagging. McCarthy made a provocative speech to the Women's Republican Club of Wheeling, West Virginia, on February 9, 1950. He held up a piece of paper, which he said was a list of 205 known communists in the State Department.

The audience was electrified. The speech was reported nationally, and the nation likewise was stunned. McCarthy suddenly became famous and, over the next four years, spearheaded a legislative crusade to root out communists in government and other positions of power. *Crusade* is a word McCarthy and his followers would have been comfortable with. Others called what happened a *witch hunt*. (And no one ever bothered actually to examine that piece of paper the senator waved in Wheeling.)

McCarthy pointed fingers, raised suspicions, leveled charges. Due process of law, the rules of evidence, and the presumption that a person is innocent until *proven* guilty mattered not at all to "Tail Gunner Joe" McCarthy. He gained chairmanship of the powerful Senate Subcommittee on Governmental Operations and, from this post, launched investigations of the Voice of America broadcasting service and the U.S. Army Signal Corps. That McCarthy pointed a finger was quite enough to ruin a reputation and destroy a career— even if no actual evidence of subversion or disloyalty was presented. Those called to testify before the committee were asked to "name names," expose other individuals with communist affiliations. If the witnesses refused, they were found to be in contempt of Congress and subject to imprisonment. If a witness exercised his constitutional right not to testify against himself—a right guaranteed in the Fifth Amendment—McCarthy (and much of the public, it seemed) presumed him guilty.

McCarthy was aided in his witch hunt by a slick young lawyer named Roy Cohn, who was instrumental in one of the most highly publicized phases of the witch hunt, an investigation of communist influence in the Hollywood film industry. A parade of executives, producers, directors, and movie stars appeared before the Senate committee. Some witnesses "named names." Some refused. Those who failed to "cooperate" with the committee and those who stood accused were *blacklisted*—which meant that no studio would hire them.

The McCarthy witch hunts were certainly not born of fantasy. Many influential Americans did have ties to communist organizations—though most of these associations had come and gone with the 1930s, when intellectuals and liberals flocked to socialist and communist groups in order to oppose fascism, which was then menacing the world. The Cold War also spawned a veritable legion of spies, including those who communicated U.S. atomic secrets to the Soviets, thereby enabling the U.S.S.R. to develop an atomic bomb in 1949 and a hydrogen bomb in 1954.

McCarthy, however, made no real effort to separate fact from fantasy, and even after the Republican party captured the White House in 1952, he continued his strident attacks. In 1954, McCarthy accused the entire U.S. Army of being riddled with communists. This blow was sufficient to provoke President Eisenhower—a career army man—to encourage Congress to form a committee to investigate McCarthy's attempts to coerce army brass into granting preferential treatment for a former aide, Private G. David Schine.

From April to June 1954, the "Army-McCarthy Hearings" were carried on an infant medium called television. The nation was riveted—and, not incidentally, sales of television sets soared. Joseph McCarthy was exposed for the reckless, self-serving demagogue that he was. Censured by action of the Senate later that year, he was overtaken by the alcoholism that had always dogged him. McCarthy died in 1957, at the age of 49.

Main Event

On June 19, 1953, Julius Rosenberg (born 1918) and his wife, Ethel Greenglass Rosenberg (born 1915), became the first United States civilians in history to be executed for espionage. Their trial and their punishment were sources of great bitterness and controversy during the Cold War.

Julius Rosenberg, a member of the Communist party, had been employed as an engineer by the U.S. Army Signal Corps during World War II. He and Ethel were accused of supplying Soviet agents with atomic bomb secrets during 1944–45. Their chief accuser was Ethel's brother, David Greenglass, who had worked on the "A-bomb" project at Los Alamos, New Mexico, and had fed the Rosenbergs secret information. Because Greenglass turned state's witness, he received a 15-year sentence, whereas, under the Espionage Act of 1917, the Rosenbergs were sentenced to death on April 5, 1951. The sentence provoked protests worldwide—including accusations of anti-Semitism—but President Eisenhower, convinced of the couple's guilt, refused to commute the sentences.

Word for the Day

The *A-bomb*, or atomic bomb, first tested and used in 1945, operates on the principle of nuclear fission—the splitting of the nuclei of uranium or plutonium atoms—which suddenly releases an incredible amount of explosive energy. The *H-bomb* (hydrogen bomb), first tested in 1952, is a *fusion* rather than *fission* device, joining the nuclei of hydrogen atoms together in an uncontrolled nuclear reaction. The hydrogen bomb releases about 1,000 times more energy than an atomic bomb.

Police Action in Korea

The Cold War was not just a contest of rattling sabers and strong language. As eastern Europe had fallen behind an Iron Curtain, so China, the world's most populous nation, became a communist nation in 1949. China was long the subject of a struggle between communist forces (led primarily by Mao Tse-tung) and capitalist-nationalist forces (whose strongest leader was U.S. World War II ally Chiang Kai-shek). Elsewhere in Asia,

Word for the Day
Congress never
declared war
against North
Korea or China.
Officially, the
conflict was called a
police action—a localized war
without a declaration of war.

communist factions were positioning themselves to take power. After World War II, Korea was divided along the 38th parallel between a Soviet occupation zone in the north and a U.S. zone in the south. In November 1947, the United Nations resolved to create a unified independent Korea, but the communists barred free elections in the north. Only in the U.S. southern zone were elections held, and on August 15, 1948, the Republic of Korea was born. In North Korea, the communists created the Democratic People's Republic of Korea in September.

Invasion, Counterstrike, Invasion

On June 25, 1950, communist-backed forces from the north invaded South Korea. The United States secured a United Nations sanction against the invasion and contributed the lion's share of troops to repel it. World War II hero Douglas MacArthur was put in command of the U.N. forces.

The North Korean troops—trained by the Soviets and the Chinese—quickly pushed the South Koreans back toward the southern tip of the Korean peninsula. MacArthur struggled to hold the critical southern port of Pusan to buy time until reinforcements arrived. He then executed a controversial landing at Inchon, on the west coast of Korea, *behind* North Korean lines. The landing was a stunning success—perhaps MacArthur's single greatest military feat—and by October 1, 1950, the North Koreans had been pushed out of South Korea. U.N. forces were now arrayed along the 38th parallel.

Within the Truman administration debate raged over whether to cross the 38th parallel and invade North Korea. President Truman compromised, authorizing the crossing, but taking steps to avoid provoking the Chinese and the Soviets directly. No U.N. troops would enter Manchuria or the U.S.S.R., and only South Koreans would operate along international borders. On October 7, the U.N. General Assembly called for the unification of Korea and authorized MacArthur to invade. On October 19, the North Korean capital of Pyongnang fell, and the North Korean armies were pushed far north, to the Yalu River, the nation's border with Manchuria.

The war seemed to be over—but then, between October 14 and November 1, some 180,000 communist "volunteers" crossed the Yalu from China. MacArthur launched an offensive on November 24, only to be beaten back by massive Chinese resistance, which pushed U.N. troops back across the 38th parallel. The South Korean capital of Seoul fell to the communists in January 1951.

Meatgrinder

Halting their retreat south of Seoul, U.S. and other allied troops began probing northward once again in an offensive that front-line soldiers dubbed the "meatgrinder." By March 1951, U.N. forces had returned to the 38th parallel and established a strong defensive position.

Old Soldiers...

In light of the Chinese intervention, General MacArthur demanded permission to retaliate against the Chinese by bombing Manchuria. President Truman and the United Nations—fearing that direct aggression against China would trigger nuclear war with the Soviets—turned MacArthur down. The confrontation was controversial, and many Americans—including Senator Joseph McCarthy—vociferously sided with the general against the president. Contrary to the accepted military practice of refraining from publicly differing with the civilian administration, MacArthur loudly blamed his military setbacks in Korea on Truman's policies. Finally, on March 25, 1951, just after Truman had completed preparation of a cease-fire plan, MacArthur broadcast an unauthorized and provocative ultimatum to the enemy commander. In response to this insubordination, Truman relieved MacArthur of command in Korea on April 11.

Thrust, Counterthrust, and Stalemate

General Matthew B. Ridgway assumed command of U.S. and U.N. forces after the dismissal of MacArthur, and Lieutenant General James A. Van Fleet led the U.S. 8th Army northward. But on April 22, nearly half a million Chinese troops initiated an offensive, driving the 8th Army to within five miles of Seoul. On May 10, the Chinese launched a second offensive, concentrating on the eastern portion of the U.N. line; however, Van Fleet counterattacked in the west, north of Seoul, taking the communists entirely by surprise. In full retreat, the communists suffered their heaviest casualties of the war and withdrew into North Korea. By the beginning of summer 1951, the war was stalemated at the 38th parallel. For the next two years, both sides, now dug in, pounded one another fruitlessly.

Peace Table

Armistice negotiations began at the behest of the Soviets in June 1951 and dragged on for two years. It took until July 26 even to establish an agenda for the conference. The participants decided that an armistice would require agreement on a demarcation line and demilitarized zone, impartial supervision of the truce, and arrangements for return of prisoners of war. The toughest single issue involved the disposition of POWs. U.N.

negotiators wanted prisoners to decide for themselves whether they would return home; the communists, fearful of mass defection, held out for mandatory repatriation. In an effort to break the negotiation stalemate, General Mark Clark, who had succeeded Ridgway, stepped up bombing raids on North Korea. At last, during April 1953, the POW issue was resolved; a compromise permitted freed prisoners to choose sides, but under supervision of a neutral commission.

The Unhappiest Ally

After this long and frustrating process, the only individual who remained thoroughly displeased was Syngman Rhee (1875–1965), president of South Korea. Rhee desired nothing less than unification of Korea and wholly voluntary repatriation as absolute conditions for cease-fire. So he threw a monkey wrench into the proceedings by suddenly ordering the release of 25,000 North Korean prisoners who wanted to live in the South. To regain Rhee's cooperation, the United States promised him a mutual security pact and long-term economic aid. Nevertheless, the armistice signed on July 27, 1953, did not include South Korea. Still, the cease-fire held, and the shooting war was over.

Stats

Just how many Chinese and North Korean troops were killed in the Korean War is unknown, but estimates range between 1.5 and 2 million, in addition to at least a million civilians. The U.N. command lost 88,000 killed, of whom 23,300 were American. Many more were wounded. South Korean civilian casualties probably equaled those of North Korea.

The Korean War did succeed in containing communism—confining it to North Korea—but in all other respects, this costly conflict was inconclusive, except that it provided a precedent for intervention in another Asian war. This time the war would take place in a divided Vietnam, beginning in the next decade.

The Least You Need to Know

➤ Jubilation at the end of World War II was short lived, as the Western capitalist nations and the eastern European and Asian communist nations squared off for a Cold War.

➤ A policy of "containing" communism and a fear of touching off a nuclear World War III dominated American foreign policy in the postwar years.

Chapter 30

From the Back of the Bus to the Great Society (1947–1968)

In This Chapter

➤ The African-American struggle for civil rights

➤ Start of the "space race"

➤ Bay of Pigs and Cuban Missile Crisis

➤ Idealism and social reform in the Kennedy and Johnson years

➤ Assassinations

With the ruins of war-ravaged Europe still smoldering, much of the world's population remained hungry, politically oppressed, or both. But Americans, having triumphed over evil incarnate in the form of Nazi and Japanese totalitarianism and enjoying the blessings of liberty, had much to be proud of. True, the postwar world was a scary place, with nuclear incineration just a push of a button away. Childhood, which Americans prized as a time of carefree innocence, was now marred by air raid drills that regularly punctuated the school day. In an increasingly confusing world, America's children were also menaced by a much-discussed and debated wave of "juvenile delinquency." Yet, all in all, 1950s America was a rather complacent place—prosperous, spawning a web of verdant (if rather dull) suburbs interconnected by new highways built under the Interstate Highway Act of 1956.

Postwar suburbia was an expression of the long-held American dream: a house of one's own, a little plot of land, a clean and decent place to live. But if suburban lawns were green, the suburbs themselves were white. As usual, African-Americans had been excluded from the dream—or, at least, relegated to the very back of it.

Executive Order 9981

On July 26, 1948, President Harry S Truman (1884–1972) issued Executive Order 9981, which mandated "equality of treatment and opportunity to all persons in the Armed Services without regard to race." African-Americans had regularly served in the armed forces since the Civil War, but always in separate—segregated—units, though usually under white officers. Truman's order did not use the word *integration*, but when he was asked point-blank if that is what the order meant, the president replied with his characteristic directness: "Yes."

Executive Order 9981 did much more than integrate the armed forces. It began a gradual revolution in American society. For many soldiers, sailors, and airmen, the army or navy or air force (itself newly created as a service branch independent from the army in 1947), became their first experience of integration. In even more immediate terms, Executive Order 9981 meant that the mom and pop owners of the tavern just beyond the post gate had to open their businesses to all personnel, white and black. If a local lunch counter refused to serve a black soldier, for example, it could be declared "off-limits" by the post commander—and there would be no one to serve.

The Dream Deferred

Of course, the integration of the armed forces did not completely transform American society, let alone transform it overnight. Racial prejudice was deeply ingrained in American life, and in some places, particularly the South, prejudice was even protected by law. In most Southern states, the "Jim Crow" legislation that had been passed during the bitter years following Reconstruction remained on the books in one form or another. Theoretically, Southern society was segregated such that publicly funded facilities (like schools) provided "separate but equal" service. In practice, services and facilities were certainly separate, but hardly equal. In the South, African-Americans were treated as an underclass. This was true in subtler ways up North as well, where segregation was often *de facto* rather than *de jure*.

Following both world wars, African-Americans migrated in large numbers from the rural South to the industrial cities of the North. Industry welcomed their cheap labor, but many whites, fearing they would lose their jobs to the newcomers, met them with hostility. Up North, blacks typically found themselves restricted to menial labor and compelled to live in slum districts that became known as ghettoes. In effect, the entire American nation was both separate *and* unequal.

Rosa Parks Boards a Bus

On December 1, 1955, Montgomery, Alabama, was a typical Southern city, its social fabric shot through with the threads of major injustice and trivial humiliation carefully (if no longer quite consciously) interwoven to keep blacks "in their place." Rosa Parks (b. 1913) boarded a city bus to return home from her job. Like any other commuter, she was tired after a hard day's work. She settled into a seat in the forward section of the bus.

In most parts of the world, this mundane action would have gone entirely unnoticed. But in Montgomery in 1955, it was a crime for a black person to sit in the front of a city bus. Told to yield her place to a white person, Parks refused, was arrested, and jailed.

The arrest sparked a boycott of Montgomery city buses. If the town's African-Americans could not ride in the front of the bus, they would not ride at all. Although most of Montgomery's African-American population depended on the buses, they maintained the boycott for more than a year, focusing national attention on Montgomery and, more importantly, on the issues of civil rights for African-Americans.

Main Event

The year before Rosa Parks's bus ride, the U.S. Supreme Court effectively declared segregation illegal when, on May 17, 1954, it handed down a decision in the case of *Brown v. Board of Education of Topeka, Kansas*. The decision was the culmination of a long series of lawsuits first brought against segregated school districts by the National Association for the Advancement of Colored People (NAACP) in the 1930s. Repeatedly, the Supreme Court ruled consistently with its 1896 decision in *Plessy v. Ferguson* that found "separate but equal" accommodations for blacks constitutional as long as all *tangible* aspects of the accommodations were, indeed, equal. But in 1954, Thurgood Marshall (1908–93; in 1967, he would become the first African-American appointed to the Supreme Court) and other NAACP lawyers demonstrated that segregated school systems were inherently unequal because of *intangible* social factors. The high court agreed. Desegregation of the nation's schools became the law of the land. In some places, the process of integration proceeded without incident; in others, it was accompanied by violent resistance that required the intervention of federal marshals and even federal troops.

Emergence of Martin Luther King, Jr.

The Reverend Martin Luther King, Jr., pastor of the Dexter Avenue Baptist Church in Montgomery, emerged during the Montgomery boycott as moral and spiritual leader of the developing civil rights movement. Born on January 15, 1929, in Atlanta, Georgia, the son of a prominent local minister, King was educated at Morehouse College, Crozer Theological Seminary, and Boston University, from which he received a doctorate in 1955. Along with the Reverend Ralph Abernathy and Edward Nixon, King entered the national spotlight during the boycott. He used his sudden prominence to infuse the national civil rights movement with what he had learned from the example of India's great leader, Mahatma Gandhi, who taught the principle of *satyagraha*—"holding to the truth" by nonviolent civil disobedience. Rosa Parks's protest was a classic example.

After Montgomery, King lectured nationally and became president of the Southern Christian Leadership Conference (SLC). He conducted major voter registration drives, demonstrations, marches, and campaigns in Albany, Georgia (December 1961–August 1962), Birmingham, Alabama (April–May 1963), and Danville, Virginia (July 1963). In August 1963, King organized a massive March on Washington, where he delivered one of the great speeches in American history, declaring "I Have a Dream."

Voice from the Past

Martin Luther King, Jr., spoke these words from the steps of the Lincoln Memorial, Washington, D.C., on August 28, 1963:

"...I have a dream that one day on the red hills of Georgia sons of former slaves and the sons of former slave owners will be able to sit down together at the table of brotherhood. I have a dream that one day even the state of Mississippi, a state sweltering with the heat of injustice, sweltering with the heat of oppression, will be transformed into an oasis of freedom and justice.

"I have a dream that my four little children will one day live in a nation where they will not be judged by the color of their skin but by the content of their character. I have a dream today. I have a dream that one day down in Alabama, with its vicious racists, with its governor having his lips dripping with the words of interposition and nullification, one day right there in Alabama little black boys and black girls will be able to join hands with little white boys and white girls as sisters and brothers.

"...This is our hope. This is the faith that I go back to the South with. With this faith we will be able to hew out of the mountain of despair a stone of hope..."

In 1964, King was internationally recognized with the Nobel Peace Prize, then went on to conduct desegregation efforts in St. Augustine, Florida. King organized a voter-registration drive in Selma, Alabama, leading a march from Selma to Montgomery in March 1965, which was met by angry white mobs. King expanded the civil rights movement into the North and began to attack not just legal and social injustice, but economic inequality.

While King was planning a multiracial "poor people's march" on Washington in 1968, aimed at securing federal funding for a $12-billion "Economic Bill of Rights," he flew to Memphis, Tennessee, to support striking sanitation workers. In that city, on April 4, Martin Luther King, Jr., fell to a sniper's bullet.

Or Does It Explode?

The assassination of Dr. King, brilliant apostle of nonviolent social change, sparked urban riots across a number of the nation's black ghettoes. These riots were not the first of the decade. Despite the nonviolent message of Dr. King, racial unrest had often turned violent. NAACP leader Medgar Evers was assassinated in Jackson, Mississippi, in 1963; Birmingham, Alabama, was the site of the bombing of a black church, in which four girls were killed; three civil rights activists—including two whites—were killed in Mississippi while working to register black voters. On August 11, 1965, a six-day riot ripped apart the Watts section of Los Angeles after a police patrolman attempted to arrest a man for drunk driving. Riots broke out the following summer in New York and Chicago, and in 1967 in Newark, New Jersey, and Detroit. Following the King assassination in 1968, more than 100 cities erupted into violence.

> **Voice from the Past**
> The great African-American poet Langston Hughes (1902–1967) asked in a poem called "Harlem," "What happens to a dream deferred? / Does it dry up / like a raisin in the sun? ...*Or does it explode?*"

Emergence of Malcolm X and the Black Power Movement

The racial violence of the 1960s was extreme evidence of the pent-up frustration and outrage long simmering within black America. Back in 1916, Jamaican-born Marcus Mosiah Garvey (1887–1940) came to New York to recruit followers for his Universal Negro Improvement Association and by 1921 claimed a million members. The organization, which had as its aim the establishment of a new black nation in Africa, was called "militant" by whites accustomed to seeing African-Americans behave passively and submissively.

Not until the emergence of Malcolm X in the early 1960s was African-American militancy given compelling and eloquent direction. Malcolm X had been born Malcolm Little in

Omaha, Nebraska, in 1925. He turned bitter and rebellious after his father, an activist preacher, was murdered in 1931, presumably for advocating the ideas of Marcus Garvey.

Malcolm Little moved to Harlem, where he became a criminal and, convicted of burglary, was imprisoned from 1946 to 1952. While in prison, he became a follower of Elijah Muhammad (1897–1975), leader of the Lost-Found Nation of Islam, popularly called the Black Muslims. Rejecting his surname as a "slave name," Malcolm Little became Malcolm X and, upon his release from prison, served as a leading spokesman for the Black Muslim movement.

What Malcolm X said galvanized many in the black community, giving young black men in particular a sense of pride, purpose, and potential, even as his rhetoric intimidated and outraged many whites, who saw Malcolm X as one of several angry young activists. These included such figures as Stokley Carmichael, who called for "total revolution" and "Black Power"; H. Rap Brown, leader of the Student National Coordinating Committee (SNCC), who exhorted angry blacks to "burn this town down" in a 1967 speech in Cambridge, Maryland; and Huey Newton, leader of the militant Black Panther Party, which many whites saw as little more than a national street gang. By the mid 1960s, the civil rights movement was split between the adherents of King's nonviolence and those who, having lost patience with American society, followed a more aggressive path.

In fact, Malcolm X evolved ideas that were quite different from those not only of King, but of the young militants. Malcolm X split with the Black Muslims and founded the Organization of Afro-American Unity in June 1964, advocating a kind of socialist solution to the corruption of American society that had led to racial hatred and the subjugation of blacks. His original message, that the "white man" was (quite literally) the devil incarnate, had become transformed into a religiously inspired quest for racial equality. The quest was tempered by a conviction that black America had to look within, and not to white America, for the means to freedom and progress.

The evolution of Malcolm X was cut short on February 21, 1965, when he was gunned down by three Black Muslims during a speech at Harlem's Audubon Auditorium. His *Autobiography* (dictated to Alex Haley, who would later gain fame as the author of *Roots*, a sweeping novel of black history), published just after his assassination, became an extraordinarily influential document in expanding and redefining the civil rights movement.

The journey of black America, like the life of Malcolm X, remained incomplete during the 1960s and remains incomplete to this day. The fact is that African-Americans generally live less affluently, amid more crime, and with less opportunity than white Americans. Yet the range of black leaders of the 1950s and 1960s, from Rosa Parks, to Martin Luther King, Jr., to Malcolm X, brought hope and social visibility to black America.

Sputnik and the New Frontier

Despite growing racial disharmony, the United States was a fairly self-satisfied place in the 1950s. Then, on October 4, 1957, the world learned that the Soviet Union had successfully launched a 184-pound satellite into earth orbit. Called Sputnik I, its radio transmitter emitted nothing more than electronic beeps, but it sent shock waves through the American nation. Suddenly, the U.S.S.R., our adversary in the postwar world, the embodiment of godless communism, had demonstrated to the world its technological superiority. The launching of Sputnik began a "space race," in which the United States came in dead second during the early laps. The Soviets put a man, "cosmonaut" Yuri Gagarin, into orbit four years after Sputnik and one month before American "astronaut" Alan B. Shepard was launched on a 15-minute suborbital flight on May 5, 1961.

Sputnik shook Americans out of their complacency. The 1960 presidential race, between Eisenhower's vice president, Richard M. Nixon, and a dashing, youthful senator from Massachusetts, John F. Kennedy, almost ended in a tie. But the nation rejected the security of Eisenhower's man and voted into office a candidate who embodied a new energy, vigor, and challenge.

JFK

At 43, John F. Kennedy was the youngest elected president in American history (Theodore Roosevelt was slightly younger when he assumed office after the assassination of William McKinley). Kennedy's administration established the Peace Corps (an organization of volunteers assigned to work in developing nations), created the Alliance for Progress (which strengthened relations with Latin America), and set a national goal of landing an American on the moon before the end of the 1960s. Despite these accomplishments, Kennedy is best remembered for the *magic* (there is no better word) he and his beautiful wife, Jacqueline, brought to the White House and the national leadership.

"The Torch Has Been Passed…"

Intelligent (his books included the Pulitzer Prize-winning *Profiles in Courage*), handsome, idealistic, athletic, irreverently witty, and a war hero, Kennedy declared in his inaugural address that the "torch has been passed to a new generation"—of which *he* was clearly the embodiment. Mired in a depressing Cold War, plagued by social problems, continually anxious over impending nuclear war, worried that the Soviets and the Chinese were winning the hearts and minds of the world, Americans eagerly embraced the attractive optimism of JFK.

Bay of Pigs and Brink of Armageddon

Although he was adored by many, Kennedy never succeeded in winning the support of Congress. He and his brother, Attorney General Robert F. Kennedy (1925–68), sought to further civil rights but were repeatedly thwarted by Congress. Kennedy tried to create programs to fund broad educational initiatives, only to see them diluted by Congress. He also introduced a program to provide medical care for the elderly, which was delayed by Congress.

Early in Kennedy's administration, the nation suffered the tragic humiliation of a bungled attempt to invade Cuba, which was under the communist rule of Fidel Castro (b. 1926). In March 1960, President Eisenhower had approved a CIA plan to train anti-Castro Cuban exiles for an invasion to overthrow the Cuban leader. Kennedy allowed the preparations to proceed, and some 1,500 exiles landed on April 17, 1961, at Bay of Pigs on the island's southwestern coast.

The result was unmitigated disaster. Not only had the attack's secrecy been breached, but Kennedy, fearing Soviet reprisal, decided not to authorize promised U.S. air support. Worse, the CIA had badly misread the political climate of revolutionary Cuba. The general uprising the CIA believed would be set off by the landing simply did not happen. By April 19, the invasion was crushed and 1,200 survivors were captured. (They were released in December 1962, in exchange for $53 million worth of U.S. medicines and provisions.)

Soviet premier Nikita Khrushchev saw the failure of the Bay of Pigs as a sign of the new administration's weakness. Khrushchev quickly rushed in to exploit this flaw by covertly sending nuclear-armed missiles to Cuba plus the technical and military personnel to install and operate them. An American U-2 spy plane photographed the missile bases under construction, and on October 22, 1962, President Kennedy addressed the nation on television, announcing a naval blockade of the island. Kennedy demanded that the Soviets withdraw the missiles, and by October 24, the blockade was in place.

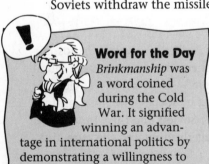

Word for the Day
Brinkmanship was a word coined during the Cold War. It signified winning an advantage in international politics by demonstrating a willingness to push a dangerous situation to the brink of nuclear war.

The idea of hostile nuclear warheads parked a mere 90 miles from the United States was terrifying, but so was the prospect of a naval battle off the coast of Cuba, which might ignite a thermonuclear war. For the next four days, Americans braced themselves for "the big one." Offices and factories staged air raid drills, as did the nation's schools, where children practiced "duck and cover": ducking under their desks and covering their heads.

Few had much hope that such maneuvers would help one survive a full-scale thermonuclear assault.

On October 28, Premier Khrushchev backed down, offering to remove the missiles under U.N. supervision. For his part, President Kennedy pledged never again to attempt to invade Cuba, and he also removed U.S. ICBMs (intercontinental ballistic missiles) from Turkish bases near the Soviet border. On October 29, the blockade was lifted, and JFK had scored a signal victory in Cold War "brinkmanship."

An Autumn Day in Dallas

Late in November 1963, President Kennedy visited Texas to bolster his popularity as he geared up for the reelection campaign. The presidential aircraft—Air Force One—touched down at Dallas's Love Field on the morning of the 22nd, and the president was given a gratifyingly warm greeting. A man who enjoyed contact with voters, who did not hesitate to "press the flesh," Kennedy declined to ride beneath the bulletproof bubble top normally affixed to the armored presidential limousine. As the motorcade passed by a warehouse building called the Texas School Book Depository, three shots rang out, the second of which ripped into the president's head, fatally wounding him. Texas governor John Connally, riding in the front seat of the car, was also grievously wounded, but recovered.

The accused assassin, captured later in the day (though not before murdering Dallas police officer J.D. Tippett), was Lee Harvey Oswald, a misfit who had lived for a period in the Soviet Union, having renounced his U.S. citizenship. As he was being transferred from the city to the county jail, Oswald was assassinated himself on November 24 by Dallas nightclub owner and small-time mobster Jack Ruby.

LBJ

Lyndon Baines Johnson (1908–73), the popular Texas senator tapped by Kennedy as vice president to improve his standing in the South and West, took the oath of office inside Air Force One. Jacqueline Kennedy, her elegant pink dress stained with her husband's blood, looked on. One of Johnson's first acts was to appoint a commission, headed by Supreme Court Chief Justice Earl Warren, to investigate the assassination. Despite the Warren Commission's finding that Oswald had acted alone, rumors and theories of elaborate conspiracies—some involving the CIA, FBI, Mafia, and Cuba's Castro—developed and persist to this day.

War on Poverty

Americans had much to admire as well as much to criticize about the "thousand days" of the Kennedy administration, but the youthful president's sudden, terrible martyrdom cast an aura of enchantment and heroism over Kennedy and his programs. President Johnson was able to refashion the JFK social programs that had floundered in Congress and, in the name of the slain president, oversee their passage into law. When Johnson ran for president in his own right in 1964, he called upon America to build a "Great Society," one that "rests on abundance and liberty for all."

The phrase *Great Society* became, like FDR's New Deal, the label for an ambitious, idealistic package of legislation, including Medicare, which helped finance medical care for Americans over 65; elementary, secondary, and higher education acts to enhance education and provide financial aid to college students; and legislation relating to what Johnson called a War on Poverty.

Civil Rights Act of 1964

Of all the creations of the Great Society, none has had more lasting and profound impact than the Civil Rights Act of 1964. The act banned segregation and discrimination in public accommodations such as restaurants, theaters, and hotels, and it barred employers from discriminatory hiring practices based on race.

The Civil Rights Act of 1964 was followed the next year by a Voting Rights Act, which destroyed the last vestiges of local legislation intended to prevent or discourage African-Americans from voting. In 1968, at the end of the Johnson years, another civil rights act rendered discrimination by landlords and realtors illegal.

President Johnson's Great Society was built in part on the memory of JFK and was also a result of the black political and social activism of the 1950s and 1960s. By the end of the Johnson years, equality in America was certainly not fully *de facto*—a fact of life—but it was at least *de jure*—a condition of law.

The Least You Need to Know

➤ The modern civil rights movement began with the integration of the armed forces in 1947 and developed through a nonviolent program of civil disobedience led by Dr. Martin Luther King, Jr., and others.

➤ Although John F. Kennedy attempted to create an ambitious program of civil rights and social legislation, it was the administration of Lyndon Baines Johnson that secured passage of legislation creating the "Great Society."

Chapter 31

Vietnam (1946–1975)

In This Chapter

➤ Background of the Vietnam War

➤ Escalation and deception

➤ Protest on the home front

➤ U.S. withdrawal and communist victory

In 1964, the beacon of the Great Society shone brightly. Motivated by the memory of JFK and energized by the moral passion of Lyndon Johnson, the program of social reform, even more ambitious than the New Deal had been, seemed unstoppable.

Then, on August 2, 1964, the American destroyer *Maddox*, conducting electronic espionage in international waters, was attacked by North Vietnamese torpedo boats. Undamaged, *Maddox* was joined by a second destroyer, the *C. Turner Joy*. On August 4, both ships claimed to have been attacked. Although evidence of the second attack was thin (later it was discovered that the second attack had not occurred), President Johnson ordered retaliatory air strikes and asked Congress for support. On August 7, the U.S. Senate passed the Tonkin Gulf Resolution, giving LBJ almost unlimited authority to expand American involvement in a long-standing war in a part of the world few Americans knew or cared much about.

That war would wreck the Great Society, nearly tear the United States apart, spawn an idealistic albeit drug-oriented youth counterculture, and cost the lives of 58,000 young Americans.

Flashback

World War II left much of the world, including Southeast Asia, dangerously unstable. During the 19th century, France had colonized Laos, Cambodia, and Vietnam, and when France caved in to Germany in 1940, the Japanese allowed French colonial officials puppet authority in Southeast Asia until the Allied liberation of France in 1945. Japan then seized full control, purging the French police agencies and soldiery that had kept various nationalist groups in check. In Vietnam, Ho Chi Minh (1890–1969) led the most powerful of these independence-seeking groups, the Viet Minh. Aided by U.S. Office of Strategic Services (OSS) personnel, Viet Minh fought a guerrilla war against the Japanese occupiers.

When the war in Europe ended, Allied forces were free to turn their attention to Vietnam (and the rest of Southeast Asia). Nationalist Chinese troops (under Chiang Kai-shek) occupied northern Vietnam. The British secured southern Vietnam for re-entry of the French, who ruthlessly suppressed supporters of Ho Chi Minh. A state of low-level guerrilla warfare developed, which escalated sharply when Chiang Kai-shek, hoping to checkmate communist ambitions in the region, withdrew from northern Vietnam and turned that region over to French control.

The March to Dien Bien Phu

Like Chiang Kai-shek, U.S. leaders feared communist incursions in Southeast Asia and began to supply the French with funding, military equipment, and—on August 3, 1950—the first contingent of U.S. military "advisors." By 1953, the United States was funding 80 percent of the cost of France's war effort.

France assigned General Henri Eugene Navarre to strike a decisive blow on the strategically located plain of Dien Bien Phu, near Laos. President Eisenhower stepped up military aid, but despite Navarre's massing of troops, Dien Bien Phu fell to the forces of Ho Chi Minh on May 7, 1954. This disaster was followed by a string of Viet Minh victories, and, in a July peace conference, the French and the Viet Minh concluded a cease-fire and agreed to divide Vietnam along the 17th parallel.

Domino Theory

During the thick of the Dien Bien Phu campaign, on April 7, 1954, President Eisenhower presented reporters with his rationale for aiding the French—a foreign power—in their fight against communism in Vietnam—a remote country. "You have a row of dominoes set up," he explained, "you knock over the first one, and what will happen to the last one is the certainty it will go over very quickly." This off-handed metaphor was immediately christened the *domino theory*, and it became the basis for an escalating U.S. involvement in Vietnam.

American "Advisors"

As a condition of the armistice agreement concluded in Geneva between Ho Chi Minh and the French, the divided Vietnam was to hold elections within two years to reunify. South Vietnam's President Ngo Dinh Diem assumed that Ho Chi Minh would win a popular election; therefore, he declined to abide by the Geneva accords, refusing to hold the promised elections. The United States, more concerned with blocking communism than with practicing democracy in Vietnam, backed Diem's position. Under John F. Kennedy, who succeeded Eisenhower in 1961, the number of military "advisors" sent to Vietnam steadily rose. By June 30, 1962, 6,419 Americans were in South Vietnam. President Kennedy reported to the press that no U.S. combat forces were in the country, but he did admit that the "training units" were authorized to return fire if fired upon.

Flaming Monks and the Fall of Diem

The Kennedy administration's desire to stop the falling dominoes caused U.S. officials to turn a blind eye toward the essential unpopularity and corruption of the Diem regime. Diem's cronies were put into high civil and military positions, and although a small number of urban South Vietnamese prospered under Diem, the rural majority fared poorly. Moreover, the Catholic Diem became tyrannical in his support of the nation's Catholic minority and openly abused the Buddhist majority. The world was soon horrified by a series of extreme protest demonstrations: Buddhists monks doused themselves in gasoline and set themselves ablaze in the streets of Saigon.

By mid-1963, the Kennedy administration determined that the Diem regime was no longer viable. President Kennedy secretly allowed the CIA to plot the murder of Diem in a U.S.-backed military coup that overthrew him on November 1, 1963. Diem's death unleashed a series of coups that made South Vietnam even more unstable over the next two years and encouraged the communists to escalate the war, now fueled by increasing Soviet and Chinese aid.

Rolling Thunder

Hindsight, according to a well-worn cliché, is always 20/20, and historians critical of the Kennedy administration often blame JFK for miring the nation in a hopeless war. Actually, evidence exists that, in the months and weeks before his assassination, President Kennedy, recognizing that only the Vietnamese could ultimately resolve the conflict, was planning a withdrawal. Perhaps. What is certain is that Kennedy's successor, Lyndon B. Johnson, moved vigorously to oppose North Vietnamese insurgents, authorizing the CIA to oversee diversionary raids on the northern coast while the navy conducted electronic espionage in the Gulf of Tonkin. The new president also named General William Westmoreland to head the Military Assistance Command, Vietnam (MACV) and increased the number of military "advisors" to 23,000. Nevertheless, faced with a succession of weak Saigon governments, President Johnson continued to weigh the odds. The domino theory was persuasive, but the conflict began to look increasingly hopeless. In February 1965, LBJ sent his personal advisor, McGeorge Bundy, on a fact-finding mission to Saigon.

Suddenly, action by the Viet Cong moved the president's hand. On February 7, Viet Cong units attacked U.S. advisory forces and the headquarters of the U.S. Army 52nd Aviation Battalion, near Pleiku, killing nine Americans and wounding 108. Bundy, Westmoreland, and U.S. Ambassador Maxwell Taylor recommended a strike into North Vietnam. Operation Flaming Dart retaliated against an enemy barracks near Dong Hoi, provoking a Viet Cong counterstrike on February 10 against a U.S. barracks at Qui Nhon. The next day, U.S. forces struck back with a long program of air strikes deep into the North. Code named Rolling Thunder, the operation formally began on March 2, 1965, and marked the start of a course of escalation as 50,000 new ground troops were sent to Vietnam, ostensibly to "protect" U.S. air bases.

Escalation and Vietnamization

Johnson's strategy was to continue a gradual escalation of the war, bombing military targets in a war of attrition that would not provoke overt intervention from China or the U.S.S.R. This scheme proved to be a no-win strategy that only prolonged the war. In an aggressive military campaign, success is measured by objectives attained—cities captured, military targets eliminated—but in a war of attrition, the only measure of success is body count. To be sure, American forces produced a massive body count among the enemy, but, just as Buddhist monks were willing to set themselves aflame, this enemy was prepared to die.

Stats

In 1965, 75,000 Americans were fighting in Vietnam. In 1966, the number jumped to 375,000, and to half a million by 1968.

Motivated by nationalistic passion, the North Vietnamese did more than militarily infiltrate the South. Special political cadres won widespread support from the rural populace of the South. With this support, the Viet Cong enjoyed great mobility throughout the country, often fighting from a complex network of tunnels that were all but invisible. True, the growing numbers of U.S. troops were successful in clearing enemy territory. Yet U.S. numbers were never great enough to *occupy* that territory, and, once cleared, battle zones were soon overrun again.

President Johnson and his advisors began to recognize that the war would not be won by U.S. intervention, and military efforts were increasingly directed toward *Vietnamization*—giving the ARVN (Army of the Republic of Vietnam) the tools and training to take over more and more of the fighting, so that U.S. forces could ultimately disengage. That word, *Vietnamization*, was endlessly repeated as a mantra of American war policy, even as it became increasingly apparent that the South Vietnamese did not support their own government and had little will to fight.

Hearts and Minds

In the early stages of the war, President Kennedy had spoken of the need to win the "hearts and minds" of the Vietnamese people. And even as America's technologically advanced weaponry (including napalm incendiary bombs and highly toxic chemical agents to defoliate the jungle and expose the enemy) destroyed the country, the hearts and minds of the people remained elusive targets.

Hell, No! We Won't Go!

The fact is that American war policy had not only failed to win the hearts and minds of the Vietnamese, but it was rapidly losing influence over the hearts and minds of citizens of the United States. President Johnson increasingly relied on the Selective Service system—the draft—to supply troops. Relatively well-off young people could often avoid conscription through student deferments (college enrollment skyrocketed during the war) and by other means. Less-privileged and minority youth bore the brunt of the draft, a fact that stirred resentment and unrest, especially in the African-American community.

But antiwar sentiment was hardly confined to black America. What rapidly evolved into a full-blown antiwar movement began with leftist college students and peace activists. And as more Americans came home in "body bags," the movement spread into the main-stream. College campuses first served as centers of discussion about and against the war, and then they became the staging areas for demonstrations, including a series of marches on Washington starting in 1965 and continuing through 1968 and again in 1971.

Antiwar protest widened what was popularly called the *generation gap*, pitting young people against "anyone over 30." The antiwar movement became associated with a general counterculture movement, which featured young people in long hair (for both sexes) and wearing what to their elders seemed bizarre gypsy-hobo outfits. Such young-sters called themselves *hippies* and ostentatiously indulged in "recreational" drugs (such as marijuana and the hallucinogenic LSD) and "recreational" sex. Government officials assumed that the entire peace movement was backed by communists and used the FBI as well as the CIA (illegally) to infiltrate antiwar organizations. True, some organizations associated with the movement were undoubtedly subversive; however, most protesters were mainstream individuals, aged 20 to 29, who were simply disgusted and outraged by the war.

The student fringe of the peace movement became increasingly vocal during the 1960s, with demonstrations—sometimes destructive—disrupting and even temporarily closing down some college campuses. In mass demonstrations across the country, young men burned their draft registration cards and chanted, "Hell, no! We won't go!" So-called "confrontations" between demonstrators and police or even National Guardsmen became commonplace.

Main Event

The most visible and violent "confrontation" of the 1960s took place August 26–29, 1968, in Chicago, during the Democratic National Convention. Earlier, on March 31, 1968, President Johnson had announced to a stunned nation that he would not run for reelection. However, probably the most electable antiwar candidate, Robert F. Kennedy, was assassinated on June 6, following his victory in the California primary. Hubert H. Humphrey then became the most likely candidate, and he did not oppose the war. Some 10,000 individuals massed in Grant and Lincoln parks along Chicago's lakefront to protest the war, to protest the nomination of Humphrey ("Dump the Hump!" they chanted), and to vent rage against Chicago mayor and Democratic "boss" Richard J. Daley, whom they scorned as a racist and even a fascist.

The Light at the End of the Tunnel

By the end of 1967, it was clear that the Vietnam War was gruesomely stalemated. President Johnson repeatedly went before the nation, assuring television viewers that there was "light at the end of the tunnel." But the increasing numbers of U.S. casualties created a *credibility gap* between what the administration claimed and what the public believed.

Tet Offensive

In this period of growing doubt, Hanoi staged a series of massive offensives, first along the border, with attacks against the U.S. base at Khe Sanh, then against South Vietnamese provincial capitals and principal cities beginning on January 30, 1968, a Vietnamese lunar holiday called Tet. The offensive, which included an assault on the U.S. embassy in Saigon, was costly to U.S. and ARVN forces, but even more costly to the Viet Cong. However, the three-week campaign was a devastating psychological victory for the communists and convinced many Americans, including politicians and policy makers, that the war was unwinnable.

With American casualties now topping 1,000 a month, it was hard to believe official military pronouncements that Tet was by no means a defeat. Tet hardened public opposition to the war and sharply divided legislators, with *hawks* (war supporters) on one side, and *doves* (peace advocates) on the other.

Resignation of Johnson

On March 31, President Johnson made two surprise television announcements. He declared that he would restrict bombing above the 20th parallel, thereby opening the door to a negotiated settlement of the war, and he announced that he would not seek another term as president. Johnson recognized that his advocacy of the war was tearing the nation apart.

Cease-fire negotiations began in May, only to stall over Hanoi's demands for a complete bombing halt and NLF (National Liberation Front) representation at the peace table. Johnson resisted but in November agreed to these terms. Despite the boost this move gave the sagging presidential campaign of Democrat Hubert Humphrey, Richard M. Nixon (whom many had counted out of politics after he lost the race for California governor in 1962) emerged victorious in the presidential contest.

Nixon's War

Richard Milhous Nixon (1913–94) was a man who believed in winning at any cost. To ensure victory in the 1968 election, he made repeated—though vague—promises to end the war. Yet, after he was elected, Nixon did not hesitate to *expand* the war into neighboring Laos and Cambodia. Nixon had evolved a grand strategy with his foreign policy advisor, Henry Kissinger (b. 1923). The strategy called for improving relations with the Soviets (through trade and an arms-limitation agreement) in order to disengage Moscow from Hanoi, and for normalizing relations with China. After the U.S.S.R. and China had cut the North Vietnamese loose, Nixon and Kissinger reasoned, the United States could negotiate a "peace with honor" in Vietnam.

> **Word for the Day**
> The object of the Nixon–Kissinger diplomacy was to achieve *détente* with the Soviet Union and China, a condition of increased diplomatic, commercial, and cultural contact designed to reduce tensions.

The strategy didn't work. The Soviets announced their recognition of the Provisional Revolutionary Government (PRG) formed by the NLF in June 1969, and the peace talks foundered.

Paris, Cambodia, and Laos

As peace negotiations went round and round in Paris, the Nixon administration sought to accelerate the Vietnamization process by turning more and more of the responsibility for the war over to ARVN forces, which, however, continued to perform poorly. Despite the discouraging results, U.S. casualties did drop, and President Nixon was able to begin troop withdrawals.

Main Event

On March 16, 1968, a U.S. infantry company commanded by Lieutenant William L. Calley marched into the South Vietnamese hamlet of My Lai, supposedly a Viet Cong sanctuary/stronghold. The company massacred 347 unarmed civilians, including women, old men, and children, some of whom were herded into ditches and shot. The grisly scenes were recorded by army photographers.

The "My Lai Incident" was not made public until 1969, and then only through the efforts of Vietnam veteran Ronald Ridenhour, who threatened to go to the media with what he had heard about the massacre if the U.S. Army failed to initiate an inquiry. That proceeding resulted in the court martial of several soldiers, of whom only Calley was convicted on March 29, 1971.

For many Americans, My Lai symbolized the essential brutality of the Vietnam War, a conflict in which the defenders of democracy were seen as slaughterers of innocent women and children. As to Calley, some people saw him as likewise a victim, thrust into a war in which everyone was a potential enemy. Sentenced to life imprisonment, Calley was released in September 1974 when a federal court overturned the conviction.

With the failure of diplomacy, Nixon turned to force, striking at communist supply and staging areas in Cambodia. This incursion triggered angry protests at home, including a demonstration at Kent State University in Ohio on May 4, 1970. The event resulted in the killing of four unarmed students and the wounding of nine more when inexperienced National Guardsmen fired on them. Subsequently, 100,000 demonstrators marched on

Washington, and Congress registered its own protest by rescinding the Tonkin Gulf Resolution. Nixon withdrew troops from Cambodia but stepped up bombing raids, and when communist infiltration continued unabated, the U.S. supplied air support for an ARVN invasion of Laos in February 1971.

By the end of 1971, withdrawals had reduced troop strength to 175,000 in Vietnam, somewhat calming protests at home but destroying front-line morale, as remaining troops saw themselves pawns in a lost cause. Drug and alcohol abuse assumed epidemic proportions among soldiers, who were openly rebellious; some transformed search-and-destroy missions into "search-and-avoid" operations, the object of which was to get home safely.

> **Word for the Day**
> Officers who ordered their men into dangerous situations risked *fragging*—that is, assassination by their own troops—typically by *fragmentation* grenade.

Death for Easter

In March 1972, the communists launched a new invasion, initially routing ARVN troops until President Nixon retaliated by redoubling air attacks, mining Haiphong harbor, and establishing a naval blockade of the North. Following the communist "Easter Offensive," Henry Kissinger and North Vietnamese representative Le Duc Tho finally formulated an agreement. The terms were to withdraw U.S. troops, return POWs, and lay the foundation for a political settlement through establishment of a special council of reconciliation. South Vietnamese president Nguyen Van Thieu rejected the peace terms because they permitted Viet Cong forces to remain in place in the South.

Bombs for Christmas

The fact that Nixon's negotiator, Kissinger, had been able to announce that "peace is at hand" assured the president reelection in 1972. Once in office, however, Nixon supported Thieu, repudiating the peace terms Kissinger had negotiated. Nixon then ordered massive B-52 bombing raids north of the 20th parallel, which forced the North Vietnamese back to the negotiating table.

The agreement reached after the bombing was not materially different from what Kissinger had originally concluded. This time, President Thieu was ignored.

Paris Accords and the Fall of Saigon

On January 31, 1973, the United States and North Vietnam signed the Paris Accords, which brought U.S. withdrawal and the return of the POWs, some of whom had been languishing in North Vietnamese prisons for nearly a decade. A four-party Joint Military

Commission and an International Commission of Control and Supervision supervised the cease-fire. However, the Nixon administration continued to send massive amounts of aid to the Thieu government, and both the North and South freely violated the accords. To pressure the North into abiding by them, the United States resumed bombing Cambodia and menaced North Vietnam with reconnaissance overflights.

But a war-weary Congress had turned against the president, whose administration (as you shall see in the next chapter) was now wallowing and disintegrating in the Watergate Scandal. In November 1973, Congress passed the War Powers Act, which required the president to inform Congress within 48 hours of deployment of U.S. military forces abroad; the act also mandated the forces' withdrawal within 60 days if Congress did not approve. In 1974, U.S. aid to South Vietnam was reduced from $2.56 billion to $907 million, and to $700 million in 1975.

What hopes Thieu held out for support from the Nixon administration were dashed when the U.S. president, facing impeachment, resigned in August 1974. Beginning in early 1975, the dispirited South suffered one military defeat after another. After Congress rejected President Gerald Ford's request for $300 million in supplemental aid to South Vietnam, Nguyen Van Thieu hurriedly resigned his office. He left the leadership of his nation to Duong Van Minh, whose single official act was unconditional surrender to the North on April 30, 1975. A dramatic, frenzied evacuation of Americans remaining in Vietnam followed. The spectacle of U.S. personnel being airlifted by helicopter from the roof of the U.S. embassy in Saigon was humiliating and heartbreaking. At the cost of over $150 billion and 58,000 Americans killed, the Vietnam War had ended in defeat for South Vietnam and (as many saw it) for the United States as well.

The Least You Need to Know

➤ U.S. involvement in the Vietnam War was an extreme result of the Cold War policy of the "containment" of communism.

➤ The Vietnam War was the most unpopular and divisive war in American history, wrecking the grand social programs of Lyndon Johnson and badly undermining popular faith in the federal government and the nation's leaders.

Part 8
Identity Crisis

By the late 1960s, a deep division opened up between a rebellious under-30 generation and their elders, with youngsters developing a colorful separate culture compounded of "psychedelic" art and music, as well as (on a more sinister note) drugs such as LSD and marijuana. The nation reached a great technological and human pinnacle in the successful lunar mission of Apollo 11, and the Cold War began to thaw. Yet Americans were stunned by the revelation of democracy's failings in The Pentagon Papers *and by the Watergate scandal that forced President Nixon to resign from office in 1974.*

The so-called women's liberation movement was finally taken seriously. But if men were now compelled to readjust their attitudes and egos, so was the entire nation, as it found itself held hostage to the oil sheiks of the Middle East, the industrial giants of Japan, a sluggish economy at home, and the religious fanaticism of the Ayatollah Khomeini of Iran. This section recalls a most unquiet period in our history.

Of Love, the Moon, and Dirty Tricks (1968–1974)

Who were the victims of the Vietnam War? Two, perhaps three million Indochinese died, and 58,000 American lives were lost. Many thousands more were wounded, some disabled for life. U.S. Vietnam veterans were not welcomed home with parades but were looked on with guilt and suspicion. By some Americans, veterans were seen as "baby killers"; by others, they were regarded as damaged goods—young men who may have escaped physical wounds but who bore psychological scars that made adjustment to civilian life difficult if not impossible.

The fact is that all America was a victim of the war, which had created a rift—to use a term from the era, a *credibility gap*—between citizens and government. Vietnam killed human beings, and it also killed trust.

Tune In, Turn On, Drop Out

Since the early 20th century, illegal drug abuse had been associated with the fringes of society, with desperate and disturbed individuals, and to some extent, with urban African-Americans. By the 1950s, addiction to such narcotics as heroin was becoming a major and highly visible problem in many American cities and was linked to the increasing incidence of violent street crime. Yet drug use was still far from a mainstream affliction.

This all changed by the mid 1960s. A new generation of middle-class youth, characterized by relative affluence and the advantages of education, became passionately dedicated to forms of music and other types of popular art that expressed a turning away from much that had been accepted as the American dream: material prosperity, a successful career, a happy marriage, a house set amid a green lawn and surrounded by a white picket fence. Youngsters craved the experience of new music (a development of the rock 'n' roll that had started in the 1950s) and new clothing—colorful, wild, casual, sometimes evoking the bygone world of British Edwardian extravagance and sometimes suggesting the realm of that ultimate thorn in the side of the American dream, the hobo. As they looked with distrust on their elders ("anyone over thirty"), 1960s youth indulged in so-called recreational drugs. True, previous generations had had their overindulgences, especially alcohol, but for many of those coming of age in the 1960s, drugs became an integral part of everyday life.

Main Event

No generation was influenced more thoroughly by popular music than that of the 60s. The roots of rock may be found in African-American popular music, especially the blues, and was first popularized among white youngsters in the 1950s by a cadre of young pop performers, most notably Elvis Presley, who electrified the nation by his 1956 appearance on TV's popular *Ed Sullivan Show*. But by the early 1960s, American rock had hit the doldrums and was losing its young audience.

Then in 1964, a quartet of "Mod"-clothed, mop-headed British teenagers calling themselves the Beatles toured the United States. Influenced by American rockers Chuck Berry and Presley, guitarists John Lennon and George Harrison, bass player Paul McCartney, and drummer Ringo Starr infused this American-born music with a new vitality, freshness, and electricity. Their 1964 tune, "I Want to Hold Your Hand," unleashed "Beatlemania" in this country and paved the way, first for a "British invasion" of other English bands and then for the development of a redefined American rock idiom.

Rock music became the ceaseless anthem of the decade, the beat of rebellion and of the solidarity of youth.

With thermonuclear war an ever-present danger, with an ongoing war escalating in Vietnam—a meatgrinder into which American youth were regularly tossed—and with social justice still an elusive goal in America, there was much to protest and reject in mainstream society. Marijuana was one form of protest, alternative, and escape (all rolled up into a cigarette called a *roach* or *joint*). Sex (which many youth in the 1960s saw as a synonym for love) was another. Yet another alternative was religion—not the "outworn" faiths of the Judeo-Christian West, but the apparently less materialistic beliefs of the East. The decade spawned a series of spiritual leaders, or *gurus*, including the Maharishi Mahesh Yogi (b. 1911?), who introduced a generation to Transcendental Meditation. Mahesh gained renown as spiritual counselor to a bevy of celebrities, including the Beatles.

A guru of a different kind exhorted his followers to "expand" their minds with a hallucinogenic drug called LSD, which (it was claimed) offered users a universe of "psychedelic" experience. "My advice to people today is as follows," proclaimed Harvard psychologist and LSD advocate Timothy Leary (1920–96) in 1966: "If you take the game of life seriously, if you take your nervous system seriously, if you take your sense organs seriously, if you take the energy process seriously, you must turn on, tune in, and drop out."

By taking drugs—"turning on"—one would "tune in" to what was really worthwhile in life and, as a consequence, be prompted to "drop out" of life in the hollow mainstream. The phrase became the banner slogan of a generation: *Turn on, tune in, drop out.*

Word for the Day
D-lysergic acid diethylamide, also known as LSD, LSD-25, and *acid*, is a hallucinogenic drug discovered in 1943 by Swiss chemist Albert Hofmann. LSD produces powerful sensory distortions, with visual (and sometimes auditory) hallucinations. In the 1960s, such LSD experiences were called *acid trips* and were thought to be mind or consciousness expanding.

Summer of Love

Americans who had, to one degree or another, turned on, tuned in, and dropped out characteristically called themselves *hippies* (derived from *hip*, slang for being attuned to the latest social trends). The hippie movement, despite its association with drug-induced escapism, was certainly not all negative. The movement placed emphasis on kindness, on affection, on looking out for one's fellow being, on caring for the natural environment, on social justice, on freedom of expression, on tolerance, on fostering creativity, on general peaceful coexistence, and on other life-affirming values. Naive from today's perspective, perhaps, hippies seemed to be engaged in a mass attempt to *will* the world to return to innocence. And if love was often confused with sex, the word *love* took on a more general meaning as well, as in the biblical injunction to love thy neighbor.

For many who remember the 1960s fondly, the era was summed up in the summer of 1969, called the *summer of love* and capped by an open-air rock-music festival held on a farm near Woodstock, New York, August 15–17, 1969. The most popular rock music performers of the time drew perhaps 500,000 fans, who indulged in three days of song, drugs, sex, and (there is no other word for it) love. Woodstock immediately became a cultural icon, symbol of a generation's solidarity in rebellion against the Establishment (a collective label given to those who controlled the status quo) and its war in Vietnam. Woodstock was a symbol, too, of a generation's hope for a better world.

The Eagle Has Landed

As much as the counterculture wanted to believe it, the Establishment did not fail in all it put its hand to. Beginning with the launch of Sputnik I in 1957, the United States had consistently come in second to the Soviet Union in the space race. In 1961, President Kennedy made a speech in which he set a national goal of putting a man on the moon before the end of the decade. At the time, few Americans thought this goal was realistic, but on July 20, 1969, at 4:17 p.m. (Eastern Daylight Time), the people of a world shaken by a multitude of fears, gnawed by myriad acts of injustice, and racked by a terrible war in Southeast Asia, watched live television pictures of two American astronauts setting foot on the lunar surface, a quarter million miles from earth.

"That's one small step for man," Neil Armstrong declared as he hopped down off the ladder of the lunar excursion module (LEM) *Eagle*, "and one giant leap for mankind." The successful mission of Apollo 11 was a national—and human—triumph in a time of bitterness, pain, doubt, and rejection of long-cherished values.

Pentagon Papers

Unfortunately, the government that put men on the moon was capable of moral lapses as deep as its lunar aspirations were lofty. During June 1971, the *New York Times* published a series of articles on a secret government study popularly called *The Pentagon Papers*. The 47-volume document, compiled between 1967–1969 by Defense Department analysts, meticulously revealed how the federal government had systematically deceived the American people with regard to its policies and practices in Southeast Asia. Among many other things, the study showed how the CIA had conspired to overthrow and assassinate South Vietnam president Diem, and it revealed that the Tonkin Gulf Resolution was actually drafted months in advance of the attack on the destroyer *Maddox* and the apparent attack on the *C. Turner Joy*, the events that supposedly prompted the resolution.

In 1971, Daniel Ellsberg, an MIT professor and government consultant who had access to the study and who had become disgusted and disillusioned with the Vietnam War, leaked *The Pentagon Papers* to the *Times*. The Department of Justice attempted to block publication of the document, but the Supreme Court upheld freedom of the press and ruled in favor of the newspaper. Although Ellsberg (whom some deemed a hero, others a traitor) was indicted for theft, espionage, and conspiracy, the charges were dismissed in 1973 because the government had acted illegally in obtaining evidence. Part of the govern-ment's illegal action included, at the behest of the Nixon administration, burglar-izing the office of Ellsberg's psychiatrist to find material to embarrass the whistle blower.

The revelations of *The Pentagon Papers* marked a low point of popular faith in the Ameri-can government and the continued prosecution of the Vietnam War. The effect of these documents was profoundly depressing precisely because Americans had long taken for granted that theirs was a free, open, honest, and noble government—as Abraham Lincoln had put it, "the last best hope of the world."

SALT, China, and the Middle East

Last best hope. President Nixon, who had risen to power in Congress through his uncom-promising, at times virulent stance against communism, now worked with his advisor Henry Kissinger to engineer *détente* with the Soviets and with the communist Chinese. His most immediate motivation was to cut them loose from North Vietnam, but the ramifications of the Nixon–Kissinger diplomacy extended far beyond the Vietnam War. The consummate "cold warrior," Richard M. Nixon initiated the long thaw that ulti-mately ended the Cold War.

In 1968, the United Nations sponsored the Nuclear Non-Proliferation Treaty, which sought to limit the spread of nuclear weapons by persuading nations without nuclear arsenals to renounce acquiring them in return for a pledge from the nuclear powers that they would reduce the size of their arsenals. The following year, the United States began negotiations with the Soviet Union to limit strategic (that is, nuclear-armed) forces. These Strategic Arms Limitation Talks (SALT) produced a pair of important arms-control agree-ments in 1972. Then, from 1972 to 1979, the talks of SALT II were conducted, extending provisions formulated in 1972. Although the U.S. Senate failed to ratify SALT II, the two nations generally abided by its arms-limitation and arms-reduction provisions.

Perhaps even more remarkable was President Nixon's February 1972 journey to China, where he was received in Beijing by Chairman Mao Tse-tung, the very incarnation of the communism Nixon had spent his life opposing. In a single stroke of diplomacy, Nixon reversed the long-standing U.S. policy of refusing to recognize China's communist government, and by January 1979 (under President Jimmy Carter), full diplomatic relations were established between the nations.

The third of Nixon's major triumphs in diplomacy came in the war-torn Middle East. Following the Arab–Israel War in 1973, Nixon's emissary Henry Kissinger presided over negotiations that led to a cease-fire, troop disengagement, and ultimately, the founda-tions of a more lasting peace in the region.

Real Life

When Richard Nixon was buried at his boyhood home in Yorba Linda, California, following his death in 1994, the nation, almost in spite of itself, paid homage to a president who betrayed his oath of office—the only chief executive in U.S. history to resign office.

Born on January 9, 1913, Nixon overcame a financially pinched childhood and excelled in school, becoming a successful lawyer, then serving in the navy during World War II. Returning from the war, Nixon ran for Congress from California's 12th district in 1946, handily winning after he attacked his Democratic opponent, Jerry Voorhis, as a communist. From that point on, Nixon focused on communism as his principal political theme. Reelected to the House in 1948, Nixon defeated Congresswoman Helen Gahagan Douglas in a 1950 Senate race, accusing her of communist leanings ("pink right down to her underwear").

In 1952, the 39-year-old Nixon was tapped as running mate of Dwight D. Eisenhower and served as vice president through Ike's two terms. Nixon earned particular respect in 1955 when he effectively and confidently filled in for Eisenhower as the president recovered from a heart attack.

In 1960, Nixon became the Republican candidate for president, only to lose the election by a mere 100,000 votes to John F. Kennedy. Discouraged, Nixon ran for California governor two years later and was defeated, telling reporters that they wouldn't "have Nixon to kick around anymore."

But Nixon returned as a presidential candidate in 1968, defeating Democrat Hubert H. Humphrey. As president, Nixon reached out to the Soviet Union and China, beginning a gradual thaw in the Cold War. Through foreign policy advisor (later secretary of state) Henry Kissinger, Nixon engineered a painful U.S. withdrawal from Vietnam. On the domestic front, he developed what he called the "New Federalism," cutting back on federal programs and shifting power as well as responsibility back onto state and local governments.

The 1972 elections swept Nixon back into office for a second term; however, his campaign tactics involved a myriad of illegal activities, and, after a lengthy congressional inquiry, Nixon resigned office on August 9, 1974. He accepted a pardon from his successor, Gerald R. Ford, and spent the rest of his life writing works of autobiography and foreign policy. He died cloaked in the mantle of elder statesman.

CREEP

Brilliant, even noble on the international front, Richard Nixon never won total trust and confidence at home. A vigorous, typically merciless political campaigner, Nixon had a reputation for stopping at nothing to crush his opponent. "Tricky Dick," he was called, and never affectionately.

As the 1972 elections approached, there was little doubt that Nixon would be reelected. Henry Kissinger had announced that peace in Vietnam was "at hand," international relations were dramatically improving, and Americans were generally loath to (in Lincoln's homely phrase) change horses in midstream. Yet, oddly, none of this optimism was enough for the president. He directed his reelection organization, the Committee to Reelect the President—known (incredibly enough) by the acronym CREEP—to stack the deck even more thoroughly in his favor. The committee engaged in a campaign of espionage against the Democratic party and a program of dirty tricks aimed at smearing Democratic challengers.

Plumbers

On June 17, 1972, during the presidential campaign, five burglars were arrested in the headquarters of the Democratic National Committee at the Watergate office building in Washington, D.C. This was hardly front-page news—except that these burglars were really "Plumbers." That's what the White House secretly called the men, because their mission was to plug any leaks (security breaches) that developed or might develop in the aftermath of the publication of *The Pentagon Papers*. The Plumbers served the Nixon administration as a kind of palace guard, assigned to do jobs that lay beyond the chief executive's constitutional mandate. One such job involved planting electronic bugs (listening devices) at the headquarters of the political opposition.

The five Plumbers included three anti-Castro Cuban refugees, all veterans of the ill-fated Bay of Pigs invasion, and James McCord, Jr., former CIA agent and now "security" officer for CREEP. McCord reported directly to CREEP's head, Nixon's campaign manager, U.S. Attorney General John Mitchell. In a slapstick security faux pas, one of the burglars carried in his pocket an address book with the name of E. Howard Hunt. A former CIA agent (he'd been in charge of the Bay of Pigs operation) and writer of spy novels, Hunt was assistant to Charles Colson, special counsel to President Nixon. Hunt's address? "The White House."

What President Nixon tried to dismiss as a "third-rate burglary" pointed to conspiracy at the very highest levels of government. In September, the burglars and two co-plotters—Hunt and former FBI agent G. Gordon Liddy, CREEP's general counsel—were indicted on charges of burglary, conspiracy, and wiretapping. After their convictions, Nixon's aides, one after the other, began to talk.

All the President's Men

Despite the arrests and early revelations, President Nixon won reelection, but soon after he began his second term, the Watergate conspiracy rapidly unraveled. As each of the "president's men" gave testimony to federal authorities, the conspiracy tightened around Nixon's inner circle. In February 1973, the Senate created an investigative committee headed by North Carolina Senator Sam Ervin, Jr. As the Army–McCarthy Hearings had done two decades earlier, so the Watergate Hearings riveted Americans to their television sets. After each key disclosure, the president announced the resignation of an important aide, including John Ehrlichman and H.R. Haldeman, his closest advisors. Nixon's counsel, John W. Dean III, was dismissed. Patiently, persistently, and with the cunning of a country lawyer educated at Harvard, the drawling Ervin elicited testimony revealing crimes far beyond Watergate:

➤ that Mitchell controlled secret monies used to finance a campaign of forged letters and false news items intended to damage the Democratic party

➤ that major U.S. corporations had made illegal campaign contributions amounting to millions

➤ that Hunt and Liddy had in 1971 burglarized the office of Daniel Ellsberg's psychiatrist in order to discredit *The Pentagon Papers* whistle blower

➤ that a plan existed to physically assault Ellsberg

➤ that Nixon had promised the Watergate burglars clemency and even bribes in return for silence

➤ that L. Patrick Gray, Nixon's nominee to replace the recently deceased J. Edgar Hoover as head of the FBI, turned over FBI records on Watergate to White House counsel John Dean

➤ that two Nixon cabinet members, Mitchell and Maurice Stans, took bribes from shady financier John Vesco

➤ that illegal wiretap tapes were in the White House safe of Nixon advisor John Ehrlichman

➤ that Nixon directed the CIA to instruct the FBI not to investigate Watergate

➤ that Nixon used $10 million in government funds to improve his personal homes

➤ that during 1969–70, the U.S. had secretly bombed Cambodia without the knowledge (let alone consent) of Congress

In the midst of all this turmoil, Vice President Spiro T. Agnew was indicted for bribes he had taken as Maryland governor. He resigned as vice president in October 1973 and was replaced by Congressman Gerald Ford of Michigan. Finally, it was revealed that President

Nixon had covertly taped White House conversations; the tapes were subpoenaed, but the president claimed "executive privilege" and withheld them. Nixon ordered Elliot L. Richardson (who had replaced the disgraced John Mitchell as attorney general) to fire special Watergate prosecutor Archibald Cox. On October 20, 1973, Richardson refused and resigned in protest; his deputy, William Ruckelshaus, likewise refused and was fired. The duty to discharge Cox fell to Nixon's solicitor general, Robert H. Bork, and this "Saturday night massacre" served only to suggest that Nixon had much to hide.

At length, the president released transcripts of some of the White House tapes (containing $18^1/_2$ minutes of suspicious gaps), and on July 27–30, the House Judiciary Committee recommended that Nixon be impeached on three charges: obstruction of justice, abuse of presidential powers, and attempting to impede the impeachment process by defying committee subpoenas. Nixon released the remaining tapes on August 5, 1974, which revealed that he had taken steps to block the FBI's inquiry into the Watergate burglary. On August 9, 1974, Richard Milhous Nixon became the first president in U.S. history to resign from office.

The Least You Need to Know

➤ As World War I had produced in America a lost generation, so Vietnam spawned a youth counterculture movement, founded on idealism, rock music, sexual freedom, and "recreational" drugs.

➤ The turbulent Nixon years saw men land on the moon and the Cold War begin to thaw, but the era ended in the gravest national crisis since the Civil War.

Chapter 33

Women, Crisis, and a Call to the Great Communicator (1963–1980)

The 1960s marked a period of self-examination in the United States, an era of sometimes liberating reflection and sometimes debilitating self-doubt. During the decade, women joined African-Americans and other minorities in calling for equal rights and equal opportunity. In the course of the following decade, all Americans were forced rethink attitudes about growth, expenditure, and the natural environment as the fragility of the nation's sources of energy was dramatically exposed. Then, in 1980, after 20 years of often painful introspection, Americans elected a president whose resume included two terms as California's governor and a lifetime as a movie actor. His message to the nation was to be proud and feel good—a message Ronald Wilson Reagan's fellow Americans eagerly embraced.

A Woman's Place

The sweet land of liberty was largely a man's world until 1920, when women, at long last, were given the constitutional right to vote. Yet that giant stride changed remarkably little about American society. The first presidential election in which women had a voice brought Warren G. Harding (1865–1923) into office, embodiment of the status quo, whose very campaign slogan promised a "return to normalcy." No, it would take a second world war to bring even temporary change to gender roles and sexual identity in the United States.

From Rosie the Riveter to The Feminine Mystique

The national war effort spurred into action by the December 7, 1941, surprise attack on Pearl Harbor required maximum military force and maximum industrial production. But if the men were off fighting the war, who would run the factories? Women answered the call in massive numbers, invading traditionally male workplaces. Posters exhorting workers to give their all for war production often depicted a woman in denim overalls and bandana, wielding a rivet gun like an expert. She was Rosie the Riveter, symbol of American womanhood in World War II.

For most American women, the war was their first experience of life in a workplace other than the home. Women faced new responsibilities but also tasted new freedom and independence. Yet when the war ended, the women, for the most part, quit their jobs, married the returning soldiers, and settled into lives as homemakers.

Throughout the 1950s, relatively few women questioned their role in the home. With the beginning of the 1960s, however, the American economy started a gradual shift from predominantly manufacturing-based to service-based industries, and women soon began finding job opportunities in these venues. Propelled in part by the powerful advertising medium of television, the 1960s were also driven by headlong consumerism. Increasing numbers of women found it necessary (or desirable) to earn a second income for their product-hungry families.

In 1963, writer Betty Friedan sent a questionnaire to graduates of Smith College, her alma mater. She asked probing questions about the women's satisfaction in life, and the answers she received were sufficiently eye opening to prompt her to write a book, *The Feminine Mystique*. Its thesis, based on the Smith questionnaire and other data, was that American women were no longer universally content to be wives and mothers. They were, in fact, often the unhappy victims of a myth that the female of the species could gain satisfaction only through marriage and childbearing. *The Feminine Mystique*, an instant bestseller, struck a chord that caused many women to reexamine their lives and the roles in which society had cast them.

The Power of the Pill

In 1960, shortly before Friedan's book appeared, the U.S. Food and Drug Administration approved the world's first effective oral contraceptive, the birth-control pill, which was soon dubbed more simply "The Pill." It was destined not only to bring radical change to the nation's sexual mores—contributing to the so-called *sexual revolution* of the 1960s—but also to liberate women from the inevitability of life tied to the nursery. Now, a women could choose to delay having children (or not to have them at all) and use the time to establish a career.

NOW and Ms.

Three years after publishing *The Feminine Mystique*, Friedan helped found the National Organization for Women and served as NOW's first president. An organized feminist movement—popularly called *women's liberation* or (sometimes derisively) *women's lib*—crystallized around NOW. The organization advocated equality for women in a general social sense and in the workplace, liberalized abortion laws, and passage of the Equal Rights Amendment (ERA), a proposed constitutional amendment declaring that "equality of rights under the law shall not be denied or abridged by the United States nor by any State on account of sex." ERA was drafted by feminist Alice Paul (1885–1977) of the National Woman's Party and introduced in Congress in 1923, where it was essentially ignored until NOW took up its cause in 1970.

By the end of the 1960s, the women's liberation movement was in full swing. In 1972, journalist and feminist Gloria Steinem started *Ms.* magazine, which became a popular, entertaining, and immensely profitable vehicle for the feminist message.

Word for the Day

The rise of feminism brought many changes and proposed changes to American society, including the modification of *sexist* (gender-biased) language. For example, the word *mankind* excluded women; feminists preferred *humankind*. The use of *Mrs.* and *Miss* suggested to feminists that a woman's value was unfairly bound to her marital status (in contrast, men are addressed simply as *Mr.*, whether married or not). The abbreviation *Ms.* (pronounced *mizz*) was widely adopted as a more equitable female counterpart to *Mr.*

NOW met with opposition not only from conservative men but also from many women, some of whom claimed that the feminist movement ran contrary to the natural (or God-given) order; other women feared the movement would defeminize women and lead to the disintegration of the family. By the 1970s, NOW was also under attack from more radical feminists, such as Shulamith Firestone, Kate Millet, and Ti-Grace Atkinson, for being too conservative. Nevertheless, NOW and the entire range of feminist activism have had an impact on American life. More women occupy corporate executive positions today than ever before; in state legislatures, the number of women serving doubled between 1975 and 1988; and by the late 1980s, 40 of 50 states had laws mandating equality of pay for men and women in comparable jobs.

Main Event

In 1973, the Supreme Court ruled in the case of *Roe v. Wade*, which had its origin in a suit brought by a woman against the state of Texas for having denied her the right to an abortion. In a 7-to-1 vote, the high court determined that women have a constitutional right to abortion during the first three months of pregnancy.

Abortion is the most controversial right women have asserted, and the *Roe v. Wade* decision gave rise to a so-called *Right to Life* anti-abortion movement. Usually motivated by religious conviction, Right to Life advocates have campaigned for a constitutional amendment banning abortion (except in cases of rape, incest, or threat to the mother's life). In recent years, some opposition to abortion has been fanatical, leading to the bombing of abortion clinics and the murder of medical personnel.

ERA Sunset

Thanks to NOW, the Equal Rights Amendment was approved by the House of Representatives in 1971 and by the Senate in 1972. The amendment was then sent to the states for ratification, and when the necessary three-fourths majority of states failed to ratify it by the original March 1979 deadline, a new deadline of June 30, 1982, was fixed. Yet, by this date, ratification was still three states short of the 38 needed. Reintroduced in Congress on July 14, 1982, ERA failed to gain approval and was dead as of November 15, 1983.

The failure of ERA points to the limits of what the feminist movement has achieved. Despite gains, far fewer women than men hold high elective office or sit on the boards of major corporations, and despite legislation, women continue to earn, on average, significantly less than men.

Stats

1993 U.S. Bureau of Labor statistics reveal continued inequality of pay for men and women. Among white adults earning hourly wages, 1,290,000 men (over age 16) earned $4.25 or less, compared with 2,177,000 women at this level.

12,415,000 men were paid $10 or more, compared with only 7,186,000 women. (Figures for blacks and those of Hispanic origin show narrower gaps between men and women at the lower range, but wider gaps at the top.)

A Meeting of the Sheiks

Citizens of the United States, men and women, have always cherished their liberty, and after 1908, when Henry Ford introduced his Model T, they have increasingly identified a part of that liberty with the automobile. With six percent of the world's population, the United States consumes a third of the world's energy—much of it in the form of petroleum. Through the 1960s, this posed little problem. Gasoline was abundant and cheap. Indeed, at the start of the decade, U.S. and European oil producers slashed their prices, a move that prompted key oil nations of the Middle East—Iran, Iraq, Kuwait, and Saudi Arabia, plus Venezuela in South America—to band together as the Organization of Petroleum Exporting Countries (OPEC) on September 14, 1960, to stabilize prices. (More nations joined later.) Beginning in 1970, OPEC began to press for oil price hikes, and on October 17, 1973, OPEC temporarily embargoed oil exports to punish nations that had supported Israel in its recent war with Egypt. Chief among the embargo's targets was the United States.

The effects of the OPEC embargo were stunning. Not only did prices shoot up from 38.5 cents per gallon in 1973 to 55.1 cents by June 1974, gasoline shortages were severe in some areas. Americans found themselves stuck in gas lines stretching from the pumps and snaking around the block.

Cruising full speed ahead since the end of World War II, Americans were forced to come to grips with an energy crisis, cutting back on travel and on electricity use. The public endured an unpopular, but energy- (and life-) saving 55-mile-an-hour national

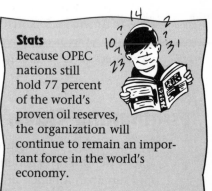

Stats
Because OPEC nations still hold 77 percent of the world's proven oil reserves, the organization will continue to remain an important force in the world's economy.

speed limit, in addition to well-meaning, if somewhat condescending lectures from President Jimmy Carter, who characteristically sported a cardigan sweater on TV appearances because he had turned down the White House thermostat as an energy-conserving gesture. In a modest way, Americans learned to do without, and oil consumption was reduced by more than 7 percent—enough to prompt some OPEC oil price rollbacks by the early 1980s. By this time, too, OPEC's grip on key oil producers had slipped as various member producers refused to limit production.

Made in Japan

The energy crisis came on top of an economic crisis, characterized by a combination of inflation and recession christened *stagflation* (stagnant growth coupled with inflation). The crisis had begun during the Nixon–Ford years and continued into the Carter presidency. By the mid 1970s, the heady consumerism of the 1960s was on the wane, and the dollar bought less and less. To use a phrase popular during the period, the economy was in the toilet.

And so, it seemed, was the American spirit. Accustomed to being preeminent manufacturer to the world, American industry was losing ground to other nations, especially Japan. All but crushed by World War II, Japan had staged an incredible recovery, becoming a world-class economic dynamo. By the 1970s, Japanese automobiles especially were making deep inroads into the U.S. automotive market. Not only were the Japanese vehicles less expensive than American makes, they were more fuel efficient (which meant fewer dollars spent on increasing gasoline costs), and they were more dependable.

The Chrysler Corporation, smallest of the Big Three automakers (behind General Motors and Ford), found itself on the verge of bankruptcy and, in 1980, sought federal aid. The government-backed loan was ultimately paid back and the Chrysler recovery became a celebrated comeback story (the company's CEO, Lee Iacocca, was elevated nearly to the status of American folk hero). However, the $1.5 billion bailout of America's 17th largest corporation was as controversial as it was depressing. Patriotic Americans felt vaguely humiliated—even as more and more of them climbed behind the wheel of a Toyota or Mitsubishi.

Frightening Cities, Crumbling Bridges

Driving through an American city, circa 1975, in one of those Japanese imports could be a pretty depressing experience as well. The post-World War II building boom had developed suburban America, and throughout the 1950s, many middle-class families left the old cities for the new suburbs. The pace of this exodus accelerated following the racial violence that plagued many cities during the 1960s. Social commentators began to speak of *white flight*—though, in fact, the abandonment of inner city for suburb was as much a matter of economics as it was of race; middle-class blacks fled just as quickly as their white neighbors. The result was cities that rotted at their cores. With the urban economic base dramatically reduced, businesses followed residents to outlying areas, and once-vibrant downtown districts became ghetto ghost towns. Throw into this dismal mix the often-ineffective efforts of a chronically underfunded public education system plus a steady increase in the abuse of illegal narcotics, and it seemed that many U.S. municipalities had been reduced to forbidding urban jungles.

Main Event

Americans have typically had a love-hate relationship with their nation's greatest city, New York. But during the 1970s, Gotham became an unwilling emblem of all that was going wrong with urban America. Poverty, decay, crime, and corruption were bigger there than anywhere else and always under the national spotlight. In 1975, Mayor Abe Beame issued the astounding statement that his city could not pay its creditors. New York City, cultural center of the nation and home of Wall Street, was broke.

President Gerald Ford did not help matters when he steadfastly resisted extending federal aid to the city to prevent it from defaulting, and the *New York Daily News* trumpeted an instantly famous headline: "FORD TO NY: DROP DEAD!"

Fortunately, through the efforts of Democratic leaders such as Texas representative Jim Wright, Congress voted emergency loans amounting to $2.3 billion, the city avoided bankruptcy, ultimately recovered, and paid back the loan—with interest.

But deteriorating cities weren't the only symptoms of a crisis in the national economy and spirit. The American infrastructure was in need of a general repair. The very roads that had carried the middle class out of the inner city were typically cratered with potholes. And a growing proportion of the nation's bridges—physical expressions of the necessity and desire to join town to town and citizen to citizen—were failing inspection, too old, too neglected to bear the traffic for which they had been designed.

Meltdown

The single most terrifying event that suddenly and dramatically forced Americans to question their faith in U.S. technology, big business, and government regulation occurred on March 28, 1979. A nuclear reactor at the Three Mile Island electric generating plant, near the Pennsylvania capital of Harrisburg, lost coolant water, thereby initiating a partial meltdown of the reactor's intensely radioactive core.

Nuclear energy had long been a subject of controversy in the United States. During the late 1950s and early 1960s, the peaceful use of the atom was seen as the key to supplying cheap and virtually limitless energy to the nation. But by the 1970s, environmentalists and others were questioning the safety of atomic power, which was also proving far more expensive than had been originally projected. By the end of the decade, a beleaguered nuclear power industry was on the defensive. By remarkable coincidence, just before the Three Mile Island accident, a popular movie dramatized the consequences (and attempted corporate cover-up) of a nuclear power plant accident. The movie was called *The China Syndrome*, an allusion to the theory that a full-scale meltdown of a reactor's core would burn so intensely that the material would, in effect, sear its way deep into the earth—clear down to China, experts grimly joked.

The movie was very much on people's minds when a shaken Pennsylvania governor Richard Thornburgh appeared on television to warn residents to remain indoors and advised pregnant women to evacuate the area. The partial meltdown had already released an amount of radioactive gases into the atmosphere.

Although evidence exists that plant officials improperly delayed notifying public authorities of the accident, backup safety features in the plant did successfully prevent a major disaster of the proportions of the Chernobyl meltdown on April 26, 1986, in the Soviet Ukraine, which would kill 31 persons immediately and untold additional numbers later. Nevertheless, Three Mile Island seemed to many people just one more in a long string of terrible failures of American commerce, technology, and know-how.

The Ayatollah

The year 1979 brought a shock of a different kind to national pride. A revolution in Iran, led by the Ayatollah Ruhollah Khomeini (1900–89), toppled longtime U.S. ally Muhammad Reza Shah Pahlavi, the Shah of Iran, who fled into exile in January 1979. In October, desperately ill with cancer, the Shah was granted permission to come to the United States for medical treatment. In response to this gesture, on November 4, 1979, 500 Iranians stormed the U.S. embassy in Tehran and took 66 embassy employees hostage, demanding the return of the Shah.

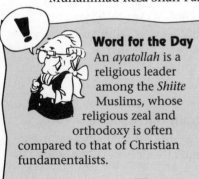

Word for the Day
An *ayatollah* is a religious leader among the *Shiite* Muslims, whose religious zeal and orthodoxy is often compared to that of Christian fundamentalists.

While President Carter refused to yield to this demand, the Shah voluntarily left the United States in early December. Still, the hostages remained in captivity (except for 13 who were black or female, released on November 19–20). Stalemated and frustrated, President Carter authorized an army Special Forces unit to attempt a rescue on April 24, 1980. The mission had to be aborted, and although its failure did not result in harm to the hostages, it seemed yet another humiliating defeat for a battered superpower.

Not until November 1980 did the Iranian parliament propose conditions for the liberation of the hostages, including a U.S. pledge not to interfere in Iranian affairs, the release of Iranian assets frozen in the U.S. by President Carter, the lifting of all U.S. sanctions against Iran, and the return of the Shah's property to Iran. An agreement was signed early in January 1981, but the Ayatollah Khomeini deliberately delayed the release of the hostages until January 20, the day Jimmy Carter left office and Ronald Reagan was inaugurated. Although the new president, in an act of great grace and justice, sent Carter as his special envoy to greet the returning hostages at a U.S. base in West Germany, many Americans saw the Iran hostage crisis as a failure of the Carter administration, and the release was regarded as a kind of miracle performed by the incoming president.

The Great Communicator

Depressed and downcast, a majority of the American people looked to smiling, unflappable Ronald Reagan for even more miracles. Certainly, his own life had much magic to it. Born above a grocery store in Tampico, Illinois, in 1911, Reagan worked his way through college, became a sportscaster and then an actor—less than a spectacular talent, perhaps, but with 53 films and many TV appearances to his credit, he was never out of work. Reagan left acting to enter politics with a strong stop-communism and end-big-government message. In 1966 he handily defeated incumbent Democrat Pat Brown for the governor's office in California and served two terms, during which he made a national reputation as a tax cutter. Delivering a feel-good message to the nation and promising large tax cuts, a vast reduction in government ("getting government off our backs"), and a return to American greatness, Reagan defeated the incumbent Carter by a wide margin in 1980. Even those who bitterly opposed what they saw as a shallow conservatism admitted that Reagan deserved the title of *The Great Communicator*.

The Least You Need to Know

➤ The 1960s and 1970s saw Americans reexamining themselves and struggling to redefine their nation in an effort to renew the American dream.

➤ Ronald Reagan took his sweeping victory over Jimmy Carter in 1980 as a mandate for a rebirth of patriotism and a revolution in economics.

Part 9
New World Order

An economically and spiritually beleaguered America was highly receptive to the tax-cutting promises and patriotic feel-good message of Ronald Reagan. While the 1990s saw the end of the Cold War breakup of the Soviet Union—leaving the United States as the world's only superpower—the decade was also marked by profound dissatisfaction with domestic "politics as usual" and also by a sinister undercurrent of political rage that exploded into incidents of "homegrown" terrorism. As we see in this concluding section, sensational criminal cases—the videotaped police beating of Rodney King and the televised murder trial of O.J. Simpson—revealed the persistence of deep national divisions along racial lines, yet the evolution of electronic media, especially the emergence of personal computers linked by the Internet, suggested an enduring passion to make the ideals of democracy a reality.

Chapter 34

A New Economy, a Plague, a Fallen Wall, and a Desert in Flames (1980–1991)

In This Chapter

➤ Rise and fall of Reaganomics

➤ The AIDS crisis

➤ Victory in the Cold War and the Persian Gulf

➤ Iran-Contra scandal

The presidency of James Monroe (1817–25) ushered in an "era of good feelings," a time of perceived national well-being. Much the same happened during the two terms of Ronald Reagan, the most popular president since Ike Eisenhower. Where President Carter took a stern moral tone with the nation, admonishing his fellow Americans to conserve energy, save money, and generally do with a little less, President Reagan congratulated his countrymen on the fact of being Americans and assured them that all was well—or *would* be well, just as soon as he got "big government off our backs."

For a time, business boomed during the Reagan years—though the boom was largely the result of large-scale mergers and acquisitions, the shifting back and forth of assets, rather than any great strides in production. True, too, the Reagan administration saw the beginning of the end of the Cold War and the disintegration of the Soviet Union, which the president called an "evil empire." Yet, during the Reagan years, the national debt also rose from a staggering $1 trillion to a stupefying $4 trillion. And the period was convulsed by a terrible epidemic of a new, fatal, and costly disease, AIDS, which the administration met largely with indifference and denial.

Many things good and bad befell the Reagan years, yet, for the most part and for most people, only the good seemed to stick. The bad slid off Ronald Reagan with such ease that the press dubbed him the "Teflon president."

Supply Side and Trickle Down

Following his inauguration, President Reagan lost no time in launching an economic program formulated by his conservative economic advisors. The program was quarterbacked by Office of Management and Budget (OMB) director David Stockman (b. 1946), whose ascetic appearance seemed to signal his ruthlessness as a slasher of taxes and domestic social welfare spending. The new administration marched under the banner of *supply-side economics*, a belief that the economy thrives by stimulating the production of goods and services (the *supply side*) because (according to advocates of the theory) supply creates demand. Make it, and people will buy it. Government's proper role is to stimulate production by reducing taxes as well as reducing regulation of industry. Yet, even as taxes are reduced, supply-side economics also demands that the government operate on a balanced budget, since deficit spending encourages destructive inflation.

The Reagan revolution turned on three major policies: a reduction in government regulation of commerce and industry; aggressive budget cutting; aggressive tax cutting—not for middle- and lower-income individuals, but for the wealthy and for businesses. Reducing the tax burden on the rich was supposed to free up more money for investment, the benefits of which would ultimately "trickle down" to the less well off in the form of more and better jobs.

If *trickle down* was a hard concept for many to swallow, Reagan's insistence that a *reduction* in tax rates would actually *increase* government revenues seemed downright bizarre to some. When Ronald Reagan and the man who would be his vice president, George Bush, were battling one another in the Republican primaries, Bush branded the notion *voodoo economics*—a phrase that would come back to haunt Bush in subsequent campaigns. But conservative economist Arthur Laffer (b. 1940) theorized that tax cuts would stimulate increased investment and savings, thereby ultimately increasing taxable income and generating more revenue. President Reagan made frequent reference to the "Laffer Curve," which illustrated this process.

Plausible or not, a majority of the American people were prepared to take the leap with their new president. In 1981, a bold program was hurried through a sometimes bewildered Congress, including a major tax cut, a staggering $43 billion cut in the budget for domestic programs, and broad cutbacks in environmental and business regulation. The "Great Communicator" overcame all resistance. When catastrophe struck on March 30, 1981, in the form of would-be assassin John Hinckley, Jr., the 70-year-old president's calm and heroic response to his having been shot in the chest drew even more support for his programs.

Main Event

President Reagan had been in office only two months when he exited the Washington Hilton Hotel on March 30, 1981, after delivering a speech. Six shots rang out, fired from a .22-caliber revolver loaded with explosive "Devastator" bullets. Secret Service agent Timothy J. McCarthy and Washington police officer James Delahanty were hit, as was White House press secretary James S. Brady, who suffered a severe head wound.

The president was bundled into his limousine, where it was discovered that he, too, had been wounded in the chest. Fortunately, the bullet, lodged in his lung, had failed to explode and was removed in an emergency surgical operation. "I hope you're all Republicans," the president quipped to his surgeons.

The shooter, 25-year-old John Warnock Hinckley, Jr., was the drifter son of a wealthy Denver oil engineer. Hinckley was obsessed with screen actress Jodie Foster, who had made a sensation as a teenage prostitute in "Taxi Driver," a 1976 film dealing in part with political assassination. Hinckley apparently decided to kill the president to impress Foster.

A jury found Hinckley not guilty by reason of insanity, and he was confined to a psychiatric hospital. All of his victims recovered, except for Brady, who was left partially paralyzed. Brady became a passionate advocate of federal regulation of handguns—a policy President Reagan had himself opposed.

Greed Is Good

A relatively small number of people made a lot of money as a result of Reaganomics. Most of the new wealth was generated not by the stimulated production that the supply-side theory promised, but by a frenzied crescendo of corporate acquisitions and mergers. The stock market buzzed and churned in a way that (for some) disturbingly recalled the late

Real Life

The words put into Gordon Gecko's mouth were paraphrased from a real-life Wall Street manipulator, Ivan Boesky, who told the graduating class of the School of Business Administration at the University of California, Berkeley, on May 18, 1986: "Greed is all right, by the way...I think greed is healthy. You can be greedy and still feel good about yourself."

1920s. Companies were bought and either merged for efficiency (with resulting loss of jobs) or broken up, their component parts and assets sold at a profit to stockholders (with resulting loss of jobs). Unemployment generated by the high-level financial manipulations of the 1980s was hard on the man and woman on the street, but the movement of masses of wealth benefitted those who could afford to invest in the right companies at the right time. The average American may have been raised to believe that businesses existed to make products and provide employment, but the manipulators of wealth insisted that companies existed exclusively to enrich investors, and if that meant destroying a company, breaking it up, so be it. In the words of Gordon Gecko, a fictional tycoon played by Michael Douglas in the popular movie "Wall Street" (1987), "Greed is good."

Word for the Day

During the Reagan years, the Wall Street word for the day was *arbitrage*— the art of buying securities, commodities, or currencies in one market and immediately (sometimes simultaneously) selling them in another market to profit from price differences. *Arbitrageurs* like Ivan Boesky acted on take-over bids and impending mergers, buying blocks of the target company's stock at a low price, with the hope of selling them at a much higher price when the merger occurred. If the merger failed to occur, losses could be devastating.

Early confidence in Reaganomics faltered when the recession of the Nixon-Ford-Carter years deepened further, and public-opinion polls began to suggest that many people believed the tax cuts had benefited only the rich. Inflation did roll back, though interest rates remained high, as did unemployment. However, by 1983, acquisitions, mergers, and arbitrage had made the stock market a very active place, and prices began to rise sharply. This change, combined with relatively low inflation and (at last) rising production, as well as slowly decreasing unemployment, happily portended recovery.

What hopeful observers tended to ignore was the prodigiously growing national debt— under a president whose economic theory called for a *balanced* budget—and the flimsy sources of the profits being turned on Wall Street. Arbitrage is a high-risk business, which is made less risky if one has inside information, special knowledge of impending mergers, for example. The trouble is that such inside trading is illegal, and beginning in 1985, Wall

Street was rocked by a series of massive insider trading scandals. Trader Dennis B. Levine pleaded guilty to making $12.6 million by trading on non-public information, and arbitrageur Ivan Boesky likewise admitted buying huge blocks of stock as a result of receiving inside information. Not all the money made on Wall Street was illegal, but much of it rested on very shaky ground.

To finance the buyout of companies, traders turned to *junk bonds*, high-risk investments (usually issued by a company without an established earnings history or burdened by poor credit) acquired cheaply and paying a high rate of interest. Such transactions, called *leveraged buyouts* (the takeover of a company financed by borrowed funds) were pioneered in the 1970s by the Wall Street firm of Kohlberg Kravis Roberts and brought to a point of frenzy by Michael R. Milken. Often, junk bonds were purchased with very little hope that the issuing company would ever repay the loan, but in the short run, interest payments were so high that the underlying "junkiness" of the bond hardly seemed to matter.

Real Life

Michael R. Milken (b. 1946) was a star executive at the prestigious Wall Street trading firm of Drexel Burnham Lambert, Inc. He engineered a number of high-stakes, high-profile corporate takeovers through the use of high-yield junk bonds, making many of his clients and himself enormously wealthy in the process. However, it was subsequently discovered that much of Milken's trading was based on illegal inside information, and in 1989, a grand jury handed down a 98-count indictment against him for violating federal securities and racketeering laws. When Milken pleaded guilty to securities fraud and related charges in 1990, the government dropped the insider trading and racketeering charges, which carried greater penalties. His 10-year sentence was later reduced to three, and Milken returned to the world of finance upon his release. His spectacular rise and equally dramatic fall mirrored the course of the economy and cast a harsh light on the era's questionable business ethics.

Black Monday

The junk being bought and sold hit the fan on October 19, 1987, when the Dow Jones Industrial Average (key measure of stock market performance) plunged 508 points—almost double the fall in the 1929 crash that brought on the Great Depression. As Herbert Hoover had assured the American public that "prosperity was just around the corner," President Reagan dismissed the crash as "some people grabbing profits." Fortunately, the market gradually recovered—but the high-flying era of Reaganomics had careened to a gut-wrenching end.

Stats

On "Black Monday," October 19, 1987, $870 billion in equity simply evaporated as the market dropped from a Dow of 2,246.73 to 1,738.41 points.

"Gay Plague" and a Blind Eye

While many Americans stared with envy, admiration, or disgust at the Wall Street roller coaster, they turned a blind eye to the growing legion of homeless people who haunted the nation's large cities and even many of its smaller towns. Certainly, the Reagan administration, having drastically cut back federal welfare funding, did little enough for America's poorest. The administration likewise turned away from a terrifying plague that developed initially among homosexual men but was soon also diagnosed in heterosexual men, in women, and in children.

Word for the Day

AIDS—Acquired Immune Deficiency Syndrome—is caused by infection with the Human Immunodeficiency Virus (HIV), which attacks immune system cells, ultimately producing severe suppression of the body's ability to resist other infections.

The disease is transmitted sexually, through the blood (for example, through transfusion with infected whole blood or plasma), and during birth, from infected mothers to their children.

Stats

Since the first AIDS cases were formally reported in 1981, approximately a half-million AIDS cases and more than a quarter-million AIDS-related deaths have been reported in the United States. It is believed that another million Americans have been infected with HIV through the mid-1990s but have not developed clinical AIDS symptoms.

320

Throughout the 1980s, grass-roots AIDS organizations—including, most notably, Gay Men's Health Crisis (GMHC) and AIDS Coalition to Unleash Power (ACT UP)—mobilized. The organizations accused the government of failing to respond to an epidemic perceived to affect socially marginal groups—homosexuals and intravenous drug abusers (who contract the disease by sharing hypodermic needles tainted with infected blood). President Reagan failed even to make public mention of the disease until April 1987, fully six years after health officials had determined that the epidemic was under way. Only through the efforts of AIDS activists was federal funding increased—from $5.6 million in 1982 to more than $2 billion a decade later.

"Mr. Gorbachev, Tear Down This Wall!"

If the Reagan administration did not engage AIDS vigorously, it did not hesitate to take on the Soviet Union, assuming an aggressive stance against what the president called "an evil empire." Defense spending was dramatically stepped up, dwarfing domestic budget cuts in welfare and other programs.

The president also acted aggressively to meet perceived military threats throughout the world, sending U.S. marines in the summer of 1982 to Lebanon as a peacekeeping force. On October 23, 1983, more than 200 of these troops were killed in their sleep when a truck laden with 25,000 pounds of TNT was driven into the marines' Beirut headquarters building. Just two days after this disaster, the president ordered an invasion of the island nation of Grenada in the West Indies. Cuban troops had been sent to the tiny country (population 110,100) at the behest of its anti-American dictatorship, and the president was determined to protect the approximately 1,000 U.S. citizens there. The president also saw a successful liberation of the country as a kind of emotional compensation for the death of the marines in Beirut.

Ronald Reagan's saber rattling was gratifying to some Americans and alarming to others, who were distressed by the stalemate of U.S.–Soviet arms-control talks as a fresh deployment of American nuclear missiles began in Europe during November 1983. Reagan protested to his critics that the build-up was needed to counter Soviet advances, yet the strategy produced no tangible positive diplomatic results.

Voice from the Past

"So in your discussions of the nuclear freeze proposals, I urge you to beware the temptation of pride—the temptation blithely to declare yourselves above it all and label both sides equally at fault, to ignore the facts of history and the aggressive impulses of an evil empire, to simply call the arms race a giant misunderstanding and thereby remove yourself from the struggle between right and wrong, good and evil."

—Ronald Reagan, statement made on March 8, 1983

Star Wars Arm Wrestle

During 1983, President Reagan announced the most spectacular, ambitious, elaborate, and expensive military project in world history. It was called the Strategic Defense Initiative (SDI), but the popular press dubbed the system "Star Wars," after the popular George Lucas science-fiction movie of 1977. Using an orbiting weapons system, the idea was to create a shield against intercontinental ballistic missile attack by destroying incoming ICBMs before they began their descent. The weaponry was so far beyond even the foreseeable cutting edge as to be fanciful: X-ray and particle-beam devices (as yet theoretical) operated by supercomputers that had to be programmed by other computers. Critics pointed out that Star Wars was not only a violation of the 1972 ABM (antiballistic missile) treaty, but a temptation to thermonuclear war because it promised to make such a war survivable. Others suggested that the system could never be made to work, and still others protested that the staggering cost of the program—$100 to $200 billion—would permanently cripple the nation.

Yet Presidents Reagan and George Bush pursued Star Wars to the tune of $30 billion, even though the program produced few demonstrable results. Finally, in 1993, anonymous SDI researchers revealed that at least one major space test had been "fixed" to yield successful results. Caspar Weinberger, who had served as President Reagan's secretary of defense, initially denied these charges, but subsequently claimed that the test in question—and perhaps the entire Star Wars program—had been an elaborate decoy. The program (Weinberger said) had been designed solely to dupe the Soviet Union into spending a huge proportion of its resources on a Star Wars program of its own—a program that U.S. scientists already knew was unworkable.

The Wall Falls

Whether one views Star Wars—and the rest of the gargantuan Reagan defense budget—as a vast misjudgment, which quadrupled the national debt from one to four trillion dollars, or as a costly but brilliant strategy to win the Cold War, the fact is that the Cold War *did* end. The government of the Soviet Union was first liberalized and then fell apart, the nation's economy in tatters and the people clamoring for democratic capitalist reforms. Even though Mikhail Gorbachev (b. 1931), general secretary of the Soviet Communist party (1985–91) and president of the U.S.S.R. (1988–91), introduced unheard of liberal reforms, President Reagan prodded him to go even further. In 1987, standing near the Berlin Wall, brick, stone, and razor-wire symbol of a half-century of communist oppression, the president made a stirring speech calling out to the Soviet leader: "Mr. Gorbachev, open this gate! Mr. Gorbachev, tear down this wall!" Two years later, Berliners began chipping away at the wall, tearing it down piece by piece, as a liberalized Soviet Union merely looked on.

Although communist hardliners staged a revolt against Gorbachev in 1991, progressive junior army officers refused to follow KGB (Soviet secret police) directives, and the attempted coup failed. Gorbachev then disbanded the Communist party and stepped down as leader of the Soviet Union. Boris Yeltsin (b. 1931), radical reformist president of the Russian Republic, assumed leadership not of the Union of Soviet Socialist Republics—which ceased to exist—but of a loose commonwealth of former Soviet states.

Word for the Day

Americans learned two important Russian words during the 1980s. *Perestroika* (literally, *restructuring*) was how Gorbachev described his program of liberal political and economic reforms. *Glasnost (openness)* described how the traditionally secretive and closed USSR would now approach its own people and the rest of the world.

Ollie, Iran, and the Contras

The debate still rages over whether the policies of Ronald Reagan *won* the Cold War or whether the Soviet Union, shackled to a financially, intellectually, and morally bankrupt system of government, simply *lost* the half-century contest. Another episode of unorthodox world diplomacy continues to provoke controversy as well.

In November 1986, President Ronald Reagan confirmed reports that the U.S. had secretly sold arms to its implacable enemy, Iran. The president at first denied, however, that the purpose of the sale was to obtain the release of U.S. hostages held by terrorists in perpetually war-torn Lebanon, but he later admitted an arms-for-hostages swap. Then the plot thickened—shockingly—when Attorney General Edwin Meese learned that a portion of the arms profits had been diverted to finance so-called Contra rebels fighting against the leftist Sandinista government of Nicaragua. As part of the ongoing U.S. policy of containing communism, the Reagan administration supported right-wing rebellion in Nicaragua, but Congress specifically prohibited aid to the Contras. The *secret* diversion of the *secret* arms profits was blatantly unconstitutional and illegal.

A lengthy investigation gradually revealed that, in 1985, a cabal of Israelis had approached National Security Advisor Robert MacFarlane with a scheme in which Iran would use its influence to free the U.S. hostages held in Lebanon in exchange for arms. Secretary of State George Schultz and Secretary of Defense Caspar Weinberger objected to the plan, but (MacFarlane testified) President Reagan agreed to it. In a bizarre twist, U.S. Marine lieutenant colonel Oliver (Ollie) North then modified the scheme in order to funnel profits from the arms sales to the Contras.

As was the case with Watergate during the 1970s, investigation and testimony implicated officials on successively lofty rungs of the White House ladder—through national security advisors John Poindexter and MacFarlane, through CIA director William J. Casey (who died in May 1987), and through Defense secretary Caspar Weinberger. Few people believed that President Reagan had been ignorant of the scheme, but even if he had been the unwitting dupe of zealots in his administration, the implications were bad enough, painting a picture of a passive chief executive blindly delegating authority to his staff.

In the end, Ollie North was convicted on three of 12 criminal counts against him, but the convictions were subsequently set aside on appeal; Poindexter was convicted on five counts of deceiving Congress, but his convictions were also set aside; CIA administrator Clair E. George was indicted for perjury, but his trial ended in mistrial; and Caspar Weinberger was indicted on five counts of lying to Congress. All of those charged were ultimately pardoned by President Reagan's successor, George Bush. Although the 1994 report of special prosecutor Lawrence E. Walsh scathingly criticized both Reagan and Bush, neither was charged with criminal wrongdoing.

Desert Shield and Desert Storm

President Reagan's second term, marred by the Iran-Contra affair, a bumbling performance at the 1986 summit with Mikhail Gorbachev, and the 1987 stock market crash, nevertheless saw the "Teflon president" emerge personally unscathed. Vice President George Bush sailed to easy victory in the presidential race of 1988. Where the "Great Communicator" Reagan had been charismatic, however, Bush was perceived as testy, and, with the economy faltering (the principal issue was high unemployment), his popularity rapidly slipped in the polls. Bush seemed doomed to a one-term presidency.

Then, on August 2, 1990, Iraqi president Saddam Hussein, a dictator whose florid mustache recalled Josef Stalin and whose ruthless actions summoned to mind Adolf Hitler, ordered an invasion of the small, oil-rich Arab state of Kuwait. It was the beginning of a tense and dramatic crisis, but it was also President Bush's finest hour. His administration brilliantly used the United Nations to sanction action against Iraq, and with masterful diplomacy, the president assembled an unprecedented coalition of 31 nations to oppose the invasion. Particularly delicate was acquiring the support of the Arab countries while keeping Israel, which was even subject to attack by Iraqi SCUD

Stats
Combined U.S. and coalition forces in the Gulf War amounted to 530,000 troops as opposed to 545,000 Iraqis. U.S. and coalition losses were 149 killed, 238 wounded, 81 missing, and 13 taken prisoner (they were subsequently released). Iraqi losses have been estimated in excess of 80,000 men, with overwhelming loss of materiel.

missiles, out of the fray. As to the U.S. commitment, it was the largest since Vietnam: more than a half million troops, 1,800 aircraft, and some 100 ships.

Indeed, comparisons with Vietnam were plentiful, made principally by Americans who objected to trading "blood for oil" and who feared that the nation would become mired in another hopeless conflict. The fact was that Middle East oil had become essential to the Western economy. But the issues also went far beyond this commodity. President Bush was one of the last of the generation of U.S. leaders who had fought in World War II. He well knew what can happen when an international bully like Saddam Hussein, in command of the fifth largest army in the world, is allowed to operate unchecked.

In early August 1990, King Fahd of Saudi Arabia invited American troops into his country to protect the kingdom against possible Iraqi aggression. Called Operation Desert Shield, this was a massive, orderly buildup of U.S. forces. In January 1991, the U.S. Congress voted to support military operations against Iraq in accordance with a U.N. Security Council resolution, which set a deadline of January 15, 1991, for the withdrawal of Iraqi forces from Kuwait. When Saddam Hussein failed to heed the deadline, Operation Desert Shield became Operation Desert Storm, a massively coordinated lightning campaign against Iraq from the air, the sea, and on land. After continuous air attack beginning January 17, the ground war was launched at 8:00 p.m. on February 23 and lasted exactly 100 hours before Iraqi resistance collapsed and Kuwait was liberated.

Real Life

The only thing Americans cherish more than their cynicism is their heroes, and the Persian Gulf War produced one in General H. Norman Schwarzkopf, overall commander of operations Desert Shield and Desert Storm. Born in Trenton, New Jersey, on August 22, 1934, Schwarzkopf graduated from West Point in 1956. He served with distinction in numerous staff strategic and personnel management assignments, as well as in field command in Vietnam and in the 1983 invasion of Grenada.

During the Persian Gulf War, Schwarzkopf commanded a combined U.S.-coalition force of 530,000 troops opposed to 545,000 Iraqis and achieved overwhelming victory. Frequently appearing on television press conferences during the conflict, he impressed the American public with his forthrightness, military skill, and soft-spoken humanity. "Any soldier worth his salt," Schwarzkopf declared, "should be antiwar. And still there are things worth fighting for." Much honored, he retired after the war.

New World Order

Bush, who consistently earned high marks from the American public for his conduct of foreign relations, now enjoyed overwhelming popular approval in the wake of the successful outcome of the Persian Gulf War. But Bush did not bask alone in the war's afterglow. Military success in the Gulf seemed to exorcise the demons of failure born in the Vietnam War, and with the liberalization and ultimate collapse of the Soviet Union, Americans felt that their nation was in the vanguard of what President Bush called a "new world order." Not only had the long ideological struggle between communism and democracy ended in a victory for democracy, but a bully from the Third World, Saddam Hussein, had been defeated—and he was defeated with the cooperation of many nations and to the applause of most of the world.

The Least You Need to Know

➤ President Reagan started a conservative revolution in America, introducing supply-side economics and undoing much of the welfare state that had begun with FDR.

➤ The Reagan-Bush years saw victory in the 50-year Cold War (as well as victory in the brief but dangerous Persian Gulf War) but at the cost of quadrupling an already staggering national debt and sidelining such domestic issues as welfare and the AIDS crisis.

Democracy (1992–)

Writing about what *has* happened is much easier than writing about what *is* happening. Because we don't live in the future, it's no mean feat to say one current event is histori- cally significant, but another one isn't. The history of our times has yet to be written. So this closing chapter is nothing more than a moistened finger lifted to the prevailing winds. By the time you read this, some of these winds may be forgotten breezes, and I may well have overlooked the coming storms.

The Economy, Stupid

In 1980 and again in 1984, the American electorate voted Ronald Reagan into office with gusto. In 1988, Americans had relatively little enthusiasm for either Democrat Michael Dukakis, governor of Massachusetts, or Republican George Bush, vice president of the United States. Nor was there wild enthusiasm in 1992, when the incumbent Bush was opposed by the youthful governor of Arkansas, Bill Clinton. However, during the Bush administration, the American dream seemed somehow to have slipped farther away. True, the world was probably a safer place than it had been at any time since the end of World War II (but it was still a dangerous world), and the United States had acquitted itself in the best tradition of its long democratic history by resolving the Persian Gulf War. Yet the electorate felt that President Bush habitually neglected domestic issues and focused exclusively on international relations. Candidate Bill Clinton's acerbic campaign manager, James Carville, put it directly, advising Governor Clinton to write himself a reminder lest he forget the issue on which the election would be won or lost: "It's the economy, stupid."

Third Party Politics

The *economy*. It was not that America teetered on the edge of another depression in 1992. Although homeless men, women, and even children could be seen on corners and in doorways of the nation's cities, there were not the long bread lines or crowded soup kitchens of the 1930s. But a general sense existed among the middle class, among those who had jobs and were paying the rent, that *this* generation was not doing "as well as" previous generations. Sons were not living as well as fathers, daughters not as well as mothers. The pursuit of happiness, fueled in large part by cash, had become that much more difficult, and a majority of voters blamed it on George Bush. Bill Clinton entered the White House by a comfortable margin, but if voters rejected Bush, a sizable minority of them also rejected Clinton.

Stats
Even though Perot dropped out of the race for a time (stunning his many supporters), he won 19,237,247 votes, an astounding 19 percent of the popular vote total.

For the first time since Theodore Roosevelt ran as a Bull Moose candidate in 1912, a third-party contender made a significant impact at the polls. Presenting himself as a candidate dissatisfied with both the Republicans and Democrats, billionaire Texas businessman H. Ross Perot (b. 1930) told Americans that they were the "owners" of the nation and that it was about time they derived benefit from such ownership.

The New Right

The Perot candidacy was not the only evidence of widespread discontent with politics as usual. Americans who had come of age in the 1960s, the era of the Great Society and of protest against the Vietnam War, tended to take liberalism for granted, as if it were naturally part and parcel of the American way. Beginning in the 1970s, however, a conservative counter-movement gained increasing strength. Its values rested upon the family as traditionally constituted (father, mother, kids), a strong sense of law and order, reliance on organized religion, a belief in the work ethic (and a corresponding disdain for the welfare state), a passion for decency (even to the point of censorship), and a desire for minimal government.

> ### Word for the Day
>
> After World War II, from 1947 to 1961, the birth rate sharply rose in America. This period was described as a *baby boom*, and those born during this time were *baby boomers*. Those born between 1961 and 1972, typically college educated but chronically pessimistic and vaguely dissatisfied with career possibilities, have been dubbed *Generation X*, a label drawn from a novel of that name by Douglas Coupland.

Right to Life

Many who have identified themselves with the new right hold passionately to a belief that abortion, even in the first trimester of pregnancy (when the fetus cannot survive outside of the womb), is tantamount to murder. The so-called *Right to Life* movement has spawned a fanatic fringe, whose members have bombed abortion clinics and have intimidated, assaulted, and even murdered physicians who perform abortions. However, the mainstream of the movement has relied on legal means to effect social change, with the ultimate object of obtaining a constitutional amendment barring abortion. The Right to Life movement became so powerful a political lobby that the Republican party adopted a stance against abortion as part of its 1992 platform.

Regardless of one's attitude toward abortion—whether *pro life* or *pro choice*—many Americans are alarmed by a trend among particular political candidates and even entire political parties to become identified with single issues—such as abortion, gun control, prayer in schools, gay rights—rather than with an array of issues, let alone a philosophy of government.

> ### Word for the Day
>
> During the 1980s and 1990s, Americans heard a great deal about *PACs*. A PAC—Political Action Committee—is a special interest group, lobby, or pressure group organized to raise money for specific political activity.

Christian Right

The First Amendment to the Constitution specifies that "Congress shall make no law respecting an establishment of religion." Church and state are explicitly separated in the United States; but the government freely invokes the name of God in most of its enterprises. Our currency bears the motto "In God We Trust," both houses of Congress employ full-time chaplains, and (despite occasional protests) the Pledge of Allegiance most of us grew up reciting at the start of each school day describes the United States as "one nation, under God." While many Americans shake their heads over their perception that religious worship has somehow gone out of fashion in America, most opinion polls agree that approximately 96 percent of the population believes in God. A 1993 survey was able to turn up fewer than one million Americans willing to identify themselves as atheists—out of a total U.S. population, according to the 1990 census, of 248,709,873.

The rise of the so-called Christian Right—religiously motivated conservatism—should surprise no one, though it has worried many, who see in overt unions of religious faith and politics a threat to First Amendment freedoms. At present, the most significant political manifestation of the Christian Right is the powerful lobbying group called the Christian Coalition, which was spun off of the unsuccessful 1988 presidential campaign of religious broadcaster Pat Robertson (b. 1930). Based in Washington, D.C., the coalition boasts a membership of 1.6 million and has claimed responsibility for the Republican sweep of the Congress during the midterm elections of 1994. In 1995, the organization spent more than a million dollars mobilizing its "born-again" evangelicals behind the conservative "Contract with America" promulgated by Speaker of the House Newt Gingrich. While some people have welcomed what they see as a return of morality to American political life, others see the Christian Right as narrow, coercive, and intolerant.

Word for the Day
"In God We Trust" is plain enough English. The Great Seal of the United States, reproduced on the dollar bill, also includes two phrases of Latin: *Annuit coeptis* ("He has favored our undertakings") and *Novus ordo seclorum* ("A new order of the ages").

Real Life
Newt (Newton Leroy) Gingrich (b. 1943), elected U.S. Congressman from Georgia's 6th District in 1979, became Speaker of the House in 1995. Intensely, abrasively partisan, the eloquent Gingrich brilliantly masterminded the Republican party's so-called "Contract with America." This conservative legislative agenda promised smaller government, more responsive government, and a renewal of a sense of opportunity in American life. Gingrich has drawn ardent admiration from conservatives and equally intense contempt from liberals.

The Age of Rage

In turn, the Christian Right has viewed liberal America as too tolerant of lifestyles and beliefs that seem alien or offensive to certain religious principles, or that apparently threaten the moral fiber of the nation.

This is hardly a new dialogue. Right and left have been taffy-pulling national life since well before the Revolution. Indeed, Americans may be too accustomed to thinking in terms of right versus left; for another body of belief appears to want little to do with either side. In its mildest form, this group has expressed itself in a third political party, the Libertarians, founded in 1971. Libertarians oppose laws that limit personal behavior (including laws against prostitution, gambling, sexual preference), advocate a free market economy without government regulation or assistance, and support an isolationist foreign policy (including U.S. withdrawal from the United Nations).

But look around and listen. It's not Libertarian dialogue that you hear. It's rage. Most of the time, it's part of the background, the Muzak that marks the tempo of our times: angry slogans on bumper stickers, the endless staccato of sound bites reeling out from the television tube, the jagged litany that issues from talk-radio DJs, and the remarkable volume of violence that plays across movie screens. Sometimes the rage explodes, front and center.

> **Stats**
> In the 1980 presidential election, Libertarian candidate Ed Clark polled 920,859 votes, but candidate David Bergland received only 227,949 votes in 1984. Ron Paul garnered 409,412 votes in 1988, and Andre Marrou received 281,508 votes in 1992.

Waco and Oklahoma City

April 19, 1993, saw the fiery culmination of a long standoff between members of a fundamentalist religious cult called the Branch Davidians and federal officers. Followers of David Koresh (his real name was Vernon Howell) holed up in a fortified compound outside of Waco, Texas, and resisted the intrusion of agents from the U.S. Treasury Department's Alcohol, Tobacco and Firearms Unit (ATF). The agents were investigating reports of a stockpile of illegal arms as well as rumors of child abuse in the compound. When ATF officers moved in on the compound on February 28, the cultists opened fire, killing four ATF agents. Koresh was wounded in the exchange, and at least two of his followers were killed. For the next 51 days, the FBI laid siege to the Branch Davidians, until April 19, when the agents commenced an assault with tear gas volleys. The Branch Davidians responded by setting fire to their own compound, a blaze that killed more than 80 cultists, including 24 children. Millions witnessed both the February 28 shoot-out and the April 19 inferno on television.

Millions also saw the bloody aftermath of the bombing of the Alfred P. Murrah Federal Office Building in Oklahoma City on April 19, 1995, which resulted in the deaths of 169 persons. Timothy McVeigh and Terry Nichols were the two young men indicted in connection with the bombing. The men were associated with the "militia movement," a phrase describing militant groups organized in several states after the raid in Waco and a 1992 government assault on Randy Weaver, a white supremacist, and his family in Ruby Ridge, Idaho.

The incidents at Waco and Ruby Ridge, together with passage of relatively mild federal gun-control legislation, inspired the formation of these armed cadres. The groups were opposed not only to what they deemed excessive government control of everyday life, but also to what they saw as a United Nations plot to take over the United States in a drive toward "One World Government." Few Americans could understand how bombing a federal office building—which contained no military installations, no CIA secret headquarters, but only such ordinary offices as the local Social Security unit—could be deemed a blow against tyranny. Among those killed and injured were a number of children at play in the building's daycare center.

A Tale of Two Trials

The rage that has characterized the 1990s is not always politically motivated. Two trials commanded national attention.

Rodney King

On March 3, 1991, Rodney King, an African-American, was arrested for speeding on a California freeway. By chance, a witness carrying a camcorder videotaped the arrest: a brutal beating by four nightstick-wielding Los Angeles police officers. The tape was broadcast nationally, sending shockwaves of outrage from coast to coast. Incredibly, the officers were acquitted on April 30, 1992, by an all-white jury in the upscale California community of Simi Valley. Five days of rioting, arson, and looting erupted in Los Angeles, especially in the city's predominantly black South-Central neighborhood. (In a second, later trial on federal civil rights charges, two of the officers were convicted.)

The first verdict and the riots that followed—the worst urban disorder since the New York "Draft Riots" during July 13–16, 1863—were heartbreaking, suggesting that we as a nation had not come very far in learning to live

Voice from the Past

"People, I just want to say, you know, can we all get along? Can we get along? Can we stop making it, making it horrible for the older people and the kids?"

—Rodney King, spoken during the Los Angeles riots, May 2, 1992 harmoniously and productively together. Yet the sad episode was also a demonstration of how technology could serve the ends of democracy. For despite the jury's verdict, the beating, videotaped and broadcast, united most of the nation not in rage but in outrage. As those brutal images flickered across television screens everywhere, unquestioning belief in law and order dissolved. Middle-class whites were forced to ask themselves, *Is this what it means to be black in America?* At the very least, those millions who saw the beating had to ponder: *This is exactly what American democracy was created to prevent.*

O.J. Simpson

Television brought another racially charged legal battle into the nation's living rooms when O.J. Simpson, an African-American who had made it big as a football star and, later, sports broadcaster, was tried for the brutal murder of his ex-wife, Nicole Brown Simpson, and her friend Ronald Goldman. For almost a year, the televised "Trial of the Century" riveted a significant portion of the population. On October 3, 1995, after having been sequestered for 266 days and then deliberating for less than four hours, the Los Angeles jury found Simpson not guilty. While television had once again united the nation in focus on a single event, the televised verdict revealed a deep national division along racial lines. Whites overwhelmingly deemed the decision a miscarriage of justice, whereas the majority of African-Americans believed Simpson had been the innocent victim of racist police officers determined to frame him for the murder of his white ex-wife and her white friend.

E Pluribus Unum

Many Americans complained during the long Simpson trial that the media, in devoting coverage to every minute detail of the tortuous legal maneuvering that characterized the proceedings, gave short shrift to many other important stories of the year. Perhaps. But the televised trial did have much to teach us about our nation; about what it means to live in a country based on the presumption of innocence; about what it means to be black—or white—in the United States; about how access to wealth may influence the outcome of a trial.

Main Event

The very last year of the 19th century saw the invention of radio—at the time called the "wireless telegraph"—by the Italian-Irish inventor Guglielmo Marconi (1874–1937). Twenty-one years later, Pittsburgh's station KDKA made what is generally considered the first commercial radio

continues

broadcast in the United States (an announcement of election results), and electronic mass media was born. In 1933, a Russian-born American engineer for RCA, Vladimir Zworykin (1889–1982), having invented and patented in 1925 the "iconoscope" (basis of the modern "picture tube"), broadcast a television image over a radio-wave relay between New York and Philadelphia. It took well over a decade for the new medium to catch on with the American public, but in 1948, when an ex-vaudeville comic named Milton Berle (b. 1908) began cavorting across the small screen (often attired in drag), Americans got hooked. Berle's *Texaco Star Theater* dominated the airwaves through 1956, sales of TV sets soared, more programming was developed, and television became the dominant American entertainment medium. Soon, it also displaced the newspaper as the dominant news medium as well.

Radio and television are essentially one-way media, broadcasting to a passively receptive audience. The development of the personal computer, especially as linked to other computers through such networks as the vast Internet, represents an emerging *interactive* medium, in which there may be many parties in an exchange of entertainment, news, and information.

The modern personal computer has its most direct origins in the "analytical engine" invented by Thomas Babbage and Lady Lovelace in 1822–37, in computational theory developed by the British mathematician Alan Turing in the 1930s, and in ENIAC, the first electronic computer, unveiled at the University of Pennsylvania in 1946. From that time until the 1970s, computers were big and expensive, requiring a team of experts to program and to operate. In the 1970s, a number of companies introduced much smaller and cheaper computers, which could fit on a desktop, and, on August 12, 1981, IBM introduced the PC—personal computer—the first truly practical desktop machine. Since then, the machines have grown cheaper and more powerful each year, and one is hard pressed to find a desk—in offices as well as homes—that doesn't sport a PC.

From Leave It to Beaver to Sesame Street to the Internet

The Simpson trial also reminded us—if we needed reminding—of how profoundly mass media, particularly television, shapes our perceptions, even as it mirrors them. Back in the late 1950s and early 1960s, television programs depicted the American family as a collection of ethnically nondescript, vaguely Protestant white people living in white-painted, picket-fenced colonial-style suburban homes: the Ward, June, Wally, and Theodore "Beaver" Cleaver of *Leave It to Beaver*. This is how we liked to think of ourselves back then, and television obliged.

Then television brought us *Sesame Street* in 1969, a series aimed at entertaining and teaching children, but one that also depicted an urban neighborhood populated by whites, blacks, Hispanics, Asians, as well as people with handicaps and disabilities. The journey from *Leave It to Beaver* to *Sesame Street* consumed a decade in which a majority of Americans became more mindful and more accepting of the essence of democracy: *From many, one.*

And that mindfulness may just be the engine driving popular fascination with yet another technology. As little as two decades ago, the world of computers was an arcane realm that commanded relatively little interest and less understanding from most folks. Use the word *Internet* much before the 1990s, and you might as well have come from outer space.

Now it is difficult to get through a day without hearing some reference to the Internet. For an increasing number of Americans, few days go by without a personal visit to it.

A network of computer networks, the Internet is an *information superhighway* and also a forum, the ultimate town square, a place where ideas can be aired, shared, and debated. As yet, the Internet is unregulated by any government agency. Is the Internet democracy? No. Democracy cannot be reduced to this or that technology. But the Internet is an *expression* of democracy, a fervent wish to be democratic, to hear and to be heard, to share, to communicate, to connect with one's neighbors— next-door and around the world—and to be at the center of a great web that offers infinite centers (since, on the Internet, the *center* is wherever you happen to be).

Stats

In 1984, 18 percent of people over age 18 regularly used computers. In 1993, the figure was 36 percent. Significantly, 56 percent of children aged 3 to 17 regularly used computers in 1993.

Will the Internet make democracy any easier? Maybe, maybe not. But, more important, after the more than 200 years since the Constitution was written with pen and ink in the painstakingly graceful hand of the 18th century, the binary 0s and 1s, the light-speed ebb and flow of electrons through the Internet continue to embody the passion, the ideals, the dreams of those who founded the nation and those who have nurtured it for so long. Whether penned with a quill or tapped out on a keyboard, the message is the same: *E pluribus unum*—From many, one.

Word for the Day

The *Internet* is an international web of interconnected government, education, and business computer networks. At last estimate, at least 25 million people access the Internet, which many regard as a kind of electronic community.

The Least You Need to Know

➤ The 1990s have been characterized by discontent, political extremism, and rage that threaten democracy, but also by a renewed passion to gather and share information and ideas, the very elements that keep democracy strong.

➤ A revolution in electronic media, born in large part of an impulse to democracy, may well promote and preserve democratic values in the next millennium.

Presidents of the United States

Here is a list of our presidents, including the name of each, his term(s) in office, his party affiliation, and his vice president(s). While several chief executives have served more than one term, only one president, Grover Cleveland, is counted twice, since he is the only one who served two *nonconsecutive* terms.

1. **George Washington**, 1789–97
   No party
   John Adams

2. **John Adams**, 1797–1801
   Federalist
   Thomas Jefferson

3. **Thomas Jefferson**, 1801–09
   Democratic-Republican
   Aaron Burr (1801–05); George Clinton (1805–09)

4. **James Madison**, 1809–17
   Democratic-Republican
   George Clinton (1809–12); no vice president (April 1812–March 1813);
   Elbridge Gerry (1813–14); no vice president (November 1814–March 1817)

5. **James Monroe**, 1817–25
   Democratic-Republican
   Daniel D. Tompkins

6. **John Quincy Adams**, 1825–29
   Democratic-Republican
   John C. Calhoun

7. **Andrew Jackson**, 1829–37
   Democratic
   John C. Calhoun (1829–32); no vice president (December 1832–March 1833);
   Martin Van Buren (1833–1837)

8. **Martin Van Buren**, 1837–41
   Democratic
   Richard M. Johnson

9. **William H. Harrison***, 1841
   Whig
   John Tyler

10. **John Tyler**, 1841–45
    Whig
    No vice president

11. **James Knox Polk**, 1845–49
    Democratic
    George M. Dallas

12. **Zachary Taylor***, 1849–50
    Whig
    Millard Fillmore

13. **Millard Fillmore**, 1850–53
    Whig
    No vice president

14. **Franklin Pierce**, 1853–57
    Democratic
    William R. King (1853); no vice president (April 1853–March 1857)

15. **James Buchanan**, 1857–61
    Democratic
    John C. Breckinridge

16. **Abraham Lincoln***, 1861–65
    Republican
    Hannibal Hamlin (1861–65); Andrew Johnson (1865)

17. **Andrew Johnson**, 1865–69
    Democratic/National Union
    No vice president

18. **Ulysses S. Grant**, 1869–77
    Republican
    Schuyler Colfax (1869–73); Henry Wilson (1873–75); no vice president
    (November 1875–March 1877)

19. **Rutherford B. Hayes**, 1877–81
    Republican
    William A. Wheeler

20. **James A. Garfield***, 1881
    Republican
    Chester A. Arthur

21. **Chester A. Arthur**, 1881–85
    Republican
    No vice president

22. **Grover Cleveland**, 1885–89
    Democratic
    Thomas A. Hendricks (1885); no vice president (November 1885–March 1889)

23. **Benjamin Harrison**, 1889–93
    Republican
    Levi P. Morton

24. **Grover Cleveland**, 1893–97
    Democratic
    Adlai E. Stevenson

25. **William McKinley***, 1897–1901
    Republican
    Garret A. Hobart (1897–99); no vice president (November 1899–March 1901);
    Theodore Roosevelt, 1901

26. **Theodore Roosevelt**, 1901–09
    Republican
    No vice president (1901–05); Charles Fairbanks (1905–09)

27. **William Howard Taft**, 1909–13
    Republican
    James S. Sherman, 1909–12; no vice president (October 1912–March 1913)

28. **Woodrow Wilson**, 1913–21
    Democratic
    Thomas R. Marshall

29. **Warren G. Harding***, 1921–23
    Republican
    Calvin Coolidge

30. **Calvin Coolidge**, 1923–29
    Republican
    No vice president (1923–25); Charles G. Dawes (1925–29)

31. **Herbert Hoover**, 1929–33
    Republican
    Charles Curtis

32. **Franklin Delano Roosevelt***, 1933–45
   Democratic
   John Nance Garner (1933–41); Henry A. Wallace (1941–45); Harry S Truman (1945)

33. **Harry S Truman**, 1945–53
   Democratic
   No vice president (1945–49); Alben W. Barkley (1949–53)

34. **Dwight David Eisenhower**, 1953–61
   Republican
   Richard M. Nixon

35. **John F. Kennedy***, 1961–63
   Democratic
   Lyndon B. Johnson

36. **Lyndon B. Johnson**, 1963–69
   Democratic
   No vice president (1963–65); Hubert H. Humphrey, (1965–69)

37. **Richard M. Nixon****, 1969–74
   Republican
   Spiro T. Agnew (1969–73); no vice president (October–December 1973);
   Gerald R. Ford (1973–74)

38. **Gerald R. Ford**, 1974–77
   Republican
   No vice president (August–December 1974); Nelson Rockefeller (1974–77)

39. **Jimmy Carter**, 1977–81
   Democratic
   Walter F. Mondale

40. **Ronald Reagan**, 1981–89
   Republican
   George Bush

41. **George Bush**, 1989–93
   Republican
   Dan Quayle

42. **Bill Clinton**, 1993–
   Democratic
   Al Gore

* *Died in office*
** *Resigned during second term*

Further Reading

If this book has succeeded in whetting your appetite for more American history, you're in luck. You have thousands of books to choose from. The following list is restricted to *general* and *survey* works, which are not only interesting, but contain bibliographies to guide your reading in more specialized areas.

Andrews, Charles M. *The Colonial Period of American History.* 1934-38; reprint ed., New Haven: Yale University Press, 1964.

Andrist, Ralph K. *The Long Death: The Last Days of the Plains Indians.* New York: Macmillan/Collier, 1969.

Axelrod, Alan. *A Chronicle of the Indian Wars from Colonial Times to Wounded Knee.* New York: Prentice Hall General References, 1992.

Blum, John M., et al. *The National Experience: A History of the United States Since 1865.* 2 vols. New York: Harcourt, Brace, and World, 1968.

Bowman, John S. *The World Almanac of the American West.* New York: Modern Library, 1967.

Brandon, William. *Indians.* New York: American Heritage, 1985.

Brogan, Hugh. *The Penguin History of the United States of America.* London and New York: Penguin, 1985.

Davis, Kenneth C. *Don't Know Much About History: Everything You Need to Know About American History but Never Learned.* New York: Avon, 1990.

Debo, Angie. *A History of the Indians in the United States.* Norman: University of Oklahoma Press, 1977.

Foner, Eric, et al. *The Reader's Companion to American History*. Boston: Houghton Mifflin, 1991.

Foote, Shelby. *The Civil War: A Narrative*. 3 vols. New York: Random House, 1974.

Genovese, Eugene. *Roll, Jordan, Roll: The World the Slaves Made*. New York: Random House/Vintage, 1976.

Gibson, Charles. *Spain in America*. New York: Harper and Row, 1966.

Hofstadter, Richard. *The American Political Tradition*. New York: Knopf, 1948.

Lamar, Howard R. *The Reader's Encyclopedia of the American West*. New York: Crowell, 1977.

McPherson, James M. *Battle Cry of Freedom: The Civil War Era*. New York: Ballantine, 1988.

Prucha, Francis Paul. *The Great Father: The United States Government and the American Indian*. Lincoln: University of Nebraska Press, 1984.

Quinn, David B., ed. *North American Discovery Circa 1000-1612*. New York: Harper and Row, 1971.

Smelser, Marshal, and Joan R. Gundersen. *American History at a Glance*. New York: Harper and Row, 1978.

Smith, Page. *A New Age Begins: A People's History of the American Revolution*. 2 vols. New York: Viking Penguin, 1976.

Washburn, Wilcomb. *The Indian in America*. New York: Harper and Row, 1975.

Williams, Juan. *Eyes on the Prize: America's Civil Rights Years, 1954-1965*. New York: Penguin, 1987.

Woodward, C. Vann. *The Strange Career of Jim Crow*. New York: Oxford University Press, 1966.

Zinn, Howard. *A People's History of the United States 1492-Present*. New York: Harper Perennial, 1995.

Index

C

Queen Isabella I of Castile, 13
San Salvador, 13
Santa Maria, 13
Santangel, Luis de, 13
Santo Domingo, 16
spherical earth theory, 12
Common Sense, Paine, Thomas, 81-82
communism, 243
Company of Cathay, 30
Concord, Battle of (Revolutionary War), 79
Confederate States of America, 164
   Baylor, John Robert, Arizona Rangers, 193
   Greenhow, Rose O'Neal, 165-166
   Hill, A. P., 172
   Jackson, Stonewall, 166, 172
   Lee, Robert E., 167-168
   Pickett, George, 173
Connecticut Compromise, 98-99
conquistadors, 20-24
Constitution
   13th Amendment, 179
   14th Amendment, 179
   18th Amendment, 239
   19th Amendment, 237
   Bill of Rights, 102-103
Constitutional Convention, 98-100
   Connecticut Compromise, 98-99
   Federalist Papers, The, 99-100
   Three-Fifths Compromise, 99
   Washington, George, 98
Constitutional Union party, 163
Continental Army, Washington, George, 80
Contract with America, 330
Convention of 1818, 125
Cooke, William F., 154
Coolidge, Calvin, 240, 339
Cornwallis, Lord, 90
Coronado, Francisco Vazquez de, 22

corporate acquisitions and mergers in the 1980s, 317-318
Cortés, Hernan, 21
cotton gin, 142
counterculture movement, Vietnam War, 285, 294
coureurs de bois, 49
cowboys, 202-203
Cowpens, Battle of the (Revolutionary War), 90
Crane, Hart, 237
Crawford, William H., 124
Crazy Horse, 195
credibility gap, 293
   Johnson, Lyndon B., 286
Credit Mobilier, 189
CREEP (Committee to Reelect the President), Nixon, Richard, 299
Crittenden Compromise, 164
Croatoan, 32
Crocker, Charles, 160
Crockett, Davy, 152
Croker, Thomas, 217
Cromwell, Oliver, 38
Cuban missile crisis, 278
Currency Act, 75
Custer, George Armstrong, 195, 197
Czolgosz, Leon, 218

D

D-Day (WWII), 254
Daley, Richard, 286
Darwin, Charles, *On the Origins of Species by Means of Natural Selection*, 206
Davis, Jefferson, 164, 188
Dawes, Charles, 79
de Guzmán, Don Enrique, 13
Dean III, John W., 300
Declaration of Independence, 82
Declaration of Rights and Grievances, 75
decline of urban areas in 1970s, 308
Deere, John, Grand Detour Plow, 151, 184

Delaware River, Washington, George, 86
Democratic party, 129
   Clinton, William, 327
   Daley, Richard, 286
   Humphrey, Hubert, 286
   Kennedy, John F., 277-279
   Roosevelt, Franklin Delano, 243-245
   Tammany Hall, 216
   Wilson, Woodrow, 227-232
Democratic-Republican party, 101
   Adams, John Quincy, 129
   Jefferson, Thomas, 104, 106, 108-112
   Monroe, James, 123
desegregation, 273
Desert Storm, 325
Dezhnev, Ivanov, Northeast Passage, 29
Dickinson, John, Articles of Confederation, 96
Diem, Ngo Dihn, Vietnam War, 283
Dien Bien Phu, Vietnam War, 282
Dinwiddie, Robert, 64
Displaced Persons Plan (WWII), 263
Domino Theory, Eisenhower, Dwight D., 282
Don Luis de la Cerda, 13
Douglas, Stephen A., 162
   election of 1860, 163-164
   Lincoln, Abraham, debates, 162-163
Douglass, Frederick, 144
doves (peace advocates), Vietnam War, 287
draft dodgers, Vietnam War, 286
Drake, Francis, 22
Dreiser, Theodore, 237
drug abuse, rise of, 294-296
Du Bois, W. E. B., 238
Dumbarton Oaks Conference, United Nations, 262
Dutch West India Company, 51
Dutch West Indies, Stuyvesant, Peter, 52

Jungle, The, Sinclair, Upton, 217
junk bonds, 319

K

Kai-Shek, Chiang, 250
Kalb, Baron de, 88
Kansas
    Bleeding Kansas, 162
    Brown, John, 162
Kansas-Nebraska Act, 138, 147, 162
Karlsefni, Thorfinn, 10
Kearny, Stephen Watts,
    Mexican War, 156
Kelly, John, 217
Kennedy, John F., 277-279, 340
    assassination, 279
    Bay of Pigs invasion, 278
    Peace Corps, 277
    Vietnam War, 285-286
        Diem regime CIA plot, 283
        escalation, 283
Kennedy, Robert F., 278, 286
Kent State demonstration,
    Vietnam War, 288
Keokuk, 134
Key, Francis Scott, "Star-
    Spangled Banner," 120
Keystone Bridge Company,
    Carnegie, Andrew, 206
Khomeini, Ayatollah Ruhollah, 310
Khrushchev, Nikita, Cuban
    missile crisis, 278
Kieft, William, 52
Kinetoscope, 209
King George's War, 62
King, Jr., Martin Luther
    274-275
King Philip's War, 58
King, Rodney, 332
King William's War, 58-59
King's Mountain, Battle of
    (Revolutionary War), 90
Kino, Eusebio, 25
Kissinger, Henry, 287, 297
Kitty Hawk, North Carolina, 210
Knights of Labor, 214

Kocluszko, Tadeusz, 88
Korean War, 267-270
Koresh, David, 331-332
Ku Klux Klan, 180

L

La Follette, Robert M., 217
La Navidad, 15
labor strikes, 215-216
Lafayette, Marquis de, 88
Laffer Curve, 316
laissez-faire expansionism, 129
Lake Champlain, Battle of, 121
Lake George, Battle of
    (French-Indian War), 67
land bridge
    Bering Sea, 4
    Chukchi Sea, 4
Las Casas, Bartolome de, 23-26
Laud, William, 38
Lazarus, Emma, 213
League of Nations, Wilson,
    Woodrow, 234-236
Leary, Timothy, 295
Leave It to Beaver, 334
Lee, Richard Henry, 82
Lee, Robert E., 167-168
Leif the Lucky, see *Eriksson, Leif*
LEM (lunar excursion module), 296
Leon, Juan Ponce de, Puerto
    Rico, 20
leveraged buyouts, 319
Lewis and Clark Expedition, 111
Lewis, Meriwether, 111
Lexington, Battle of
    (Revolutionary War), 79
Liberator, The, 144
Libertarian party, 331-332
Liddy, G. Gordon, 299
Lincoln, Abraham, 135,
    161-162, 171-172, 338
    assassination, 177-179
    Douglas, Stephen A.,
        debates, 162-163
    election of 1860, 163
    Emancipation Proclamation, 169
    Fugitive Slave Act, 164
    Gettysburg Address, 173

Homestead Act, 184
Kansas-Nebraska Act, 162
Railway Act, 189
Republican party, 162
Thanksgiving, 40
Wade-Davis Reconstruction
    Bill, 179
Lincoln, Benjamin, 89
Little Bighorn, Battle of, 197
Lobsterbacks, 84
Locke, John, 82
Logan, Harvey, 204
Longfellow, Henry Wadsworth
    Evangeline, 66
    Paul Revere's Ride, 79
Longley, Bill, 204
Lookout Mountain, Battle of
    (Civil War), 175
Louisiana
    Cajuns, 66
    secession, 163
Louisiana Purchase, 110-112
LSD, 295
Luciano, Lucky, 246
Luks, George, 224
Lusitania (WWI), 228

M

MacArthur, Douglas, 250-251, 268
MacDonough, Thomas, 121
MacFarlane, Robert, 323
Machu Picchu citadel, Incas, 7
Mackenzie, Ranald, 197
Madison, James, 116, 337
    Bill of Rights, 102
    Federalist Papers, The, 100
Magellan, Ferdinand, 19
Maharishi Mahesh Yogi, 295
Malcolm X, 275-276
Manhattan Project, Roosevelt,
    Franklin Delano, 258
Manhattan Purchase, Minuit,
    Peter, 51
manifest destiny, 155
Marbury v. Madison, 109
March to the Sea, Sherman,
    William Tecumseh, 176
Marconi, Guglielmo, 333
marijuana, 295
Marion, Francis, 89

O

Q-R

Quakers, 42-43, 142
Quartering Act, 75
Quaternary Period, 4
Quebec, 48
Queen Anne's War, 60
Queen Elizabeth I, Walter
  Raleigh, 32
Queen Isabella I of Castile, 13
Queenston, Battle of (War of
  1812), 117

radical feminism, 306
radio, 333-335
Radisson, Pierre-Spirit and
  Medart Chouart, Hudson's
  Bay Company, 50
railroads
  Baltimore and Ohio
    Railroad, 187
  Credit Mobilier, 189
  Railway Act, 189
  Rock Island Line, 187
  transcontinental railroad,
    188
    Golden Spike, 190
    Promontory Summit, 190
  Union Pacific, 189
Railway Act, 189
Raleigh, Walter, 31-32
Randolph, Edmund, Virginia
  Plan, 98-100
Reagan, Ronald, 311, 315-316,
  340
  assassination attempt, 317
  Great Communicator, 311
  Iran-Contra Affair, 323
  Laffer Curve, 316
  SDI (Strategic Defense
    Initiative), 322
  supply-side economics, 316
  trickle-down economics, 316
Reaganomics, 317
reapers, horse-drawn,
  McCormick, Cyrus, 150
Reconstruction Acts, 179
recreational drugs, 294
Red River War (Indian Wars),
  196
Red Scare, 235

Reform party, Perot, Ross, 328
religious alternatives in the
  1960s, 295
Remington, Frederick, 225
Republican party, 129, 184
  Bush, George, 322
  Eisenhower, Dwight D., 255
  Lincoln, Abraham, 162
  Nixon, Richard, 287-289
  Reagan, Ronald, 315-316
  Roosevelt, Theodore,
    218-220
Revere, Paul, 79
Revolutionary War
  Allen, Ethan, 80
  Arnold, Benedict, 85, 90
  Battle of Bunker Hill, 80-81
  Battle of Concord, 79
  Battle of King's Mountain,
    90
  Battle of Lexington, 79
  Battle of Monmouth, 88
  Battle of Saratoga, 87
  Battle of the Cowpens, 90
  Battle of Yorktown, 91
  Boone, Daniel, 89
  Burgoyne, John, 86
  Canada, 85
  Carleton, Guy, 85
  Charleston, 89
  Cherokees, 89-90
  Clark, George Rogers, 88
  Common Sense, 81
  Cornwallis, Lord, 90
  Dawes, Charles, 79
  Declaration of
    Independence, 82
  France, 87-88
  Franklin, Benjamin, 95
  Gage, Thomas, 79
  Gates, Haratio, 89
  Green Mountain Boys, 80
  Hamilton, Harry, 88
  Hessians, 86
  Howe, William, 85
  Iroquois Indians, 89
  Jay, John, 95
  Kalb, Baron de, 88
  Kocluszko, Tadeusz, 88
  Lafayette, Marquis de, 88
  Lincoln, Benjamin, 89
  Marion, Francis, 89

Minutemen, 79
Olive Branch Petition, 81
Philadelphia, 87
Prescott, Samuel, 79
Revere, Paul, 79
Rochambeau, Comte de, 91
Siege of Boston, 84
Smith, Francis, 79
Spain, 87-88
Steuben, Baron von, 88
Sullivan, John, 89
Sumter, Thomas, 89
Treaty of Paris, 96
Valley Forge, Pennsylvania,
  88
Washington, George, 85
  Continental Army, 80
  Delaware River, 86
Rhode Island, Williams, Roger,
  41-42
Richelieu, 47, 48
Ridgway, Matthew B., Korean
  War, 269
Right to Life movement, 306,
  329
Riis, Jacob August, *How the
  Other Half Lives*, 214
Rio Grande Pueblos, 8
Roanoke, 31-35
Roaring Twenties, 236
Robertson, Pat, 330
Rochambeau, Comte de, 91
Rock Island Line, 187
rock music, 294
Rockefeller Foundation, 206
Rockefeller Institute of Medical
  Research, 206
Rockefeller, John D., 205-206
Roe v. Wade, 306
Roebling, Washington
  Augustus, 209
Rolfe, John, 34
Rolling Thunder Operation,
  Vietnam War, 284
Rommel, Erwin, Germany,
  251-252
Roosevelt, Eleanor, 244
Roosevelt, Franklin Delano,
  243-245, 340
  Agricultural Adjustment
    Administration, 245
  CCC (Civilian Conservation
    Corps), 244

U

V

X-Z

When You're Smart Enough to Know That You Don't Know It All

For all the ups and downs you're sure to encounter in life, The Complete Idiot's Guides give you down-to-earth answers and practical solutions.

Lifestyle

The Complete Idiot's Guide to Learning French on Your Own
ISBN: 0-02-861043-1 ▪ $16.95

The Complete Idiot's Guide to Learning Spanish on Your Own
ISBN: 0-02-861040-7 ▪ $16.95

The Complete Idiot's Guide to Successful Gambling
ISBN: 0-02-861102-0 ▪ $16.95

The Complete Idiot's Guide to Hiking and Camping
ISBN: 0-02-861100-4 ▪ $16.95

The Complete Idiot's Guide to Choosing, Training, and Raising a Dog
ISBN: 0-02-861098-9 ▪ $16.95

The Complete Idiot's Guide to Trouble-Free Car Care
ISBN: 0-02-861041-5 ▪ $16.95

The Complete Idiot's Guide to Trouble-Free Home Repair
ISBN: 0-02-861042-3 ▪ $16.95

The Complete Idiot's Guide to Dating
ISBN: 0-02-861052-0 ▪ $14.95

The Complete Idiot's Guide to Cooking Basics
ISBN: 1-56761-523-6 ▪ $16.99

The Complete Idiot's Guide to the Perfect Wedding
ISBN: 1-56761-532-5 ▪ $16.99

The Complete Idiot's Guide to the Perfect Vacation
ISBN: 1-56761-531-7 ▪ $14.99

The Complete Idiot's Guide to Getting and Keeping Your Perfect Body
ISBN: 0-02-861051-2 ▪ $14.95

The Complete Idiot's Guide to First Aid Basics
ISBN: 0-02-861099-7 ▪ $16.95

Personal Business

The Complete Idiot's Guide to Getting Into College
ISBN: 1-56761-508-2 ▪ $14.95

The Complete Idiot's Guide to Terrific Business Writing
ISBN: 0-02-861097-0 ▪ $16.95

The Complete Idiot's Guide to Surviving Divorce
ISBN: 0-02-861101-2 ▪ $16.95

The Complete Idiot's Guide to Managing Your Time
ISBN: 0-02-861039-3 ▪ $14.95

The Complete Idiot's Guide to Speaking in Public with Confidence
ISBN: 0-02-861038-5 ▪ $16.95

The Complete Idiot's Guide to Winning Through Negotiation
ISBN: 0-02-861037-7 ▪ $16.95

The Complete Idiot's Guide to Managing People
ISBN: 0-02-861036-9 ▪ $18.95

The Complete Idiot's Guide to Starting Your Own Business
ISBN: 1-56761-529-5 ▪ $16.99

The Complete Idiot's Guide to a Great Retirement
ISBN: 1-56761-601-1 ▪ $16.95

The Complete Idiot's Guide to Protecting Yourself From Everyday Legal Hassles
ISBN: 1-56761-602-X ▪ $16.99

The Complete Idiot's Guide to Getting the Job You Want
ISBN: 1-56761-608-9 ▪ $24.95

Personal Finance

The Complete Idiot's Guide to Buying Insurance and Annuities
ISBN: 0-02-861113-6 ▪ $16.95

The Complete Idiot's Guide to Doing Your Income Taxes 1996
ISBN: 1-56761-586-4 ▪ $14.99

The Complete Idiot's Guide to Getting Rich
ISBN: 1-56761-509-0 ▪ $16.95

The Complete Idiot's Guide to Making Money with Mutual Funds
ISBN: 1-56761-637-2 ▪ $16.95

The Complete Idiot's Guide to Managing Your Money
ISBN: 1-56761-530-9 ▪ $16.95

The Complete Idiot's Guide to Buying and Selling a Home
ISBN: 1-56761-510-4 ▪ $16.95

You can handle it!
Look for The Complete Idiot's Guides at your favorite bookstore,
or call 1-800-428-5331 for more information.